Tea

WORLD ENGLISH 2

SECOND EDITION

Real People • Real Places • Real Language

Kristen L. Johannsen/Rebecca Tarver Chase, Authors

Rob Jenkins, Series Editor

NATIONAL GEOGRAPHIC LEARNING | CENGAGE Learning

Australia • Brazil • Japan • Korea • Mexico • Singapore • Spain • United Kingdom • United States

World English Level 2 Teacher's Edition
Real People, Real Places, Real Language
Kristen L. Johannsen, Author
Rebecca Tarver Chase, Author
Rob Jenkins, Series Editor

Publisher: Sherrise Roehr

Executive Editor: Sarah Kenney

Senior Development Editor: Margarita Matte

Development Editor: Brenden Layte

Assistant Editor: Alison Bruno

Editorial Assistant: Patricia Giunta

Media Researcher: Leila Hishmeh

Senior Technology Product Managers:
  Scott Rule, Lauren Krolick

Director of Global Marketing: Ian Martin

Senior Product Marketing Manager:
  Caitlin Thomas

Sr. Director, ELT & World Languages:
  Michael Burggren

Production Manager: Daisy Sosa

Content Project Manager: Andrea Bobotas

Senior Print Buyer: Mary Beth Hennebury

Cover Designer: Aaron Opie

Art Director: Scott Baker

Creative Director: Chris Roy

Cover Image: PAUL CHESLEY/
National Geographic Creative

Compositor: MPS Limited

Cover Image

Hong Kong's skyline at night

For product information and technology assistance, contact us at
Cengage Learning Customer & Sales Support, 1-800-354-9706

For permission to use material from this text or product,
submit all requests online at **cengage.com/permissions**
Further permissions questions can be emailed to
permissionrequest@cengage.com

World English 2 Teacher's Edition: 978-1-285-84840-2

National Geographic Learning
20 Channel Center Street
Boston, MA 02210
USA

Cengage Learning is a leading provider of customized learning solutions with office locations around the globe, including Singapore, the United Kingdom, Australia, Mexico, Brazil, and Japan.

Cengage Learning products are represented in Canada by Nelson Education, Ltd.

Visit National Geographic Learning online at ngl.cengage.com

Visit our corporate website at www.cengage.com

Printed in the United States of America
Print Number: 04 Print Year: 2017

WORLD ENGLISH STUDENT BOOK WALK-THROUGH

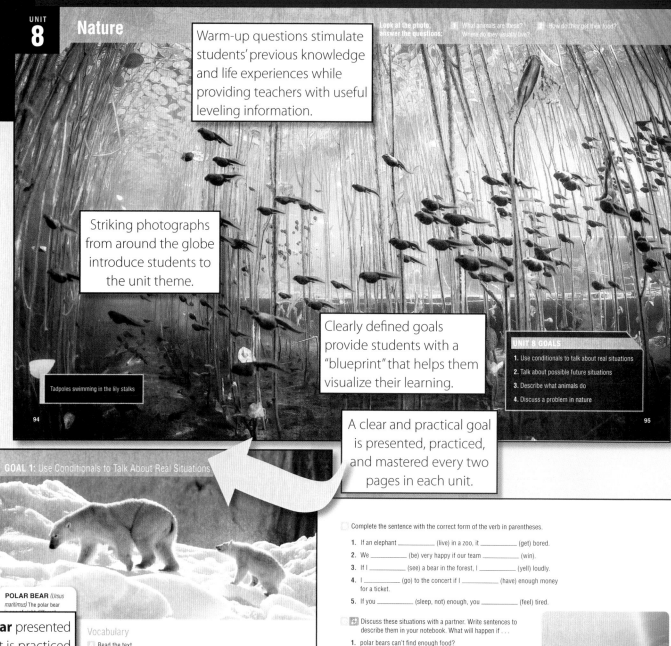

UNIT **8** **Nature**

Look at the photo, answer the questions: 1 What animals are these? Where do they usually live? 2 How do they get their food?

Warm-up questions stimulate students' previous knowledge and life experiences while providing teachers with useful leveling information.

Striking photographs from around the globe introduce students to the unit theme.

Clearly defined goals provide students with a "blueprint" that helps them visualize their learning.

UNIT 8 GOALS

1. Use conditionals to talk about real situations
2. Talk about possible future situations
3. Describe what animals do
4. Discuss a problem in nature

Tadpoles swimming in the lily stalks

94

95

A clear and practical goal is presented, practiced, and mastered every two pages in each unit.

A **GOAL 1**: Use Conditionals to Talk About Real Situations

POLAR BEAR *(Ursus maritimus)* The polar bear

Grammar presented in the unit is practiced through a variety of activities, each designed to reinforce students' knowledge of how the language works and ensure accuracy and appropriateness in their use of English.

Vocabulary

A Read the text.

B Match the words in blue to their meanings.

1. to look for animals and kill them
2. an animal that other animals kill to eat
3. animals that kill other animals
4. the place where an animal usually lives
5. a kind of animal or plant
6. doesn't exist any more, all dead
7. to keep safe from danger
8. in nature, not controlled by people

Grammar: Real conditionals in the future

A Study the sentence and answer the questions.

Condition   Result
If we don't protect these bears, they will b

1. Is the condition possible or not possible
2. Is the result now or in the future?

Real conditionals in the future	
We use the real conditional for situations that can happen in the future.	**If you look** out the trai of wild deer.
Conditional sentences have two clauses: the condition clause and the result clause.	Condition: *if* + subject Result: subject + *will/b*
The condition clause can be at the beginning or end of the sentence.	**If you talk** loudly, the birds will fly away. The birds are going to fly away **if you talk** loudly.

96 Unit 8

Complete the sentence with the correct form of the verb in parentheses.

1. If an elephant _____ (live) in a zoo, it _____ (get) bored.
2. We _____ (be) very happy if our team _____ (win).
3. If I _____ (see) a bear in the forest, I _____ (yell) loudly.
4. I _____ (go) to the concert if I _____ (have) enough money for a ticket.
5. If you _____ (sleep, not) enough, you _____ (feel) tired.

Discuss these situations with a partner. Write sentences to describe them in your notebook. What will happen if . . .

1. polar bears can't find enough food?
2. the polar bear's habitat disappears?
3. people put more polar bears in zoos?
4. people protect polar bears?
5. polar bears become extinct?

▲ An Alaskan brown bear near Nonvianuk Lake, Katmai National Park, Alaska

Conversation

6 Close your book and listen to the conversation. What is Katie afraid of?

Mike: Let's go camping in the national park.
Katie: I'm not sure that's a good idea. There are black bears in the park.
Mike: That may be, but there aren't very many, and they stay away from people.
see a bear, I'll be really scared. They're so dangerous!
ars won't hurt you if you leave them alone.

the conversation with a partner. Switch roles and e it again.

wo new conversations. Choose from the topics below.

each/sharks   3. the nature reserve/snakes
ampground/wolves   4. your own idea

Real Language

You can say *That may be (true), but . . .* to show that you disagree with the other person's idea.

Frequent **Conversation** activities motivate students to practice natural language themselves after practicing with a model dialog.

GOAL CHECK Use conditionals to talk about real situations

Look at the problems in the box. How will these issues affect nature? Talk about them with a partner.

Goal Check activities on each spread highlight measurable outcomes and provide accessible navigation for teachers and students.

T-4

Nature 97

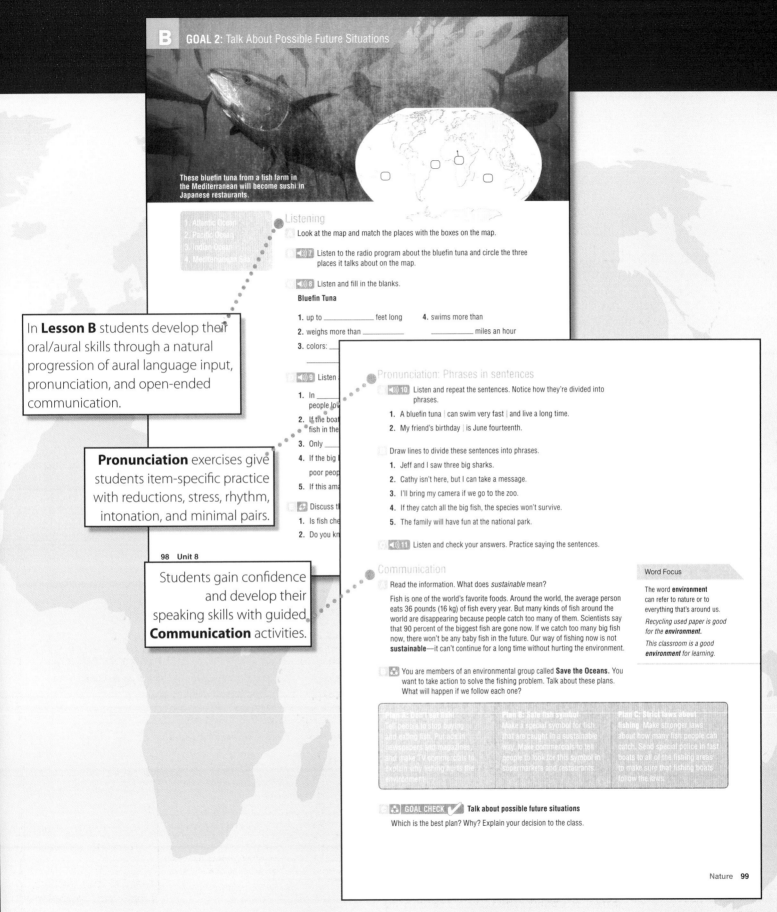

B **GOAL 2:** Talk About Possible Future Situations

These bluefin tuna from a fish farm in the Mediterranean will become sushi in Japanese restaurants.

1. Atlantic Ocean
2. Pacific Ocean
3. Indian Ocean
4. Mediterranean Sea

Listening

Look at the map and match the places with the boxes on the map.

🔊 7 Listen to the radio program about the bluefin tuna and circle the three places it talks about on the map.

🔊 8 Listen and fill in the blanks.

Bluefin Tuna

1. up to _____ feet long
2. weighs more than _____
3. colors: _____

4. swims more than _____ miles an hour

🔊 9 Listen

1. In _____ people lov
2. If the boat fish in the
3. Only _____
4. If the big poor peop
5. If this ama

Discuss t
1. Is fish ch
2. Do you kn

98 Unit 8

> In **Lesson B** students develop their oral/aural skills through a natural progression of aural language input, pronunciation, and open-ended communication.

> **Pronunciation** exercises give students item-specific practice with reductions, stress, rhythm, intonation, and minimal pairs.

> Students gain confidence and develop their speaking skills with guided **Communication** activities.

Pronunciation: Phrases in sentences

🔊 10 Listen and repeat the sentences. Notice how they're divided into phrases.

1. A bluefin tuna | can swim very fast | and live a long time.
2. My friend's birthday | is June fourteenth.

Draw lines to divide these sentences into phrases.

1. Jeff and I saw three big sharks.
2. Cathy isn't here, but I can take a message.
3. I'll bring my camera if we go to the zoo.
4. If they catch all the big fish, the species won't survive.
5. The family will have fun at the national park.

🔊 11 Listen and check your answers. Practice saying the sentences.

Communication

Read the information. What does *sustainable* mean?

Fish is one of the world's favorite foods. Around the world, the average person eats 36 pounds (16 kg) of fish every year. But many kinds of fish around the world are disappearing because people catch too many of them. Scientists say that 90 percent of the biggest fish are gone now. If we catch too many big fish now, there won't be any baby fish in the future. Our way of fishing now is not **sustainable**—it can't continue for a long time without hurting the environment.

You are members of an environmental group called **Save the Oceans.** You want to take action to solve the fishing problem. Talk about these plans. What will happen if we follow each one?

Word Focus

The word **environment** can refer to nature or to everything that's around us.

Recycling used paper is good for the environment.

This classroom is a good environment for learning.

Plan A: Don't eat fish!	Plan B: Safe fish symbol	Plan C: Strict laws about fishing
Tell people to stop buying and eating fish. Put ads in newspapers and magazines, and make TV commercials to explain why fishing hurts the environment.	Make a special symbol for fish that are caught in a sustainable way. Make commercials to tell people to look for this symbol in supermarkets and restaurants.	Make stronger laws about how many fish people can catch. Send special police in fast boats to all of the fishing areas to make sure that fishing boats follow the laws.

♻ **GOAL CHECK** ✔ **Talk about possible future situations**

Which is the best plan? Why? Explain your decision to the class.

Nature 99

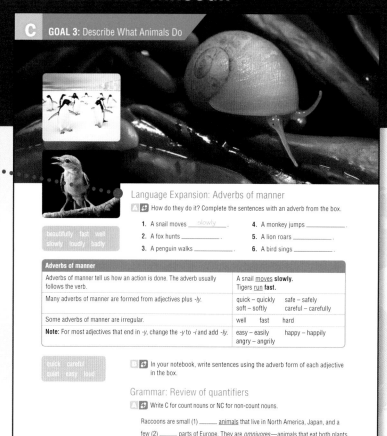

C GOAL 3: Describe What Animals Do

Language Expansion sections focus on specific areas that help learners' build language strategies and become more competent users of English.

Language Expansion: Adverbs of manner

A How do they do it? Complete the sentences with an adverb from the box.

beautifully fast well
slowly loudly badly

1. A snail moves _____slowly_____ .
2. A fox hunts _____ .
3. A penguin walks _____ .
4. A monkey jumps _____ .
5. A lion roars _____ .
6. A bird sings _____ .

Adverbs of manner	
Adverbs of manner tell us how an action is done. The adverb usually follows the verb.	A snail moves **slowly**. Tigers run **fast**.
Many adverbs of manner are formed from adjectives plus -ly.	quick – quickly safe – safely soft – softly careful – carefully
Some adverbs of manner are irregular.	well fast hard
Note: For most adjectives that end in -y, change the -y to -i and add -ly.	easy – easily happy – happily angry – angrily

quick careful
quiet easy loud

B In your notebook, write sentences using the adverb form of each adjective in the box.

Grammar: Review of quantifiers

A Write C for count nouns or NC for non-count nouns.

Raccoons are small (1) _____ animals that live in North America, Japan, and a few (2) _____ parts of Europe. They are *omnivores*—animals that eat both plants and animals. A raccoon's usual diet is (3) _____ nuts and (4) _____ fruit. They

---

D GOAL 4: Discuss a Problem in Nature

Reading

A What are some reasons animals are endangered? Talk about your ideas with a partner.

B Look at the list of ways we can protect endangered animals. Check (✓) the ideas you predict you will read about in the article. Compare your answers with a partner.

1. _____ stop poaching
2. _____ create advertisements about conservation
3. _____ prevent droughts
4. _____ put land under conservation
5. _____ support nature tourism

C Read the article. Write the dates next to the events.

1. _____ 20 lions remain in Kunene
2. _____ John Kasaona is born
3. _____ drought hits Namibia
4. _____ war begins
5. _____ war ends

D List two good things in your notebook about the community-based conservation program. Compare your answers with a partner.

Many elephants are killed for their tusks.

TED Ideas worth spreading

John Kasaona
Community-Based Conservationist

HOW POACHERS BECAME CARETAKERS

When John Kasaona was a boy growing up in Namibia, his father took him into the **bush** to teach him how to take care of the family's livestock. His father said, "If you see a cheetah eating our goat, walk up to it and smack it on the backside." A cheetah is a very nervous animal. If a person **confronts** it, it will probably run away. John also learned how to deal with a lion by standing very still and making himself look very big. These were useful lessons for a boy who

[...] wildlife **conservationist**. As Kasaona says, [...] important if you are in the field to know what [...] what to run from."

[...] was born in 1971. At that time, Namibia [...] problems. The country was at war from 1966 [...]. Because of the fighting, many people had [...]. This caused a secondary problem—**poaching**. [...] example, poachers killed many black rhinos for their horns, which were very valuable. To make things even worse, around 1980, a terrible drought killed people, livestock, and wildlife. By 1995, there were only 20 lions left in the Kunene region in the northwest of the country, where Kasaona's family lives. Many other sp[...]

Magazine-style readings are a springboard for opinion sharing and personalization, and provide opportunities for students to use the grammar and vocabulary presented earlier in the unit.

"We knew conservation would fail if it didn't work to improve the lives of the local communities."
– John Kasaona

Many readings, such as this one, now focus on TED speakers and talks, promoting student comprehension of interesting topics.

John Kasaona's idea worth spreading is that there is good news from Africa. Protecting wildlife is a great way to transform communities — and countries. Watch Kasaona's full TED Talk on TED.com.

answer was surprising: work with local poachers. It seemed crazy, but it also made sense. After all, if you spend your time hunting for animals, you will know where they live and how they behave. So IRDNC hired a group of poachers, including Kasaona's own father, to help protect wildlife in Namibia.

Since then, the situation has changed dramatically. The Kunene region now has more than 130 lions. The black rhino, almost extinct in 1982, has come back, and there are now many free-roaming black rhinos in Kunene. Most importantly, more land than ever is under conservation. That protected land generates money from tourism for Namibia to use in education, health care, and other important programs for its people.

John Kasaona explains, "We were successful in Namibia because we dreamed of a future that was much more than just a healthy wildlife." Kasaona created a model for other nations to follow by starting the largest community-led conservation program in the world.

bush land far from towns and cities
confront to challenge (someone) in a forceful way
conservationist someone who works to protect animals, plants, and natural resources
poaching killing an animal illegally
species a group of animals or plants that are similar

Communication activities allow students to take content and apply it to real-world situations.

Poaching endangers species in their natural habitats.

Communication

A Think about two or three problems in nature in your country. What is happening? What are the causes? Share your ideas with a partner.

Writing

A Complete the sentences about a problem in nature in your country.

1. If we believe in conservation, we will _____.
2. If _____, many animals will be saved.
3. [peo]ple want to make positive changes, they will _____.

Writing activities reinforce the structures, vocabulary, and expressions learned in the unit.

... *so*, and *even though* in the correct places in the paragraph. ...990s, many species of animals were endangered in Namibia. ...ation was serious, (1)_____ conservationists needed ...way to protect the animals. They found one, (2)_____ it wasn't what you would expect: they asked poachers for help. (3)_____ this seemed crazy, I think it was a great idea. If we want to protect endangered species, we need to consider every solution.

Writing Strategy
Conjunctions

Conjunctions are used to connect ideas within sentences.

C Write a paragraph in your notebook giving your opinion about a problem in nature in your country. Be sure to use the connectors in Exercise **B**.

D **GOAL CHECK** ✓ Discuss a problem in nature

Work with a group. Share your ideas from Exercise **A** about proble[ms] in nature. In your opinion, what is the most important problem to solve? What are two or three ways to help?

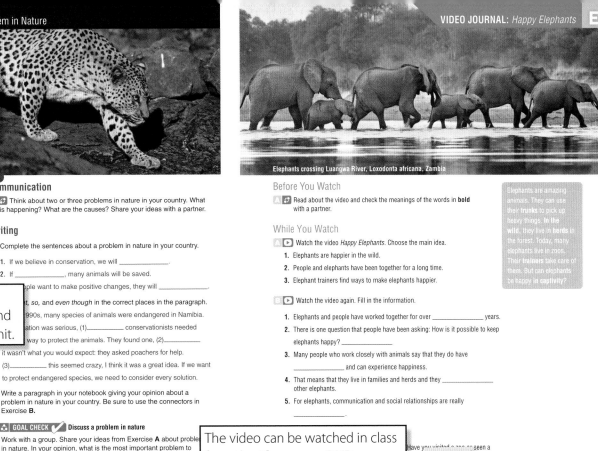

Elephants crossing Luangwa River, Loxodonta africana, Zambia

Before You Watch

A Read about the video and check the meanings of the words in **bold** with a partner.

While You Watch

A Watch the video *Happy Elephants*. Choose the main idea.

1. Elephants are happier in the wild.
2. People and elephants have been together for a long time.
3. Elephant trainers find ways to make elephants happier.

B Watch the video again. Fill in the information.

1. Elephants and people have worked together for over _____ years.
2. There is one question that people have been asking: How is it possible to keep elephants happy? _____
3. Many people who work closely with animals say that they do have _____ and can experience happiness.
4. That means that they live in families and herds and they _____ other elephants.
5. For elephants, communication and social relationships are really _____.

Elephants are amazing animals. They can use their **trunks** to pick up heavy things. **In the wild**, they live in **herds** in the forest. Today, many elephants live in zoos. Their **trainers** take care of them. But can elephants be happy **in captivity**?

Have you visited a zoo or seen a[n animal] living [in captivity?] [Why] why not?

The video can be watched in class from the **Classroom DVD** or students can watch it individually on the **Student CD-ROM**.

Students conclude the unit by watching an authentic but carefully-graded National Geographic video clip. This application of students' newly acquired language skills is a part of the ongoing unit assessment system and serves as a motivating consolidation task.

This **World English Teacher's Edition** is designed to make your preparation as simple as possible, allowing you to maximize actual classroom teaching time. It features page-by-page suggestions on how to teach the course, answer keys to the Student Book and Workbook, culture notes, extension activities, audio scripts of listening passages not printed in the Student Book, and video scripts.

A snapshot from the course **Scope and Sequence** provides a quick reference as the teacher presents the new unit to students.

The **Unit Theme Overview** provides teachers with all the background information that they will need as they work through the unit. It also gives them a quick preview of the type of activities the students will do throughout the unit.

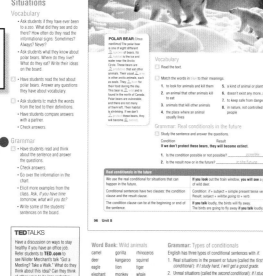

Step-by-step teaching suggestions are provided on every page of the unit.

Detailed **Grammar** explanations are provided for teacher reference in Lessons A and C.

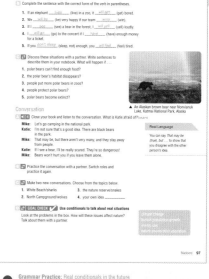

An additional **Grammar Practice** activity can be used when necessary for re-teaching and review. There are also additional Grammar worksheets at the back of the Teacher's Edition.

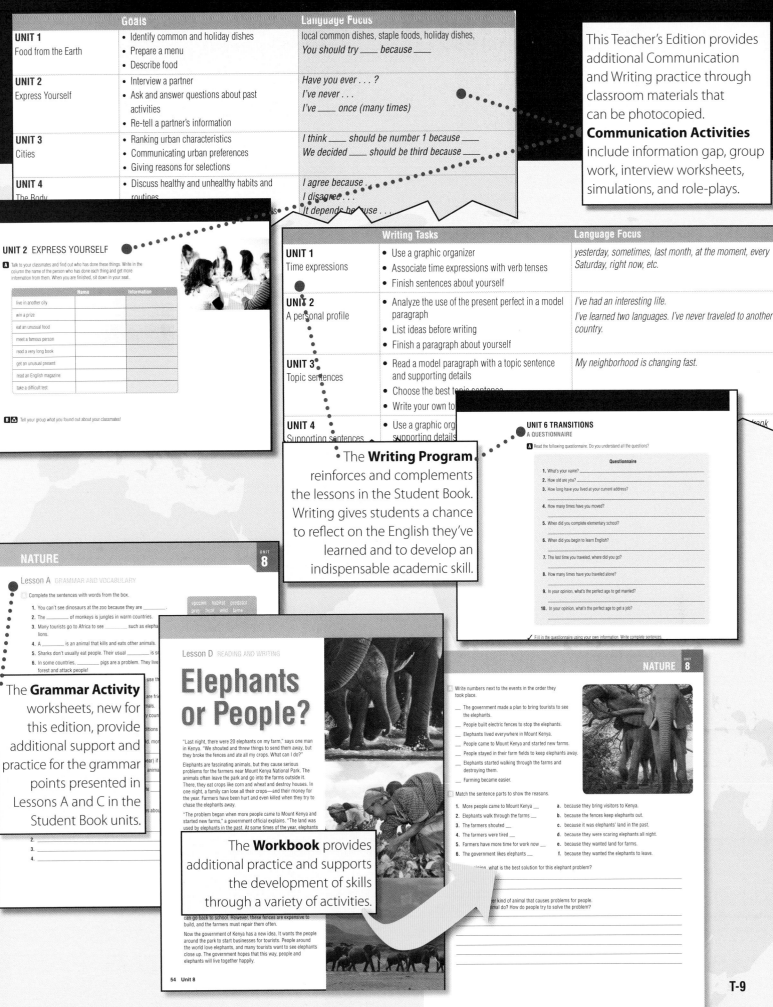

	Goals	Language Focus
UNIT 1 Food from the Earth	• Identify common and holiday dishes • Prepare a menu • Describe food	local common dishes, staple foods, holiday dishes, *You should try ___ because ___*
UNIT 2 Express Yourself	• Interview a partner • Ask and answer questions about past activities • Re-tell a partner's information	*Have you ever . . . ?* *I've never . . .* *I've ___ once (many times)*
UNIT 3 Cities	• Ranking urban characteristics • Communicating urban preferences • Giving reasons for selections	*I think ___ should be number 1 because ___* *We decided ___ should be third because ___*
UNIT 4 The Body	• Discuss healthy and unhealthy habits and routines	*I agree because . . .* *I disagree . . .* *It depends because . . .*

This Teacher's Edition provides additional Communication and Writing practice through classroom materials that can be photocopied. **Communication Activities** include information gap, group work, interview worksheets, simulations, and role-plays.

UNIT 2 EXPRESS YOURSELF

A Talk to your classmates and find out who has done these things. Write in the column the name of the person who has done each thing and get more information from them. When you are finished, sit down in your seat.

	Name	Information
live in another city		
win a prize		
eat an unusual food		
meet a famous person		
read a very long book		
get an unusual present		
read an English magazine		
take a difficult test		

B Tell your group what you found out about your classmates!

	Writing Tasks	Language Focus
UNIT 1 Time expressions	• Use a graphic organizer • Associate time expressions with verb tenses • Finish sentences about yourself	*yesterday, sometimes, last month, at the moment, every Saturday, right now, etc.*
UNIT 2 A personal profile	• Analyze the use of the present perfect in a model paragraph • List ideas before writing • Finish a paragraph about yourself	*I've had an interesting life.* *I've learned two languages. I've never traveled to another country.*
UNIT 3 Topic sentences	• Read a model paragraph with a topic sentence and supporting details • Choose the best topic sentence • Write your own to	*My neighborhood is changing fast.*
UNIT 4 Supporting sentences	• Use a graphic org supporting details	

The **Writing Program** reinforces and complements the lessons in the Student Book. Writing gives students a chance to reflect on the English they've learned and to develop an indispensable academic skill.

UNIT 6 TRANSITIONS
A QUESTIONNAIRE

A Read the following questionnaire. Do you understand all the questions?

Questionnaire

1. What's your name? _____
2. How old are you? _____
3. How long have you lived at your current address? _____
4. How many times have you moved? _____
5. When did you complete elementary school? _____
6. When did you begin to learn English? _____
7. The last time you traveled, where did you go? _____
8. How many times have you traveled alone? _____
9. In your opinion, what's the perfect age to get married? _____
10. In your opinion, what's the perfect age to get a job? _____

✓ Fill in the questionnaire using your own information. Write complete sentences.

NATURE
UNIT 8

Lesson A GRAMMAR AND VOCABULARY

Complete the sentences with words from the box.

species habitat predator prey hunt wild tame

1. You can't see dinosaurs at the zoo because they are _____.
2. The _____ of monkeys is jungles in warm countries.
3. Many tourists go to Africa to see _____ such as elephants lions.
4. A _____ is an animal that kills and eats other animals.
5. Sharks don't usually eat people. Their usual _____ is sm
6. In some countries, _____ pigs are a problem. They live forest and attack people!

The **Grammar Activity** worksheets, new for this edition, provide additional support and practice for the grammar points presented in Lessons A and C in the Student Book units.

2. _____
3. _____
4. _____

Lesson D READING AND WRITING

Elephants or People?

"Last night, there were 20 elephants on my farm," says one man in Kenya. "We shouted and threw things to send them away, but they broke the fences and ate all my crops. What can I do?"

Elephants are fascinating animals, but they cause serious problems for the farmers near Mount Kenya National Park. The animals often leave the park and go into the farms outside it. There, they eat crops like corn and wheat and destroy houses. In one night, a family can lose all their crops—and their money for the year. Farmers have been hurt and even killed when they try to chase the elephants away.

"The problem began when more people came to Mount Kenya and started new farms," a government official explains. "The land was used by elephants in the past. At some times of the year, elephants

The **Workbook** provides additional practice and supports the development of skills through a variety of activities.

can go back to school. However, these fences are expensive to build, and the farmers must repair them often.

Now the government of Kenya has a new idea. It wants the people around the park to start businesses for tourists. People around the world love elephants, and many tourists want to see elephants close up. The government hopes that this way, people and elephants will live together happily.

NATURE
UNIT 8

Write numbers next to the events in the order they took place.

___ The government made a plan to bring tourists to see the elephants.
___ People built electric fences to stop the elephants.
___ Elephants lived everywhere in Mount Kenya.
___ People came to Mount Kenya and started new farms.
___ People stayed in their farm fields to keep elephants away.
___ Elephants started walking through the farms and destroying them.
___ Farming became easier.

Match the sentence parts to show the reasons.

1. More people came to Mount Kenya ___
2. Elephants walk through the farms ___
3. The farmers shouted ___
4. The farmers were tired ___
5. Farmers have more time for work now ___
6. The government likes elephants ___

a. because they bring visitors to Kenya.
b. because the fences keep elephants out.
c. because it was elephants' land in the past.
d. because they were scaring elephants all night.
e. because they wanted land for farms.
f. because they wanted the elephants to leave.

r opinion, what is the best solution for this elephant problem?

_____

er kind of animal that causes problems for people.
imal do? How do people try to solve the problem?

_____
_____
_____
_____

Overview

The new edition of **World English** uses rich, engrossing National Geographic text, photos, art, and videos to involve students in learning about real people, real places, and real language.

In this edition, newly added TED Talks and Readings also bring some of the world's most important and interesting speakers to the classroom.

Each unit is divided into three two-page lessons, a three-page Reading, Writing, and Communication lesson, and a Video Journal.

A concrete objective at the beginning of every lesson focuses students' attention on what they will be learning. At the end of the lesson, a personalization activity gives students an opportunity to apply what they've learned and lets both teachers and students check student progress.

Unit Opener

Each unit opens with a two-page spread featuring a striking photo. These photos have been chosen both to illustrate the unit theme and to provide material for discussion. Before beginning the unit, teacher and students can describe the picture, name as many things as they can in it, and make guesses about when and where the photo was taken. The two discussion questions then lead students into the topic and introduce several key vocabulary items.

In this Teacher's Edition, a Unit Theme Overview is provided to orient you to the scope of the unit and to give additional information that may be useful in discussing the unit theme. Throughout the lesson notes, For Your Information boxes contain additional facts about the topic of a listening passage, reading, or video.

Vocabulary

Lessons A and C both begin with a short activity presenting lexical items related to the unit theme. In Lesson A, the vocabulary section introduces the core words that students will need to discuss and learn about the unit topic. These are presented in context, with text or pictures to aid students in understanding. After completing the exercises in this section, students have a written record of the meanings of the words, which they can refer to later. The lesson notes in this Teacher's Edition contain a Word Bank of supplementary vocabulary that can be used in activities or taught as enrichment.

Grammar

World English features an explicit grammar syllabus, with individual grammar points tied to the unit theme. Two different grammar points are taught in Lesson A and Lesson C. They are used in the opening presentation of the lessons along with the vocabulary items and then explicitly presented in a box with examples, rules, and usage notes.

Students first do controlled practice with the structure in writing, then freer production in writing, and finally use the structure in controlled speaking practice. Every grammar point is followed by a Conversation section that gives further practice in the use of the structure.

The lesson notes in this Teacher's Edition contain a brief summary of each grammar point for teacher reference, as well an additional Grammar Practice Activity.

New to this edition are Grammar worksheets in the back of the Teacher's Edition. Each unit has two worksheets, one for each of the grammar points in Lessons A and C.

Conversation

Each unit contains two model conversations highlighting both the vocabulary and the grammar for the lesson. Students first listen to the conversation with their books closed and answer one general comprehension question. Next, they listen again while reading the conversation. They are then ready to practice the conversation, taking turns with both roles before making their own conversations based on the model and incorporating specified information along with their own ideas.

Listening

Lesson B starts off with a listening activity. After a warm-up to introduce the subject of the activity, students listen to a conversation, radio program, or interview multiple times, completing a series of written tasks of graded difficulty. The first time, they are asked to listen for the gist or main ideas; subsequent activities ask them to find numbers, details, or further information. A post-listening task helps students to explore and personalize what they've heard.

Audioscripts for all listening activities begin on page T-169.

Pronunciation

The pronunciation component of **World English** emphasizes stress, intonation, reductions, and other features to make learners' English more natural and comprehensible to a wide international audience. Students first learn to recognize a feature of English pronunciation and then to produce it. Examples are presented on the audio recording in the context of the unit theme. Students begin by listening, then repeat with the audio recording, and then practice freer production of the features while interacting with a partner.

If a particular pronunciation point is especially challenging for your students, it can be practiced in a number of ways. You can have the entire class repeat the items in chorus, then the two halves of the class, then rows or columns of students, and finally you can call on individual students to pronounce the items. When students practice in pairs, circulate around the room listening and correcting.

Communication

In contrast to the controlled speaking practice in the Conversation sections, the Communication activities give freer practice with the structures and vocabulary that the students have learned. These activities are designed to allow personal expression, but still within a controlled field of language, so that all students can feel confident of success. While students are doing these activities, you should circulate around the class to help with vocabulary and ideas as needed and to make note of errors and interesting responses to discuss with the class after the end of the activity.

The lesson notes in this Teacher's Edition include Expansion activities for further discussion around the theme of the listening passage. For classes where more practice of free communication is desired, this book also contains 12 Communication Activity Worksheets, which may be photocopied, one for each unit. The activities, which require 15 to 30 minutes of class time each, reinforce the vocabulary and structures from the unit while giving students another opportunity to express their own ideas in English.

Language Expansion

The first part of Lesson C is a Language Expansion activity that is meant to broaden students' vocabulary around the unit theme by introducing a closely related group of lexical items. These are presented in context and are used immediately in writing and then speaking, giving students more options when doing the Grammar and Conversation activities that follow in Lesson C.

Reading

Lesson D is centered around a reading passage, which is followed by a Communication activity that prepares students for writing. All of the reading passages in **World English** are abridged and adapted from authentic articles in National Geographic publications or TED Talks. To help students read for interest and enjoyment, unfamiliar vocabulary is explained either with glosses in a Word Focus box or in a picture dictionary illustration.

The lesson notes in this Teacher's Edition include a Web search activity and a suggestion for a simple project that can be done as a follow-up for each reading passage.

Writing

The writing activities in Lesson D of **World English** flow from the subject of the reading passage and are always preceded by a Communication activity in which students discuss and explore the topic further. This generates ideas and forms a natural prewriting sequence. Writing tasks are short and simple and range from writing single sentences in the lower levels, through writing groups of sentences, on up to writing an entire paragraph.

The writing activities in the units emphasize helping students put their ideas into written form. Where a more structured approach to writing is desired, this Teacher's Edition contains a complete Writing Program, which may be photocopied. These optional writing worksheets, one for each unit, provide instruction and practice in a sequence of writing skills graded to the level of the course.

Video Journal

Each unit of **World English** concludes with an authentic National Geographic three- to four-minute video, with a voice-over that has been specially edited for language learners. The video segments recycle the themes and language of the main unit, bringing them to life in colorful locations around the globe. A Before You Watch activity presents new words that students will hear and gives information about the setting of the video. Students watch the video several times while completing While You Watch activities that ask them first to find general themes and then to locate specific information. They give their response to the video in an After You Watch activity.

The responses to the video draw the strands of the unit together and allow students to demonstrate what they've learned.

TED Talks

In this new edition, students also watch a TED Talk every three units. These videos are accompanied by four-page sections which review the vocabulary and grammar content of the previous three units and also allow students to build upon prior instruction to communicate about issues that affect their community and the world.

Special Features in the Student Book

Real Language This feature highlights high-frequency expressions from everyday language that will make students' speech sound natural and confident. To present them, point out their use in the activity and discuss other situations when they might be useful. If desired, have students work in pairs to create conversations using the expressions.

Word Focus These boxes present and explain additional vocabulary used in an activity, as well as introduce commonly used collocations.

WORLD ENGLISH 2

SECOND EDITION

Real People • Real Places • Real Language

Kritin L. Johannsen/Rebecca Tarver Chase, Authors

Rob Jenkins, Series Editor

Australia • Brazil • Japan • Korea • Mexico • Singapore • Spain • United Kingdom • United States

World English Level 2
Real People, Real Places, Real Language
Kirsten L. Johannsen and Rebecca Tarver Chase, Authors
Rob Jenkins, Series Editor

Publisher: Sherrise Roehr

Executive Editor: Sarah Kenney

Senior Development Editor: Margarita Matte

Development Editor: Brenden Layte

Assistant Editor: Alison Bruno

Editorial Assistant: Patricia Giunta

Media Researcher: Leila Hishmeh

Senior Technology Product Manager: Scott Rule

Director of Global Marketing: Ian Martin

Senior Product Marketing Manager:
    Caitlin Thomas

Sr. Director, ELT & World Languages:
    Michael Burggren

Production Manager: Daisy Sosa

Content Project Manager: Andrea Bobotas

Senior Print Buyer: Mary Beth Hennebury

Cover Designer: Aaron Opie

Art Director: Scott Baker

Creative Director: Chris Roy

Cover Image: PAUL CHESLEY/
    National Geographic Creative

Compositor: MPS Limited

For product information and technology assistance, contact us at
Cengage Learning Customer & Sales Support, 1-800-354-9706

For permission to use material from this text or product,
submit all requests online at **cengage.com/permissions**
Further permissions questions can be emailed to
permissionrequest@cengage.com

World English 2 ISBN: 978-1-285-84870-9
World English 2 + CD-ROM ISBN: 978-1-285-84836-5
World English 2 + Online Workbook ISBN: 978-1-305-08953-2

National Geographic Learning
20 Channel Center Street
Boston, MA 02210
USA

Cengage Learning is a leading provider of customized learning solutions with office locations around the globe, including Singapore, the United Kingdom, Australia, Mexico, Brazil, and Japan.

Cengage Learning products are represented in Canada by Nelson Education, Ltd.

Visit National Geographic Learning online at ngl.cengage.com

Visit our corporate website at www.cengage.com

Printed in the United States of America
1 2 3 4 5 6 7 8 9 10   16 15 14

Thank you to the educators who provided invaluable feedback during the development of the second edition of the *World English* series:

AMERICAS

Brazil

Renata Cardoso, Universidade de Brasília, Brasília
Gladys De Sousa, Universidade Federal de Minas Gerais, Belo Horizonte
Marilena Fernandes, Associação Alumni, São Paulo
Mary Ruth Popov, Ingles Express, Ltda., Belo Horizonte
Ana Rosa, Speed, Vila Velha
Danny Sheps, English4u2, Natal
Renata Zainotte, Go Up Idiomas, Rio de Janeiro

Colombia

Eida Caicedo, Universidad de San Buenaventura Cali, Cali
Andres Felipe Echeverri Patiño, Corporación Universitaria Lasallista, Envigado
Luz Libia Rey, Centro Colombo Americano, Bogota

Dominican Republic

Aida Rosales, Instituto Cultural Domínico-Americano, Santo Domingo

Ecuador

Elizabeth Ortiz, COPEI-Copol English Institute, Guayaquil

Mexico

Ramon Aguilar, LEC Languages and Education Consulting, Hermosillo
Claudia García-Moreno Ávila, Universidad Autónoma del Estado de México, Toluca
Ana María Benton, Universidad Anahuac Mexico Norte, Huixquilucan
Martha Del Angel, Tecnológico de Monterrey, Monterrey
Sachenka García B., Universidad Kino, Hermosillo
Cinthia I. Navarrete García, Universidad Autónoma del Estado de México, Toluca
Alonso Gaxiola, Universidad Autonoma de Sinaloa, Guasave
Raquel Hernandez, Tecnológico de Monterrey, Monterrey
Beatriz Cuenca Hernández, Universidad Autónoma del Estado de México, Toluca
Luz María Lara Hernández, Universidad Autónoma del Estado de México, Toluca
Esthela Ramírez Hernández, Universidad Autónoma del Estado de México, Toluca
Ma Guadalupe Peña Huerta, Universidad Autónoma del Estado de México, Toluca
Elsa Iruegas, Prepa Tec Campus Cumbres, Monterrey
María del Carmen Turral Maya, Universidad Autónoma del Estado de México, Toluca
Lima Melani Ayala Olvera, Universidad Autónoma del Estado de México, Toluca
Suraya Ordorica Reyes, Universidad Autónoma del Estado de México, Toluca
Leonor Rosales, Tecnológico de Monterrey, Monterrey
Leticia Adelina Ruiz Guerrero, ITESO, Jesuit University, Tlaquepaque

United States

Nancy Alaks, College of DuPage, Glen Ellyn, IL
Annette Barker, College of DuPage, Aurora, IL
Joyce Gatto, College of Lake County, Grayslake, IL
Donna Glade-Tau, Harper College, Palatine, IL
Mary "Katie" Hu, Lone Star College – North Harris, Houston, TX
Christy Naghitorabi, University of South Florida, St. Petersburg, FL

ASIA

Beri Ali, Cleverlearn (American Academy), Ho Chi Minh City
Ronald Anderson, Chonnam National University, Yeosu Campus, Jeollanam
Michael Brown, Canadian Secondary Wenzhou No. 22 School, Wenzhou
Leyi Cao, Macau University of Science and Technology, Macau
Maneerat Chuaychoowong, Mae Fah Luang University, Chiang Rai
Sooah Chung, Hwarang Elementary School, Seoul
Edgar Du, Vanung University, Taoyuan County
David Fairweather, Asahikawa Daigaku, Asahikawa
Andrew Garth, Chonnam National University, Yeosu Campus, Jeollanam
Brian Gaynor, Muroran Institute of Technology, Muroran-shi
Emma Gould, Chonnam National University, Yeosu Campus, Jeollanam
David Grant, Kochi National College of Technology, Nankoku
Michael Halloran, Chonnam National University, Yeosu Campus, Jeollanam
Nina Ainun Hamdan, University Malaysia, Kuala Lumpur
Richard Hatcher, Chonnam National University, Yeosu Campus, Jeollanam
Edward Tze-Lu Ho, Chihlee Institute of Technology, New Taipei City
Soontae Hong, Yonsei University, Seoul
Chaiyathip Katsura, Mae Fah Luang University, Chiang Rai
Byoug-Kyo Lee, Yonsei University, Seoul
Han Li, Aceleader International Language Center, Beijing
Michael McGuire, Kansai Gaidai University, Osaka
Yu Jin Ng, Universiti Tenaga Nasional, Kajang, Selangor
Somaly Pan, Royal University of Phnom Penh, Phnom Penh
HyunSuk Park, Halla University, Wonju
Bunroeun Pich, Build Bright University, Phnom Penh
Renee Sawazaki, Surugadai University, Annaka-shi
Adam Schofield, Cleverlearn (American Academy), Ho Chi Minh City
Pawadee Srisang, Burapha University, Chanthaburi Campus, Ta-Mai District
Douglas Sweetlove, Kinjo Gakuin University, Nagoya
Tari Lee Sykes, National Taiwan University of Science and Technology, Taipei
Monika Szirmai, Hiroshima International University, Hiroshima
Sherry Wen, Yan Ping High School, Taipei
Chris Wilson, Okinawa University, Naha City, Okinawa
Christopher Wood, Meijo University, Nagoya
Evelyn Wu, Minghsin University of Science and Technology, Xinfeng, Hsinchu County
Aroma Xiang, Macau University of Science and Technology, Macau
Zoe Xie, Macau University of Science and Technology, Macau
Juan Xu, Macau University of Science and Technology, Macau
Florence Yap, Chang Gung University, Taoyuan
Sukanda Yatprom, Mae Fah Luang University, Chiang Rai
Echo Yu, Macau University of Science and Technology, Macau

The publisher would like to extend a special thank you to Raúl Billini, English Coordinator, Mi Colegio, Dominican Republic, for his contributions to the series.

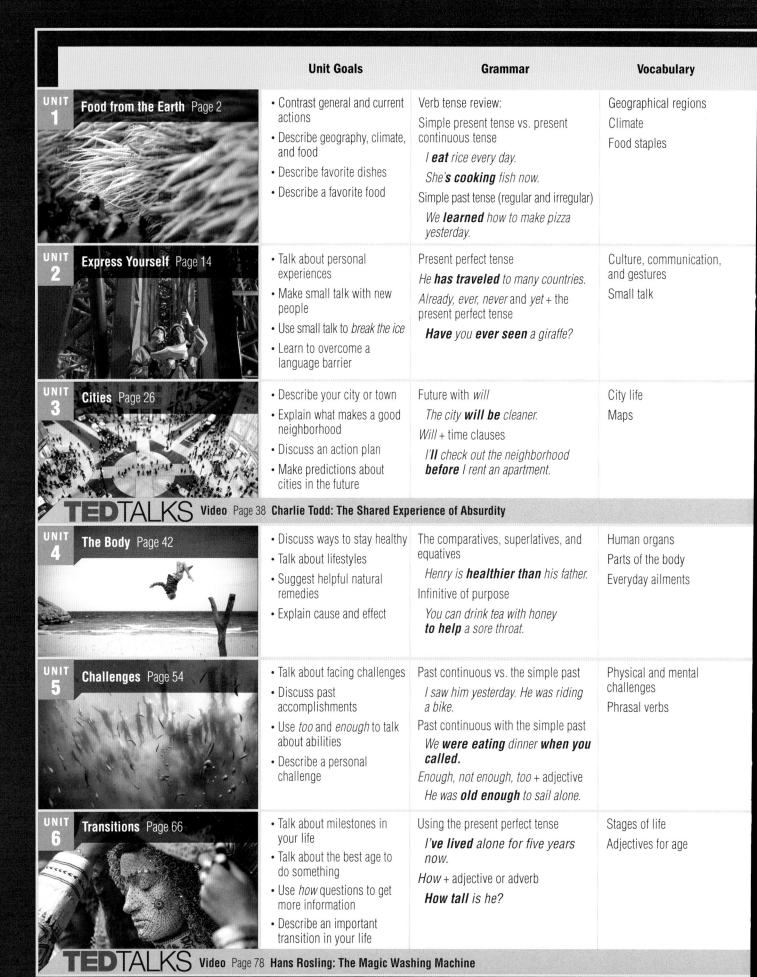
TEDTALKS   Video   Page 38   **Charlie Todd: The Shared Experience of Absurdity**

TEDTALKS   Video   Page 78   **Hans Rosling: The Magic Washing Machine**

Listening	Speaking and Pronunciation	Reading	Writing	Video Journal

Focused listening
 	
An interview:
  Rice farming
	Comparing different regions:
	  discussing their climate
	  and their food
	
	Linking sounds:
	  final consonant followed
	  by a vowel
		National Geographic:
		"A Slice of History"
			Responding to
			an e-mail
				National Geographic:
				"Forbidden Fruit"

General listening Conversations: Small talk	Talking about what you have or haven't done Making small talk *Have* or *has* vs. contractions	**National Geographic:** "Taking Pictures of the World"	Writing opinions	**National Geographic:** "Orangutan Language"
General and focused listening A radio interview: Jardin Nomade in Paris	Discussing good and bad elements in a neighborhood Predicting the future of cities Emphatic stress	**TED**TALKS "How Food Shapes Our Cities"	Writing a paragraph with predictions about cities in the future	**National Geographic:** "Fes"
Focused listening Discussions: Different lifestyles	Talking about food and exercise that are good for you Suggesting easy remedies Linking with comparatives and superlatives	**National Geographic:** "Tiny Invaders"	Writing an excuse for a sick child	**National Geographic:** "The Human Body"
General listening An interview: Jenny Daltry, herpetologist	Discussing challenges Talking about abilities Words that end in *–ed*	**National Geographic:** "Arctic Dreams and Nightmares"	Writing a paragraph about a challenging experience	**National Geographic:** "Searching for the Snow Leopard"

General and focused
listening
 	
A radio program:
  Healthy tips from an
  Okinawan centenarian
	Talking about something
	you did
	
	Discussing the best age for
	life transitions
	
	The schwa sound /ə/ in
	unstressed syllables
		TEDTALKS
		"Living Beyond Limits"
			Writing a paragraph
			to describe a life
			transition
				National Geographic:
				"Nubian Wedding"

	Unit Goals	Grammar	Vocabulary
UNIT 7 **Luxuries** Page 82	• Explain how we get luxury items • Talk about needs and wants • Discuss what makes people's lives better • Evaluate the effect of advertising	Passive voice (present tense) *Jewelry **is given** as a gift.* Passive voice with *by* *This blouse **was made by** well-paid workers.*	Luxury items Import/export items Past participles of irregular verbs
UNIT 8 **Nature** Page 94	• Use conditionals to talk about real situations • Talk about possible future situations • Describe what animals do • Discuss a problem in nature	Real conditionals in the future *If I **have** time tomorrow, I'll **call** you.* Review of quantifiers *Raccoons eat **many** different kinds of food.*	Nouns and adjectives to describe animals Adverbs of manner
UNIT 9 **Life in the Past** Page 106	• Discuss life in the past • Contrast different ways of life • Compare today with the past • Talk about historical wonder	*Used to* *Native Americans **used to** make their shoes out of deerskin.* Passive voice in the past *Igloos **were built** with blocks of ice.*	Life in the past Separable phrasal verbs

TEDTALKS Video Page 118 **Beverly and Dereck Joubert: Life Lessons from Big Cats**

	Unit Goals	Grammar	Vocabulary
UNIT 10 **Travel** Page 122	• Talk about preparations for a trip • Talk about different kinds of vacations • Use English at the airport • Discuss the pros and cons of tourism	Expressing necessity *I **must** make a reservation.* Expressing prohibition *You **must not** take pictures here.*	Travel preparations At the airport
UNIT 11 **Careers** Page 134	• Discuss career choices • Ask and answer job-related questions • Talk about career planning • Talk about innovative jobs	Modals for giving advice *You **should** choose a career that fits your personality.* Indefinite pronouns ***Everyone** in the audience **was** laughing.*	Careers and jobs Participial adjectives
UNIT 12 **Celebrations** Page 146	• Describe a festival • Compare holidays in different countries • Talk about celebrations • Share opinions about holidays	Comparisons with *as…as* *New Year's is **as** exciting **as** National Day.* *Would rather* *I**'d rather** have a big party.*	Festivals and holidays Expressions for celebrations

TEDTALKS Video Page 158 **Sylvia Earle: My Wish—Protect Our Oceans**

Listening	Speaking and Pronunciation	Reading	Writing	Video Journal
Focused listening Discussions: The world flower market	Discussing luxuries and necessities Talking about improving your life Sentence stress—content words vs. function words	**National Geographic:** "Perfume: The Essence of Illusion"	Writing a print ad	**National Geographic:** "Coober Pedy Opals"
General and focused listening A radio program: The bluefin tuna	Talk about issues that affect nature Role-playing to promote environmental action to make oceans sustainable Phrases in sentences	**TED**TALKS "How Poachers Became Caretakers"	Writing a paragraph to give an opinion	**National Geographic:** "Happy Elephants"
General and focused listening A lecture: The Sami people	Talking about how technology has changed our lives Discussing daily life in the past Reduction of *used to*	**National Geographic:** "Lord of the Mongols"	Writing a paragraph on one of the New 7 Wonders of the World	**National Geographic:** "Searching for Genghis Khan"
General and focused listening Conversations: Vacations	Planning a dream vacation Making your way through the airport Reduction of *have to, has to, got to*	**National Geographic:** "Tourists or Trees?"	Writing a paragraph about how tourists can help a place they visit	**National Geographic:** "Adventure Capital of the World"

General and focused listening
 	
An interview:
  A restaurant owner
  in Thailand
	Discussing career choices
	
	Intonation in questions
		TEDTALKS
		"Making Filthy Water Drinkable"
			Writing a letter giving advice	**National Geographic:**
				"Trinidad Bird Man"

General and focused listening
 	
Discussions:
  Local celebrations or
  holidays
	Comparing different international celebrations
	
	Talking about personal celebrations
	
	Question intonation with lists
		National Geographic:
		"Starting a New Tradition"
			Writing a substantiated opinion	**National Geographic:**
				"Young Riders of Mongolia"

BACKGROUND – LEARNING AND INSTRUCTION

Learning has been described as acquiring knowledge. Obtaining knowledge does not guarantee understanding, however. A math student, for example, could replicate any number of algebraic formulas, but never come to an *understanding* of how they could be used or for what purpose he or she has learned them. If understanding is defined as the ability to use knowledge, then learning could be defined differently and more accurately. The ability of the student to use knowledge instead of merely receiving information therefore becomes the goal and the standard by which learning is assessed.

This revelation has led to classrooms that are no longer teacher-centric or lecture driven. Instead, students are asked to think, ponder, and make decisions based on the information received or, even more productive, students are asked to construct learning or discover information in personal pursuits, or with help from an instructor, with partners, or in groups. The practice they get from such approaches stimulates learning with a purpose. The purpose becomes a tangible goal or objective that provides opportunities for students to transfer skills and experiences to future learning.

In the context of language development, this approach becomes essential to real learning and understanding. Learning a language is a skill that is developed only after significant practice. Students can learn the mechanics of a language but when confronted with real-world situations, they are not capable of communication. Therefore, it might be better to shift the discussion from "Language Learning" to "Communication Building." Communication should not be limited to only the productive skills. Reading and listening serve important avenues for communication as well.

FOUR PRINCIPLES TO DEVELOPING LEARNING ENVIRONMENTS

Mission: The goal or mission of a language course might adequately be stated as the pursuit of providing sufficient information and practice to allow students to communicate accurately and effectively to a reasonable extent given the level, student experiences, and time on task provided. This goal can be reflected in potential student learning outcomes identified by what students will be able to do through performance indicators.

World English provides a clear chart within the table of contents to show the expected outcomes of the course. The books are designed to capture student imagination and allow students ample opportunities to communicate. A study of the table of contents identifies the process of communication building that will go on during the course.

Context: It is important to identify what vehicle will be used to provide instruction. If students are to learn through practice, language cannot be introduced as isolated verb forms, nouns, and modifiers. It must have context. To reach the learners and to provide opportunities to communicate, the context must be interesting and relevant to learners' lives and expectations. In other words, there must be a purpose and students must have a clear understanding of what that purpose is.

World English provides a meaningful context that allows students to connect with the world. Research has demonstrated pictures and illustrations are best suited for creating interest and motivation within learners. National Geographic has a long history of providing magnificent learning environments through pictures, illustrations, true accounts, and video. The pictures, stories, and video capture the learners' imagination and "hook" them to learning in such a way that students have significant reasons to communicate promoting interaction and critical thinking. The context will also present students with a desire to know more, leading to life-long learning.

Objectives (Goals)

With the understanding that a purpose for communicating is essential, identifying precisely what the purpose is in each instance becomes crucial even before specifics of instruction have been defined. This is often called "backward design." Backward design means, in the context of classroom lesson planning, that first desired outcomes, goals, or objectives are defined and then lessons are mapped out with the end in mind, the end being what students will be able to do after sufficient instruction and practice. Having well-crafted objectives or goals provides the standard by which learners' performance can be assessed or self-assessed.

World English lessons are designed on two-page spreads so students can easily see what is expected and what the context is. The goal that directly relates to the final application activity is identified at the beginning. Students, as well as instructors, can easily evaluate their performance as they attempt the final activity. Students can also readily see what tools they will practice to prepare them for the application activity. The application activity is a task where students can demonstrate their ability to perform what the lesson goal requires. This information provides direction and purpose for the learner. Students, who know what is expected, where they are going, and how they will get there, are more apt to reach success. Each success builds confidence and additional communication skills.

Tools and Skills

Once the lesson objective has been identified and a context established, the lesson developer must choose the tools the learner will need to successfully perform the task or objective. The developer can choose among various areas in communication building including vocabulary, grammar and pronunciation. The developer must also choose skills and strategies including reading, writing, listening, and speaking. The receptive skills of reading and listening are essential components to communication. All of these tools and skills must be placed in a balanced way into a context providing practice that can be transferred to their final application or learner demonstration which ultimately becomes evidence of communication building.

World English units are divided into "lessons" that each consists of a two-page spread. Each spread focuses on different skills and strategies and is labeled by a letter (A-E). The units contain the following lesson sequence:

> A: Vocabulary
> B: Listening and Pronunciation
> C: Language Expansion
> D: Reading/Writing
> E: Video Journal

Additional grammar and vocabulary are introduced as tools throughout to provide practice for the final application activity. Each activity in a page spread has the purpose of developing adequate skills to perform the final application task.

LAST WORD

The philosophy of *World English* is to provide motivating context to connect students to the world through which they build communication skills. These skills are developed, practiced, and assessed from lesson to lesson through initially identifying the objective and giving learners the tools they need to complete a final application task. The concept of performance is highlighted over merely learning new information and performance comes from communicating about meaningful and useful context. An accumulation of small communication skills leads to true and effective communication outside of the classroom in real-world environments.

Rob Jenkins, Series Editor

Food from the Earth

About the Photo

This photo was taken by American photographer Kelly Lannen. The photo shows heirloom carrots at a farmer's market. The term *heirloom* is given to plants and vegetables that were grown before large-scale agriculture began. They are considered tastier and more nutritious than the hybrid vegetables we are used to seeing at the supermarket.

- Introduce the theme of the unit. Ask students, *What kinds of food grow in this country? Where do they grow?*

- Direct students' attention to the picture. Have students describe what they see.

- Have students work with a partner to answer the questions. Compare answers with the class, compiling a list on the board.

- Ask these questions orally or by writing them on the board for students to answer in pairs: *What are some famous foods from other countries? What foods do we buy from other countries?*

- Go over the Unit Goals with the class.

- For each goal, elicit any words students already know and write them on the board.

UNIT
1

Food from the Earth

Heirloom carrots sold in a farmer's market

2

UNIT 1 GOALS	Grammar	Vocabulary	Listening
• Contrast general and current actions • Describe geography, climate, and food • Describe favorite dishes • Describe a favorite food	Simple present tense vs. present continuous tense *I **eat** rice.* *She**'s cooking** fish now.* Simple past tense (regular and irregular) *We **learned** how to make pizza yesterday.*	Geographical regions Climate Food staples	Focused listening An interview: rice farming

Unit Theme Overview

- The theme for this unit is how climate and geography affect people's food and way of eating. It begins by examining staple foods in different parts of the world, and then moves on to look at how foods have become international.

- The world has over 50,000 edible plants. According to the United Nations Food and Agricultural Organization, just three of them (rice, corn, and wheat) make up 60 percent of the calories consumed in the world every day. They are the staple foods for four billion people. Rice is the staple food of over half the human race. Most people in the world live on one or several of these staple foods: rice, wheat, corn, millet, sorghum, potatoes, cassava, yams, taro, and animal products (meat, milk, eggs, cheese, and fish).

- Over time, patterns in staple foods are changing. Consumption of rice is increasing as incomes in Asia rise and people can afford more rice. Consumption of roots like yams and taro is decreasing, because more people in Africa and the Pacific are moving to cities where it is easier to buy grains.

- Only a part of the diet is staple foods, however. People also eat a wide variety of complementary foods, and in the last 500 years, improvements in transportation have helped to make many foods truly global. For example, coffee originally grew only in Ethiopia; chocolate came from Central America; pasta originated in China. These and many other foods are now enjoyed in virtually every country of the world.

UNIT 1 GOALS

1. Contrast general and current actions

2. Describe geography, climate, and food

3. Describe favorite dishes

4. Describe a favorite food

3

Speaking	Reading	Writing	Video Journal
Comparing different regions: discussing their climate and their food **Pronunciation:** Linking sounds: Final consonant followed by a vowel	**National Geographic:** A Slice of History	Responding to an e-mail	**National Geographic:** Forbidden Fruit

Teacher Tip

Going over the Unit Goals is an important stage in the lead-in to each unit. It is helpful for students to know what they are going to be learning so they can activate prior knowledge, either in English or their first language. Activating what students already know about a topic helps them organize and understand the new knowledge.

Contrast General and Current Actions

Vocabulary

A • Have students look at the picture and describe what they see.

• Ask students if they ever read (or write) blogs. If necessary, explain that a blog is a Web site where people write their personal ideas about topics that interest them. Tell students that they are going to read what a woman wrote in a travel blog about a trip to Turkey. If necessary, point out Turkey on a map.

• Have students read the blog post.

• Go over any unfamiliar words with the students. Point out the two irregular plurals: *cattle* (cows and bulls) and *sheep*. Ask a few comprehension questions, for example, *What food is mentioned in the blog? Where are there mountains? What is the weather like on the coast?* etc.

B • Have students work individually to find and write the words with the given meanings.

• Have students compare answers with a partner.

• Check answers.

Grammar

• Review the simple present tense. Ask, *What do you do every day? What do you eat for breakfast? Who cooks at your house?* Write answers on the board, and underline the verbs. Elicit/Give the name of the tense: simple present tense.

• Review the present continuous tense. Ask, *What are you doing now?* (possible answers: *learning English, sitting in class, reviewing grammar,* etc.) *What am I doing?* (possible answers: *asking questions, writing on the board,* etc.) Write answers on the board, and underline the verbs. Elicit/Give the name of the tense: present continuous tense.

• Go over the information in the chart, contrasting the two tenses.

A | **GOAL 1:** Contrast General and Current Actions

Vocabulary

A Read part of a travel blog.

This is my first visit to Turkey. It's a wonderful place! The people are friendly and the meals are delicious. Farmers here grow many different crops, including many kinds of fruit. They also grow a lot of wheat, and the bread in Turkey is really good. Of course, the geography and climate in different parts of Turkey affect the kind of food farmers can produce in each region. In Central Anatolia, the land is almost flat, and the weather is usually warm and dry. It's a good place to grow crops and to raise animals such as cattle and sheep. High up in the mountains of eastern Turkey, farmers also keep animals since they can't grow crops. Today I'm visiting the coast of the Mediterranean Sea in southern Turkey. The weather here is hot and humid, but the fish and seafood are excellent!

▲ Armenian church on Akdamar Island, Turkey

B Write the words in blue next to the correct meaning.

1. ___farmers___ people who produce food
2. ___region___ an area of a country or of the world
3. ___crops___ plants grown for food
4. ___mountains___ very high parts of the land
5. ___humid___ describes air with a lot of water in it
6. ___coast___ land near the ocean
7. ___flat___ describes land without mountains
8. ___geography___ features of a place, such as rivers
9. ___meals___ breakfast, lunch, and dinner
10. ___climate___ normal weather in a certain place

Grammar: Simple present vs. present continuous tense

Simple present tense		Present continuous tense	
I **eat** rice She **cooks** fish They **bake** bread We **have** fruit for breakfast	every day.	I'm **eating** rice She's **cooking** fish They're **baking** bread We're **having** mangos for breakfast	now.
Use the simple present tense to talk about habits and things that are generally true. *Use the present continuous tense to talk about actions and events that are happening now.*			

4   Unit 1

Word Bank:
Land and climate

desert	rainy
dry	river
frozen	rocky
lake	snowy
marsh	valley
monsoon	

Expansion Activity

Have students write a similar blog post on a sheet of paper or on a class or school Web site. Tell them to describe the food in a place they have visited—in their own country or in another country.

A Complete each sentence with the simple present or present continuous form of the verb in parentheses.

1. My mother and I ___cook___ a meal together every afternoon. (cook)
2. In Mexico, most people ___eat___ a big meal in the afternoon. (eat)
3. Right now, my mother and I ___are making___ a dish called *enchiladas*. (make)
4. I really like enchiladas. Sometimes I ___have___ them for breakfast! (have)
5. Now my mother ___is telling___ the whole family to come to the table. (tell)
6. We ___enjoy___ at least one meal together every day. (enjoy)

B Take turns with a partner doing the following.

1. Tell your partner what you usually eat for breakfast and lunch. (Use the simple present tense.)
2. Tell your partner three things people you know are doing right now. (Use the present continuous tense.)

Conversation

A 2 Close your book and listen to the conversation. What do Julie's cousins usually eat? *meat and potatoes and a lot of vegetables*

Tom: What are you doing?
Julie: I'm looking at pictures from my vacation.
Tom: Oh, can I see? Where did you go?
Julie: I visited my cousins in the south. It's very flat there—no mountains or hills, and it's pretty dry for most of the year.
Tom: What about food? What do your cousins usually eat?
Julie: Meals are very simple there. It's basically meat and potatoes and a lot of vegetables. But they grow wheat everywhere, so pasta is becoming popular.
Tom: That sounds good.
Julie: Yes, I really like the food there.

▲ Enchiladas with rice

B Practice the conversation with a partner. Switch roles and practice it again.

C How is the geography and food in your part of the world similar to or different from the place Julie describes? Work in small groups and share your answers to the question.

D **GOAL CHECK** ✔ **Contrast general and current actions**

Complete this sentence three times. Two of the sentences should be true, but one should be untrue: *I usually _____, but today I'm _____.*

Read your sentences to your partner in any order. Your partner will guess which sentence is false.

> I usually wear glasses, but today I'm wearing contact lenses.

> And I usually carry my phone to class, but today I'm letting my sister use my phone.

Grammar: Simple present vs. present continuous

The simple present is used in four types of situations.

1. Habitual activities: *Koreans eat rice every day.*
2. General facts: *Bananas grow in hot climates.*
3. States, feelings, or perceptions: *This soup tastes salty.*
4. Things that happen all the time: *I live in Tokyo.*

The present continuous is used in two types of situations.

1. Actions that are happening right now: *I'm doing my homework.*
2. Ongoing activities that started in the past and will continue in the future: *Jack is taking tennis lessons.*

A • Have students work individually to complete the sentences with the verbs in the correct tense.
- Have students compare answers with a partner.
- Check answers.

B • Divide the class into pairs and have them take turns talking about what they usually eat and about what people they know are doing.
- Ask students to tell the class an interesting sentence they heard from their partner.

Conversation

A • Have students close their books. Write the question on the board: *What do Julie's cousins usually eat?*
- Play the recording. 2
- Check answers.

B • Play or read the conversation again for the class to repeat.
- Practice the conversation with the class in chorus.
- Have students practice the conversation with a partner, then switch roles and practice it again.

C • In groups of four, have them compare the geography and food in their country with the place described in the recording.
- Have each group report on the similarities and differences they discussed.

D **GOAL CHECK** ✔

- Model the activity. Write three sentences about yourself on the board. One of them must be untrue. Have students guess which one isn't true.
- Have students write three sentences about themselves. Remind them to follow the model.
- In pairs, have them take turns reading and guessing.
- Have several students share a true sentence about their partner with the class.

Describe Geography, Climate, and Food

Listening

A
- Have students look at the picture and describe what they see. Ask, *What is the geography like in this region? The climate? What do you think is a staple food in this region?* Write *staple food* on the board and give an example.
- Divide the class into pairs and have them answer the questions.
- Compare answers with the class.

B
- Tell students they are going to listen to an interview about farming rice. Have them read the questions.
- Play the recording one or more times. 🔊 3
- Check answers.

C
- Tell students to listen again to find the information.
- Play the recording one or more times. 🔊 3
- Have students compare answers with a partner.
- Check answers.

Communication

A
- Review the idea of regions. With the class, talk about and list on the board the different regions of their countries.
- Divide the class into pairs and have them complete the chart about two regions of their choice.

B
- Combine pairs to make groups of four. Have pairs take turns describing and guessing regions.
- Point out the Word Focus box. Ask, *What crops do farmers raise near here? What crops do they grow in other parts of this country?*
- Direct students' attention to the Engage! box. Have students discuss the question in pairs or groups, or talk about it as a class. Elicit reasons why farmers would need to grow more food (increase in population, improving people's health).

B   GOAL 2: Describe Geography, Climate, and Food

Listening

A 🔄 Look at the picture. Discuss these questions with a partner.

1. What are important foods that everyone in your country eats?
2. Where in the world do farmers grow rice? *in colder places, like Japan and Korea, but not in water.* **Answers will vary. Most rice grows in paddies. Other types of rice are grown**
3. Why do they grow it there? *Rice usually needs a lot of water to grow.*

▲ People working in a rice paddy.

Word Focus

Farmers **raise crops** or **grow crops.**

Engage!

Do you think farmers and scientists need to find ways to increase food production? Why?

B 🔊 3 Listen to the interview. Circle the correct letter.

1. Who is the interviewer talking to?

   a. a restaurant owner   **(b.)** a rice farmer   **c.** a news reporter

2. What is happening in the rice paddy today? People are . . .

   (a.) planting rice plants.   **b.** planting seeds.   **c.** letting water into the paddy.

3. What kind of climate does rice need?

   a. hot and dry   **(b.)** warm and wet   **c.** cool and humid

C 🔊 3 Listen again and answer the questions.

1. Why doesn't the rice farmer plant seeds like other farmers? *He gets a much larger crop if he starts with young plants.*

2. How is the rainfall this year? *There has been a lot of rain.*

3. What happens to the water in the rice paddy after the rice plants grow? *The farmer lets the water run out.*

4. What happens to the rice plants after they're dry? *The farmer cuts the rice plants and cleans them.*

Communication

A 🔄 Talk with a partner about two different regions in your country. Describe the land, the climate, and the food.

	Region #1	Region #2
land		
climate		
staple foods		

B 🔗 Get together with another pair of students. Describe your two regions and have the other students guess the names of the regions.

6   Unit 1

For Your Information: Rice

The rice plant is native to southern Asia and some parts of Africa. But after centuries of trade, it is grown around the world. It is not known where or when rice was first cultivated, but there is evidence of rice grown in both India and China about 5,000 years ago. Today, the largest rice-growing countries are China, India, Egypt, and Indonesia. Most rice is consumed where it is grown—only about five percent of the world's rice is exported.

A Welsh fisherman rakes the sand to harvest small shellfish.

Pronunciation: Linking words together

When a word ends in a consonant sound, and the next word starts with a vowel sound, the words are linked together.

We cut the rice plants and clean them.   **We grow a lot of rice.**

A 🔊 **4** Listen to the sentences. Notice the pronunciation of the linked words. Listen again and repeat the sentences.

1. I usually like a tomato with breakfast.

2. Staple foods are the most important foods.

3. We're eating dinner now.

4. Paul and I don't like fish very much.

5. Farmers work on weekends and holidays.

6. Rain falls in all regions of the world.

B 🔁 Underline the sounds that link together. Then read the sentences to a partner.

1. Hal enjoys pizza.

2. Wheat bread is very popular.

3. Corn grows well in Mexico.

4. A ham and cheese sandwich is my favorite lunch.

5. My friend is eating sushi.

6. Dry grasslands are good places to raise animals.

C 🔁 **GOAL CHECK** ✔ **Describe geography, climate, and food**

Tell a partner about your ideal place. It can be a real or imagined place. Describe the geography and climate there as well as the food people usually eat.

Food from the Earth   **7**

Pronunciation

- Present the rule about linking words. Write the sentences on the board and help students understand that the words with the arrows run into each other when spoken.

A
- Tell students to listen to the linking of the underlined words in the recording.
- Play the recording. 🔊 **4**
- Tell students to listen again and repeat the sentences.
- Play the recording. 🔊 **4**
- If desired, have students read the sentences to a partner, linking the indicated sounds.

B
- Have students underline the sounds that link.
- Check answers.
- Have students read the sentences to a partner. Walk around helping with difficulties.

C ⚙ **GOAL CHECK** ✔

- Have students think about their ideal place (real or imagined). Have them write notes about the geography, climate, and food there. Provide vocabulary as necessary.
- Divide the class into pairs and have them take turns describing their ideal place.
- Have several students share something about their partner's ideal place with the class.

Expansion Activity

Have students go online to get information about a staple food in another country. Where does it grow? How do people cook it? Why is it common in that part of the world? Have them write down several facts about the staple food and present them to the class or to a small group.

Describe Favorite Dishes

Language Expansion

- Have students look at the illustration. Ask, *Which of these foods have you tried? Which ones do you like? Which ones can grow in this country?*

A
- Have students think about their personal knowledge of these foods and answer *true* or *false*.
- Have students compare answers with a partner.
- Check answers.

B
- Have students discuss the questions with a partner.
- Compare answers as a class.

Grammar

- Review the simple past tense by asking, *What did you do yesterday?* Write answers on the board, underlining the verb: *I went shopping.* Give/Elicit the name of the tense: simple past tense.

- Go over the information in the chart, reminding students that many common verbs are irregular (the past tense cannot be formed with -*ed*) and must be learned one by one.

- Point out the time expressions in the Word Focus box. Have students make sentences using the expressions from the box. Prompt them with questions as necessary, *What did you do yesterday? When did you start studying English?* etc.

- Direct students' attention to the Engage! box. Have students write sentences about their life using the time expressions in the Word Focus box and words from the Grammar chart.

- Have different students share their sentences with the class and write them on the board.

Language Expansion: Staple food crops

A What do you know about staple food crops? Circle T for *true* or F for *false*.

Corn
Wheat
Rice
Oats
Soybeans
Lentils
Black Beans
Red Beans
Potatoes
Yucca
Yams

1. Potatoes are originally from South America.   (T)   F
2. India is one of the world's largest producers of wheat.   (T)   F
3. Lentils are a kind of legume.   (T)   F
4. Soy sauce is made from soybeans.   (T)   F
5. Yucca grows in (under) the ground.   (T)   F
6. China is the world's largest consumer of rice.   (T)   F

B Discuss the questions with a partner.

1. In what parts of the world do people eat these staple foods?
2. What other staple foods do you know about?
3. What staple foods do you usually eat?

> People eat a lot of soybeans in Asian countries.

> Right, or they eat foods made from soybeans, like *tofu* and *miso*.

Word Focus

With the simple past, we often use:

yesterday/the day before **yesterday**

days/weeks/years/months **ago**

last week/month/year

Engage!

Write sentences about your own life in a notebook. Use the simple past and words from the grammar chart, for example: *I **ate** sushi at a party last month, and I liked it!*

Grammar: Simple past tense

Simple past tense	
We **learned** how to make pizza	yesterday.
Too much rain **fell**	last November.
I **ate** sushi for the first time	in 2006.
*Some verbs are regular in the simple past tense. They have an -*ed* ending.	*Some verbs are irregular in the simple past tense. They have many different forms.

learn – learned	want – wanted	see – saw	take – took
arrive – arrived	need – needed	eat – ate	fall – fell
play – played	help – helped	drink – drank	try – tried
ask – asked	show – showed	go – went	meet – met
travel – traveled		send – sent	be – was/were
		give – gave	

Grammar Strategy

In order for students to internalize irregular past forms, having the opportunity to use them communicatively is an important stage in the learning process (for example, using them to express something about themselves, as in the Engage! activity). Remind students that using new language forms immediately will help them remember them more effectively. As well as writing sentences, have students ask and answer questions in pairs, using irregular verbs in the past.

Word Bank: More everyday foods

bread	fish	soup
cheese	meat	stew
curry	milk	tofu
dumplings	oatmeal	tortillas
eggs	pasta	

A Complete the conversation. Use the simple past tense of the verbs in parentheses.

Mary: Tell me about yourself, Pedro.

Pedro: Well, I love to travel. Last year I __traveled__ (travel) to Greece.

Mary: Wow! You __went__ (go) to Greece?

Pedro: Yes, and I __met__ (meet) my friend Vasilys and his family there. They __showed__ (show) me around Athens and __introduced__ (introduce) me to many new foods.

Mary: That sounds like fun.

Pedro: It was. I __ate__ (eat) seafood and lamb, and I __tried__ (try) a dish made from rice and grape leaves. It __was__ (be) delicious!

B Complete these sentences about the past. Use your own information.

1. Yesterday, I ate _____ .
2. Last week, I went _____ .
3. On the first day of this class, I learned _____ .
4. Last month, _____ .
5. In 2012, _____ .
6. Ten years ago, _____ .

Conversation

A 🔊 **5** Close your book and listen to the conversation. What is Albert eating? What is it made from? *couscous, wheat*

Albert: You should try this! My aunt made it.

Mary: Mmmm . . . Delicious! What is it?

Albert: It's called *couscous*. It's made from wheat.

Mary: And what's this on top of the couscous?

Albert: Mostly vegetables and some kind of sauce.

Mary: How did your aunt learn to cook it?

Albert: Her great-uncle married a woman from North Africa. That's where couscous is from. They always ate it on special occasions.

Mary: What an interesting family history!

Albert: Yeah, and a great family recipe.

B 🔄 Practice the conversation. Switch roles and practice it again. Tell your partner about some foods you like that come from other parts of the world.

C 🔄 **GOAL CHECK** ✔ **Describe favorite dishes**

Look at the staple foods on page 8. Tell your partner about dishes you like to eat that are made with these staple foods. When was the last time you ate each dish?

Real Language

When we say something is *made from* other things, we're talking about its ingredients.

▲ North African couscous

> I really like Indian *biryani*. It's a rice dish with vegetables and spices. I ate it last month at a restaurant.

Food from the Earth **9**

Grammar:
Simple past tense

The simple past tense is used to talk about single or repeated occurrences in the past, during a time period that is finished.

> *I saw Anna yesterday.*
>
> *Jason worked every day last week.*

Grammar Practice: Simple past tense

Have students write five sentences about their lives in the past. (For example, *I went to Mexico last summer.*) Four of the sentences should be true, and one should be false. Then divide the class into groups of three or four students. After the group has heard each student's list, they ask questions to try to decide which sentence is not true. This activity can be used to help students get to know each other in a new class.

A
- Have students work individually to fill in the past tense form of each verb.
- Have students compare answers with a partner.
- Check answers.
- Direct students' attention to the Real Language box. Point out the expression and ask about common foods in students' countries: *What is [kimchi] made from?*

B
- Have students complete the sentences with true information about themselves.
- Ask students to share their sentences with a partner.

Conversation

A
- Have students close their books. Write the questions on the board: *What is Albert eating? What is it made from?*
- Play the recording. 🔊 **5**
- Check answers.

B
- Play or read the conversation again for the class to repeat. Then practice again with the class in chorus.
- Have students practice the conversation with a partner, then switch roles and practice it again.
- Have students tell each other about food they like from around the world. Point out the example, and tell students about a food you like.
- Have several students tell the class about a food their partner likes.

C 🔄 **GOAL CHECK** ✔

- Divide the class into pairs and have them look at the staple foods on page 8 again. Ask, *What dishes are made with potatoes? Lentils?*
- Have students tell their partner about dishes they eat made with the different staple foods and when they last ate them.
- Have several students share with the class something about the dishes their partner likes.

Describe a Favorite Food

Reading

- Introduce the topic of the reading. Ask, *Do you eat pizza? What is it made of? Where did pizza come from? How old do you think it is?*

A
- Have students read the directions and the three options. Have them read the title and the first line of each paragraph.
- Have students decide how the article is organized.
- Check answer, and have students underline the expressions that show the article is organized over time (*thousands of years ago, over time, slowly, in the late 1800s, now*).

B
- Have students read the article. Tell them to circle any words they don't understand.
- Go over the article with the class, answering any questions from the students about vocabulary.
- Have students complete the sentences with words from the article.
- Check answers.

C
- Individually, have students make a list of food from other places.
- Divide the class into pairs and have them talk about the food on their lists and where it is from.
- With the class, compile a list on the board of foods and their countries of origin.

Communication

- Tell students they are going to invent a new pizza. Write on the board, *sauce, toppings,* and *crust.* Elicit examples for each one.

A
- Divide the class into groups of three or four. Tell them to invent their own kind of pizza. They should agree on a name, the toppings, sauce, and type of crust.
- Have groups present their new pizza ideas. If desired, finish with a whole-class vote for the best pizza.

D | GOAL 4: Describe a Favorite Food

Reading

A Read the title and the first sentence of each paragraph. How is the reading organized?

- **a.** by importance, from least important to most important
- **(b.)** over time, from earliest to latest
- **c.** comparison and contrast, showing similarities and differences

B Read the whole article and complete each sentence.

1. People thousands of years ago made flat bread on hot _____rocks_____ .

2. _Native American_ people ate tomatoes before European people.

3. Cooks in _____Naples_____ put tomatoes on flat bread.

4. _____Italians_____ brought pizza to the United States.

5. People eat lamb and tofu on pizza in _____India_____ .

C 🔁 Make a list of popular foods that came from other countries. Where did these foods come from? Tell a partner.

> People here eat a lot of curry. I think it came from India.

> Right. There's an Indian restaurant downtown. They have wonderful curry.

Communication

A 👥 Work in a small group. Invent a new kind of pizza for Lombardi's restaurant. You should all agree on the toppings, the sauce, and the type of crust.

Naples, Italy

A SLICE OF HISTORY

What do you like on your pizza? Cheese? Tomatoes? Sausage? People may disagree on their favorite ingredients, but many people agree that pizza is a favorite food. Where and when did people start making pizza? To find out, we have to travel back in time.

Thousands of years ago, people used ancient types of wheat and other grains to make flat bread on the hot rocks of their **campfires.** At some point in time, early cooks started putting other kinds of food on the bread—using the bread as a plate. It was the world's first pizza **crust!**

For Your Information: Pizza

- The largest pizza in the world was made in Johannesburg, South Africa, in 1990. It was 37.4 meters (122.7 feet) across, and was made with 500 kilograms (1,102.3 pounds) of flour, 800 kilograms (1,763.7 pounds) of cheese, and 900 kilograms (1,984.1 pounds) of tomato puree.

- Pizza restaurants in many countries deliver to people's homes. The longest pizza delivery in the world was from Cape Town, South Africa, to Sydney, Australia, in 2001.

- The most expensive pizza in the world was sold at a charity auction in 2007 for almost $4,000. It was made with caviar and smoked salmon and decorated with edible gold.

Over time, pizza began to look more like the food we know today. When European explorers arrived in the Americas, they saw Native American people eating tomatoes. When they brought tomatoes back to Europe, however, people there wouldn't eat them. They thought eating tomatoes could make them ill.

Slowly, however, Europeans discovered that tomatoes were delicious and safe to eat. Cooks in Naples, an Italian city, began putting tomatoes on their flat bread. The world's first true pizza shop opened in Naples in 1830. People there ate pizza for lunch and dinner. They even ate it for breakfast!

In the late 1800s, many Italians moved to the United States. They brought pizza with them. The first American pizzeria, or pizza restaurant, was Lombardi's in New York City. It opened its doors in 1905. Now pizza is one of the three most popular foods in the USA, but Americans are not the only pizza lovers.

People now eat around five billion pizzas a year, and everyone has their favorite kind. Brazilians love green peas on their pizza. Russians like fish and onions. People in India use lamb and tofu. The Japanese think seafood on pizza is good. Some pizzas truly sound **strange,** yet all of them share two things. Each begins with bread. And each is a **slice** of history.

Food from the Earth 11

After Reading

Web search: Have students search online using the term *pizza recipe* to find a recipe that sounds interesting. Divide the class into groups and have them talk about the recipes they found. Which is the most unusual, delicious, or easy to make?

Project: As a follow-up to the communication activity, have students write and perform a television commercial for their new kind of pizza, with all members of the group acting in the commercial.

Describe a Favorite Food

Writing

A
- Go over the e-mail message with the class. Ask, *Who is the e-mail from? Who is it to? What does Ronald want to know?* Elicit possible answers for the questions in the e-mail?

- Tell students to imagine they are answering the e-mail with advice for students who are coming to visit their country. Have them write down their e-mails.

Communication

A
- Divide the class into pairs and have them exchange their e-mails. Have them compare their answers to Ronald's questions.

- Compare answers with the class, and write on the board lists of typical breakfast, lunch, and dinner foods, and other traditional dishes the visitors should try.

B 🔁 **GOAL CHECK** ✔

- Divide the class into pairs and have them discuss foods from their region or country that are eaten in other places.

- Compare answers with the class.

D **GOAL 4:** Describe a Favorite Food

Food vendor at the Damnoen Saduak Floating Market in Thailand.

Writing

A Read the email and write a response. Be sure to answer all the questions.

From: Ronald Ferguson

To: _____

Subject: Help! My students have some questions for you.

Hi there,

How is everything there? I hope you're doing well, and I hope you can answer some questions from my students. Our class will visit your country next month, and the students are asking me about the food. Here are some of their questions:

What do people usually eat for breakfast there?
Do you have pizza and hamburger restaurants?
What are some traditional dishes we can try?

Is there a staple food that people eat every day?
What are some good things to eat for lunch and dinner?

Thank you very much! I look forward to our visit next month. Maybe you can join us for a good meal.

Your friend,
Ronald

Communication

A 🔁 Share your e-mail with a partner. Did your partner answer all of Ronald Ferguson's questions? Did you and your partner answer any of the questions differently?

B 🔁 **GOAL CHECK** ✔ **Describe a favorite food**

Discuss the questions with a partner.

1. What foods from your country are now popular in other places?

2. Why do you think people like these foods?

12 **Unit 1**

Teacher Tip: Correcting writing

You can save a lot of time reviewing student papers by using peer correction. Before students turn in a paper, have them exchange their work with a partner and mark any mistakes or problems they see on their partner's paper. Then, have them make the corrections on their own papers before handing them in to you for grading.

a floating market

Before You Watch

A 🔁 Discuss the following questions with a partner. Use the adjectives in the box.

1. What are some foods that have a very strong smell?

2. After you prepare food with a strong smell in your home, how can you get rid of the odor?

> smelly   delicious
> fragrant   disgusting

While You Watch

A ▶ Watch the video *Forbidden Fruit*. Match the people to the actions.

1. Hotel staff __c__
2. Hotel guests __a__
3. Hotel cleaning staff __b__

a. try to bring durian fruit into hotel rooms.
b. use a special machine in smelly hotel rooms.
c. watch for people bringing in durian fruit.

B ▶ Watch the video again and write the correct answer.

1. How old are durian trees when they begin to produce fruit? __15 years old__
2. How many American dollars can one durian fruit cost? __$50__
3. Where do hotel owners want people to eat durian fruit? __outside in the fresh air__

After You Watch / Communication

A 🔁 Write a guide for tourists visiting your country. Describe three foods that are popular in your culture, but that people from other cultures might find disgusting or intolerable. Give reasons why tourists should try those foods.

B 👥 You are a group of hotel owners in Malaysian Borneo. Brainstorm a list of ways to prevent people from bringing durian fruit into their hotel rooms.

▲ Durian fruit

Food from the Earth   **13**

Video Journal: *Forbidden Fruit*

Before You Watch

- Have students look at the pictures and describe what they see. Tell them they are going to watch a video about a fruit that is forbidden (not allowed) in Kuching, Malaysia. If students are not familiar with durians, have them guess why a fruit would be forbidden.

A
- Go over the adjectives in the box.
- Have students discuss the questions with a partner, using the adjectives in the box.
- Compare answers with the class.

While You Watch

A
- Tell them to watch the video and match the people to the actions.
- Play the video.
- Have students compare answers with a partner.
- Check answers.

B
- Have students read the questions. Have them watch again and write their answers.
- Play the video.
- Have students compare answers with a partner.
- Check answers.

After You Watch / Communication

A
- Divide the class into pairs. Go over the directions.
- Call on pairs to tell the class what they've written about one food.

B
- Divide the class into groups of three or four. Have them list as many ideas as they can for how to keep durians out of hotels. Set a five-minute time limit, and encourage them to think of both serious and funny methods.
- Have each group share their list with the class. Compile a list on the board. With the class, discuss the most useful/funniest ideas.

For Your Information: Durian

- The durian fruit is native to Indonesia and Malaysia. The fruit can grow up to 30 centimeters (12 inches) long and usually weighs 1–4 kilograms (2–9 pounds).

- Durian is sometimes called *the king of fruits*, but opinions vary. The fruit has a very strong odor, which some people find fragrant and others find

intensely disgusting (It is sometimes compared with rotting garbage or dirty socks.). Despite this, many people love the flavor, and durian is used in candy, ice cream, and milk shakes.

- Today, durians are grown all around Southeast Asia. Thailand is the main exporter of durians.

Express Yourself

About the Photo

This photo was taken by British photographer Monty Rakusen. Rakusen does a lot of corporate photography, including working with companies in the heavy industry sector. Consequently, he is not adverse to photo shoots that involve difficulty and danger, such as climbing a 200-meter tower or scaling the side of a tanker out at sea. This photo shows a moment in heavy industry. Here, Rakusen has captured the immensity and power of the huge cranes as they tower high above the two workers who stand below discussing them.

- Introduce the theme of the unit. Ask, *When do you talk to people you don't know? What do you talk about with people you don't know? Do you talk about different things with people you know?*

- Direct students' attention to the picture. Have students describe what they see.

- Have students answer the questions with a partner.

- Compare answers with the class.

- Ask these questions orally or by writing them on the board for students to answer in pairs: *What are some gestures that you sometimes use? What do they mean? Why do we smile at people?*

- Go over the Unit Goals with the class.

- For each goal, elicit any words students already know and write them on the board; for example, the names of different nationalities and languages, difficulties they have communicating with someone who speaks a different language, etc.

Crane workers on a construction site

14

UNIT 2 GOALS	Grammar	Vocabulary	Listening
• Talk about personal experiences • Make small talk with new people • Use small talk to *break the ice* • Learn to overcome a language barrier	Present perfect tense He **has traveled** to many countries. Signal words: *yet, already, ever, never* **Have** you **ever eaten** Indian food?	Culture, communication, and gestures Small talk	Listening for general understanding Conversations: small talk

UNIT 2 GOALS

1. Talk about personal experiences

2. Make small talk with new people

3. Use small talk to *break the ice*

4. Learn to overcome a language barrier

Unit Theme Overview

- Different cultures have different rules for, and patterns of, communicating. In this unit, students will learn about and consider some of these cultural differences.

- Communication can be broken down into two basic types: *nonverbal* and *verbal*. Nonverbal communication includes facial expressions, eye contact, gestures, and rules for distance and touching during conversations. Cultures have widely differing rules for nonverbal communication. For instance, Latin Americans and Arabs tend to stand closer together when speaking than Japanese and North Americans do. This unit briefly introduces some of these differences.

- Verbal communication includes matters such as directness and indirectness, display of emotion in speaking, and even the types of topics that are appropriate to discuss with different types of people. This unit focuses on making small talk with a new acquaintance, a skill students will find useful when making cross-cultural contact. Students learn about and practice making small talk and then consider different ways of *breaking the ice* when meeting someone for the first time. Small talk is an especially important skill for learners of English as an international language.

Speaking	Reading	Writing	Video Journal
Talking about what you have or haven't done Making small talk **Pronunciation:** *Have* or *has* vs. contractions	**National Geographic:** Taking Pictures of the World	Writing opinions	**National Geographic:** Orangutan Language

Talk About Personal Experiences

Vocabulary

A • Have students look at the picture and describe what they see. Ask, *Do you think they know each other well? What do you think they are talking about?*

• Ask, *What are some problems in talking with people from another culture?* Elicit ideas like language, customs, knowing how to be polite, etc. Tell students that they are going to read about communicating with people from other cultures.

• Point out the expressions in the Word Focus box. Have students read the article. Ask some comprehension questions, for example, *When you learn a language, what else do you learn? What do they say in China when they say hello to someone? Why is a smile important?*

B • Have students write the words next to the correct meanings.

• Have students compare answers with a partner.

• Check answers.

Grammar

• Review the present perfect tense. Tell the class, *I've been very busy so far today. I've taught three classes. I've checked homework. I've talked to students. What about you? What have you done?* Elicit answers with the present perfect tense. Ask students, *Have you eaten lunch/had other classes today?* Elicit, *Yes, I have./No, I haven't.*

• Go over the information in the chart. Write the following sentences on the board. Tell the class that these are examples of the three uses of the present perfect tense explained in the chart.

I have been a nurse for five years.

I have seen that movie six times.

I have eaten lunch, so I'm not hungry now.

A   GOAL 1: Talk About Personal Experiences

Vocabulary

A Read the article.

▲ A photographer talks with a Nepalese woman.

Every culture around the world has different customs and ways of communicating. When you learn a language, you learn more than words. You also learn a lot of rules. You learn what kind of greetings to use in different situations. For example, in English, we use formal and informal greetings. In China, a traditional greeting is "Have you eaten today?" In addition, there are rules for making small talk when you meet a person. Once you have learned the rules of a language, you can communicate more easily and avoid misunderstandings.

People in different cultures also have different ways of using their bodies to communicate. We use our heads and our hands to make gestures, for example. But there's one kind of communication that's the same everywhere. A smile can always connect people.

B Write the words in blue next to the correct meaning.

1. _____rules_____ instructions for what is allowed
2. _____smile_____ happy facial expression
3. _____gestures_____ movements used to communicate
4. _____connect_____ to join together
5. _____culture_____ behaviors special to a country or people
6. _misunderstandings_ problems caused when one is not understood
7. _____customs_____ usual ways of doing things
8. _____small talk_____ informal talk about everyday topics
9. _____traditional_____ describes customs from long ago
10. _____greetings_____ language used when we meet someone

Grammar: Present perfect tense

Present perfect tense
Subject + **has/have** + **(not)** + **past participle** He **has traveled** to many countries. He **has not been** in Korea before.
We use the present perfect tense: *to talk about something that started in the past and continues now. *to talk about something that happened several times in the past. *to talk about something in the past that is connected with the present.

Word Focus

follow a rule = do something the correct way

make small talk = talk about things that aren't important

16   Unit 2

Word Bank:
Communication

appropriate	interrupt
assume	nonverbal
frown	shake hands
glance	silence
honest	stare
inappropriate	verbal

Grammar: Present perfect tense

The present perfect tense emphasizes the connection between past and present situations. It is used for:

a. situations that began in the past and continue into the present: *Jane **has been** an administrative assistant for 27 years.*

b. experience in general, when the specific time is not important: *I **have** already **seen** that movie (so I know what it's about).*

A Complete the sentences. Use the present perfect form of the verb in parentheses.

1. I ___have met___ (meet) many Canadians, but I __haven't been/have not been__ (not, be) to Canada.

2. Jason doesn't want to watch a movie tonight. He ___has watched___ (watch) movies every night for the past week.

3. Sam ___has traveled___ (travel) to Argentina four times. He loves it there!

4. My husband and I ___have been___ (be) married for six years.

5. It's my friend's birthday, but I ___haven't bought/have not bought___ (not, buy) her a present yet!

6. I think Lee will do well on the test. He ___has studied___ (study) a lot for it.

B ⟳ Complete the questions. Ask a partner to answer them. Write some questions of your own in your notebook.

Have you ever . . .

1. eaten _____ food?

2. seen a movie from _____ (country)?

3. gone to _____ ?

4. played _____ ?

5. talked to _____ ?

> **Have you ever eaten Indian food?**

> **No, never.**

> **Yes, once/many times. It's really good!**

Conversation

A 🔊 6 Close your book and listen to the conversation. Why is the woman worried? *She has never been to Mexico before.*

Annie: Guess what? I'm going to spend a month in Mexico City.
Rick: That's great! What are you going to do there?
Annie: I'm going to work in my company's office there. I'm a little worried, though. I've never been to Mexico before.
Rick: But you've met lots of people from Mexico, and you've taken Spanish lessons.
Annie: That's true. And I guess I've learned something about Mexican customs.
Rick: It sounds to me like you're ready to go.

B ⟳ Practice the conversation with a partner. Switch roles and practice it again. Tell your partner how you might feel about going to another country.

C ⟳ **GOAL CHECK** ✔ **Talk about personal experiences**

Which of these things have you done or not done? Use the present perfect to tell a partner about your experiences.

talk to someone from another culture

communicate with gestures

speak a foreign language

make small talk with a stranger

Real Language

We use *Guess what?* in informal conversations to say that we have interesting news.

▲ Palace of Bellas Artes, Mexico City

Express Yourself **17**

A
• Have students work individually to fill in the present perfect tense of the given verbs.
• Have students compare answers with a partner.
• Check answers.
• Discuss the reason why the present perfect was used in each sentence.

B
• Have students work individually to complete the questions and write at least two of their own.
• Divide the class into pairs and have them take turns asking and answering their questions.
• Call on student pairs to share their most interesting question and answer.

Conversation

A
• Have students close their books. Write the question on the board: *Why is the woman worried?*
• Play the recording. 🔊 6
• Check answers.
• Point out the expression in the Real Language box and explain that we use this with people we know well.

B
• Play or read the conversation again for the class to repeat. Then practice it again with the class in chorus.
• Have students practice the conversation with a partner, then switch roles and practice it again.
• Have students discuss how they would feel about going to another country to work or study.

C ⟳ **GOAL CHECK** ✔

• Have students read the directions and the list. Have them write notes. Elicit *Wh*-question words and possible follow-up questions. Write the question words on the board.
• Assign new pairs and have them talk about the things they have/haven't done. Remind them to ask follow-up questions.
• Have several students share with the class something interesting about their partner.

Speaking Strategy

Remind students that taking notes and preparing what they want to say before speaking, both in and out of class (speaking activities/presentations/phone calls/interviews), will help them communicate more effectively. By brainstorming ideas first, they activate the vocabulary and grammar they will need.

Grammar Practice: I have . . .

Tell students to write five true sentences about themselves on a sheet of paper using the present perfect tense. Give examples: *I have never driven a car. I have seen my favorite movie 12 times.* Tell students NOT to write their names on the paper. When all students have finished, collect the papers. Read each group of sentences to the class and have them guess which of their classmates wrote them.

Make Small Talk with New People

Listening

A • Have students look at the picture and describe what they see. Tell students they are going to hear two conversations between people meeting for the first time. Have them read the directions.

• Play the recording one or more times. ◀)) 7

• Have students compare answers with a partner.

• Check answers.

B • Have students read the directions.

• Play the recording one or more times. ◀)) 7

• Have students compare answers with a partner.

• Check answers.

C • Have students work with a partner to think of more possible topics of conversation.

• Share ideas with the class.

• If desired, have students role-play the continuation of each conversation with a partner.

Pronunciation

• Review the idea of contractions: short forms that combine two words and are used in fast or informal speech.

A • Tell the students to listen and repeat.

• Play the recording one or more times. ◀)) 8

B • Tell students to listen to the sentences and circle the one they hear.

• Play the recording one or more times. ◀)) 9

• Have students compare answers with a partner.

• Check answers.

• Have students practice reading the pairs of sentences to a partner.

B **GOAL 2:** Make Small Talk with New People

Listening

A ◀)) 7 These people are meeting for the first time. Listen to their conversations. Where are the people?

Conversation 1 The speakers are in _____.
   a. a hospital   **(b.)** a school   c. an airport

Conversation 2 These people are in _____.
   a. a restaurant   **(b.)** an apartment   c. an office building

B ◀)) 7 Listen again. What do the people make small talk about?

Conversation 1 They make small talk about _____.
   (a.) classes   b. weather   c. clothes

Conversation 2 They make small talk about _____.
   a. sports   b. TV shows   **(c.)** the neighborhood

C 🔁 Work with a partner. What will they talk about next? Think of two more ideas for each conversation. *Possible answers: Conversation 1: classes they've taken before, reasons for taking these classes Conversation 2: different kinds of restaurants, places to go shopping*

Pronunciation: *Have* or *has* vs. contractions

In statements with the present perfect tense, ***have*** and ***has*** are sometimes pronounced completely, but in informal speaking, contractions may be used.

A ◀)) 8 Listen and repeat.

Have	Contraction	*Has*	Contraction
I have	I've	she has	she's
you have	you've	he has	he's
we have	we've	it has	it's
they have	they've		

B ◀)) 9 Listen and circle the sentences you hear.

1. **(a.** I have never gone skiing.**)**   b. I've never gone skiing.
2. a. He has been to Colombia three times.   **(b.** He's been to Colombia three times.**)**
3. **(a.** Linda has taken a scuba diving class.**)**   b. Linda's taken a scuba diving class.
4. **(a.** They have already eaten breakfast.**)**   b. They've already eaten breakfast.
5. **(a.** We have had three tests this week.**)**   **(b.** We've had three tests this week.**)**
6. **(a.** Michael has found a new job.**)**   b. Michael's found a new job.

Remember that has *is pronounced with a /z/ sound.*

She **has** *already watched that movie, so she doesn't want to see it again.*

Remember to link words together when the word after a contraction begins with a vowel sound.

I've always *liked that restaurant. They serve delicious food there.*

18 Unit 2

For Your Information: Small talk

In many English-speaking cultures, people do not like to stand in silence for a long time with another person, even someone they don't know. It's considered polite to make small talk with strangers in situations that involve waiting together. It's also polite to make small talk at a party with other guests whom you don't know. Suitable topics for small talk are always general, not personal (such as sports, the weather, or upcoming holidays). They may also involve the situation that the two people are in—such as how they met the host at a party or how often they take the bus they are waiting for.

Communication

A Read the information.

> English-speakers often make small talk when they meet someone new. They have a conversation to get to know the other person. In general, small talk should make people feel more comfortable—not less comfortable—so the topics should not be very personal. For example, "Which department do you work in?" is a good question at work, but "How much money do you make?" is too personal.

B Circle the topics that are good for small talk when you meet someone for the first time. Then add two more ideas. Compare your ideas.

(school)   money   family   (work)   (sports)   religion   _____   _____

C Read the situations. Circle the best question for each situation. Then practice conversations with a partner.

Situation 1 At work, Min-Hee talks to Judy. It's Judy's first day at her job.
   a. How old are you?   (**b.**) Are you new in this city?

Situation 2 Andrei is from Russia. He talks to Eduardo at the International Students' Club. It's Eduardo's first meeting.
   (**a.**) Where are you from?   **b.** Do you practice a religion?

Situation 3 Mark lives in apartment 104. He meets Lisa, his new neighbor.
   (**a.**) Which apartment do you live in?   **b.** Are you married?

D Which are good questions to ask when you meet someone new? Circle the letters.

(**a.**) Which classes are you taking now?

(**b.**) Who is your teacher?

c. What was your score on the placement test?

(**d.**) Have you studied at this school before?

(**e.**) When did you start working here?

f. How much did you pay for that car?

(**g.**) Have you lived here for a long time?

h. How much money do you earn here?

E GOAL CHECK ✔ **Make small talk with new people**

Pretend you are meeting your classroom partner for the first time (on the first day of class, waiting for the bus, or in another situation). Talk for two minutes.

Communication

A • Go over the information about small talk.

• Ask, *How is this different from what you do? How is it similar?*

B • Have students work with a partner to choose the best topics.

• Check answers.

• Have each pair of students choose two more subjects.

• Compare answers with the class. Discuss why each suggestion is or isn't appropriate. Possible topics: the weather, holidays, news events, other people at a party, classes a person is taking, job duties.

C • Go over the situations with the class. Have students work with a partner to choose the best questions.

• Check answers.

• Have students practice conversations for each situation with a partner.

D • Have students work with a partner to choose questions that are appropriate for a first meeting.

• Check answers.

E GOAL CHECK ✔

• Divide the class into pairs. Have each pair of students choose a situation for a first meeting. Then time the class for two minutes as they practice making small talk in that situation.

• At the end of two minutes, discuss the questions students used and which ones worked well for initiating a friendly conversation.

Culture Note

In English-speaking cultures, it is usually considered rude to ask a person's age if you don't know him or her well. In the past, this was because many people (especially women) wanted others to think they were younger than they actually were. The question is still somewhat sensitive. It is also inappropriate to ask people (especially women) if they are married. This sounds as though the questioner is expressing a romantic interest!

Use Small Talk to *Break the Ice*

Language Expansion

A • Focus students' attention on the expression *break the ice* in the lesson title. Explain that many people feel shy when they meet someone new. If they can find an interesting topic to talk about, they will feel more comfortable.

• Go over the questions in the box, and talk about ways to answer them. Point out that responses should lead to a longer conversation. For example, if someone asks *Are you enjoying yourself?* at a party, you shouldn't just answer, *Yes.* You should add something like, *I really like this music. Do you know who the singer is?*

• Have students write down possible answers for each question.

• Compare answers with the class.

B • Have students work with a partner to choose a situation. Remind them to try to add information to their responses as they make small talk. Then have them carry on a conversation for as long as they can. (Have them aim for at least two to three minutes.)

• Have students change partners and choose a different situation.

• Call on one or two pairs to present their conversation to the class.

• Direct students' attention to the Engage! box. Ask how many students in the class are shy and how many are outgoing. Do the outgoing students have any good tips for talking to new people?

Grammar

• Go over the information about *already*, *ever*, and *yet* in the chart. Ask different students questions, for example, *Have you eaten lunch yet? Have you ever studied French?* etc.

C   **GOAL 3:** Use Small Talk to *Break the Ice*

Language Expansion: Starting a conversation

A Read the questions in the box. Think of different ways to answer them.

> **Engage!**
>
> Are you shy or outgoing when you meet new people? Do you like to make small talk?

> **Starting a conversation**
> How do you like this weather? Are you enjoying this class?
> Did you hear about _____ ? (something in the news, for example)
> How long have you been waiting? (for the elevator, the bus, the meeting to begin, etc.)

B ⚡ Choose one of the situations. Try to make small talk for as long as you can. Then change partners and practice again with another situation.

> waiting in line in the office cafeteria   walking in the park
> at a welcome party for new students   at the airport

Grammar: *Already, ever, never, and yet*

Already, ever, never, and *yet* + the present perfect		
already	Use *already* in questions and affirmative statements to emphasize that something has happened in the past.	**Has** Roberta **already left**? We **have already studied** this.
(not) yet	Use *yet/not yet* in questions or negative statements for emphasis.	**Have** you **done** the dishes **yet**? Melanie **hasn't eaten** lunch **yet**.
(not) ever never	Use *ever/never (not ever)* in questions or negative statements to talk about something that has or has not happened at any time before now.	**Have** you **ever** seen a giraffe? We **have never** played tennis in the rain. We **haven't ever** gone to Canada.

20   Unit 2

Word Bank: More questions for small talk

Have you always lived in this city?

Do you like living here?

What do you do?

What are you studying?

Who do you think will win the big game?

Which department do you work in?

Grammar: *Already* and *yet*

Already indicates that something has happened before now. When used in a question, it anticipates a positive answer. *Yet* is more neutral. When used in a question, it shows that the speaker doesn't know whether or not something has happened. Compare:

> Have you **already** eaten? (It's very late for dinner.)
> Have you eaten **yet**? (It's dinner time now.)

A Read the page from Marcy's journal. What has she already done? What has she not done yet? Complete the sentences.

1. She has already _taken a cooking class_ .
2. She has already _learned to speak Spanish_ .
3. She has not _visited her cousins in Colombia_ yet.
4. _She has not played Australian rugby yet._ .

Things I Want to Do in My Life

take a cooking class (✓)

visit my cousins in Colombia

learn to speak Spanish (✓)

play Australian rugby

B Read the conversation between Marcy and a classmate. Fill in each blank with one word.

John: Have you ever traveled to another country?

Marcy: No, I have _never_ left this country, but I want to go to Colombia someday. Some of my cousins live there.

John: I see. Have _you_ already met your Colombian cousins?

Marcy: Yes, I have _met_ them. They came here last year.

John: That's nice. Are there any other countries you want to visit?

Marcy: I want to visit Australia someday. _Have_ you ever been there?

John: No, I haven't _ever_ been there. Why do you want to go?

Marcy: Well, I learned the rules for Australian rugby last year, but I _have_ not played the game yet. Maybe I can play it in Australia!

▲ Cathedral in Bolivar Square in Bogota, Colombia

C 🗨 Have a conversation with your partner about things you have and haven't yet done in your life. Use small talk to break the ice first.

Conversation

A 🔊 10 Close your book and listen to the conversation. What do the speakers decide to do about the homework?
call each other and talk about it

Tom: Excuse me. Are you in my history class?

Rita: Yes! I saw you in class yesterday. I'm Rita.

Tom: Hi, Rita. I'm Tom. Is this your first class with Mr. Olsen?

Rita: Yes, it is, but I've heard good things about him. What about you?

Tom: I've taken his classes before, and they've always been good.

Rita: That's nice. Have you already done the homework for tomorrow?

Tom: No, not yet. What about you?

Rita: Not yet. Maybe we can call each other to talk about it.

Tom: That's a great idea! I'll give you my number.

B 🗨 Practice the conversation. Then practice the conversation with subjects you are studying and teachers from your school.

C 👥 **GOAL CHECK** ✔ Use small talk to *break the ice*

Move around the class. Walk up to five classmates and ask *icebreaker* questions.

> Have you ever taken a class with Ms. Lee before?

> Yes, I took an art class with her.

A • Have students complete the sentences with information from the list.
• Have students compare answers with a partner.
• Check answers.

B • Have students work individually to complete the sentences.
• Have students compare answers with a partner.
• Check answers.

C • Have students write a list of things they want to do in their life. Remind them to include things they have already done and check them, as in Marcy's list in **A**.
• Divide the class into pairs and have students have conversations about what they have and haven't yet done. Remind them to use the small talk questions to start the conversation.
• Have several pairs present their conversation to the class.

Conversation

A • Have students close their books. Write the question on the board: *What do the speakers decide to do about the homework?*
• Play the recording. 🔊 10
• Check answers.

B • Play or read the conversation again for the class to repeat.
• Practice the conversation with the class in chorus.
• Have students practice the conversation with a partner, then switch roles and practice it again.

C 👥 **GOAL CHECK** ✔

• Have students move around the room and start conversations with their classmates. Tell them to talk to five people and to try to use a different question with each person.
• Have several students share one of the icebreaker questions they asked and the answer they got.

Grammar Practice: *Already, yet, never, ever*

Match students with a partner. Tell them to get as much information as they can from their partner about these activities, using *already, yet, never,* and *ever* in their conversation.

1. visit another country
2. study another foreign language (not English)
3. use English online
4. meet a famous person
5. your idea: _____

Compare answers with the class.

Learn to Overcome a Language Barrier

Reading

- Have students look at the pictures and describe what they see. Ask, *Who do you think took these photos?* Elicit the idea of a *professional photographer.* Introduce the topic of the reading. Tell students they are going to read about a famous photographer. Ask students, *What do photographers do? What are some good things about their job? What are some bad things?*

A
- Divide the class into pairs and have them discuss the questions.
- Compare answers with the class.

B
- Point out the words in the Word Focus box. Have students read the article. Tell them to circle any words they don't understand.
- Go over the article with the class, answering any questions from the students about vocabulary.
- Have students work individually to answer *true* or *false* and change the false sentences to make them true.
- Have students compare answers with a partner.
- Check answers.

Communication

A
- Have students read the directions and the list of actions. Individually, have them add other ideas to the list.
- Divide the class into pairs and have them discuss which actions are helpful and which are not.
- Have each pair share what other actions they added and write lists on the board of helpful and not helpful actions.

Reading

A 🔁 Discuss these questions with a partner.

1. Have you ever taken a picture of people you didn't know? How did you do it?

2. What kinds of photographs do you like? What makes those photographs good?

B Circle **T** for *true* or **F** for *false*. Then correct the false sentences.

1. Griffiths has never traveled to England. (has traveled) T (F)

2. Griffiths has never traveled to Antarctica. (T) F

3. Petra is a very old city in Jordan. (T) F

4. Griffiths can only connect with English-speakers. T (F)
   (can connect with people even when she does not speak their language)

5. Most people do ~~not~~ want Griffiths to take their picture. T (F)

6. Volunteering is one way to begin a photography career. (T) F

Communication

A 🔁 Which actions can help people from different cultures to communicate? Which actions are not helpful for communication? Talk with a partner.

smile at people you don't know	pretend to understand everything
use gestures to communicate	ask people about words in their language
say nothing if you don't know the right word	other _____

Word Focus

landscapes = broad view of the land
overwhelmed = very emotional
rewarding = a valuable experience

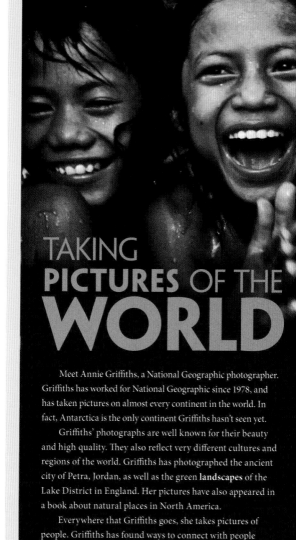

TAKING PICTURES OF THE WORLD

Meet Annie Griffiths, a National Geographic photographer. Griffiths has worked for National Geographic since 1978, and has taken pictures on almost every continent in the world. In fact, Antarctica is the only continent Griffiths hasn't seen yet.

Griffiths' photographs are well known for their beauty and high quality. They also reflect very different cultures and regions of the world. Griffiths has photographed the ancient city of Petra, Jordan, as well as the green **landscapes** of the Lake District in England. Her pictures have also appeared in a book about natural places in North America.

Everywhere that Griffiths goes, she takes pictures of people. Griffiths has found ways to connect with people of all ages and nationalities even when she does not speak their language. "The greatest privilege of my job is being allowed into people's lives," she has said. "The camera is like a passport, and I am often **overwhelmed** by how quickly people welcome me."

For Your Information: Annie Griffiths Belt

Annie Griffiths Belt studied photojournalism at the University of Minnesota in the United States and has worked for a number of magazines, including *LIFE, Geo, Smithsonian, Paris Match,* and *Stern.* She also spent a part of every year taking photographs for charity organizations such as Habitat for Humanity. She is a Fellow with the International League of Conservation Photographers, and her book *Last Stand: America's Virgin Lands* raised $250,000 for conservation projects. She has written a memoir about her work called *A Camera, Two Kids and a Camel.* She lives in the United States with her husband, Don, and two children, Lily and Charlie.

Portrait by Annie Griffiths

Knowing how to *break the ice* has helped to make Griffiths a successful photographer, but experts say that anyone can learn to connect with new people. When people speak the same language, greetings and small talk can make strangers feel more comfortable with each other. When people don't speak the same language, a smile is very helpful.

Griffiths has some advice if you are thinking about a career in photography. You can volunteer to take pictures for someone who can't afford to hire a professional photographer, for example. Griffiths also recommends studying and learning from good photos taken by professional photographers.

Remember, the next time you look at a beautiful photograph, you might be looking at the work of Annie Griffiths. And the next time you meet a new person, don't be afraid to break the ice. The connection you make could be very **rewarding.**

Express Yourself 23

After Reading

Web search: Have students go online and search the term *Annie Griffiths* to view her photographs. Ask each student to describe a photo that they especially liked.

Project: Ask each student to choose a photograph of a person in another country from a magazine or Web site to bring to class. Working in groups, have students talk about what the photographer probably did to break the ice with the person in the picture.

Learn to Overcome a Language Barrier

Writing

A
- Tell students to complete the sentences with their own ideas.
- Have students exchange books with a partner. Ask students to mark corrections and suggestions for improvements to their partner's answers.

B
- Have students help you begin developing the paragraph on the board. Write one or two sentences.
- Have students write their own paragraph using their ideas from **A.**

Communication

A
- Have students write a list of places they have traveled to (or want to visit, if they haven't traveled.) Ask, *How did you communicate with the people in these places?* Have students write notes on their list. Remind them that just keywords are necessary, not sentences.
- Divide the class into groups of three or four. Have them talk about where they have traveled to and how they communicated.
- Have each group write a list of "Do's and don'ts" for communicating with people who speak a different language. This can be done as a poster activity, if resources are available.
- Have each group share their list with the class, either as a gallery walk (if posters were made) or by writing a group list on the board.

B | **GOAL CHECK** ✔
- Have students work with a partner to talk about jobs that require an employee to overcome language barriers quickly, and have them think of ways to do this.
- Compare answers with the class. Possible jobs include journalist, tour guide, international businessperson, doctor, and social worker.

▲ Ancient acacia trees near the red sand dunes of the Namib Desert

Writing

A Complete the sentences with your own ideas.

1. Annie Griffiths' work is interesting because _____ .
2. Griffiths takes good "people pictures" because _____ .
3. For me, traveling is _____ because _____ .
4. For me, connecting with new people is _____ because _____ .
5. The next time I need to "break the ice," I will _____ .

B Use your ideas from exercise **A** to complete the paragraph in your notebook.

Today I read about a National Geographic photographer. Her name is Annie Griffiths, and _____

_____

_____

> Do smile at people.

> Don't expect them to know your language.

Communication

A Talk to your classmates about some places you have traveled. How did you communicate with the people in those places? Then make a list of *Do's* and *Don'ts* for communicating with people who speak a different language.

B | **GOAL CHECK** ✔ **Learn to overcome a language barrier**

In what professions do people need to overcome language barriers quickly in order to do their jobs? Talk with your partner about different ways they can do this.

Teacher Tip: Starting and ending group work

To make group work go smoothly, it's helpful to use clear signals for beginning and ending a task. Some ideas:

- Write starting and ending times on the board *(Group work starts: 10:15; Group work ends: 10:25).*
- Tell your students that group work ends when you clap your hands three times.
- Train your students to stop talking and raise their hands when they see you raise your hand. The room will fall silent without you interrupting.

Shumaker and Inda perform certain exercises on the computer.

At the National Zoo in Washington, D.C., Rob Shumaker runs the Orangutan Language Project. Orangutans are large, intelligent **primates**. They aren't able to speak like humans, but they can learn to connect **symbols** to real objects. Shumaker believes the language program is mentally **stimulating** for the orangutans. The program is **voluntary,** so the animals can choose to participate or not. It's part of a zoo **exhibit** which educates people about the problems orangutans face in the wild.

Before You Watch

A Read about the video and look up the meanings of the words in bold.
primates: animals like monkeys; symbols: pictures with a meaning; stimulating: very interesting; voluntary: you decide if you want to do it; exhibit: a show to look at

While You Watch

A ▶ Watch the video and circle the correct answers.

1. In Malay, the word *orangutan* means "person of the (jungle | (forest))."
2. The orangutans in the video are Inda and (Miki | (Azie)).
3. The orangutans work with symbols on ((a computer) | paper).
4. The orangutans are ((brother and sister) | mother and son).
5. Wild orangutans could become extinct in ((10 to 12) | 8 to 10) years.

B ▶ Watch the video again and answer the questions in your notebook.

1. Where do orangutans come from? Indonesia and Malaysia
2. What choices does the zoo give the orangutans? where to go
3. How old is Inda, the female orangutan? 20 years old
4. What do zoo officials hope exhibits like Think Tank will do? educate the public (and increase conservation efforts)

After You Watch / Communication

A 🔄 Brainstorm several ways that animals communicate. Do you think animal communication is very different from human communication?

B 👥 You have the opportunity to create a new way to write English. Think of ten English words that are difficult to spell. Make a word list with a better way to write the words. Share your word list with the class. (Can your classmates guess all the words?)

Express Yourself 25

Video Journal: *Orangutan Language*

Before You Watch

- Have students look at the pictures and describe what they see. Ask, *What do you know about orangutans?*
- Ask the class, *How do animals communicate? Do you think animals can talk?*

A • Have students read the video summary and look up the words in bold in a dictionary.
- Go over the summary of the video and check understanding by asking comprehension questions.

While You Watch

A • Tell students to watch the video and circle the answers.
- Play the video.
- Have students compare answers with a partner. Play the video again as necessary.
- Check answers.

B • Have students answer questions in their notebooks.
- Tell students to watch the video again and write the answers.
- Have students compare answers with a partner.
- Check answers.

After You Watch / Communication

A • Divide the class into pairs and have them discuss the questions.
- On the board, write ways that animals communicate. Discuss similarities and differences with human communication.

B • Explain that spelling can be difficult. Divide the class into small groups to write their list of words.
- Have each group write their "improved" words on the board. Can the class understand all the words?

For Your Information: Orangutans

Orangutans are the largest tree-dwelling animals in the world. They live in the forests of Indonesia and Malaysia. The males are about 145 centimeters (4 feet, 9 inches) in height and weigh over 118 kilograms (260 pounds), and females are around 127 centimeters (4 feet, 2 inches) in height and weigh around 45 kilograms (100 pounds). Their usual diet is fruit, but they also eat insects, honey, and bird eggs. They are very intelligent. They use tools to get fruit, and scientists have seen orangutans using leaves to make rain hats!

Cities

About the Photo

This photo shows the new pedestrian crossing at Oxford Circus in London. Oxford Circus is one of the most popular destinations in the world, with more than 200 million visitors a year. This amount of people combined with city center traffic obviously causes congested sidewalks. Based on crossings in Tokyo's Shibuya district, the new design stops traffic in all directions, allowing pedestrians to cross the road in any direction, both straight ahead and diagonally. This eases sidewalk congestion, especially around the underground station entrances and exits.

- Introduce the theme of the unit. Call on students to name cities they have visited, and list them on the board. Ask, *What was it like?*
- Direct students' attention to the picture. Have students describe what they see.
- Have students discuss the questions with a partner. Have them write two lists, one for each question.
- Compare answers with the class, compiling two lists on the board.
- Ask these questions orally or by writing them on the board for students to answer in pairs: *What can you see downtown in our city/town? Which cities in our country have skyscrapers? What's the name of your neighborhood? What are some good things about your neighborhood?*
- Go over the Unit Goals with the class.
- For each goal, elicit any words students already know and write them on the board; for example, the names of places and buildings in cities, vocabulary for things in their neighborhood, etc.

Japanese-inspired 'Shibuya' style crossing at Oxford Circus in London

26

UNIT 3 GOALS	Grammar	Vocabulary	Listening
• Describe your city or town • Explain what makes a good neighborhood • Discuss an action plan • Make predictions about cities in the future	Future with *will* *The city **will** be cleaner.* *Will* + time clauses *I'll check out the neighborhood **before** I rent an apartment.*	City life Maps	General and focused listening A radio interview: Jardin Nomade in Paris

UNIT 3 GOALS

1. Describe your city or town

2. Explain what makes a good neighborhood

3. Discuss an action plan

4. Make predictions about cities in the future

Unit Theme Overview

- Only 100 years ago, 20 percent of the world's population lived in urban areas. By 1990, still less than 40 percent lived in cities. But as of 2010, more than half the global population lives in an urban area, even though cities make up only three percent of the earth's surface. A United Nations forecast predicted that by 2050, the percentage of people living in cities will rise to 70 percent.

- Although this trend is occurring around the world, the biggest migrations to cities are taking place in developing countries in Asia and Africa. This massive movement is driven by a search for greater economic and educational opportunities. However, many of the newcomers will find themselves in difficult conditions. About one billion people now live in slums around the world, without access to clean water, sanitation, or adequate housing.

- Nonetheless, some experts view this migration to the cities as a positive step for development, asserting that cities are engines for economic growth. They further point out that in most of the developed countries of Europe and North America, 70 percent of the population is urban.

- In this unit, students will learn to describe their own city and neighborhood and will consider the features and attributes of a good neighborhood. They will learn and practice the vocabulary for reading a city map. They will talk about improving their neighborhoods and their cities, and in the reading, they will learn about future trends in the cities of the world. In the unit's Video Journal, they will see how one of the oldest cities in the world is working to preserve its heritage.

Speaking	Reading	Writing	Video Journal
Discussing good and bad elements in a neighborhood Predicting the future of cities **Pronunciation:** Emphatic stress	**TED Talks:** How Food Shapes Our Cities	Writing a paragraph	**National Geographic:** Fes

27

Describe Your City or Town

Vocabulary

A • Have students look at the picture and describe what they see. With the class, read the first opinion of urban life. Go over the words in blue, and help students work out their meanings by using context clues and their own knowledge about cities.

• Repeat the same steps with the second opinion.

• Have students tell a partner which opinion they agree with and explain their reasons.

• Call on students to give their opinions to the class. After several students have spoken, take a class poll with a show of hands to see which position they agree with.

B • Have students work individually to write the correct words.

• Have students compare answers with a partner.

• Check answers.

• Direct students' attention to the Word Focus box. Go over the expressions in the box. Ask, *Where do people get in* **traffic jams**? *What time of day? Is* **population growth** *a problem in our city/country?*

Grammar

A • This activity introduces *will* for predictions. Have students work individually to mark their predictions for their city or town in 2030.

• Have students compare answers with a partner.

• Ask the class more *yes/no* questions about the city with *will*, such as *Do you think more people will live in apartments? Will the city have more than (one million) people?* etc.

▲ Shibuya Crossing outside Shibuya Station in Tokyo, Japan

Word Focus

traffic jam = so many cars in the street that they can't move

population growth = more people living in a place

Vocabulary

A Read the opinions. Which one do you agree with?

Opinion 1

"Urban life is great! There is good public transportation, like trains and buses. And we also have highways where cars can go fast. People can find good jobs. And after work, there is great nightlife in restaurants and dance clubs. Cities get bigger every year because they are the best places to live."

Opinion 2

"City life is terrible! Cities are so crowded, with too many people in a small area, and the population grows every year. There is too much traffic, because people want to drive everywhere. It's always noisy. A lot of people want to live in a rural area, but there aren't many jobs. It's better to live in a suburb and commute to a job by car."

B Write the words in blue next to the correct meaning.

1. _____urban_____ in the city
2. _____highways_____ roads where cars go fast
3. _____commute_____ travel to your job
4. _____public transportation_____ trains, buses, and subways
5. _____population_____ number of people
6. _____nightlife_____ things to do in the evening
7. _____traffic_____ cars moving on a street
8. _____crowded_____ too full
9. _____noisy_____ too loud
10. _____rural_____ in the country

Grammar: Future with *will*

A ⚡ What do you think? Circle **Y** for *yes* or **N** for *no*. Compare your answers with a partner's answers.

In the year 2030 . . .

1. My city will be bigger than it is now.   Y   N
2. People will drive cars in the city.   Y   N
3. Houses will be smaller than they are now.   Y   N
4. Cities will have many parks and green spaces.   Y   N

Word Bank: City streets

bench	phone booth
bus stop	sidewalk
corner	streetlight
intersection	street sign
newsstand	taxi stand
parking garage	traffic light
parking meter	trash can

Grammar: *Will*

In this lesson, students are taught to use *will* for making predictions. *Going to* is used in a similar way for future prediction. *Will* has these additional uses for future time:

• statements of fact: *The play* **will** *start at 8:00.*

• promises: *I* **will** *help you tomorrow.*

• decisions made at the time of speaking:

   *I'**ll** have a hamburger and iced tea.*

Will		
Statement	The city **will be** cleaner.	Use *will* to make predictions about things you are sure about in the future and to ask questions about the future. In speaking, use contractions with *will*: *I'll, you'll, he'll, she'll, we'll, they'll.*
Negative	People **won't drive** cars.	
Yes/No questions	**Will** houses **be** smaller?	
Wh- questions	Where **will** people **live**?	

B Complete the sentences and questions with a word from the box.

> when he not
> will be

1. Silvio will ___*be*___ in New York next April for an interesting event.

2. Will ___*he*___ enjoy New York in April? It can be cold at that time.

3. The weather will ___*not*___ be a problem.

4. ___*Will*___ he participate in The JFK Runway Run?

5. That's a great event. ___*When*___ will the race begin?

C 🔄 Ask a partner three questions about city life in the future. Use *will*.

Conversation

A 🔊 11 Close your book and listen to the conversation. Where did Mimi live when she was a child? *Seoul*

Mark: So, where are you from, Mimi?
Mimi: I live in New York now, but I grew up in Seoul.
Mark: Really? I've never been to Seoul. What's it like?
Mimi: Well, some people think it's too crowded, but it has great restaurants.
Mark: I've heard that it's very polluted.
Mimi: That's true, but it's changing now. In the future, it will be much cleaner.

B 🔄 Practice the conversation with a partner. Switch roles and practice it again.

C Check (✓) the things that are true about your city. Add some ideas of your own.

Bad things about your city		Good things about your city	
It's _____.		It has great _____.	
☐ noisy	☐ boring	☐ restaurants	☐ beaches
☐ dangerous	☐ crowded	☐ parks	☐ museums
☐ expensive	☐ polluted	☐ neighborhoods	☐ nightlife
_____	_____	_____	_____

> How will people commute in the future?

> I think they'll have personal airplanes!

▲ Bongeunsa Temple in Seoul, South Korea

D 🔄 **GOAL CHECK** ✓ **Describe your city or town**

With a partner, have a new conversation about your city. Then make new conversations about two other cities you know.

Cities **29**

- Go over the information in the chart
- Elicit more predictions with *will*. Ask, *What **will** our school be like in the year 2030?*

B
- Have students work individually to complete the sentences.
- Have students compare answers with a partner.
- Check answers.

C
- Have students work individually to prepare three questions about city life using *will*.
- In pairs, have them take turns asking questions and making predictions.
- Call on pairs to present a question and answer to the class, and list their predictions on the board.
- Discuss the likelihood of these predictions actually happening.

Conversation

A
- Have students close their books. Write the question on the board: *Where did Mimi live when she was a child?*
- Play the recording. 🔊 11
- Check answer.

B
- Play or read the conversation again for the class to repeat. Then practice again with the class in chorus.
- Have students practice the conversation with a partner, then switch roles and practice again.

C
- Have students work individually to add to each list, and check the words describing their city.
- Add students' ideas to the list on the board.

D 🔄 **GOAL CHECK** ✓

- Have students work with a partner to make conversations about their cities and two other cities.
- Invite pairs to present a conversation to the class.

Grammar Practice: *Will*

Bring in newspaper/magazine pictures showing actions. Divide the class into pairs and give each one a picture. Have students make predictions about what will happen next in the picture, using *will*: *The man **will** kick the ball. The people **will** start shouting.* Have them pass each picture to the next pair when they've finished with it. After each pair has practiced with several pictures, compare answers with the class.

Explain What Makes a Good Neighborhood

Listening

A
- Have students look at the picture and describe what they see.
- Have students answer the questions with a partner.
- Compare answers with the class.

B
- Tell students they are going to hear a radio program about an unusual park in Paris. Have them read the questions.
- Play the recording one or more times. 🔊 12
- Have students compare answers with a partner.
- Check answers.

C
- Have students read the questions and answer any they think they already know the answers to in their notebooks.
- Play the recording one or more times for students to confirm or answer the questions. 🔊 12
- Have students compare answers with a partner.
- Check answers.
- Direct students' attention to the Engage! box. Have students discuss the question in pairs or groups.
- Compare answers with the class. Ask, *What do you think about these new things?*

Pronunciation

A
- Explain that the stressed words in a sentence sound stronger.
- Play the recording and have students listen and repeat. 🔊 13

B **GOAL 2:** Explain What Makes a Good Neighborhood

▲ The Jardin Nomade in Paris

Engage!

What are some new things in your city?

Are there any <u>parks</u> in your <u>neighborhood</u>?

Yes, there are <u>two</u>.

Listening

A 🔄 Discuss these questions with a partner.

1. How often do you go to a park?
2. What do you do there?
3. What do you think about the parks in your city or town?

B 🔊 12 Listen to a radio program about a park in Paris called the Jardin Nomade. Circle the correct letter.

1. The Jardin Nomade is in _____ area.
   a. a rural   (b.) an urban   c. a suburban
2. The Jardin Nomade is amazing because it's so _____ .
   a. big   (b.) small   c. old
3. In the Jardin Nomade, people _____ .
   (a.) grow food   b. go swimming   c. enjoy art

C 🔊 12 Listen again. Answer each question in your notebook.

1. What year did the park start? ___2003___
2. How many gardens do people have in the park? ___54___
3. What do the neighbors eat there every month? ___soup___
4. How many people come to the monthly dinners? _more than a hundred_
5. How many parks like this are there in Paris now? ___40___

Pronunciation: Emphatic stress

A 🔊 13 Listen and repeat the exchanges. Notice how the underlined words sound stronger.

1. **A:** Is your city <u>expensive</u>?
   B: Yes, it's <u>really</u> expensive!
2. **A:** Do you like living in an <u>apartment</u>?
   B: No, I like living in a <u>house</u> much more.
3. **A:** Is your neighborhood <u>new</u> or <u>old</u>?
   B: The houses are very <u>old</u>.
4. **A:** Can you <u>walk</u> to school?
   B: No, I <u>can't</u>. It's too <u>far</u>.

30   Unit 3

Expansion Activity

Have students work in groups to plan and draw a map of a new park for their city or town on a large piece of paper. Have each group present and explain their map to the class.

For Your Information: Urban gardens

Around the world, a surprising amount of food is grown on small plots of land in urban environments. An estimated 800 million people are now involved in urban agriculture in different cities. In Mumbai, India, an urban farm was created at a school to give employment to street children and provide healthy food for slum residents. In Seattle, USA, the P-Patch program has land in 70 different neighborhoods where people can have their own gardens for a small fee.

B 🔄 Read the exchanges in exercise **A** with a partner. Stress the underlined words.

C 🔄 Take turns asking and answering three questions about your neighborhood. Stress the important words.

Conversation

A 🔊 14 Close your book and listen to the conversation. What is the problem in Sarah's neighborhood? *There's only one supermarket, so food is very expensive.*

Ben: How do you like living in your neighborhood?
Sarah: Well, it has a lot of beautiful old buildings, but there are some problems.
Ben: Like what?
Sarah: It doesn't have many different stores. There's only one supermarket, so food is very expensive.
Ben: That sounds like a pretty big problem.
Sarah: It is, but the city is building a new shopping center now. Next year, we'll have more stores.

B 🔄 Practice the conversation with a partner. Switch roles and practice it again.

C Write the words or phrases from the box in the correct column. Add two more ideas to each column.

Good things in a neighborhood	Bad things in a neighborhood
beautiful buildings	crime
public transportation	a lot of noise
trees and green space	heavy traffic
many different stores	pollution

beautiful buildings
crime
a lot of noise
heavy traffic
public transportation
pollution
trees and green space
many different stores

D 🔄 Make two new conversations. Use your ideas from exercise **C**.

E 👥 What are the three most important things for a good neighborhood? Talk about your ideas in exercise **C**. Make a new list together. Give reasons.

Most important things for a good neighborhood	Reason
1.	
2.	
3.	

F 👥 **GOAL CHECK** ✔ **Explain what makes a good neighborhood**
Explain your group's list to the class.

Cities **31**

B • Have students practice the exchanges in **A** with a partner. Walk around listening for correct stress.

C • Have students work with the same partner to ask and answer three questions about their neighborhoods, practicing stressing the important words.

Conversation

A • Have students close their books. Write the question on the board: *What is the problem in Sarah's neighborhood?*
• Play the recording. 🔊 14
• Check answer.

B • Play or read the conversation again for the class to repeat.
• Practice the conversation with the class in chorus.
• Have students practice the conversation with a partner, then switch roles and practice again.

C • Have students work individually to categorize the words and phrases.
• Check answers.
• Then ask students to add their own ideas.
• Compare answers with the class, and list the ideas on the board. See if students disagree about whether any of these items are good or bad.

D • Have students work with a partner to make new conversations about each student's neighborhood, using their ideas from **C**. Remind students to use the conversation in **A** as a model.

E • Combine pairs to form groups of four. Have them discuss the ideas they added to the chart in **C**, and then agree on one list of the three most important things for a good neighborhood.

F 👥 **GOAL CHECK** ✔
• Call on groups to present and explain their lists to the class.

Expansion Activity

Bring in newspaper or magazine photos of city neighborhoods. Divide the class into pairs or groups, give each a photo, and have them prepare a conversation about the neighborhood in the picture. Call on them to present their conversations to the class.

Discuss an Action Plan

Language Expansion

A • Explain that there are special words that are used on maps. With the class, go over the meanings of the words in the box.

• Have students write the words in the correct spaces.

B • Go over the model conversation with the class. Before modeling the answer, locate the train station on the map together.

• Divide the class into pairs and have them practice asking and answering the questions.

• Check answers.

• Have students take turns asking and answering their own questions about the map.

Grammar

A • Have students read the sentences, think about their meanings, and circle the answers.

• Have students compare answers with a partner.

• Check answers.

C **GOAL 3:** Discuss an Action Plan

Language Expansion: Using maps

A Study the map. Write the word from the box in the correct space.

South
symbols
East
key
West
scale

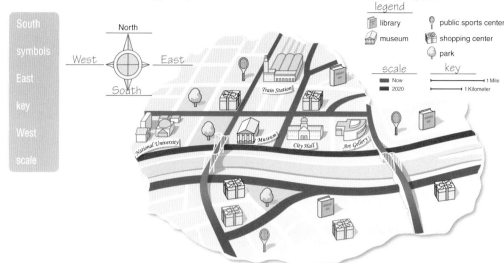

legend

📖 library   🏸 public sports center
🏛 museum   🏬 shopping center
🌳 park

scale   key
■ Now |————| 1 Mile
■ 2020 |————| 1 Kilometer

North
West — East
South

B 🔄 Take turns asking and answering the questions.

Where's the train station?

It's in the north of the city.

1. In which parts of the city are the libraries?
   They're in the north, the east, and the south of the city.
2. Where are the public sports centers?
   They're in the north and the east of the city.
3. Where will the new road be?
   It will be north of the river.
4. How many shopping centers does the city have now? How many do you think it will have in 2020? *It has four shopping centers now. It will have six shopping centers in 2025.*
5. What do you think this city needs?
   Answers will vary.

Grammar: *Will* + time clauses

A Study the sentences and circle the correct letter.

I will finish my homework <u>before I go to bed</u>.

1. What will you do first?
   ⓐ Finish my homework.   **b.** Go to bed.
2. The word *before* shows the action that happens . . . .
   a. first   **ⓑ** second

I will wash the dishes <u>after I eat dinner</u>.

1. What will you do first?
   a. Wash the dishes.   **ⓑ** Eat dinner.
2. The word *after* shows the action that happens . . . .
   ⓐ first   **b.** second

32 Unit 3

Word Bank: City buildings

apartment building   hospital
bank   office building
bus station   post office
department store

Grammar: *Will* + time clauses

A time clause is a clause that gives information about when something happened. In this lesson, students learn to use time clauses to talk about actions in the future:

*I'**ll** watch TV **after** I finish my homework.*

These time clauses are also used to talk about other time frames.

The past: *I watched TV **after** I finished my homework.*

Habitual present: *I watch TV **after** I finish my homework.*

☐ ⟳ Use the words below and the information in the note to make sentences with time clauses.

1. find a place for the meeting/make an invitation (after)

2. make a list of things to talk about/give invitations to all the neighbors (before)

3. make a list of things to talk about/have the meeting (before)

4. have the meeting/ask the city government for a sports center (after)

5. talk to newspaper reporters/ask the city government for a sports center (after)

May 2 find place for the meeting
May 3 make invitation
May 5–12 give invitations to neighbors
May 13 make list of things to talk about
May 25 have the meeting
May 26 ask city government for sports center
May 27 talk to newspaper reporters

Conversation

☐ ⟳ Practice the conversation. What does Jennie want for her neighborhood? a library

Jennie: This neighborhood really needs a library.
Dan: You're absolutely right. But how can we get one?
Jennie: I think we should have a neighborhood meeting to talk about it.
Dan: That's a good idea. And after we have the meeting, we'll write a letter to the newspaper.
Jennie: Great! I'll help you.

☐ ⟳ Make new conversations to talk about places in your neighborhood.

☐ ⟳ **GOAL CHECK** ✔ **Discuss an action plan**

What does your city need? List things you can do to make your plan happen. Use time clauses to discuss when you will do each thing on the list. Then compare your list with a partner.

Answers for excercise B:

1. After we find a place for the meeting, we will make an invitation./We will make an invitation after we find a place for the meeting.

2. Before we make a list of things to talk about, we'll give invitations to all the neighbors./We'll give invitations to all the neighbors before we make a list of things to talk about.

3. Before we have the meeting, we will make a list of things to talk about./We'll make a list of things to talk about before we have the meeting.

4. After we have the meeting, we'll ask the city government for a sports center./We'll ask the city government for a sports center after we have the meeting.

5. After we ask the city government for a sports center, we'll talk to newspaper reporters./We'll talk to newspaper reporters after we ask the city government for a sports center.

Cities **33**

- Go over the information in the chart. Elicit more examples from students, for example, *Before I do my homework today, I'll eat lunch. After I go to the gym, I'll meet my friends.*

☐ • Go over the information in the note. Explain that it's an action plan. Ask, *What is the action plan for? Who is having a meeting? What do they want to ask for? What can you do at a public sports center?*

- Have students work with a partner and write the notes as sentences with time clauses.

- Check answers.

Conversation

☐ • Write the question on the board: *What does Jennie want for her neighborhood?*

- Have students read the conversation and check the answer.

- Read the conversation again for the class to repeat. Then practice again with the class in chorus.

- Have students practice the conversation with a partner, then switch roles and practice it again.

☐ • Divide the class into pairs. Have them make new conversations about their neighborhoods. Remind them to use the conversation in **A** as a model.

- Call on pairs to present their conversations to the class.

☐ ⟳ **GOAL CHECK** ✔

- Have students decide on something their city needs. Elicit an example and write it on the board. Have students help you write one or two steps of an action plan to achieve it, using *before/after*. Ask, *What do we need to do first? Then?*

- Have students write their own action plan. Remind them to use time clauses.

- Have students compare their action plans with a partner.

- Have several students tell the class about their partner's action plan.

Grammar Practice: Time clauses
Write the following stems on the board:
When will you do your homework? . . . go to bed tonight?
. . . leave your house tomorrow?
. . . buy some new clothes?
Have students take turns asking and answering the questions with a partner, using time clauses. Remind students to use *before* and *after* in their answers.

Make Predictions About Cities in the Future

Reading

A
- Have students look at the pictures and describe what they see. Ask, *What do you think the article is about?*
- Have students read the directions. Go over the words in the box. Have students write three predictions. Provide vocabulary as necessary.
- Have students compare predictions with a partner.
- Compare predictions with the class and write a list on the board.

B
- Have students read the ideas. Point out the words in the Word Bank. Have students read the article and check the ideas mentioned.
- Have students compare answers with a partner.
- Check answers.

C
- Have students read the problems and the solutions.
- Have students read the article and match the problems with the solutions.
- Have students compare answers with a partner.
- Check answers.

D **GOAL 4:** Make Predictions About Cities in the Future

Reading

A 🔄 How did people get their food in the past, and what kinds of food did they eat? How is it different from our food today? How will it change in the future? Use the words below. Share your ideas with a partner.

produce	healthy food	grow
distribute	transport	

B Check (✓) the ideas that are in the reading.

✓ **1.** Cities need safe and healthy food.

___ **2.** If we know how people in the past got food in cities, we can do the same things that they did.

___ **3.** City populations will triple by 2050.

✓ **4.** In the future, we will need to change the way we grow food.

C Match the problems and the solutions from the reading.

_c_ **1.** It takes a lot of fossil fuel to produce food.
  a. We can study ways people got food in the past.

_a_ **2.** Our ways of producing food are not efficient.
  b. We can grow food more sustainably.

_b_ **3.** We don't take care of the natural world.
  c. We can grow food closer to cities.

Carolyn Steel Architect, Food urbanist

HOW FOOD SHAPES OUR CITIES

How do you feed a city? It's an important question, but we rarely ask it. We take it for granted that we will find food in any restaurant or supermarket that we walk into. It's almost magic! Many of us don't think about **agriculture** at all. Many of us don't know who grew our food, who harvested it, or how it got from the farm to the city. But without good, healthy food, we—and our cities—won't survive.

Carolyn Steel is an architect who studies how ancient food routes shaped our modern cities. By understanding how city **dwellers** have gotten their food in the past, she thinks we can come up with better ways to produce and distribute food in the cities of the future.

By 2050, twice as many people will live in cities as do now. We will **consume** twice as much meat and **dairy** as we do today. This modern diet, heavy in meat, dairy, and processed food, requires enormous amounts of energy to produce. That energy mostly comes from fossil fuels, which are not renewable. We're also using fossil fuels to clear millions of acres of rainforest each year for planting crops and then to transport the crops to cities around the world. If we don't change the way that food is produced, we will have a serious problem. It will be very difficult to feed everyone.

How can we change our food systems so that we will be able to feed ourselves? Steel proposes producing food closer to our cities, as our ancestors did. Additionally, starting community agriculture programs in urban

---

For Your Information: Carolyn Steel

Carolyn Steel is an architect, a food urbanist, and the author of the book *Hungry City*. Born and raised in central London, Steel says she has always had a fascination with buildings and how they are inhabited. She was interested not only with the architecture of the buildings, but also in the relationship between the building and what happens within it. This interest in how things are connected led her to focus on food and architecture and the importance of food in the development of cities worldwide. Steel wants to make us aware of how the growth of cities in the past was connected to the food the inhabitants ate, and how this connection has been lost in modern cities. This loss, she argues, has a negative effect on the planet and our lives. She strongly believes that we need to re-evaluate how we grow and produce food, how far it is transported, and our relationship with nature.

"We know we are what we eat. We need to realize that the world is also what we eat . . . we can use food as a really powerful tool to shape the world."

– Carolyn Steel

17th Century London Meat

Carolyn Steel's idea worth spreading is that we really are what we eat. Food is a powerful tool we should use to create the world we want to live in. Watch Steel's full TED Talk on TED.com.

areas will allow us to grow some of our own food. Steel believes that when we can see how our food is produced, and grow some of it ourselves, it will strengthen our connection with nature. And if we are connected to the natural world, we will **value** and protect it.

agriculture the science or occupation of farming
dweller a person or animal that lives in a particular place
consume to use (fuel, time, resources, etc.)
dairy milk and food made from milk (such as butter and cheese)
value to think that (someone or something) is important or useful

35

After Reading

Either individually or in pairs, have students carry out research on the Internet and find out more about Carolyn Steel and what she does (if necessary, assign students one of these categories: as a writer/a speaker/an architect/a university professor, and other things she has done). Have them share what they find out with the class or in small groups.

Encourage students to watch Carolyn Steel's TED Talk at www.TED.com.

Communication

A • Have students look at the picture and describe what they see.

• Have students read the directions. Go over the words in the box.

• Have students write notes about how their city has been shaped by food. Provide vocabulary as necessary.

• Divide the class into pairs and have them share their ideas.

• Share ideas with the class.

Writing

A • Elicit ideas about how food in the students' cities will change in the future. Have students read the directions. Go over the words in the box.

• Have them write six ideas in order of importance. Provide vocabulary as necessary.

• Have students compare lists with a partner.

• Share and compare ideas with the class.

B • Have students complete the paragraph.

• Have students compare answers with a partner.

• Check answers.

C • Have students write their own paragraph with predictions about the future, using *will* and the words in the box. Provide extra vocabulary as necessary.

D ⚙ **GOAL CHECK** ✔

• Divide the class into groups of three or four and have them share and discuss the ideas from their paragraphs. Have them decide which ideas are the most realistic and which are the most unrealistic.

• Have each group share their conclusions with the class.

D | **GOAL 4:** Make Predictions About Cities in the Future

▲ Market in Madeira, Portugal

cold/moderate/hot	
climate	ocean
inland	hunting
fishing	immigrants
native people	

population	climate
transport	resources
traditions	environment
eating habits	

Communication

A 🔄 Share your ideas of how food has shaped your city with a partner. Think about its location, its environment, and its culture. Use the words in the box.

Writing

A How will food in your city change in the future? Write six ideas and rank them in order of importance. Use the words in the box.

____ 1. _____   ____ 4. _____

____ 2. _____   ____ 5. _____

____ 3. _____   ____ 6. _____

B Complete the paragraph with *will* or *won't* and the verb in parentheses.

In the future, the population of cities (1) ___will grow___ (grow) twice as big as it is now. We (2) ___won't be___ (be) able to keep producing food the way we do in the present. People (3) ___will need___ (need) to grow food closer to where they live.

C Write a paragraph with predictions about cities in the future. Use *will* and words in the box to make your prediction.

D ♻ **GOAL CHECK** ✔ **Make predictions about cities in the future**

Work with a group. Share your paragraphs and support your opinions with facts. Which predictions are the most/least realistic?

36   Unit 3

Teacher Tip: Encouraging use of English

A common challenge in monolingual classes is motivating students to use only English in group work. Here are some approaches to consider:

• Explain the rationale for using only English. Tell students, *We learn to speak English by speaking English.* If appropriate, tell students about your own language-learning experiences.

• Establish a clear policy. For example, you might tell students, *It's OK to ask questions in your* *native language, but for all other things we use only English.*

• Set an example for the students. Use only English for instructions and classroom management.

Bouananiya Medersa in Morocco

The Bouananiya Medersa in Fes, Morocco, is a **masterpiece** of art. It's in very bad condition now, but people are working to **restore** its walls and **fountains**. Some old buildings in Fes are in danger because **wealthy** people buy and take away pieces of them. Now, **private** organizations are trying to **preserve** these buildings for the future. They hope all people can enjoy Morocco's **heritage**.

Before You Watch

A Read about the video and check the meanings of the words in **bold**.

masterpiece: excellent art; **restore**: put into good condition again; **fountain**: water pushed into the air in a beautiful way; **wealthy**: rich; **private**: not part of the government; **preserve**: keep in good condition; **heritage**: beliefs and traditions that came from the past

While You Watch

A ▶ Watch the video. Write **T** for *true* or **F** for *false*.

___F___ **1.** In the past, the Bouananiya Medersa was a palace.

___T___ **2.** Restorers are taking old paint off the walls of the Medersa.

___F___ **3.** The government isn't interested in restoring historic buildings in Fes.

___F___ **4.** There is a problem because wealthy people want to live in the old houses in Fes.

B ▶ Watch the video again. Circle the correct answer.

1. The city of Fes was founded in the ((ninth) | eleventh) century.

2. By the 1300s, Fes was a center for ((art) | science) and learning.

3. (One or two | (five or six)) families live in each house in the medina.

4. In the future, the Medersa will be a ((museum) | school).

After You Watch / Communication

A ⚡ What are some important buildings and places in your city's heritage? Make a list and then share the information with your partner.

B 👥 Write a guide for foreign visitors to a historic place in your city. Answer these questions in your guide.

1. What happened there? What can visitors see and do there?

2. How much does it cost to visit? What hours is it open? How can visitors get there?

▲ Bouananiya Medersa in Fes, Morocco

Cities 37

Video Journal: *Fes*

Before You Watch

A • Have students look at the picture and describe what they see.

• Have students read the video summary and look up the words in bold. Confirm the meanings of the vocabulary in bold.

While You Watch

A • Tell students to watch the video and answer *true* or *false*. Have the students read the statements.

• Play the video.

• Have students compare answers with a partner.

• Check answers.

B • Tell students to watch the video again and circle the correct answer. Have the students read the statements.

• Play the video.

• Have students compare answers with a partner.

• Check answers.

After You Watch / Communication

A • Have students make a list of important places in their city (or their country, if preferred).

• Divide the class into pairs and have them compare ideas and explain why these places are important.

B • Divide the class into groups of three to four. Go over the directions.

• Have each group choose a different place (or assign groups a historic place). Have them compile their information and decorate their guide with drawings and photos.

• Display the guides on the classroom walls.

For Your Information: Fes

• Fes is the third largest city in Morocco, with a population of one million in 2010.

• The name of the city is sometimes spelled *Fez*.

• It's one of Morocco's "Four Imperial Cities" (with Marrakech, Meknes, and Rabat).

• Al-Karaouine University in Fes is the oldest continuously operating university in the world.

• The medina (old city) in Fes is believed to be the largest car-free urban area in the world.

• Popular tourist sites in Fes include the Bouananiya Medersa (in the video) and the Bab Bou Jeloud gate. Visitors can shop for brassware, leather, pottery, and other traditional crafts.

• The traditional Middle Eastern hat called the *fez* actually comes from Greece—not Fes!

The Shared
Experience
of Absurdity

Before You Watch

A • Have students look at the picture and answer the questions with a partner.

• Compare answers with the class.

B • Have students read the directions. Go over the words in the Word Bank.

• Have students read the paragraph and complete it with the words from the Word Bank. Point out that they might need to change the form of the word depending on number or tense. Remind them that they won't need all of the words.

• Check answers.

C • Have students look at the pictures on page 39 and describe what they see.

• Have students check what they think they will hear in the TED Talk.

• Compare answers.

While You Watch

A • Have students read the possible main ideas. Tell them to watch the talk and identify the main idea.

• Play the talk.

• Have them compare their answer with a partner.

• Check answer, and confirm prediction from **Before You Watch C.**

TEDTALKS   **Charlie Todd** Comedian, Founder of Improv Everywhere
THE SHARED EXPERIENCE
OF ABSURDITY

Before You Watch

Charlie Todd's idea worth spreading is that play is a good thing—however old you are. Watch Todd's full TED Talk on TED.com.

Improv Everywhere is a group that creates (1) ____pranks____ in public places. Their founder, Charlie Todd, believes that (2) ____play____ is as important for adults as it is for kids. He was (3) ___inspired___ to start the group when he couldn't find a regular theater to perform in. Now, Improv Everywhere's (4) ___diverse___ members can be found all around the world. So the next time a group of people are (5) ___improvising___ on the street or a store, you might be seeing an Improv Everywhere performance.

A 🔄 Look at the picture and answer the questions with a partner.

1. Where are these people?

2. What do people usually do here?

3. What are these people doing?

B Charlie Todd is a man who delights in creating unexpected scenes like the one in the picture above. Here are some words you will hear in his TED Talk. Complete the paragraph with the correct form of the word. Not all words will be used.

cop *n.* a police officer
diverse *adj.* made up of people or things that are different from each other
improvise *v.* to speak or perform without preparation
inspire *v.* to give (someone) an idea about what to do or create
play *n.* activities that are done especially by children for fun or enjoyment
prank *n.* a trick that is done to someone usually as a joke

C Look at the pictures on the next page. Check (✓) the information that you predict you will hear in the TED Talk.

___ **1.** We perform in many different public places.

_✓_ **2.** Our goal is to make people smile and laugh.

___ **3.** Our performances are only for paying audiences.

While You Watch

A ▶️ Watch the TED Talk. Circle the main idea.

1. Charlie Todd couldn't find work as an actor.

②Everyone needs to be creative and have fun.

3. Improv Everywhere creates pranks that are positive experiences.

38

" There is no point and [. . .] there doesn't have to be a point. We don't need a reason. As long as it's fun."

– Charlie Todd

B ▶ Look at the photos. Watch the TED Talk again and write the letter of the caption under the correct photo.

a. Improv Everywhere's pranks take place in public places.

c. Getting a high five on your way to work might make your day better.

b. Nobody expects to see characters from a movie at the library.

d. Charlie Todd wants to share a sense of fun and play.

1. _c_   2. _d_   3. _b_   4. _a_

Challenge! ♻ Some people might object to Improv Everywhere's pranks. Why? Are Improv Everywhere's pranks a good idea or a bad idea? Tell a partner. Give examples to support your idea.

39

B • Have students look at the pictures and read the captions. Tell them to match the captions with the photos as they watch the talk.

• Play the talk again.

• Have them compare answers with a partner.

• Check answers.

Challenge

• Have students read the directions and think about whether the pranks are a good idea or not, and reasons why people might not like the pranks.

• Divide the class into small groups or pairs and have them discuss the questions. Remind them they must give reasons to support their opinions.

• Compare opinions with the class.

Viewing Tip

Remind students that focusing only on the main idea, as in **While You Watch A,** is a useful listening strategy. Identifying the main idea rather than trying to understand details, especially when listening for the first time, will help them understand what the talk is about more quickly.

After You Watch

A • Have students read the paragraph and complete it with the words in the box.

• Have them compare answers with a partner.

• Play the talk again as necessary.

• Check answers.

B • Have students read the phrases and match them to the numbers they heard in the talk.

• Have them compare answers with a partner.

• Check answers.

C • Have students read the statements and circle the ones that match what Todd said in the talk.

• Have them compare their answers with a partner.

• Check answers.

TEDTALKS

Charlie Todd Comedian, Founder of Improv Everywhere
THE SHARED EXPERIENCE OF ABSURDITY

After You Watch

A Complete the summary with the words in the box.

Charlie Todd (1) _____believes_____ that we should be having more fun. In 2005, he staged an Improv Everywhere prank when he asked a group of friends to (2) _____stand_____ in the window frames of a building. Todd calls their (3) _performances_ "missions," and the (4) _____actors_____ are "secret agents." Since the first prank, Todd and his group have (5) _____completed_____ more than 100 missions and some of them have become an international (6) _____event_____.

stand	actors
believes	completed
event	performances

B Match the phrases to the information from the TED Talk.

_d_ **1.** number of high fives Rob gave   **a.** 2006

_c_ **2.** number of agents participating in "Blue Shirt" mission   **b.** 8

_e_ **3.** number of windows in the building   **c.** 80

_a_ **4.** year he was inspired to do "Blue Shirt" mission   **d.** 2,000

_b_ **5.** age of one young "secret agent"   **e.** 70

C Circle the statements that paraphrase Charlie Todd's ideas.

1. When I moved to New York, I wanted to be famous.

(2.) I started performing in public because I couldn't use a theater.

(3.) We want to create performances that make people happy.

4. Riding the subway in New York is a pleasant experience.

(5.) Adults need to learn to play again.

40

For Your Information: Charlie Todd

Charlie Todd is a New York-based comedian and actor. He created the group Improv Everywhere in 2001 and has produced, directed, performed in, and documented the more than 100 events they have staged. Improv Everywhere organizes pranks in public spaces, such as on trains, at train stations, in stores, and at the library. Its aim is to create unusual, unexpected moments that people can enjoy together—shared moments of unexpected fun. Todd wants people, adults especially, to remember that playing and having fun are important parts of life. Improv Everywhere's events are called missions and the event participants, secret agents. Some missions have been massive, involving thousands of agents, and also international; the 13th Annual No Pants Subway Ride took place on January 12, 2014 in more than 60 cities in over 25 countries around the world, and tens of thousands of participants were involved. Todd is the author of *Causing a Scene*, which tells Improv Everywhere's story.

Project

Charlie Todd and his group Improv Everywhere are on a mission to make New Yorkers laugh. They play pranks in public places, creating shared, positive experiences. Use Todd's ideas to design an improvised performance in your own city.

A Look at the list of places Improv Everywhere "agents" have performed. Circle the ones you think would be the most fun.

beach   park   public library   store   subway   car   train station

B Compare your choices in exercise **A** with a partner. Where else could you perform in your town or city? Remember that your goal is to create a positive, shared experience for the people who see your performance.

C Work with a group. Decide where you will perform and what activity you will do. Give each person in your group something specific to do. Use the table to organize your ideas.

Place	Date & Time	Activity	People

Challenge! Charlie Todd and Improv Everywhere really are everywhere— they even pulled a prank at TED. Go to TED.com and find out more about the prank they played. How did they do it?

41

Project

- Have students look at the picture and describe what they see. Have them read the project information.

A • Have students look at the list of places and choose the ones they think would be the most fun.
- Have students interview a partner and write their information in the chart.
- Have students tell the class about their partner's preferences.

B • Have students compare their choices in **A** with a partner.
- Have them add other places in their town or city.

C • Combine pairs to make groups of four. Assign each group member a role: leader, secretary, recorder, and reporter.
- Have them decide where they will perform, what they will do, and what each person in the group's role will be. The recorder should complete the table.
- Have the reporter from each group tell the class about their plan.

Challenge

- Have students read the information. In their project groups, have them research the prank Improv Everywhere did at TED. Tell them to find out what they did, how they did it, how many secret agents were involved, and how the TED audience reacted.
- Point out the Research Strategy.
- Have groups report back to the class on what they found out.

Teacher Tip: Roles in group work

It can be helpful to assign roles to students in each group. Some possibilities:

Leader—asks questions and keeps the discussion on topic

Secretary—takes notes on the group's ideas

Reporter—tells the group's answers to the class

Recorder—records the number of times each group member speaks, and tells each member how often they spoke when the activity ends

Be sure to rotate these roles often.

The Body
About the Photo

Over the years our way of life has become a lot more sedentary than it was in the past, with more time spent sitting in a car, an office, or at a computer. However, nowadays, we are much more aware of the need for regular physical activity to ensure our physical well-being. Along with a nutritious, balanced diet, physical exercise is an important element of a healthy lifestyle. Experts recommend at least twenty minutes of exercise every day, even if it is only walking. The photo, taken on a beach in Mallorca, reflects the positive benefits of being outdoors and physically active. With a healthy, active body, we have more energy and are less likely to get sick.

- Introduce the theme of the unit. Call on students to name as many parts of the body as they can remember.
- Direct students' attention to the picture. Have students describe what they see.
- Have students discuss the questions with a partner.
- Compare answers with the class.
- Ask these questions orally or by writing them on the board for students to answer in pairs: *How is your health? Excellent, good, OK, or poor? What are some things you do for better health?*
- Go over the Unit Goals with the class.
- For each goal, elicit any words students already know and write them on the board; for example, body and health vocabulary, sports and exercise vocabulary, etc.

A man doing a back flip off of a tree stump in Mallorca Island, Spain

42

UNIT 4 GOALS	Grammar	Vocabulary	Listening
• Discuss ways to stay healthy • Talk about lifestyles • Suggest helpful natural remedies • Explain cause and effect	Review of comparatives, superlatives, and equatives *The skin is the body's **largest** organ.* Infinitive of purpose *You can drink tea with honey **to help** a sore throat.*	Human organs Parts of the body Useful adjectives	Focused listening: A doctor's appointment

UNIT 4 GOALS

1. Discuss ways to stay healthy

2. Talk about lifestyles

3. Suggest helpful natural remedies

4. Explain cause and effect

43

Unit Theme Overview

- Around the world, people are becoming more concerned with maintaining good health, and the focus is shifting from medical care to everyday lifestyle choices and things that people can do to help themselves.

- Developing countries have made progress in controlling infectious diseases that once shortened people's life spans. Unfortunately, at the same time, changes in dietary habits mean that people in the developing world are now also more prone to obesity, heart disease, and other problems that were once much more prevalent in richer countries. According to the Worldwatch Institute, for the first time in human history, the number of overweight people in the world (1.1 billion) is estimated to equal the number of people who don't have enough food.

- This unit looks at the ways our lifestyle affects our health. It begins by introducing the parts and systems of the body and discussing how our daily lifestyle affects them. Students will then talk about home remedies and natural solutions for some common health problems. They will read about how the body defends itself against bacteria and viruses, and then watch a video about the marvels of the human body. Throughout the unit, the emphasis is on self-care, giving students the opportunity to consider and discuss ways to improve their health.

Speaking	Reading	Writing	Video Journal
Talking about food and ingredients that are good for you Suggesting easy remedies **Pronunciation:** Linking with comparatives and superlatives	**National Geographic:** Tiny Invaders	Writing an excuse for a sick child	**National Geographic:** The Human Body

Discuss Ways to Stay Healthy

Vocabulary

A • With books closed, ask students, *How many parts of the body can you name?* Have them point to each part they name, if possible.

• Go over the parts of the body in the illustration, pronouncing them for students to repeat.

• Have students write the correct word after each sentence.

• Check answers.

• Explain that the liver makes chemicals that your body needs and breaks down bad chemicals inside the body. If necessary, explain that arteries carry blood away from the heart and veins carry blood to the heart.

B • Tell students they will hear a conversation between a doctor and a patient. They should check the names of the body parts they hear.

• Play the recording one or more times. ◀》 15

• Have students compare answers with a partner.

• Check answers.

Grammar

• Review the formation of comparatives, superlatives, and equatives. Ask two students to stand up next to each other. Elicit a sentence with *taller*. *Ayako is taller than Yuki.* Ask two other students to stand up and elicit a sentence with *shorter*. Have a third student stand up and elicit a sentence with *shortest*. Continue with *as tall as.*

• Go over the information in the chart. Elicit more examples.

A **GOAL 1:** Discuss Ways to Stay Healthy

Vocabulary

brain — bone
artery
vein — heart
muscle
lungs
liver
small intestine — skin
large intestine

A Look at the picture. Then fill in the blanks with the vocabulary words.

1. This pushes your blood through your body: _____heart_____
2. These carry blood around your body: _____vein_____ , _____artery_____
3. These bring air into your body: _____lungs_____
4. This covers the outside of your body: _____skin_____
5. This makes your body move: _____muscle_____
6. This lets you think and remember: _____brain_____
7. This does many different things: _____liver_____
8. These digest food: _____stomach_____ , _____small intestine_____ , _____large intestine_____
9. This supports your body: _____bone_____

B ◀》 15 Listen and check (✓) the words you hear.

☐ brain	✓ lungs	☐ liver
☐ large intestine	☐ vein	☐ muscle
✓ heart	✓ stomach	✓ small intestine
☐ artery	☐ bone	✓ skin

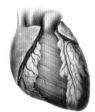

▲ human heart

▲ human fist

Grammar: The comparative, superlative, and equative

The comparative expresses similarities or differences between two people or things. Form the comparative with an adjective + *-er* + *than* or *more/less* + adjective + *than*.	The small intestine is **longer than** the large intestine. Henry is **healthier than** his father.
The superlative expresses extremes among three or more people or things. Form the superlative with *the* + adjective + *-est* or *the most/least* + adjective.	The skin is **the largest** organ in the human body. Some people think that the liver is **the most important** organ in the body.
The equative is used when people or things are the same or equal to each other. Form the equative with *(not) as* + adjective + *as*.	Your heart is **as large as** your fist. Your stomach is **not as large as** your liver.
Add *-er/-est* to most adjectives with 1 or 2 syllables. Use *more/less* or *the most/least* with adjectives of 3 or more syllables. When adjectives end in *-y*, change the *-y* to *-i* and add *-er/-est*.	
Some adjectives have irregular comparative and superlative forms: good better best / bad worse worst / far farther farthest	

44   Unit 4

Word Bank: Parts of the body

abdomen	elbow	knee
ankle	eye	mouth
back	finger	neck
bladder	foot	nerve
cheek	hand	nose
chin	hip	shoulder
ear	kidney	toe

Grammar: Comparatives, superlatives, equatives

Comparative and superlative adjectives were introduced in Student Book 1. **Comparatives** are used to describe contrasts between two things; **superlatives** describe the contrast between one thing and all the others in a group. **Equatives** are used to describe things that are equal or the same. They are presented in greater detail in a later unit.

A Complete the sentences. Use comparatives, superlatives, equatives, and the words in parentheses.

1. Walking for exercise is __better__ (good) than running.
2. Smoking is the __worst__ (bad) thing you can do to your lungs.
3. Drinking alcohol is __more harmful__ (harmful) to your liver than eating junk food.
4. I think vegetables are the __most nutritious__ (nutritious) kind of food for your brain.
5. Swimming is not the __quickest__ (quick) way to build up your arm muscles.
6. Some elderly people are __as healthy__ (healthy) as some young people.

B 🔁 Do you agree or disagree with the statements above? Use comparatives, superlatives, and equatives.

> **I agree. Running is bad for your knees.**

> **But it's harder work, so maybe it's better for your heart.**

Conversation

A 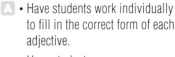 **16** Close your book and listen to the conversation. Which body parts do the speakers mention? *brain, arteries, muscles, bones*

Ron: What are you eating? It looks better than my lunch.
Valerie: It's fish stew, and it *is* good! Did you know that fish is good for your brain?
Ron: Really? Is it good for anything else?
Valerie: Well, it's also low in fat, so it's probably good for your arteries.
Ron: And it's high in protein, right? So it could help you build muscles.
Valerie: Yes, I think you're right.
Ron: My lunch isn't as good as yours. I just have a cheese sandwich.
Valerie: But cheese has a lot of calcium. That's good for your bones.
Ron: That's right! Enjoy your lunch.
Valerie: You, too.

B 🔁 Practice the conversation with a partner. Then make a new conversation using foods you know about.

C 🔁 **GOAL CHECK** ✔ **Discuss ways to stay healthy**

Talk with your partner about things you do to stay healthy. Complete these sentences:

I try to _____ .

I try not to _____ .

> **I try to get some exercise every day.**

> **I try not to eat a lot of sugar.**

Real Language

Common equative expressions include:

As soon as possible

As much as possible

The Body **45**

Grammar Practice: Comparatives, superlatives, equatives

Divide the class into pairs. Tell them to talk about themselves, and together write as many sentences as they can in three minutes, comparing themselves with their partner using comparatives and equatives. Tell them to write their sentences in the third person:

Mona has longer hair than Aisha.

Aisha is as old as Mona.

Call on pairs to read their lists to the class. Who has the longest list?

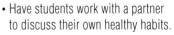

Talk About Lifestyles

Listening

A • Go over the terms in the Word Focus box. Discuss what lifestyle includes—things like eating, exercise, and other daily habits.

• Have students discuss the questions with a partner.

• Compare answers with the class. Who feels genes are more important? Who feels lifestyle is more important?

B • Tell students they are going to hear three people speaking about their health. They will label the pictures A, B, and C.

• Play the recording one or more times. ◀))) 17

• Check answers.

C • Tell students to listen again to the speakers and answer the questions. Have them read the questions.

• Play the recording one or more times. ◀))) 17

• Have students compare answers with a partner.

• Check answers.

D • Divide the class into pairs and have them take turns asking and answering the questions. Encourage them to ask their own questions. Tell them to make notes about their partner's answers.

• Have students tell the class about their partners. In classes with more than 15 students, you may prefer to divide the class into groups of five to six and have them report about their partner to their group.

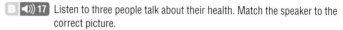

B | **GOAL 2:** Talk About Lifestyles

Word Focus

genes = parts of a cell that control physical characteristics (eye color, height, etc.)

lifestyle = how we live

Listening

A 🔁 Discuss these questions with a partner.

1. What determines how healthy you are?

2. Are your **genes** or your **lifestyle** more important?

B ◀))) 17 Listen to three people talk about their health. Match the speaker to the correct picture.

Speaker _____ _B_ _____   Speaker _____ _C_ _____   Speaker _____ _A_ _____

C ◀))) 17 Listen again and answer the questions.

Speaker A:

1. What kind of exercise does Speaker A get? _walking_

2. Which family members does Speaker A mention? _mother, grandmothers_

Speaker B:

3. What kind of exercise does Speaker B get? _He goes to the gym._

4. How often does Speaker B get sick? _every couple of months_

Speaker C:

5. Why did Speaker C change her diet when she got older? _She didn't have any energy._

6. What do some people think about Speaker C's diet? _You can't get all the nutrients you need from plant foods._

D 🔁 Work with a partner. Interview each other. Then tell the class about your partner's lifestyle. Find out about:

• Exercise: What kind? How often?

• Diet: What do you usually eat?

• Genes: Do family members have health problems?

• Stress: How much and what kind?

Ask other questions about lifestyle that you think are important.

46   Unit 4

For Your Information: Genes vs. lifestyle

The debate about the relative importance of genes and lifestyle in a person's health has continued for years, but some research indicates that the two may in fact be connected. A study in 2008 found that men with cancer actually changed their genes by changing their lifestyle. The 30 men in the study switched to a plant-based diet, walked 30 minutes a day, took vitamins, practiced yoga and meditation one hour a day, and participated in a support group. After three months, many genes that promoted cancer growth were "turned off," and genes that fought the cancer were "turned on." More research is being done to determine if this is true for other serious diseases as well.

Pronunciation: Linking with comparatives and superlatives

Linking with comparatives and superlatives
When we use the comparative **-er** or **more,** and the next word starts with an /r/ sound, the words are linked together.

When we use the superlative **-est** or **most,** and the next word starts with a /t/ sound, the words are linked together.

She'll run in a longer race next month.   We had the best time of our lives.

A 🔊 **18** Listen to the sentences. Notice how the sounds are linked. Listen again and repeat the sentences.

1. It's a stricter religion than my religion.
2. This is the best tea for your stomach.
3. My grandfather is a faster runner than I am.
4. Which exercise is the most tiring?
5. You'll need a better reason than that.

B 🔁 Underline the sounds that link together. Then read the sentences aloud to a partner.

1. This is the longest text message I've ever seen.
2. Today's news was more reassuring than yesterday's news.
3. What's the best time of the day for you to study?
4. Flower experts are trying to develop a redder rose.
5. He took the softest towel in the house.

Communication

A 👥 What are the best kinds of food and exercise for a healthy lifestyle? Rate the foods from least healthy (1) to healthiest (5). Add one idea of your own. Then do the same with the types of exercise. Compare your list with the list of another pair.

____ fruit ____ bread ____ meat ____ vegetables ____ _____

____ walking ____ running ____ swimming ____ yoga ____ _____

B 🔁 **GOAL CHECK** ✓ **Talk about lifestyles**

Talk to a partner. Who are the healthiest people you know? What are some reasons for their good health?

> **Engage!**
>
> Is your generation healthier or less healthy than your parents' generation?

> **I feel good if I eat some meat or fish every day.**

> **But is meat a healthier food than vegetables?**

The Body **47**

• Direct students' attention to the Engage! box. Have students discuss the question in pairs or small groups. Compare answers with the class.

Pronunciation

• Go over the information about linking with comparatives and superlatives.

A • Tell students to listen to the linked sounds in the sentences.

• Play the recording one or more times for students to listen and repeat. 🔊 **18**

B • Have students work with a partner to find and underline the sounds that link together.

• Check answers.

• Tell students to read the sentences aloud to their partner. Walk around helping with difficulties.

Communication

A • Tell the class that they are going to talk about things that are good for a healthy lifestyle.

• Divide the class into pairs and have them rate the lists of food and exercise from healthiest to least healthy. Have them add at least one idea of their own to each list.

• When all student pairs are finished, combine them to form groups of four. Have them compare their lists, noting similarities and differences.

• Ask the class, *Which things were on both lists? Are there things you disagreed about?*

B 🔁 **GOAL CHECK** ✓

• Reassign pairs and have them discuss the questions.

• Finish with a whole-class discussion of the healthiest people they know. What do they have in common— what's true for all of them?

Expansion Activity: Health survey

Divide the class into groups of four to six. Have each group choose an area from **Listening D** (Exercise, Diet, Family History, or Stress) and plan two survey questions. Have each student survey two classmates and, if time permits, two other people outside the class. Then have them compile their answers and present a short oral report to the class about the information they recorded.

Suggest Helpful Natural Remedies

Language Expansion

- Introduce the idea of everyday ailments (small health problems) and ask if students can name any (such as a cold, sore throat, etc.).

A
- Read the paragraph with the class. Go over any unfamiliar vocabulary.
- Ask students to find the words in the reading that fit the definitions.
- Have students compare answers with a partner.
- Check answers.

B
- Introduce the idea of natural remedies—simple things we use at home as cures for illnesses.
- Have students read the article.
- Ask, *Have you ever used any of these remedies? Did they work?*
- Have students write a list of other natural remedies they know and compare their list with a partner.
- Compare answers with the class and write a list on the board. Discuss the effectiveness of the different remedies.

garlic

lemon

olive oil

onion

ginger

> If my skin feels dry, I put some olive oil on it.

Language Expansion: Everyday ailments

For every common health problem, there's a product for sale to cure it. Are you suffering from insomnia? There's a pill to help you fall asleep. Did a pimple appear on your face? There's a cream for that. If you have a headache after a long day at work, or perhaps a sore throat and fever, you can buy something to make you feel better. Do you have indigestion because you ate the wrong kind of food? There's a pill to end the burning feeling in your stomach. If food won't stay in your stomach at all, you can take some medicine to end the nausea. Or maybe you ate too fast, so now you have the hiccups. Well, you won't find anything at the pharmacy for hiccups, but there's probably a company working on a new product right now.

A Write the words in blue next to their definition.

1. _____insomnia_____ not being able to sleep
2. _____fever_____ high body temperature
3. _____hiccups_____ a repeated sound in your throat, often from eating too quickly
4. _____nausea_____ a feeling like you are going to vomit
5. _____indigestion_____ pain in the stomach because of something one has eaten
6. _____pimple_____ a small raised spot on the skin
7. _____headache_____ a pain in your head
8. _____sore throat_____ a general feeling of pain in the throat

B Read the article about natural remedies. What other natural remedies do you know about?

A Natural Solution

Garlic for a cold? Mint for bad breath? These days, more and more people are turning to their grandparents' remedies to cure their minor illnesses. And why not? These natural remedies are usually safe, inexpensive, and best of all—they work! (At least for some of the people, some of the time.) So the next time you're looking for a cure, skip the pharmacy and head to the grocery store for:

- **lemons** to stop the hiccups (Bite into a thick slice.)
- **ginger** to end nausea (Grind it and add hot water to make a tea.)
- **milk** to cure insomnia (Drink a warm glass at bedtime.)
- **honey** to help a sore throat (Mix it with warm water and drink it slowly.)
- **onions** to relieve a headache (Put slices on your forehead, close your eyes, and relax.)

Word Bank: Remedies

chile peppers (to prevent colds)

clove oil (to stop toothache pain)

cumin seeds (for indigestion)

echinacea flowers (to prevent all kinds of illness)

fennel seeds (for bad-smelling breath)

valerian root (for insomnia)

Grammar: Infinitive of purpose

One common use of the infinitive in English is to express the desired result of an action.

The infinitive of purpose can come at the beginning or end of a sentence.

> **To stop** hiccups, I eat a spoonful of sugar.
>
> I eat a spoonful of sugar **to stop** hiccups.

Grammar: Infinitive of purpose

The infinitive of purpose gives a reason for doing something. Form an infinitive with *to* + the simple or base form of a verb.	You can drink tea with honey **to help** a sore throat. I use a sunscreen **to protect** my skin.
In order to + the base form of a verb is also a way to express the infinitive of purpose.	Nikki took an aspirin **in order to lower** her fever.
Use a comma after the infinitive of purpose when it begins a sentence.	**To stop hiccups,** I drink a glass of water.

A Match the actions with the reasons.

1. Get plenty of sleep at night __c__
2. Eat fruits and vegetables __e__
3. Take a nap __f__
4. Give children warm milk __a__
5. Ask your doctor questions __b__
6. Lift weights __d__

a. to help them fall asleep.
b. to find out the best remedy for your problem.
c. to increase your concentration during the day.
d. to make your muscles stronger.
e. to get enough vitamins in your diet.
f. to cure a headache.

Conversation

A 🔊 19 Close your book and listen to the conversation. What remedies for fatigue do the speakers talk about? *drink coffee, go for a walk*

Olivia: Hi, Ashley. Are you drinking coffee? That's new.
Ashley: Hi, Olivia. You're right. I usually don't drink coffee, but I need it today to wake up.
Olivia: You do look tired. Did you get enough sleep last night?
Ashley: No, I was worried about today's test, so it was hard to fall asleep.
Olivia: Come on. Let's go for a walk.
Ashley: Go for a walk? Why?
Olivia: To wake you up and to get some oxygen to your brain before the test.
Ashley: That's a good idea. Where do you want to go?

> **Real Language**
>
> We say *That's new* when we notice something different or unusual.

B 🔁 Practice the conversation with a partner. Find and underline the three uses of the infinitive of purpose.

C 🔁 Make a new conversation using your own ideas about health problems. Then role-play the conversation for the class.

D 🔁 **GOAL CHECK** ✔ **Suggest helpful natural remedies**

Talk to a partner. What do you usually do to cure these common problems: a headache, bad breath, sore feet, and hiccups?

The Body **49**

Grammar Practice: Infinitive of purpose

Write these phrases on the board. Divide the class into groups of three to four and have them share their ideas for how to do these things, using infinitives of purpose.

1. *sleep better (To sleep better, you should open the window.)*
2. *remember people's names*
3. *get exercise*
4. *practice English outside of class*
5. *stay healthy in winter*

Grammar

- Go over the information in the chart.
- Elicit more examples by asking students *Why do you exercise/ brush your teeth/take vitamins?* and so forth. (to get stronger/to keep my teeth clean/to have more energy)

A • Have students match the actions with the reasons.
- Have students compare answers with a partner.
- Check answers.

Conversation

A • Have students close their books. Write the question on the board: *What remedies for fatigue do the speakers talk about?*
- Play the recording. 🔊 19
- Check answers.

B • Play or read the conversation again for the class to repeat.
- Practice the conversation with the class in chorus.
- Have students practice the conversation with a partner, then switch roles and practice it again.
- Have students identify the three infinitives of purpose (to wake up, to wake you up, to get some oxygen).

C • Have student pairs choose a health problem and make a new conversation.
- Have students role-play their conversations for the class or for a small group (in large classes).

D 🔁 **GOAL CHECK** ✔

- Have students discuss remedies they know for these problems with a partner.
- Compare answers with the class. What are the most unusual remedies? Has anyone tried them? How well do they work?

Explain Cause and Effect

Reading

- Have students look at the pictures and describe what they see. Introduce the topic of the reading. Ask students, *Why do we get sick? How does sickness go from one person to another?*

A
- Have students discuss the list of actions with a partner and choose the ones that can make people sick.
- Compare answers with the class. Point out that any of these things can make you sick because they can bring germs (bacteria and viruses) into your body.

B
- Point out the words in the Word Focus box. Have students read the article. Tell them to circle any words they don't understand.
- Go over the article with the class, answering any questions from the students about vocabulary.
- Have students read the statements and choose *true* or *false*.
- Have students compare answers with a partner.
- Check answers.

C
- Divide the class into pairs and have them take turns telling about their experiences.
- Compare answers with the class. Ask, *What did you do to feel better? Was it a good remedy?*

Communication

A
- Divide the class into groups and have them list all the serious illnesses they can think of—both in their own country and other places that have been in the news. Have them talk about how these diseases move from one person to another.
- Compare answers with the class.

D **GOAL 4:** Explain Cause and Effect

Reading

A Talk to a partner. Which of these can make you sick?

- shaking hands with someone
- being outside in cold weather
- eating food
- riding a crowded bus
- touching your eye
- playing a computer game

B Circle **T** for *true* or **F** for *false*.

1. Viruses can only live inside people or animals.   T   (F)
2. All bacteria cause illnesses.   T   (F)
3. Washing your skin can prevent some illnesses.   (T)   F
4. Germs can enter the body through the eyes.   (T)   F
5. After they kill germs, antibodies stay in the body.   (T)   F
6. Vaccines kill germs in the body.   T   (F)

C Tell a partner about the last time you got sick. How did you feel? What did you do to feel better?

Communication

A Work in a small group. Make a list of serious illnesses that people in different parts of the world can get. How do people get those illnesses?

Word Focus

sense = see, hear, feel, etc.
influenza = illness
cut = opening in the skin
immune system = the body's way of preventing illness
weak = not strong

The Human Body

TINY INVADERS

The human body is truly amazing. It allows us to **sense** the world around us, to do work and have fun, and to move from place to place. In fact, the human body does its work so well that most people don't think about it very much—until they get sick.

The germs that make people sick are everywhere. You can't see them, but they're there. They're sitting on your desk. They're hiding on your computer's keyboard. They're even in the air that you are breathing.

E-coli

Word Bank:
Serious illnesses

AIDS	malaria
cancer	polio
cholera	tuberculosis
hepatitis	typhoid

For Your Information: Germs

The English word *germ* is very common in everyday use, but it is not a scientific term. It refers to both bacteria and viruses, which are very different. One very common type of drug, antibiotics, is effective against bacteria but does not kill viruses. Because people don't understand the difference, they often want to take antibiotics for illnesses that won't be helped by them.

The immune system is the body's natural defense against illness.

There are two types of germs: viruses and bacteria. Viruses use the cells inside animals or plants to live and multiply. Viruses cause illnesses such as **influenza,** or the flu. Bacteria are tiny creatures. Some bacteria are good. They can help your stomach digest food. Other bacteria aren't as good. They can cause sore throats and ear infections.

How can you stop these tiny invaders from making you sick? Your skin is the first defense against germs. One of the easiest ways to prevent some illnesses is simply by washing with soap and water. But germs can still enter the body through small **cuts** in the skin or through the mouth, eyes, and nose.

Once germs are inside your body, your **immune system** tries to protect you. It looks for and destroys germs. How does it do that? Some cells in the body actually eat germs! Other cells make antibodies. There is a different antibody for each kind of germ. Some antibodies keep germs from making you sick. Others help your body find and kill germs. After a germ is destroyed, the antibodies stay in your body. They protect you if the same kind of germ comes back. That way you will not get the same illness twice.

You can also help your immune system to fight germs by getting vaccinated. Vaccines are medicines. They contain dead or **weak** germs that cannot make you sick. Instead, they cause your body to make antibodies. If the same germ ever shows up again, then your antibodies attack it. You can also keep your body healthy by eating a healthy diet to make your immune system strong.

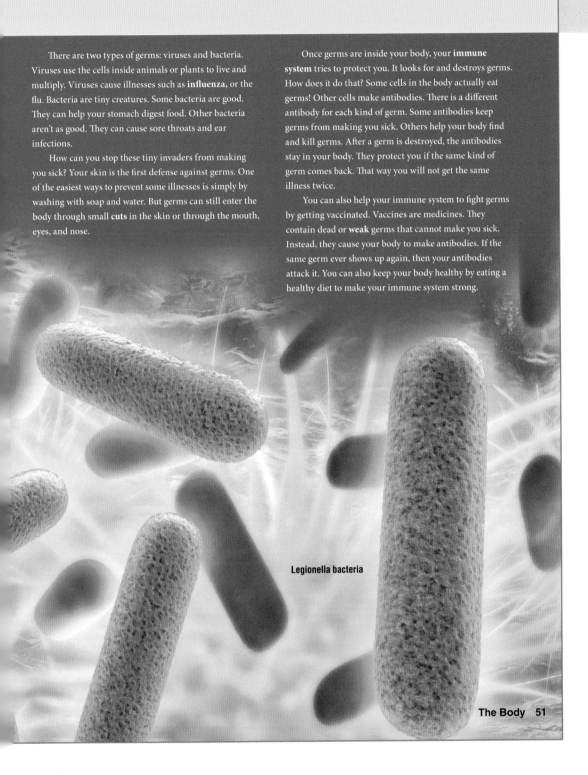

Legionella bacteria

The Body 51

After Reading

Web search: Have students research remedies for common health problems online. Tell them to choose one problem and search to find at least two simple remedies that people can use at home. Have them report the information to the class or a small group.

Project: Have students work in pairs or small groups to create a poster with pictures and information about a common health problem, such as colds, headaches, or sore feet. Tell them to include facts about what causes the problem, what happens inside the body, and simple remedies for the problem.

Explain Cause and Effect

Communication

A • Have students look at the picture and describe what they see.

• Divide the class into small groups and have them discuss the information in the chart.

• Compare answers with the class. Have each group explain their answers.

Writing

A • Tell students to imagine they are the parent of a child who has a common childhood illness. Elicit/ Give examples: a cold, the flu, a sore throat, a stomachache.

• Have students read the directions. Have them help you begin writing a note on the board. Ask, *What's wrong with my child? How did he/she get ill? Why does he/she need to stay at home?* etc. Use their ideas to write an example note on the board.

• Have them write a short note to explain the problem to the child's teacher.

• Have students exchange papers with a partner. Ask students to mark corrections and suggestions for improvements on their partner's paper.

• If desired, have students rewrite their papers, to be collected for marking.

B 🔁 **GOAL CHECK** ✔

• Have students answer the question with a partner. Remind them to think about cause and effect and to try to use infinitives of purpose.

• Compare answers with the class.

D **GOAL 4:** Explain Cause and Effect

Communication

A 👥 Talk with your classmates. How does each action on the left spread illness? Which actions on the right prevent illness?

> Shaking a person's hand can pass on bacteria.

> Staying home will help prevent spreading germs.

Ways to spread illness	Ways to prevent illness
shaking hands	Stay home when you're sick.
coughing or sneezing	Wash your hands often.
drinking from a friend's water bottle	Cover your nose and mouth.
sitting near a sick person at school	Use clean dishes for eating and drinking.
eating food without washing your hands	Exercise and eat healthy foods.

Writing

A Imagine your child is sick and cannot go to school today. Write a message to your child's teacher in your notebook. Explain how your child became ill and give reasons why you want him or her to stay at home.

_____
(date)

Dear (Mr./Ms.) _____,

_____

Sincerely,

_____

B 🔁 **GOAL CHECK** ✔ **Explain cause and effect**

Talk to a partner. What happens when viruses or bacteria enter the body?

52 Unit 4

Teacher Tip: Errors in spoken English

Giving immediate corrections to students during group and pair work is not very effective. Students are too involved in the activity and won't retain the correct form. Instead:

• Make notes on errors frequently heard during the activity and give a mini-lesson after the activity, contrasting the error and the correct form.

• Listen to different groups in rotation, write down important errors, and give the list to the group members to correct.

• For all of these activities, it's best NOT to include the name of the student who made the error.

Before You Watch

A ⚡ Brainstorm five things your body lets you do every day.

While You Watch

A ▶ Watch the video *The Human Body*. Draw lines to match the body's systems to the parts of the body or the cells they produce.

1. the circulatory system __b__   **a.** the brain, spinal cord, and nerves
2. the respiratory system __e__   **b.** the heart
3. the digestive system __d__   **c.** egg cells and sperm cells
4. the nervous system __a__   **d.** the stomach and intestines
5. the reproductive system __c__   **e.** the lungs

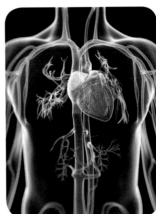

B ▶ Watch the video again. Write **T** for *true* or **F** for *false*.

1. The heart is the body's strongest muscle. __T__
2. Nutrients enter the blood from the small intestine. __T__
3. The brain is about the size of an orange. __F__
4. Another word for nerve cells is neurons. __T__

After You Watch / Communication

A ⚡ What information from the video surprised you the most? What are some things you can do to take care of your body's systems?

B 👥 Design a training program for an Olympic athlete. What will he or she eat every day? What kinds of exercise, and how often? What else will help to get your athlete into top physical condition?

The Body **53**

Video Journal:
The Human Body
Before You Watch

A • Have students look at the picture and describe what they see. Have students work with a partner to talk about five things their bodies do every day. (Examples: digest food, move, and so on.)

• Have students compare answers with a partner.

• Compare answers with the class.

While You Watch

A • Tell students to watch the video the first time and match the columns.

• Play the video.

• Have students compare answers with a partner.

• Check answers.

B • Have students read the statements. Tell students to watch the video again and choose *true* or *false*.

• Play the video again.

• Have students compare answers with a partner.

• Check answers.

After You Watch / Communication

A • Divide the class into pairs and have students discuss what they found most surprising in the video and ways of keeping body systems healthy.

B • Divide the class into groups of three to four. Have each group choose a type of athlete (such as a swimmer or a skier) and then discuss the best training program for this type of athlete. Appoint one member in each group to take notes, and another who will present the group's plan to the class.

• When all groups are ready, have them give a short oral report to the class. In large classes, have groups present to each other.

For Your Information: Amazing body facts

• In one year, your heart beats 40,000,000 times.
• Your liver performs more than 500 different functions.
• In one minute, 50,000 cells in your body will die and be replaced by new cells.
• A sneeze comes out of your mouth at more than 100 mph (160 kph).

• Your eyes blink more than 6,000,000 times in one year.
• In one year, your heart does enough work to raise one ton of weight nearly one meter (one yard) off the ground. It circulates the blood through the body about 1,000 times per day.

Challenges

About the Photo

This photo shows the start of the swimming race in the Ironman World Championship in Kailua in Kona, Hawai'i. With the swimmers on the surface and the fish swimming below, it is an amazing piece of underwater photography. It was taken by Donald Miralle, who has won many international awards for his photography including six World Press Awards. He is considered one of the most innovative photographers of his time. Miralle took this shot at the 2011 Ironman contest. An Ironman Triathlon consists of a 3.86 km (2.4 mile) swim, a 180.25 km (112 mile) bicycle ride and a 42.2 km (26.2 mile) run. They are raced in that order and without a break. There is also a strict time limit of 17 hours to complete the race.

- Introduce the theme of the unit. Ask, *What is a challenge? What are some examples of challenges faced by people you know?*

- Direct students' attention to the picture. Have students describe what they see.

- Have students discuss the questions with a partner.

- Compare answers with the class.

- Ask these questions orally or by writing them on the board for students to answer in pairs: *What is the biggest challenge you have faced in your life? What are you proud of doing?*

- Go over the Unit Goals with the class.

- For each goal, elicit any words students already know and write them on the board; for example, how to talk about actions in the past, adjectives, etc.

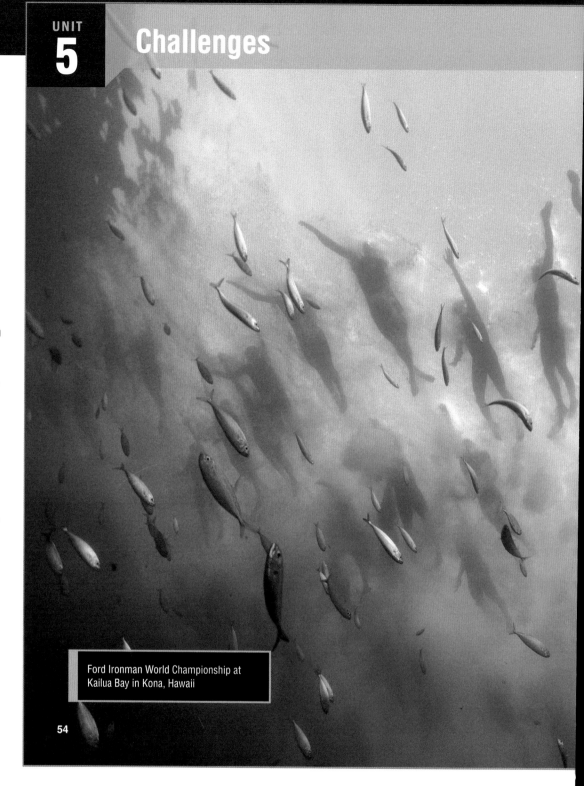

Ford Ironman World Championship at Kailua Bay in Kona, Hawaii

54

UNIT 5 GOALS	Grammar	Vocabulary	Listening
• Talk about facing challenges • Discuss past accomplishments • Use *too* and *enough* to talk about abilities • Describe a personal challenge	Simple past tense vs. past continuous tense We **were eating** dinner when you **called.** Enough, not enough, too + adjective He was **old enough** to sail alone.	Physical and mental challenges Phrasal verbs	Listening for general understanding An interview: Jenny Daltry, herpetologist

Look at the photo, answer the questions:

1 What phrase best describes the picture?

2 What do you think of when you hear the word *challenge*?

Unit Theme Overview

- People of all ages from all cultures are fascinated by challenges. *Guinness World Records*, one of the best-selling books worldwide, is filled with listings of amazing feats performed by all kinds of people: A man in Texas, in the United States, sat in a bathtub with 87 live rattlesnakes for 45 minutes. A girl in India had her artwork exhibited when she was only 11 months old. An Italian man has typed 64 entire books backwards.

- Some of these challenges are amazing in themselves—a woman in Hungary ran 247.2 kilometers (153 miles) in 24 hours. Others are amazing within the context of an individual life—such as when a blind person learns to ski. But there is something in the story of a challenge successfully met that inspires other people to consider what they may be able to achieve that now seems outside their reach.

- In this unit, students will consider many kinds of challenges—both mental and physical. They will talk about challenges they have faced in their own lives and will consider what they have accomplished. They will talk about the skills and qualities required to meet a challenge and will read and watch accounts of challenges in the wilderness—at the North Pole, in an African rain forest, and in the mountains of Central Asia.

UNIT 5 GOALS

1. Talk about facing challenges

2. Discuss past accomplishments

3. Use *too* and *enough* to talk about abilities

4. Describe a personal challenge

55

Speaking	Reading	Writing	Video Journal
Discussing challenges Talking about abilities **Pronunciation:** Words that end in *-ed*	**National Geographic:** Arctic Dreams and Nightmares	Writing about a challenging experience	**National Geographic:** Searching for the Snow Leopard

Talk About Facing Challenges

Vocabulary

A
- Have students look at the picture and describe what they see.
- Have students read the paragraph. Ask comprehension questions, for example, *Are challenges always physical? What was this person's challenge? How does she describe it? What does she want to do when she achieves her goal?* Have students listen to the recording and notice the pronunciation of the words in blue. 🔊 20
- Have different students try to explain the meaning of the words in blue.
- Point out the collocations in the two Word Focus boxes. Ask, *When did you face a challenge? What was it? How did you make progress towards your goal?*

B
- Have students match the words in blue from **A** to their meanings.
- Have students compare answers with a partner.
- Check answers.

Grammar

- Introduce the past continuous tense. Tell students, *Last night at eight o'clock, I was correcting your homework papers. My husband/friend/mother was watching TV. What about you? What were you doing at eight o'clock?* Elicit answers in the past continuous tense.
- Go over the information in the charts. Focus students' attention on the use of *when* and *while*.

▲ A young girl plays the stringed koto.

Word Focus

To face a challenge means to decide to do something new and difficult.

Word Focus

To **make progress** means to improve or get nearer to a goal over time.

Vocabulary

A 🔊 20 Listen and read about one person's challenge.

The word "challenge" might make you think of physical activities like playing sports. But mental activities such as learning a new language or a new skill can also be a challenge. For me, learning to play a musical instrument is a challenge, but also an adventure. You might feel afraid to try it, but it's as exciting as traveling to a new place, and the only equipment you need is a violin, a guitar, or in my case—a *koto*.

When I started my *koto* lessons, my goal was to learn to play this amazing instrument well enough to play for my family. Now, I'm making good progress with the help of my music teacher. She thinks I'm getting better every week! I can probably achieve my goal soon, and then I'll play the *koto* at my father's birthday party.

B Write each word in blue next to the correct meaning.

1. related to the body ___physical___
2. something new that requires effort ___challenge___
3. improvement ___progress___
4. things needed for an activity ___equipment___
5. unusual and exciting activity ___adventure___
6. succeed in making something happen ___achieve___
7. related to the mind ___mental___
8. something you hope to do over time ___goal___
9. activity that requires special knowledge ___skill___
10. surprising, interesting, and wonderful ___amazing___

Grammar: Past continuous vs. simple past

Past continuous vs. simple past	
Use the past continuous tense to talk about something in progress at a specific time in the past.	I saw Sasha yesterday afternoon. He **was teaching** his son to ride a bicycle.
Form the past continuous with *was/were* + the *-ing* form of a verb.	We **weren't watching** a movie at 8:00 last night. We **were studying** for a test.
Use the simple past tense to talk about completed actions or situations in the past.	Edmund Hillary and Tenzing Norgay **climbed** Mount Everest in 1953.

56   Unit 5

Word Bank: Achievements

earning a degree/diploma

getting a promotion at work

learning a new skill

overcoming a problem/obstacle

receiving an award

winning a game/match/contest

Grammar: Past continuous tense

The past continuous tense emphasizes an action that began before, and continued after, a point in the past. Because of this, it is often used in combination with the simple past tense in the same sentence.

   *I **was studying** when you came in.*

It can also be used with a reference to a point in time in the past:

   *I **was studying** at nine o'clock.*

Grammar: Past continuous with the simple past

Past continuous with the simple past	
Use the simple past with the past continuous to talk about a past event that interrupted something already in progress.	We **were practicing** the play **when** the lights **went** out.
Use a time clause with *when* for the action in the simple past and *while* for the action in the past continuous tense.	It **was raining** very hard **when they arrived** at the village. Sara **got** a text message **while she was talking** with her professor.
Use a comma after a time clause when it begins a sentence.	**While Ben was writing** his research paper**,** the computer stopped working.

A Complete the sentences. Use the past continuous form of the verb in parentheses.

1. William _was doing_ (do) his homework when I arrived.
2. Martina _was looking_ (look) for a job when I met her for the first time.
3. The mountain climbers _were resting_ (rest) when the storm began.
4. While Ted and I _waiting_ (wait) to see the doctor, I told him a funny story. *(were)*
5. You and your friends _were sitting_ (sit) in the coffee shop yesterday morning.

Conversation

A 🔊 21 Close your book and listen to the conversation. What was Helen's biggest challenge last year? *getting her driver's license*

Helen: What was the most difficult thing you did last year?
Paul: Do you mean the worst thing?
Helen: No, I mean your biggest challenge.
Paul: Well, getting used to a new school when my family moved was a challenge.
Helen: For me, getting my driver's license was a challenge. It was hard!

B 🔄 Practice the conversation with a partner. What was difficult about each challenge?

C 🔄 **GOAL CHECK** ✔ **Talk about facing challenges**

Talk about a challenge you have faced with a partner. What was happening in your life at that time? How did the challenge change your life, or change you?

Challenges **57**

Grammar Practice: Past continuous tense

Choose a point in the past, such as yesterday at four o'clock. Have students write ten sentences about what other people were doing at that time, using the past continuous tense. Tell them they can write about people they know or about famous people. They can use true information or their imagination.

My mother was cooking dinner.

The president was flying in a helicopter.

Have students read their sentences to a partner. Then have each pair choose one interesting sentence to read to the class.

Discuss Past Accomplishments

Listening

- Introduce the idea of animals that are endangered—they might all die out soon. Elicit well-known examples (tigers, some kinds of whales, etc.). Point out the definition in the Word Focus box.

- Tell students they are going to hear an interview with a woman who works with endangered animals.

A • Have students look at the pictures and read the directions. Discuss the questions as a class. Tell them they will hear about some of these animals in the interview.

B • Have students read the questions. Tell them to find the answers while they listen to the interview the first time.

- Play the recording one or more times. 🔊 22

- Have students compare answers with a partner.

- Check answers.

- Ask, *Which animals in the pictures were mentioned in the interview?* (answers: *panda, Siamese crocodile, Antiguan racer*) Explain that all of these animals are endangered.

C • Tell students to listen to the interview again and find the information. Have them read the questions.

- Play the recording one or more times. 🔊 22

- Have students compare answers with a partner.

- Check answers.

- Direct students' attention to the Engage! box. Have students discuss the questions with a partner. Ask, *Why are endangered animals important?* Explain that other plants and animals need the endangered animals. Talk about examples of endangered animals in the students' countries of origin.

B   **GOAL 2:** Discuss Past Accomplishments

Word Focus

endangered = If an animal is *endangered*, its population is so small that it may die out.

▲ Jenny Daltry, herpetologist and explorer

Engage!

How do you feel about crocodiles and snakes? Is it important to protect **unpopular** endangered animals?

Listening

A What do you know about these endangered animals? Which animal do you think people should work the hardest to save? Why?

▲ giant panda

▲ Siamese crocodile

▲ Antiguan racer (snake)

▲ Humboldt penguin

B 🔊 22 Listen to the interview of Jenny Daltry. Circle the correct letter.

1. What amazing thing did Jenny Daltry do?

   a. She discovered a group of Siamese crocodiles.
   b. She found a new kind of bird in Cambodia.
   c. She helped scientists protect panda bears.

2. What was her biggest challenge?

   a. walking through marshes
   b. avoiding dangerous snakes
   c. educating people about crocodiles

3. How did she achieve her goal?

   a. She explained that crocodiles are important to the marshes.
   b. She explained that crocodiles are not really dangerous.
   c. She explained that crocodiles are extinct.

C 🔊 22 Listen again. Answer the questions.

1. How many crocodiles are in the largest group? _150_

2. How many acres are now protected by the government? _over 3 million acres_

3. How do most people feel about crocodiles? _afraid_

4. What was Daltry doing when she found out about the Antiguan racer snake?
   traveling in the Caribbean

For Your Information: Siamese crocodile

The Siamese crocodile once lived in swamps, rivers, and lakes across Southeast Asia, from Vietnam to Malaysia. It is about 3 meters (10 feet) long. In 1992, scientists decided that it was completely extinct. Then, in 2005, a nest of baby crocodiles was found in Laos, and more adult crocodiles were found in Cambodia. Today, it is believed that there are only 500 of the animals left in the world. In Pang Sida National Park in Thailand, there is a program to breed the crocodiles and reintroduce them into the wild in a part of the park that is closed to visitors.

Pronunciation: Words that end in -ed

A 🔊 **23** Listen to these words that end in -ed. The -ed is pronounced in three different ways.

/t/		/d/		/ɪd/	
help	helped	listen	listened	start	started

B 🔊 **24** Listen, repeat, and check (✓) the column of the sound you hear.

Present tense	Simple past tense	-ed ending sound		
		/t/	/d/	/ɪd/
walk	walked	✓	—	—
protect	protected	—	—	✓
cross	crossed	✓	—	—
discover	discovered	—	✓	—
climb	climbed	—	✓	—
start	started	—	—	✓
need	needed	—	—	✓
close	closed	—	✓	—

C 🔄 Write down ten verbs in the present tense. Some verbs should end in *t* or *d*. Say one of your words and ask your partner to say it in the past tense. Then switch roles.

Communication

A 🔄 Work with a partner. Make a list of challenges people your age face.

B 👥 Get together with another pair of students and compare your lists. Try to agree on the two or three most difficult challenges for people your age.

C 🔄 **GOAL CHECK** ✔ **Discuss past accomplishments**

Write two or three sentences about a famous person or a person you know. Choose from the list below or use your own idea. What challenges did he or she face in the past? How did the person achieve his or her goal? Tell your partner about the person you chose.

> scientist or explorer   writer or artist   political figure   businessperson

> **Word Focus**
>
> To **achieve a goal** means to succeed in doing something you hoped to do.

Challenges **59**

Pronunciation

A
- Point out that the -ed ending for the past tense is pronounced differently in different words. Tell students to listen to the words, and notice the difference.
- Play the recording. 🔊 **23**

B
- Tell students to listen to each word, repeat it, and then check the sound of the -ed ending.
- Play the recording one or more times. 🔊 **24**
- Have students compare answers with a partner.
- Check answers.

C
- Have students write a list of ten verbs individually. Tell them to make sure that some end in *t* or *d*.
- Divide the class into pairs. Have students take turns saying a verb from their list while the other listens and says it in the past tense.
- Draw three columns on the board, /t/, /d/ and /ɪd/. Have students write their verbs in the correct column. Have students repeat the past tense forms chorally and individually.

Communication

A
- Divide the class into pairs. Have them brainstorm a list of common challenges for people their age. If students ages widely differ, let each pair choose an age to discuss.

B
- In groups of four, have them discuss their lists and agree on or rank the most difficult challenges.

C 🔄 **GOAL CHECK** ✔
- Point out the definition in the Word Focus box. Have students read the directions and write notes about the person and their goal.
- Assign new pairs to discuss the people they've chosen.
- With the whole class, discuss the people. What were some of the biggest achievements? What can we learn from them?

Expansion Activity

Following the communication exercises, have students work with a partner to make a list of advice for someone they have already met who is facing a challenge; for example, preparing for an important exam, getting a first job, or moving to a new city.

Use *Too* and *Enough* to Talk About Abilities

Language Expansion

A • Have students read the article. Ask comprehension questions, for example, *Where is Subaru from? What does he like doing? What did he do that was a challenge?* etc. Questions can be asked orally, or write them for students to answer individually or in pairs.

B • Remind students that when they don't know new vocabulary, they can use the context to guess the meaning. Point out the words in blue in the article in **A.** Have students match the phrasal verbs to their meanings.

• Have students compare answers with a partner.

• Check answers.

• Go over the information in the Phrasal verbs box. Point out that a phrasal verb is a verb plus one or two prepositions that are used together to form a meaning that is different from the meaning of the verb and the prepositions when used separately.

• Elicit more sentences with these verbs. Ask, for example, *Where did you grow up? What is something that you put up with?*

Grammar

A • Have students reread the sentences they saw in the article and circle the answers.

• Check answers.

• Direct students' attention to the Engage! box. Have students discuss the questions in pairs or small groups. Then compare answers with the class and, if desired, take a class poll with a show of hands.

C **GOAL 3:** Use *Too* and *Enough* to Talk About Abilities

▲ Subaru Takahashi, the youngest person to sail alone across the Pacific Ocean

Word Focus

Phrasal verbs are two- or three-word combinations that have a special meaning.
set + **out** = leave on a trip

Engage!

What do you think about Subaru's parents? Was he really old enough to set out alone?

Language Expansion: Phrasal verbs

A Read the article.

Subaru Takahashi was only 14 years old when he set out on an amazing adventure. His goal was to sail from Tokyo to San Francisco—alone. Subaru grew up near the sea and loved sailing. His parents thought he was old enough to sail alone, and they helped him buy a boat. He left on July 22. At first, the trip was easy. Then after three weeks, his engine broke down, so he didn't have any lights. He had to watch out for big ships at night, because it was too dark to see his boat. Five days later, his radio stopped working. Subaru was really alone then, but he didn't give up. His progress was very slow, but he kept on sailing. He almost ran out of food, and he was not fast enough to catch fish. He put up with hot sun and strong wind. On September 13, Subaru sailed into San Francisco. He was the youngest person ever to sail alone across the Pacific Ocean.

B Match each phrasal verb in blue from the article with its meaning.

1. set out _d_   **a.** accept something bad without being upset
2. give up _f_   **b.** grow from a child to an adult
3. watch out _e_   **c.** finish the amount of something that you have
4. grow up _b_   **d.** leave on a trip
5. keep on _g_   **e.** be very careful
6. run out of _c_   **f.** stop trying
7. put up with _a_   **g.** continue trying
8. break down _h_   **h.** stop working

Grammar: *Enough, not enough, too* + adjective

A Read these sentences from the article and the questions that follow. Circle **Y** for *yes* and **N** for *no*.

1. *He was old enough to sail alone.*
   Could he sail alone?   (**Y**) **N**

2. *He was not fast enough to catch fish.*
   Did he catch fish?   **Y** (**N**)

3. *It was too dark to see his boat.*
   Could people see his boat?   **Y** (**N**)

Word Bank:
Inseparable phrasal verbs

call on	go over
come across	pass away
find out	put off
get off	run into
get on	

Grammar: *Enough, not enough, too* + adjective

Enough, not enough, and *too* are used with adverbs.

   *He talks loudly **enough.**/He doesn't talk loudly **enough.**/ He talks **too** loudly.*

Enough/Not enough are also used with verbs and nouns.

   *This room is big **enough**/**not** big **enough**/**too** big.*

   *I ate **enough.***   *We have **enough** time.*

This lesson presents their use with adjectives. *Enough* is placed after the adjective, while *too* is placed before.

Enough, not enough, too + adjective

He was **old enough** to sail alone.	adjective + *enough* = The amount that you want.
He was **not fast enough** to catch fish.	*not* + adjective + *enough* = Don't have the amount that you want.
His boat was **too dark** to see.	*too* + adjective = More than the amount you want.

B Complete the sentences. Use *enough, not enough*, or *too* and the adjective.

1. Subaru's boat was <u>big enough</u> (big) for two people.
2. A boat is <u>too expensive</u> (expensive) for me to buy because I don't have much money.
3. Crossing the ocean alone is <u>too difficult</u> (difficult) for most people to do.
4. My parents say I'm <u>not old enough</u> (old) to travel alone. I have to wait until I'm 18.
5. I think Subaru's trip was <u>too dangerous</u> (dangerous) for a young person. His parents should not have let him go alone.
6. A trip to San Francisco by plane is a fun adventure, and it's <u>safe enough</u> (safe) for my family and me. Maybe we'll go there for our next vacation.

Conversation

A 🔊 25 Close your book and listen to the conversation. What does Lisa need to do before she can climb the mountain? *get good boots, go hiking every weekend, be fit/strong enough*

Lisa: Do you know what I want to do next summer? My goal is to climb Black Mountain.
Mari: Are you serious? Black Mountain is too hard to climb. Don't you need special equipment?
Lisa: I already asked about it. I just need good boots.
Mari: And you're not strong enough to climb a mountain!
Lisa: You're right, I can't do it now. But I'll go hiking every weekend. Next summer, I'll be fit enough to climb the mountain.
Mari: Well, I like hiking. I'll go with you sometimes!

B 🔄 Practice the conversation with a partner. Then have new conversations about the activities in the box.

C 🔄 **GOAL CHECK** ✔ **Use *too* and *enough* to talk about abilities**

Write down six things you want to do. Discuss whether you can do these things now. Are you old enough to do them? Are they affordable or too expensive?

> swim across a lake
> travel to _____ (another country)
> take a *karate* class

- Go over the information in the chart about *enough/not enough/too* with adjectives.

B - Have students complete the sentences with *enough/not enough/too* and the specified adjective.
- Have students compare answers with a partner.
- Check answers.

Conversation

A - Have students close their books. Write the question on the board: *What does Lisa need to do before she can climb the mountain?*
- Play the recording. 🔊 25
- Check answers.

B - Play or read the conversation again for the class to repeat.
- Practice the conversation with the class in chorus.
- Have students practice the conversation with a partner and then make new conversations using the activities in the box.
- Have one or two pairs present one of their new conversations to the class.

C 🔄 **GOAL CHECK** ✔

- Have students read the directions. Then have them write a list of at least six things they want to do. Provide vocabulary as necessary.
- Divide the class into pairs and have students discuss the things they want to do and when they can do them. Model with a student. Ask, *What do you want to do?* Then ask appropriate questions, for example, *Are you old enough to ____? Do you have enough money to ____?* etc.
- Call on several students to tell the class about something their partner wants to do and whether he or she is old enough, etc.

Grammar Practice: *Enough, not enough, too* + adjective

Write these phrases on the board:

| *run 10 kilometers* | *play chess* | *get married* |
| *buy a house* | *play with toy cars* | *ride a bicycle* |

Ask students, *Can you run 10 kilometers?* Elicit answers with *enough, not enough, too* + adjective, such as *I'm too old to run 10 kilometers./I'm not strong enough to run 10 kilometers./I'm fit enough to run 10 kilometers.* Have them discuss the phrases with a partner. Call on students to say a sentence for the class. Then challenge pairs to think of a new phrase to ask the class. Write their phrases on the board and have pairs discuss them in a similar way.

Describe a Personal Challenge

Reading

- Introduce the topic of the reading. Ask students, *Where is the Arctic? What do you know about it?*

A
- Have students read the sentences and circle their guesses. Tell them they will find the answers in the article.
- Point out the vocabulary in the Word Focus box.
- Have students read the article to check their guesses. Tell them to use the context to try to guess the meaning of any words they don't know.
- Check answers.
- Go over the article with the class, answering any questions from the students about vocabulary.

B
- Have students answer the questions, and reread the article as necessary.
- Have students compare answers with a partner.
- Check answers.

C
- Divide the class into pairs. Have them close their books and work together to retell the story of the expedition. Have them discuss what amazed them the most.
- Compare answers with the class: What did students find most impressive about the two men's achievement?

D **GOAL 4:** Describe a Personal Challenge

Reading

A What do you know about the Arctic? Circle the answers. Then read the article to check.

1. In the winter in the Arctic, it's dark _____ hours every day.
   a. 12   **b.** 20   **(c.)** 24

2. The North Pole is on _____.
   a. land   **b.** water   **(c.)** ice

3. In the Arctic, you can see _____.
   (a.) polar bears
   b. penguins
   c. polar bears and penguins

B Answer the questions in your notebook. If necessary, look back at the article.

1. What was Boerge and Mike's idea?
   to walk to the North Pole in winter
2. What happened to their food?
   a polar bear grabbed it
3. How did Boerge and Mike travel?
   They skied and swam.
4. How far did they go every day?
   15 miles (24 kilometers)
5. What happened when they were close to the Pole?
   Mike became very ill.
6. When did they get to the Pole?
   March 23

C Tell a partner about the expedition. In your opinion, what was the most amazing thing about the expedition?

> **Word Focus**
>
> **float** = to rest on top of water
>
> **tent** = portable shelter
>
> **grab** = to take suddenly
>
> **waterproof** = does not allow water to get in
>
> **GPS** = global positioning system

62   Unit 5

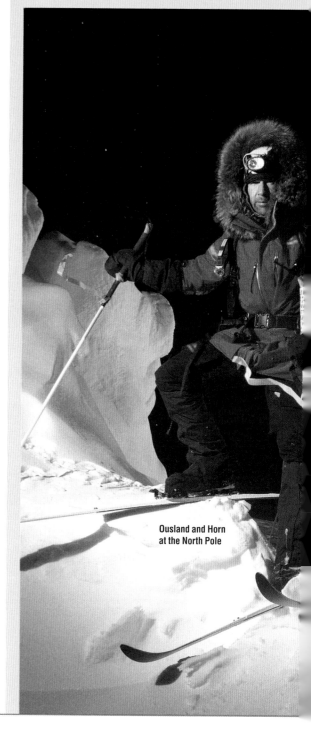

Ousland and Horn at the North Pole

For Your Information: The North Pole

The North Pole is the northernmost point on Earth. It lies in the middle of the Arctic Ocean, on sea ice above salt water that is 4,261 meters (13,980 feet) deep. Because the ice is constantly moving, it's impossible to build permanent scientific stations, such as those at the South Pole.

Surprisingly, it is not known for certain who first discovered the North Pole. The American explorer Frederick Cook claimed he reached it on April 21, 1908, but his only companions were two Inuit men who had no knowledge of science or navigation. Another American, Robert Peary, said he reached the Pole on April 6, 1909, but his navigational calculations were widely disbelieved. Most surprising of all, the first person proved to have actually seen the North Pole, Roald Amundsen, did it from an airship in 1926. He was also the first explorer to reach the *South* Pole, in 1912!

ARCTIC DREAMS AND
NIGHTMARES

Arctic Expedition

In the darkness of the Arctic night, a helicopter landed on the north coast of Russia. Boerge Ousland and Mike Horn were beginning one of the most amazing expeditions in history. It was January 22, and they planned to walk 600 miles (965 kilometers) to the North Pole—in winter.

There is no land at the North Pole, only water and ice that **floats** and moves. It's always a dangerous place, but winter is the worst time of the year. The sun doesn't come up for three months, and the temperature can be –40°F (–40°C). But Boerge grew up in Norway, and he loved skiing and climbing mountains. Mike Horn was a champion athlete from South Africa. They were ready for the challenge.

The two explorers wanted to set out right away, but the ice was moving too fast. They were waiting in their **tent** when Boerge heard a strange noise. "Mike, is that you?" Boerge asked. Suddenly, the tent ripped open. It was a polar bear! While they were looking for their guns, the bear **grabbed** some of their food. They didn't sleep very well that night.

The next day, they set out on skis and pulled their equipment behind them. When they came to open water, they had to swim. They put on **waterproof** suits over their clothes and got into the icy water five or six times a day. When they weren't in the water, they were skiing. It wasn't light enough to see, so they used headlamps.

Every day, they skied and swam north. And while they were sleeping, the ice carried them south. But they kept on for ten hours every day, covering 15 miles (24 kilometers) each day. They were making progress and getting close to the Pole when Mike became very ill. Blood was coming from his nose and ears. They had a cell phone, but Mike didn't want to give up and call for help. He took medicine, and he slowly got stronger. And every day, the sky got a little bit lighter.

On March 23, Boerge checked his **GPS.** The North Pole was 1000 yards (914 meters) away. "I've been there before," Boerge told Mike. "You've never been. You go first." "No," Mike said. "We'll do it together." And together, the two explorers walked to the Pole and took this amazing photo.

Challenges 63

After Reading

Web search: Have students gather information about another polar journey by doing an online search with the terms *Arctic* or *Antarctic* and *expedition.* Have them prepare a short oral report with information about the explorers, where they went, and their achievements.

Project: Have students work in groups to collect information about an aspect of the Arctic, such as weather, animals, marine life, or the effects of climate change on the Arctic, and give a short oral presentation to the class.

Describe a Personal Challenge

Communication

A • Elicit examples of challenges and write them on the board. Ask, *Are there some challenges we don't choose? Challenges that we have to face?* Write examples on the board.

• Divide the class into pairs and have them discuss the questions.

• Compare answers with the class.

Writing

A • Write a short paragraph about a challenging experience in your life (on the board/display on screen/on a handout). Have students identify the topic sentence and then the details that explain the topic.

• Have students read the directions and write their own paragraphs in their notebooks.

B 🔁 **GOAL CHECK** ✔

• Divide the class into pairs and have them share their paragraphs. Tell them to ask each other questions to find out more about the challenging experience.

• Have several students tell the class about their partner's challenging experience.

D | **GOAL 4:** Describe a Personal Challenge

Communication

A 🔁 Discuss the questions with a partner.

1. People face challenges for different reasons, but there is usually some reward when we accomplish our goal. What are three or four challenges in life that cannot be avoided? (For example, it can be a challenge to get along well with all of our family members or neighbors.) What are the rewards if we face those challenges?

2. Tell your partner about two or three challenges in your life that you chose for yourself. Why did you choose to do those things?

Writing

A Write a paragraph about a challenging past experience from your own life in your notebook. Finish the topic sentence below. Then add interesting details. You may want to use time expressions such as "At first," "The next day," "After that."

Topic sentence: When I was _____ years old, I decided to _____

_____

Details: It was a challenge because _____

_____

B 🔁 **GOAL CHECK** ✔ **Describe a personal challenge**

Share your paragraph with a partner. Ask your partner questions about the information in the paragraph.

Teacher Tip: Helping groups finish at the same time

A common situation in group work is that one group completes the task long before the others—or long after. Here are some approaches you can take with a group that finishes too quickly:

• Check to be sure they have understood the task and completed all parts correctly.

• Give them additional questions.

• Have the group prepare a written report of their ideas and answers.

With a group that finishes too slowly:

• Tell them to omit parts of the task.

• Take over briefly as discussion leader to help them move along.

• Set a time limit. Tell them, *I'll ask for your answers in five minutes.*

Snow Leopard running after prey

Before You Watch

A Fill in each blank with a word from the box. Use your dictionary to help you.

> altitudes   camera shy
> hunts   prey   trails

The snow leopard lives at high (1) <u>altitudes</u> in the mountains of Central Asia. There, the leopard (2) <u>hunts</u> its (3) <u>prey</u> : animals such as mountain goats and sheep. Snow leopards are (4) <u>camera shy</u> and few people have photographed them. For photographer Steve Winter, getting good pictures in these cold mountains was a physical and mental challenge. He and his team set up cameras on (5) <u>trails</u> where the leopards walk. Then they watched and waited.

While You Watch

A ▶ Watch the video. Check (✓) the activities in the box you see in the video.

B ▶ Watch the video again. Circle the best meaning for each word in **bold.**

1. Over the course of 10 months, photographer Steve Winter shot more than 30,000 **frames** in pursuit of the elusive snow leopard. (animals | (pictures))

2. As few as 3,500 snow leopards may exist in the wild. They've been **spotted** as high as 18,000 feet, and they're notoriously camera shy. ((seen) | photographed)

3. Snow leopards can **leap** seven times their own body length. (walk | (jump))

✓	driving on mountain roads
☐	cooking in a tent
☐	riding on horses
✓	fixing broken equipment
☐	touching a leopard
✓	setting up cameras

After You Watch / Communication

A Do you think Steve Winter got a lot of pictures of snow leopards? Why do you think Winter and his team decided to do such a difficult project?

Challenges   65

For Your Information: Snow Leopards

The snow leopard can survive in the cold, snowy mountains of Central Asia thanks to thick insulating fur and wide, fur-covered feet that allow them to walk more easily on the snow. They have strong legs for jumping and use their long tails for balance and as blankets to protect themselves from the cold. However, the number of snow leopards left in the wild is diminishing. They are sometimes killed by sheep and goat herders because they prey on their animals. They are hunted illegally for their fur and for their organs, which are used in Chinese medicine. In addition to this, their habitat is vanishing. As a result of these threats on their survival, conservationists are working hard to protect this rare and beautiful animal.

Video Journal:
Searching for the Snow Leopard

Before You Watch

A • Have students look at the picture and describe what they see. Elicit what they know about the snow leopard/leopards.

• Have students complete the paragraph with the words in the box. Provide dictionaries or access to an online dictionary as necessary.

• Have students compare answers with a partner.

• Check answers.

While You Watch

A • Have students read the list of activities. Tell them to check the ones they see as they watch.

• Play the video.

• Have students compare answers with a partner.

• Check answers.

B • Have students read the statements. Direct their attention to the words in bold and their possible meanings, the words in parentheses. Tell them to watch the video again and circle the correct meaning.

• Play the video again.

• Have students compare answers with a partner. Play the video again as necessary.

• Check answers.

After You Watch / Communication

A • Divide the class into groups of three or four and have them discuss the questions.

• Compare answers with the class.

Transitions

About the Photo

This photo shows a Kosovar Bosnia bride in Donje Ljubinje, a remote village on the border of Kosovo and Macedonia. Her face has been painted as part of the wedding ceremony. The tradition of painting brides' faces so intricately goes back thousands of years. According to tradition, the bride's face is painted to prevent bad luck, and the symbols in the design have special meanings. The photo was taken by the photographer Valdrin Xhemaj, who is from Kosovo himself.

- Introduce the theme of the unit. Ask, *What does transition mean?*

- Direct students' attention to the picture. Have students describe what they see.

- Have students discuss the questions with a partner.

- Talk about other kinds of transitions, compiling a list on the board; for example, *starting school, getting a driver's license, voting for the first time, getting divorced.*

- Ask these questions or write them on the board for students to answer in pairs: *Which is the most important transition in a child's life? Why? Which is the most important transition in an adult's life? Why?*

- Go over the Unit Goals with the class.

- For each goal, elicit any words students already know and write them on the board; questions with how (*How did you feel? How did your life change?*) etc.

Kosavar Bosnian bride preparing for traditional wedding in Donje Ljubinje located in the Shar Mountains between Kosovo and Macedonia

66

UNIT 6 GOALS	Grammar	Vocabulary	Listening
• Talk about milestones in your life • Talk about the best age to do something • Use *how* questions to get more information • Describe an important transition in your life	Simple past tense vs. present perfect tense I **lived** alone in 2005. I**'ve lived** alone for five years now. *How* + adjective or adverb **How tall** is he?	Stages of life Adjectives for age: *youthful, childish, mature*	General and focused listening A radio program: Healthy tips from an Okinawan centenarian

UNIT 6 GOALS

1. Talk about milestones in your life

2. Talk about the best age to do something

3. Use *how* questions to get more information

4. Describe an important transition in your life

67

Unit Theme Overview

- The great transitions in a person's life are the same around the world: birth, starting and completing an education, leaving the family home, finding a life partner, having a child, becoming a grandparent, retiring from work. Every culture has its own way of marking these transitions with celebrations and ceremonies.

- An interesting difference between cultures is the age at which people make these transitions. For example, the age at which people get married varies widely, even within regions. In Bangladesh, the average woman gets married at 16; in Burma, the average woman marries for the first time at 26. Men in Sweden marry at the average age of 32.9 years (the highest in the world) while their neighbors in Poland marry at 26.2 years.

- There are differences in the age at which people are legally considered adults, too. In Nepal, young people become adults at 16; in Tajikistan, 17; in New Zealand, 18; in Japan, 20; and in Egypt, 21. And in some countries, the issue is far more complex. In the United States, people can get married and get a driver's license at 16, join the military at 17, and vote at 18, but they must be 21 to legally consume alcohol.

- In this unit, students will reflect on the different ages and stages of life and learn about the transitions that mark them. They will talk about the best ages for different things and practice describing transitions in their own lives and in other cultures.

Speaking	Reading	Writing	Video Journal
Talking about something you did Discussing the best age for life transititons **Pronunciation:** /ə/ sound	**TED Talks:** Living Beyond Limits	Writing a paragraph to describe a life transition	**National Geographic:** Nubian Wedding

Talk About Milestones in Your Life

Vocabulary

A
- Talk about the pictures with the class. About how old is each person?
- Have students write the correct phrase for each photo.
- Check answers.

B
- Tell students to write their ideas about the ages for these transitions. Emphasize that different people will have different answers.

C
- Divide the class into pairs and have them compare their answers and explain their reasons. Point out the example in the speech bubble, and tell students to discuss the changes that take place in each transition.
- Compare answers with the class. Ask about the changes that are important in the transitions.

Grammar

- Review the present perfect tense and simple past tenses. Tell students, for example, *I have already done a lot of things today. I've already taught one class. I taught it at nine o'clock. And I've checked my e-mail. I checked it at ten o'clock. What about you? What have you done so far today? What time did you do it?* Elicit pairs of sentences with the present perfect and simple past tenses.
- Go over the information in the chart.

A GOAL 1: Talk About Milestones in Your Life

an adult	a baby
a senior citizen	
a teenager	a child

Vocabulary

A Complete the photo captions with a phrase from the box.

▲ Infancy
He's ____a baby____.

▲ Adolescence
He's ____a teenager____.

▲ Adulthood
She's ____an adult____.

▲ Old Age
He's ____a senior citizen____.

▲ Childhood
She's ____a child____.

> **A baby can't walk or talk. A child . . .**

B What do you think? At what age do people make these transitions?

1. from infancy to childhood _____
2. from childhood to adolescence _____
3. from adolescence to adulthood _____
4. from adulthood to old age _____

C Compare your answers in exercise **B** with a partner's answers. What changes take place in these transitions?

Grammar: Using the present perfect tense

Present perfect tense	
Use the present perfect to talk about actions which: 1. began in the past and continue until the present. 2. happened at an indefinite past time and which have an impact on the present. 3. happened repeatedly in the past.	1. He **has loved** music since he was a baby. (He still loves music now.) 2. Tim **has traveled** alone before, so he's not nervous about his trip to India. 3. Ken and Takako **have moved** three times.
Use the simple past for completed action or situation at a specific past time.	~~We have bought our house in 2011.~~ We bought our house in 2011.
The signal words *ever, never, already,* and *yet* are often used with the present perfect.	**Has** Justin **graduated** *already*? No, he **hasn't graduated** *yet*.

68 Unit 6

Word Bank:
Activities by age

Infancy: crawl, babble, cry

Childhood: play, go to school

Adolescence: graduate from school, date

Adulthood: get a job, get married, buy a house, have a baby

Old age: retire, enjoy grandchildren

Grammar: Present perfect tense vs. simple past tense

The present perfect tense is used to connect the past with the present.

> I**'ve** already **graduated** from college (so now I have my degree).

The simple past tense describes a completed action at a specific time.

> I **graduated** from college in 2004.

> Use the present perfect with *for* to talk about how long something has been true.
>
> Use the present perfect with *since* to talk about when a situation began.

> Simone **has had** gray hair *for* ten years.
> (That's how long.)
>
> She **has known** her best friend *since* 2004.
> (That's when they met.)

▲ City of Los Angeles, U.S.A

A Complete the sentences. Use the present perfect or simple past.

1. I ____have lived____ (live) in this apartment for five years. Before that,
   I ____lived____ (live) with my parents.

2. Leonard ____graduated____ (graduated) from high school two years
   ago. He ____hasn't graduated____ (not, graduate) from the university yet.

3. Nora ____hasn't been____ (be, not) to South America, but she
   ____traveled____ (travel) in Mexico last year.

4. We ____started____ (start) this course two months ago.
   So far, we ____have finished____ (finish) five units.

B Which of these things have you done? When did you do them? Write sentences with the present perfect or simple past tense in your notebook.

1. vote
2. get married
3. move out of your parents' house
4. find a gray hair on your head

C Compare your answers in exercise **B** with a partner's answers. At what stage of life do people usually do these things? At what age?

Conversation

A 🔊 26 Close your book and listen to the conversation. Where did Jason go? *to Los Angeles*

Rick: Have you ever traveled alone?
Jason: Yes, I have. It was fun!
Rick: Really? Where did you go?
Jason: I went to Los Angeles for a week last summer.
Rick: Did you stay in a hotel?
Jason: No, I visited my cousins. We had a great time.

B Practice the conversation with a partner. Then make a new conversation about your travel experiences.

C **GOAL CHECK** ✓ Talk about milestones in your life

Look at the stages of life on page 68. Write a question about a milestone (very important event) for each stage. Ask a partner your questions.

> **Where were you born?**

> **How long have you known your best friend?**

A
- Have students complete each sentence with the correct form of the verb in parentheses.
- Check answers.

B
- Tell students to write true sentences about themselves. Remind them to use the present perfect tense to talk about things they have done at an undefined time in the past, and the past tense to talk about exactly when they did them.

C
- Divide the class into pairs and have them compare their answers in **B**.
- Then compare answers with the class and discuss the stage of life and most usual age to do each of these things.

Conversation

A
- Have students close their books. Write the question on the board: *Where did Jason go?*
- Play the recording. 🔊 26
- Check answers.

B
- Play or read the conversation again for the class to repeat.
- Practice the conversation with the class in chorus.
- Have students practice the conversation with a partner, then make a new conversation about their own travel experiences.

C **GOAL CHECK** ✓

- Have students look at the life stages on page 68 again. Model the example question and elicit other questions for each stage. Have students write at least one question for each stage.
- Divide the class into pairs and have them ask each other their questions. Encourage them to ask each other follow-up questions to find out more information.
- Have several students tell the class something about one of their partner's life stages.

Grammar Practice: Present perfect tense vs. simple past tense

Ask, *How has your life changed in the last five years?* Have students write five sentences, such as:

I've changed jobs.

I've moved to a different apartment.

Then divide the class into pairs. Have them take turns reading a sentence to their partner.

The partner then gets more information about each sentence by asking and answering questions in the simple past tense with *when, where, why,* and so on. Discuss with the class.

Talk About the Best Age to Do Something

Listening

A • Have students look at the pictures and describe what they see. Divide the class into pairs and have them discuss the questions.
 • Compare answers with the class.

B • Tell students they are going to hear a radio program about a woman in Japan. Have them read the questions.
 • Play the recording one or more times. 🔊 27
 • Have students compare answers with a partner.
 • Check answers.

C • Tell students to listen again and find the information.
 • Play the recording one or more times. 🔊 27
 • Have students compare answers with a partner. Play the recording again as necessary.
 • Check answers.

D • Have students discuss the question in pairs.
 • Compare answers with the class. Ask, *Do you think very old people have a happy life? Why?*

Pronunciation

A • Explain that the symbol is called a *schwa* and give its pronunciation.
 • Play the recording one or more times. 🔊 28

B • Tell students to listen and repeat. After each word, they should circle the syllable (or syllables, note *national* has two unstressed syllables) with the schwa sound.
 • Play the recording one or more times. 🔊 29
 • Have students compare answers with a partner.
 • Check answers.

B **GOAL 2:** Talk About the Best Age to Do Something

▲ Portrait of a 104 year old Okinawan woman

Listening

A 🔄 Discuss these questions with a partner.

 1. Who is the oldest person you know? How old is he or she?

 2. What does this person usually do every day?

B 🔊 27 Listen to a radio program about Ushi Okushima, a woman from Okinawa, Japan. Answer the questions.

 1. Where does Ushi work? <u>a market</u>

 2. Why is Ushi unusual? <u>She's 103.</u>

C 🔊 27 Listen again and find the information needed below.

 1. More than 700 people in Okinawa <u>have celebrated their</u>
 <u>100th birthday</u>.

 2. Three reasons for this: **3.** Ushi's advice:

 a. <u>healthy food</u>   **a.** <u>Work hard.</u>

 b. <u>clean environment</u>   **b.** <u>Drink rice wine before bed.</u>

 c. <u>close relationships</u>   **c.** <u>Get a good night's sleep.</u>

D 🔄 Would you like to live to be 100? Discuss the question with a partner. Explain your reasons.

Pronunciation: The schwa sound /ə/ in unstressed syllables

A 🔊 28 Listen to the words. Notice the vowel sound of the unstressed syllables in blue. This is the schwa sound /ə/, and it's the most common vowel sound in English.

 infant   lettuce   children   population   adult

B 🔊 29 Listen and repeat the words. Circle the unstressed syllables with the /ə/ sound.

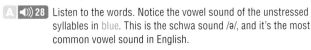

a(lone)   les(son)   per(son)   (ba)nana   par(ents)
pa(per)   chall(enge)   lan(guage)   na(tio)nal   chic(ken)

For Your Information: Centenarians

Around the world, the number of centenarians is growing rapidly. In the United States, there are now more than 50,000! Certain regions are noted for their large number of inhabitants over 100: Okinawa, Sardinia (Italy), and the Nicoya Peninsula (Costa Rica). Researchers have found that the lifestyles of elderly people in these places have a number of things in common:

People have a strong sense of purpose, they drink water containing a lot of calcium and other minerals, they have strong social and family networks, they keep working, they eat a light dinner, and they have strong spiritual beliefs.

Conversation

A 🔊 **30** Close your book and listen to the conversation. How old is Jamal? 19

Andrea:	Did you hear the big news? Jamal is getting his own apartment!
Kim:	Seriously? But he's 19! That's too young to get your own place.
Andrea:	Oh, I don't know about that.
Kim:	Do you think he's old enough?
Andrea:	Well, he's mature, and he's had a part-time job since he was 17.
Kim:	That's true . . . but I think he should wait a few years.
Andrea:	Really? What do you think is the best age to live on your own?
Kim:	I think people should get their own place after they've finished college.
Andrea:	That's a good point. I plan to live with my parents while I'm in college.

Real Language

You can say *Oh, I don't know about that* to disagree politely with someone.

B 🔄 Practice the conversation with a partner. Switch roles and practice it again.

C 🔄 Make a chart with a partner in your notebooks. Use your own ideas. Then make new conversations about Jorge and Melissa using the conversation in exercise **A** as an example.

"Jorge is too old to change jobs."	"Melissa is too young to get her own apartment."
Age: _____	Age: _____
Reasons why it is or isn't OK	Reasons why it is or isn't OK
_____	_____
_____	_____
The best age for this is _____ .	The best age for this is _____ .

D Read the opinions. How old do you think each person is?

1. "He's too old to play soccer."   Age: _____
2. "He's too young to travel alone."   Age: _____
3. "She's too old to dance."   Age: _____
4. "She's too young to drive a car."   Age: _____
5. "She's too old to learn a new language."   Age: _____
6. "He's too old to get married."   Age: _____

E 🔄 **GOAL CHECK** ✔ **Talk about the best age to do something**

Look at your answers for **D**. Compare your answers with a partner and explain your opinions. What is the best age for each of these things? Do you know someone who does these things at an unusual age?

Conversation

A
- Have students close their books. Write the question on the board: *How old is Jamal?*
- Play the recording. 🔊 **30**
- Check answers.
- Direct students' attention to the Real Language box.

B
- Play or read the conversation.
- Practice the conversation with the class in chorus.
- Have students practice the conversation with a partner, then switch roles and practice it again.

C
- Divide the class into pairs and have them read the statements and fill in ideas about the people. Then have them practice new conversations following the model in **A**.
- Call on pairs to present a conversation to the class.

D
- Have work individually to fill in the ages using their own ideas.

E 🔄 **GOAL CHECK** ✔

- Assign new partners and have them compare and discuss their answers from **D** and the two questions.
- Compare answers with the class. For each statement, call on several students to share their answers. Then discuss why someone would be too young or too old for that activity, and what the best age is for each one.

Expansion Activity

Ask students to interview an elderly person in his or her native language and get his or her advice for living a long and healthy life. Have them present the advice to the class. Are there any similarities in what different people said?

Use *How* Questions to Get More Information

Language Expansion

A
- Have students look at the picture and describe the people and their relationships.

- Divide the class into pairs and have them read the adjectives and descriptions in the box. Then have them talk about people who fit the descriptions—people they know personally or famous people.

- Ask several students to tell the class about people who fit the different descriptions.

B
- Have students work with a partner to describe the people in the pictures. Answers may vary.

- Compare answers with the class. Note that students may not be able to judge the people's ages accurately but should be able to apply the adjectives.

- Point out the two collocations with age in the Word Focus box. Ask, *What is the age limit for starting school in our country? When do people come of age in this country?*

Grammar
- Go over the adjectives/adverbs and questions in the chart.

Language Expansion: Adjectives for age

A 🔁 Do you know someone who fits any of these descriptions? Who is it? Share your answers with a partner. Use the adjectives in the box to help you.

youthful	older, but with the energy of a young person (good)
childish	older, but acting like a child (bad)
elderly	looking and acting old
mature	old enough to be responsible and make good decisions
middle-aged	not young or old (about 40–60)
in his/her twenties	between 20 and 29 (also in his *teens, thirties, forties,* etc.)
retired	stopped working full-time (often after 65)

B 🔁 Talk about these people with a partner. How old are they? Describe them with adjectives from the box.

1. *mature*

2. *youthful/middle-aged*

3. *in her teens/childish*

4. *elderly/retired*

5. *middle-aged/mature*

6. *retired/elderly*

Word Focus

age limit = the oldest or youngest age that you can do something

come of age = become an adult

> I think she's in her teens, but she looks very mature.

Grammar: *How* + adjective or adverb

How + adjective or adverb	
Adjectives give information about nouns. Use *How* + adjective to ask a question about a descriptive adjective.	Lenora is very **mature**. **How mature** is she? She's mature enough to babysit my son.
Adverbs give information about verbs. Use *How* + adverb to ask a question about an adverb.	I **learn quickly**. **How quickly** do you learn? I learned to ride a bicycle in one day!

Word Bank: Adjectives and adverbs for questions with *How . . .*

Adjectives: angry, big, boring, difficult, expensive, heavy, interesting, old, small, tall, tired, upset

Adverbs: badly, fast, slowly, well

Grammar: Questions with *how* + adjective or adverb

These questions ask for clarification of the degree of the adverb or adjective. A common example that students have already learned is *How old are you?* Note that with adverbs, this type of question is used with adverbs of manner (*well, badly,* etc.) and time (*late, early*), but not with other types of adverbs.

A 🔄 Unscramble the questions. Take turns with a partner asking the questions.

1. English how do speak well you _How well do you speak English_ ?

2. you how are old _How old are you_ ?

3. can fast you how type _How fast can you type_ ?

4. you how tall are _How tall are you_ ?

5. your family how often move does _How often does your family move_ ?

B Complete the conversations. Write questions using *how*.

1. **A:** I think Mr. Chen is too elderly to live alone.
   B: He doesn't look old to me. _How old is he_ ?

2. **A:** My brother failed his driver's license test six times because he drives so badly.
   B: Wow! _How badly does he drive_ ?

3. **A:** I can't go to the movie with you tonight, because my first class is very early tomorrow.
   B: That's too bad. _How early is it_ ?

4. **A:** I don't want to get my own apartment. It's much too expensive.
   B: Really? _How expensive is it_ ?

5. **A:** I haven't finished reading the assignment for tomorrow. I guess I read too slowly.
   B: That's a problem. _How slowly do you read_ ?

Elizabeth, in her 60s

- started on a trip around the world
- independent

reasons: _____

_____

_____

_____

Conversation

A 🔊 31 Close your book and listen to the conversation. What did Erik get? _his first credit card_

Mrs. Ryan: My son Erik just got his first credit card.
Mrs. Chen: He's still a university student.
Mrs. Ryan: That's true, but he has always been careful with money.
Mrs. Chen: Really? How careful is he?
Mrs. Ryan: He's very careful. In high school he saved enough money to buy a computer.
Mrs. Chen: Then maybe he is ready to get a credit card.

B 🔄 Practice the conversation with a partner. Switch roles and practice again.

C 🔄 Complete the descriptions on the right. Then make new conversations.

D 🔄 **GOAL CHECK** ✔ Use *how* questions to get more information

Take turns with a partner giving a description of yourself or how you do something. Ask questions with *how* to get as much information as possible.

Keisha, 19

- got her own apartment
- mature

reasons: _____

_____

_____

_____

_____

A
- Have students write the questions on the lines.
- Have students compare answers with a partner.
- Check answers.

B
- Have students write the follow-up questions.
- Have students compare answers with a partner.
- Check answers.

Conversation

A
- Have students close their books. Write the question on the board: *What did Erik get?*
- Play the recording. 🔊 31
- Check answers.

B
- Play or read the conversation again for the class to repeat.
- Practice the conversation with the class in chorus.
- Have students practice the conversation with a partner, then switch roles and practice it again.

C
- Divide the class into pairs and have them read the information and fill in ideas about the people. Then have them practice new conversations following the model in **A**.
- Call on pairs to present a conversation to the class.

D 🔄 **GOAL CHECK** ✔

- Have each student prepare a statement about themselves with an adjective or adverb. Give examples: *My parents think I'm lazy. I can cook very well.*
- Then have students take turns telling the statement to their partners, who respond asking questions with *how* to get more information; for example, *How lazy are you? How well can you cook?* etc.
- Have several students share something they found out about their partner with the class.

Grammar Practice: Questions with *how* + adverb

Write the sentence stems on the board. Have students complete each one with adverbs of manner.

Tom is a great language learner.

He works _____.

He listens _____.

He talks _____.

Risa has great parties.

She cooks _____.

She decorates her house _____.

She talks to everyone _____.

Have students ask and answer questions about the statements with *how*. For example:

Tom works carefully. How carefully does he work? He asks his brother to check his homework before he hands it in.

Describe an Important Transition in Your Life

Reading

A
- Have students read the list of activities and check the life transitions.
- Have students share their ideas with a partner, explaining the reasons for their choices.
- Compare answers with the class.

B
- Have students look at the pictures and describe what they see. Point out the definitions of the glossed words.
- Have students read the article and choose the correct options. Remind them to use the context to guess the meaning of new words.
- Have students compare answers with a partner.
- Check answers. Answer any questions students have about vocabulary.

C
- Have students read the statements.
- Have students read the article again and choose *true* or *false*.
- Have students compare answers with a partner.
- Check answers.

D
- Have students read the directions and write down their ideas about how they would react.
- Divide the class into pairs and have them share their ideas.
- Share ideas as a class.
- Ask, *What questions would you want to ask Amy Purdy if you could meet her?* Have pairs discuss and write down their questions.
- Share questions as a class.

D **GOAL 4:** Describe an Important Transition in Your Life

Reading

A 🔁 Check (✓) the items below that show a transition in life. Share your ideas with a partner.

  ✓ **1.** get a new job

  _____ **2.** go shopping

  _____ **3.** buy a car

  ✓ **4.** begin college or university

  _____ **5.** play soccer

  ✓ **6.** get married

B Read the text. Circle the correct option.

1. Amy Purdy is a champion
(cyclist | (snowboarder)).

2. She has prosthetic (arms | (legs)).

3. Purdy ((imagined) | remembered)
her new life.

4. Purdy's (book | (organization)) is
called "Adaptive Action Sports."

C Write *True* or *False* next to the statements.

  T **1.** Amy Purdy nearly died when she was 19.

  F **2.** It wasn't difficult for her to recover from her illness.

  T **3.** During her recovery, Purdy decided to control her life again.

  T **4.** She helps other people by sharing her story with them.

  F **5.** Purdy worked as a model before her illness.

D 🔁 How do you think *you* would react in Purdy's situation? Share your ideas.

74 Unit 6

TED Ideas worth spreading

Amy Purdy Professional Snowboarder

LIVING BEYOND LIMITS

Amy Purdy is a world champion snowboarder who has won two World Cup competitions. She is an actress and model. She is also a double-**amputee.**

When Purdy was 19 years old, she became ill with a rare and serious form of meningitis. It almost killed her, and even though she survived the disease, she lost her kidneys, her spleen, the hearing in her left ear, and both of her legs below her knees. Purdy says that when she finally left the hospital, she felt like she "had been pieced back together like a **patchwork** doll." She received **prosthetic** legs, but they were clumsy and heavy. At first, it was hard for her to imagine how she would learn to walk again, and even harder to imagine that one day she would be able to fly down mountains on her snowboard and travel around the world.

Purdy spent months in bed. She struggled to recover from her illness, but she felt both physically and mentally broken. Finally, she realized that she had to make a change. She says, "I knew that in order to move forward I had to let go of the old Amy and learn to **embrace** the new Amy."

Even though she still faced many struggles, Purdy took charge of her life. "It was this moment that I asked myself that life-defining question: If my life were a book and I were the author, how would I want this story to go? And I began to daydream. I daydreamed like I did as a little girl. And I imagined myself walking gracefully, helping other people through my journey, and snowboarding again," she says.

For Your Information: Amy Purdy

After having both of her legs amputated, Amy Purdy realized that there was no support or resources for action sports for people with prosthetic limbs. Prior to her illness, Purdy had been an accomplished snowboarder and skateboarder, and she wanted to continue to participate in her passions. So she put herself to work developing prosthetic legs that she could use to snowboard successfully. It wasn't an easy return to the sport, but Purdy is now a world champion adaptive snowboarder. But perhaps more importantly, Purdy is sharing what she has learned and achieved since losing her legs. She does this through the foundation she co-founded, Adaptive Action Sports, which provides support to other adaptive athletes who want to be involved in action sports. Purdy firmly believes that the obstacles we face in life should push us to be creative in reaching our goals, and she is certainly an example of this.

" . . . It's not about breaking down borders; it's about pushing off of them and seeing what amazing places they might bring us. "

— Amy Purdy

Amy Purdy's idea worth spreading is that obstacles don't have to stop us—they can help us to get creative. Watch Purdy's full TED Talk on TED.com.

Since then, Purdy has done amazing things. She has acted in music videos and movies, earned a world ranking as a snowboarder, and traveled around the world. In 2005, she founded a **non-profit** organization called "Adaptive Action Sports" to help people with physical disabilities get involved in action sports. And most importantly, she has shared her story of inspiration and imagination, encouraging us all to live beyond our limits.

amputee *a person who has had an arm or a leg removed by surgery*
patchwork *pieces of cloth that are sewn in a pattern*
prosthetic *an artificial device that replaces a missing part of the body*
embrace *to accept readily or gladly*
non-profit *not done for money*

75

After Reading

Either individually or in pairs, have students research Amy Purdy online and what she has achieved. (If appropriate, assign students to research her achievements as an adaptive athlete, model, actor, spokesperson, motivational speaker, etc.). Have them share what they find out with the class.

Encourage students to watch Amy Purdy's TED Talk at TED.com.

TEDTALKS

Communication

A • Have students read the directions and write notes about an important transition in their life, what caused it, and the effect it had on them.

• Divide the class into pairs and have them share their experiences.

• Have volunteers share their experience with the class.

Writing

A • Write on the board, *phrasal verbs,* and elicit the ones students remember from the unit. Write them on the board and have students give examples using them.

• Have students choose the correct phrasal verb to complete each sentence.

• Have students compare answers with a partner.

• Check answers.

B • Write on the board, *simple past* and *present perfect,* and have students provide examples to show how these tenses are used.

• Have students complete the paragraph.

• Have students compare answers with a partner.

• Check answers.

C ⚙ **GOAL CHECK** ✔

• Have students read the directions and write notes for their answer to the question.

• Divide the class into small groups and have them share their ideas from **Communication A** and discuss the questions. Assign each group member a role: leader, secretary, recorder, and reporter. Remind the leader to make sure that the group discusses all the questions.

• Have the reporter from each group share the group's ideas with the class.

D **GOAL 4:** Describe an Important Transition in Your Life

▲ After becoming disabled, Amy Purdy imagined—and now lives—a very full life.

Communication

A ⚡ Think about an important transition that you made in your life. What caused it? What effects did it have? Share your ideas with a partner.

Writing

A Circle the correct phrasal verbs in the sentences.

1. If you want to make a change in your life, you need to (take charge of | get over) it.

2. Transitions can be difficult, but if you (keep on | grow up) trying, you'll succeed.

3. Learning to snowboard was so challenging that Purdy nearly (set out | gave up).

B Write a paragraph in your notebook describing an important transition in your life. Include phrasal verbs in your writing.

When I was _____ years old, _____ _____. This transition was important to me because _____

C ⚙ **GOAL CHECK** ✔ **Describe an important transition in your life**

Share your ideas about transitions. What are some positive/negative reasons for making transitions?

76 Unit 6

Expansion

Have students write a paragraph about the important transition they discussed in **Communication A.** Provide them with the following model (if possible, complete the paragraph yourself and share it with students before they write their own):

When I _____, I decided to/I had to _____. It was an important transition for me because _____ .

I made this change to _____ and _____. Since then, I _____ and _____ .

Remind students to use phrasal verbs and simple past and present perfect tenses. Have students exchange papers with a partner and help each other make corrections to improve their paragraph.

VIDEO JOURNAL: *Nubian Wedding* **E**

Nubian women sing traditional songs as they arrive with gifts at the home of a newly-wedded bride

Nubia, Africa

Before You Watch

A • Talk with a partner about weddings that each of you has seen. Use the topics and the question in the box to help you.

While You Watch

A ▶ Watch the video. Number the parts of the wedding in order.

__3__ Everyone eats a special dinner.

__1__ The bride and groom sign special legal papers.

__5__ The groom puts a ring on the bride's finger.

__2__ The bride's skin is painted.

__4__ The groom leaves his parents' house.

B ▶ Watch the video again. Answer the questions.

1. When did Sheriff meet Abir? *two years ago*

2. How many days does the wedding last? *seven*

3. When does the party start each day? *early in the morning*

4. When did life change for the Nubians? *in the 1960s*

5. What do people eat at the wedding? *meat and rice*

6. Who kisses the groom? *his mother*

After You Watch / Communication

A • What surprised you the most about the Nubian wedding? How is it similar to or different from weddings in your country?

> the bride   the groom
> the party   the ceremony
> How were the two weddings similar or different?

Video Journal: *Nubian Wedding*

Before You Watch

A • Have students look at the picture and describe what they see. Ask, *How many weddings have you attended?* Go over common vocabulary for weddings (bride, groom, rings, etc.).

• Have students work with a partner or in small groups to compare the weddings they have attended. Tell them to describe the bride, the groom, the ceremony, and the party.

• Compare experiences with the class.

While You Watch

A • Point out the location of Nubia on the map and ask students what, if anything, they know about that area.

• Tell students to watch the video. Have the students read the statements.

• Play the video.

• Have students compare answers with a partner.

• Check answers.

B • Tell students to watch the video again and find the information.

• Play the video.

• Have students compare answers with a partner.

• Check answers.

After You Watch / Communication

A • Divide the class into pairs and have them discuss the questions.

• Compare answers with the class. Ask which wedding is more expensive/interesting/enjoyable— a Nubian wedding or one in their country?

Teacher Tip: Using Video

Remind students of strategies they can use to help them:

• Activate prior knowledge about the topic by looking at pictures/maps/graphs and titles before watching.

• Guess the meaning of new words from the context.

• Focus on stressed words as they are key content words.

• Focus on specific details or general idea.

• Before watching, underline key words in the questions they need to answer.

For Your Information: Nubia

Nubia is the region along the Nile River in modern Egypt and Sudan. In the past, it was an independent kingdom. Today, Arab culture predominates the area, but Nubians still have their own language, music, dances, and other traditions.

The Magic Washing Machine

Before You Watch

A • Divide the class into pairs and have them look at the picture and answer the questions.

• Compare answers with the class.

B • Have students read the directions and the words in the box. Then have them complete the paragraph.

• Have students compare answers with a partner.

• Check answers.

C • Have students look at the pictures on page 79 and predict what they will hear about in the TED Talk.

• Compare answers with the class. Write their ideas about what they will hear in the talk on the board.

While You Watch

A • Have students read the directions and the three options for the main idea of the talk. Tell them to listen the first time and focus on understanding the main idea only. Remind them that they don't need to understand everything.

• Play the talk.

• Have students compare their answer with a partner.

• Check answer.

TEDTALKS

Hans Rosling Professor of Global Health, Co-founder Gapminder.org
THE MAGIC WASHING MACHINE

Before You Watch

A 🔄 Look at the picture and answer the questions with a partner.

1. What is this device? Do you have one in your house? *a washing machine*

2. What percent of people have a modern washing machine? *about 30%*

3. How has it changed people's lives? *saves time*

B Here are words you will hear in the TED Talk. Complete the paragraph with the correct words. Not all words will be used.

> **electricity** *n.* flow of energy used as power
> **heat** *v.* to cause (something) to become warm or hot
> **load** *v.* to put (an amount of something) into or onto something
> **mesmerize** *v.* to hold the attention of (someone) entirely
> **time-consuming** *adj.* using or needing a large amount of time
> **tough** *adj.* very difficult to do or deal with

It's amazing how machines can change the world. Not so many years ago, doing laundry was a (1) *time-consuming* job. You needed to (2) _____*heat*_____ the water, add the soap and the clothes, and rub them with your hands for a long, long time. Now, we (3) _____*load*_____ the washing machine, push the button, and the machine does the rest. It's not (4) _____*tough*_____ to get your clothes clean at all. Of course, a washing machine uses (5) _____*electricity*_____ to run, and this is a problem as more people get them.

C Look at the pictures on the next page. Check (✓) the information that you predict you will hear in the TED Talk.

_____ **1.** Doing laundry is usually work for women and girls.

_✓_ **2.** People in rich countries have a lot of different machines in their homes.

_____ **3.** We should drive less and walk or ride bikes more.

While You Watch

A ▶️ Watch the TED Talk. Circle the main idea.

1. Washing machines are very popular around the world.

2. Women like to read more than they like to do laundry.

3. When people don't have to do so much hard work, they have time to do things they enjoy and their lives change in positive ways.

78

For Your Information: Hans Rosling

Dr. Hans Rosling is a global health expert from Sweden. He is a professor of international health at the Karolinska Institutet in Stockholm. Rosling spent many years in rural Africa, where he discovered an epidemic paralytic disease he named *konzo*. Rosling co-founded Medecins Sans Frontiers Sweden. He continues to be interested in the "so-called" developing world and focuses his work on helping people understand global trends, especially by dispelling the myths about the developing world.

He has been described as a "data visionary" because he presents statistics and facts in an accessible and even enjoyable manner. He co-founded a non-profit organization called Gapminder, which aims to combat ignorance about global trends and patterns. Through Gapminder, he developed free software that presents statistics in a more visually dynamic way. Rosling's aim is to raise awareness of the real state of the world by analyzing and presenting, in a digestible form, statistics, patterns, and trends.

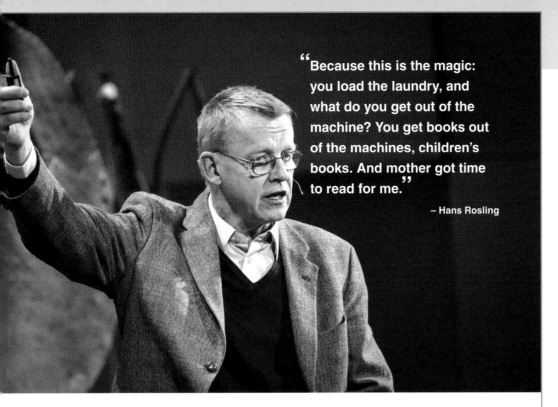

"Because this is the magic: you load the laundry, and what do you get out of the machine? You get books out of the machines, children's books. And mother got time to read for me."

— Hans Rosling

B ▶ The images below relate to the TED Talk. Watch the TED Talk again and write the letter of the caption under the correct photo.

a. Women in Sweden used to wash clothes by hand.

b. People in developed countries use half of the world's energy.

c. Having a washing machine gave Rosling's mother time to read.

2010: **12** ▪

1. _c_

2. _b_

3. _a_

Challenge! What would happen if all families around the world could use a modern washing machine? What would be the benefits and the challenges? What does Rosling think we should do about the challenges? Share your ideas with the class. Give reasons for your opinions.

B • Have students read the captions and look at the images. Tell them to listen again and match the captions to the images.

• Have students compare answers with a partner.

• Check answers.

Challenge

• Write on the board *New Technologies* and draw a chart with the following four columns: *Specific effects of new technologies, Results of everyone having a washing machine, Benefits, Challenges.* Divide the class into groups of three or four. Have them copy the chart (one per group) and discuss the questions. Then have them complete the chart with the group's ideas.

• Have each group share their ideas with the class. Complete the chart on the board, and discuss the questions as a class.

Viewing Tip

Remind students to pay more attention to the words that are stressed, as these are the content words—the words that carry meaning. Similarly, remind them that if they don't understand these content words, they should use the context and what they have already identified as the main idea to help them guess the meaning of these new words.

After You Watch

A • Have students read the summary and complete it with the words from the box. Play the talk again as necessary.

• Have students compare answers with a partner.

• Check answers.

B • Have students match the phrases to the numbers according to what Rosling said. Play parts of the talk again as necessary.

• Have students compare answers with a partner.

• Check answers.

C • Have students read the sentences and circle the ones that paraphrase Rosling's ideas.

• Have them compare answers with a partner.

• Check answers.

Project

• Ask students, *What have been key changes in your country that have led to a better quality of life? More access to education? Less time-consuming work?* Have students read the project description.

TEDTALKS

Hans Rosling Professor of Global Health, Co-founder Gapminder.org
THE MAGIC WASHING MACHINE

After You Watch

A Complete the summary with the words in the box.

| developing education improves researches washing |

Hans Rosling (1) __researches__ how people live around the world. He believes that by reducing hard work, like (2) __washing__ clothes by hand, women and girls in (3) __developing__ countries will have more time to read and study. Why is that important? Because when people have an (4) __education__, their quality of life (5) __improves__.

B Match the phrases to state information from the TED Talk.

_c_	**1.** number of people in the world	**a.** 22%
_d_	**2.** amount the richest people spend daily	**b.** $2
_e_	**3.** current total energy consumption	**c.** 7 billion
_b_	**4.** amount the poorest people spend daily	**d.** $80
_a_	**5.** future total energy consumption	**e.** 12%

C Read the statements below. Circle the ones that paraphrase Hans Rosling's opinions.

①People in rich countries use much of the energy in the world.

2. Most people in the world are not very poor.

③People who use a lot of energy shouldn't tell other people not to.

④Getting a washing machine made a big difference in his family's life.

5. We should not have more technology in the world.

Project

Hans Rosling believes that small transitions in individual lives can make a big difference in the world. As people move out of poverty and do less time-consuming work, they gain time to get an education and find better jobs. Use his ideas to survey your classmates about an important transition for people in your country.

80

In many developing countries, women do the hard work of carrying water.

A Look at the list of devices. Circle the two you think have made the biggest difference in people's lives in the last century.

microwave oven	vacuum cleaner	air conditioner
computer	cell phone	dishwasher

B 🔁 Compare your choices in exercise **A** with a partner. Are there any devices you'd like to add to the list? Think about devices that save on work and give people more time to read and get an education.

C 🔁 Take a survey. Write a question for each item. Ask each question and then ask a follow-up question for details. Use the chart to take notes.

	Question	Name	Details
1. most expensive			
2. most useful at home			
3. helped the most people			
4. caused the biggest problems			
5. caused the most pollution			

> **What's the most important device in the 21st century?**

> **I think it's the cell phone.**

> **Why do you think that?**

Presentation Strategy

Using numbers to support facts

Hans Rosling uses numbers and statistics to surprise the audience and support his argument in interesting and humorous ways.

Challenge! Hans Rosling is interested in the differences between what we *think* we know about the world and the way things really are. He's also very curious about the ways the world is going to change. Go to TED.com and find another TED Talk by Hans Rosling. What has he learned, and what predictions does he make?

81

A • Go over the words in the box.

• Have students circle the two they think have had the most impact on people's lives.

B • Divide the class into pairs and have them compare their choices in **A**. Have them discuss other devices that save time and workload and give people more time for education and reading. Have them add other items to the list.

C • Have the students read the directions and the chart. Point out the model questions and answer. Elicit other questions and possible follow-up questions for the next item in the chart. Have students write their own questions.

• Have students move around the class and survey their classmates. Remind them to write down their answers in the chart.

• Have students report back on their surveys.

Challenge

• Point out the information in the Presentation Strategy box. Ask, *What statistics did Rosling use in the talk? How did he present them?*

• Have students read the Challenge information. In pairs or individually, have students find another of Rosling's TED Talks to see what Rosling has learned about the world and what predictions he makes for the future. Have students prepare a brief presentation for the class on the talk they watched. In large classes, have them present in small groups.

Ideas Worth Sharing

• With books closed, have students share what they remember about Hans Rosling. Ask, *What is his message? What does he want to share with people? Why?*

• Have students read the information in the Ideas Worth Sharing box on page 78. Remind them that they can watch the whole talk and other talks by Rosling at TED.com.

Luxuries

About the Photo

This photo was taken by Dave Yoder, an American photojournalist based in Milan, Italy. Yoder is a National Geographic photographer and explorer. In this photo he shows guests arriving in costume for a sumptuous dinner during Carnival in Venice, Italy. The Venetian carnival tradition is most famous for its beautiful masks; many people attend the Carnival wearing both elaborate costumes, like those in this photo, and the distinctive Venetian masks. Luxury means different things to different people, but elaborate decoration; expensive, beautiful clothing; and dining in a sumptuous setting are considered luxuries by many people.

- Introduce the theme of the unit.
- Direct students' attention to the picture. Have students describe what they see.
- Have students discuss the questions with a partner.
- Compare answers with the class.
- Ask these questions orally or by writing them on the board for students to answer in pairs: *Why do people want luxury items? What other luxury items can you think of?*
- Go over the Unit Goals with the class.
- For each goal, elicit any words students already know and write them on the board; for example, vocabulary related to jobs, money, the luxury items previously discussed, etc.

Baroque dinning room for Carnival party in Venice, Italy

82

UNIT 7 GOALS	Grammar	Vocabulary	Listening
• Explain how we get luxury items • Talk about needs and wants • Discuss what makes people's lives better • Evaluate the effect of advertising	Passive voice (present tense) *Jewelry **is given** as a gift.* Passive voice with *by* *This blouse **was made by** well-paid workers.*	Luxury items Import/Export items Past participles of irregular verbs	Focused listening Discussions: the world flower market

Unit Theme Overview

- A dictionary defines a luxury item as *something expensive which is not necessary but gives you great pleasure*. In this unit, students will consider all three parts of this definition. Why are luxuries expensive? They will learn how several luxury items are produced and how the difficulty of the process (such as the raising of exotic flowers) leads to a high price. What is really necessary, and what is a luxury? Students will investigate these questions in their own lives.

- Why do luxuries give us pleasure? The answers to this question are based in emotion and culture. It's interesting to note that an item that is a treasured luxury in one culture may be totally unappreciated in another. For example, in the Arabian Peninsula, fine incense is highly valued, and people will pay thousands of dollars for the rarest varieties. A few hundred miles away, in the Indian subcontinent, incense is a cheap and common product used even by the poorest of people in their religious devotions.

- Closer to home, we all know that the same pair of sunglasses or blue jeans will have a much higher price if stamped with the name of a famous designer. Nearly all students will have strong opinions, one way or the other, about this type of luxury item. Brand names and the aura surrounding them are part of the mythology of our age.

UNIT 7 GOALS

1. Explain how we get luxury items

2. Talk about needs and wants

3. Discuss what makes people's lives better

4. Evaluate the effect of advertising

Speaking	Reading	Writing	Video Journal
Discussing luxuries and necessities Talking about improving your life **Pronunciation:** Sentence stress: content vs. function words	**National Geographic:** Perfume: The Essence of Illusion	Writing a print ad	**National Geographic:** Coober Pedy Opals

Explain How We Get Luxury Items

Vocabulary

A
- Have students look at the pictures and describe what they see.
- Have students categorize the words and phrases in the box.
- Check answers.

B
- Introduce the idea of imports and exports. Have students work with a partner to list products their country imports and exports. Prompt them if necessary: *Do factories in our country make all of our cars? Which other countries make cars for us? Do we eat all of the (rice/beef/grapes) in our country? What happens to the portion that we don't use here?*
- Call on student pairs to read their lists to the class. Compile two lists on the board.

Grammar

- Point out the lists on the board. Ask, for example, *Where do we get cars? Cars are imported from (Japan). Where do we get computers? Computers are imported from (China).* Elicit more answers from the class.
- Present the information in the chart about the active and passive voices. Explain further that the passive voice is not a verb tense—it is used together with different verb tenses. Tell students, *You can say cars are imported from Germany. You can say cars were imported from Germany last year.* Tell them that in this unit they will practice using the passive voice with the present tense. Elicit more examples of things that are *given/imported/worn.*

A GOAL 1: Explain How We Get Luxury Items

Vocabulary

▲ handmade jewelry
pearl necklace

▲ precious metals
silver, gold

▲ luxury clothing
expensive watch, silk shirt, fur coat

▲ precious stones
diamonds, emeralds

| pearl necklace   silver |
| diamonds   fur coat |
| emeralds   silk shirt |
| gold   expensive watch |

A Write each word or phrase from the box in the correct category above.

B Write three things your country imports and three things your country exports in your notebook. Share your lists with the class.

My country imports (buys from other countries)	My country exports (sells to other countries)

Grammar: Passive voice (present tense)

Notice

*Sometimes we use a *by* phrase with the passive voice.

Active voice	Passive voice
Subject + transitive verb + direct object	Direct object + *be* + past participle of transitive verb
Some people give jewelry as a gift. My country imports cars from Germany.	Jewelry **is given** as a gift (by some people). Cars are imported from Germany (by my country).
*Transitive verbs have direct objects. *Use the passive voice with transitive verbs when the focus is on the object.	*The object goes before the verb in the passive voice. *The passive voice is formed with the verb *be* plus the past participle of the main verb.

Word Bank: Luxuries

drinks: cognac, rare wines

jewelry: bracelet, cuff links, earrings, necklace, pin, ring, tie pin

precious metals: gold, platinum, silver

precious stones: diamond, emerald, ruby, sapphire

Grammar: The passive voice

The passive voice is not a tense, but a sentence construction that emphasizes the receiver of an action. As such, the passive voice can be used in any tense. The subject of a passive-voice sentence is the object that is receiving an action. The passive voice is used especially for sentences in which the agent of an action is not important or is unknown.

A Complete the sentences in the paragraph with the passive form of the verbs in parentheses.

Luxury items are expensive for a reason. Expensive watches, for example, __are made__ (make) from precious metals such as silver or platinum. Beautiful jewelry __is produced__ (produce) by people, not by machines. Precious stones such as diamonds and opals __are separated__ (separate) from tons of rock, and that requires expensive machinery. Imported luxury items __are brought__ (bring) in from distant countries, so the cost of transportation adds to their expense. Finally, a luxury item such as perfume __is made__ (make) from special ingredients that can only be found in a few places in the world.

Word Focus

mined = removed from under the Earth's surface

B Match the luxury items to the actions.

1. Pearls __d__
2. Animal skins __e__
3. Silk __b__
4. Diamonds __a__
5. Perfume __c__

a. are mined in several countries.
b. is exported from East Asian countries.
c. is sold in bottles.
d. are found inside oysters.
e. are used to make fur coats.

C Take turns. Tell a partner about a luxury item you have or want to have. Where do you get it? How do you get it? How is it made?

Conversation

A **2** Close your book and listen to the conversation. Who made Ellen's blouse? *women in a co-op*

Sandra: That's a beautiful blouse! Is it silk?
Ellen: No, it's cotton, but it is soft like silk.
Sandra: I heard that the best cotton is grown in Egypt.
Ellen: Really? A lot of cotton is grown in India, too, but I don't know which kind is better.
Sandra: Where was your blouse made?
Ellen: In Sri Lanka. It was made by women in a co-op. They work together to make clothes. Then they are sold directly to the stores, and the women keep the profit.
Sandra: That's great!

B Practice the conversation with a partner. Switch roles and practice it again.

C **GOAL CHECK** ✓ **Explain how we get luxury items**

What luxury items are popular in your country? If the items are imported, where are they made? What are they made from? Who makes them? Tell a partner.

Luxuries **85**

A • Have students look at the picture and describe what they see. Ask, *What is made from cotton?*
 • Have students work individually to fill in the passive form of each verb.
 • Have students compare answers with a partner.
 • Check answers.

B • Have students form passive sentences by matching the columns. Point out the information in the Word Focus box, and ask for examples of things that are mined (*gold, diamonds, coal*).
 • Check answers.

C • Divide the class into pairs and have them take turns telling about a luxury item.

Conversation

A • Have students close their books. Write the question on the board: *Who made Ellen's blouse?*
 • Play the recording. **2**
 • Check answers.
 • Explain further that a co-op (cooperative) is a business that is owned by the workers.

B • Play or read the conversation again for the class to repeat.
 • Practice the conversation with the class in chorus.
 • Have students practice the conversation with a partner, then switch roles and practice it again.

C **GOAL CHECK** ✓

 • Elicit luxury items that are popular in the students' country. Write a list on the board.
 • Divide the class into pairs. Have them discuss the luxury items using the questions provided. Encourage them to give as much information as possible about each item.
 • Have several pairs describe to the class one of the items they discussed.

Grammar Practice: Passive voice

Divide the class into pairs. Have them write as many sentences as they can in five minutes about things that are done at their school and the person who does them.

Math is taught by Mr. Kwan.

Computers are fixed by Mrs. Rios.

Call on students to read a sentence to the class, omitting the agent. Call on another student to repeat the sentence, adding the agent.

Talk About Needs and Wants

- Have students look at the pictures. Ask, *Has anyone ever given you flowers for a present? What was the occasion? When do people give flowers?*

A
- Tell students they are going to hear a radio program about cut flowers in three countries. Have them read the descriptions and the three items.
- Play the recording one or more times. 🔊 3
- Have students compare answers with a partner.
- Check answers.

B
- Tell students to listen again to the three speakers and write the reasons why flowers are important to each person. Tell them to give a short answer in their own words.
- Play the recording one or more times. 🔊 3
- Have students compare answers with a partner.
- Check answers.
- Ask, *Do you ever buy flowers? Why or why not? Do you like to have flowers in your house?*

Pronunciation

- Introduce the idea of content words (meaning words) and function words (grammar words). If necessary, review the names of the parts of speech, and elicit more examples for each.
- Go over the information in the chart.
- Explain that content words are stressed (sound stronger) in a sentence.

B GOAL 2: Talk About Needs and Wants

▲ Bouquets of roses for sale at a flower market

▲ a greenhouse

Listening

A 🔊 **3** Listen to three people talk about the cut-flower industry. Why is each country important to the flower industry?

1. Japan ___b___
2. Ecuador ___a___
3. The Netherlands ___c___

a. has a good climate for growing flowers.
b. imports many flowers.
c. develops new kinds of flowers.

B 🔊 **3** Listen again. Why is the flower industry important to each person?

1. Shinobu: *She celebrates the seasons with flowers in her house.*
2. Rafael: *He works in a greenhouse.*
3. Peter: *He developed a rose.*

Pronunciation: Content vs. function words

In sentences, content words have specific meaning and receive greater stress. Other words have a grammatical function and receive less stress.

Content words				
nouns	**main verbs**	**question words**	**adjectives**	**adverbs**
money	speak	why, where, how	wonderful	easily
Function words				
pronouns	**auxiliary verbs**	**the verb *be***	**articles**	**prepositions**
it, she, him	have, is, will, could	is, are, was	the, a/n	in, to, of, at

More function words
conjunctions
and, or, but, so

86   Unit 7

For Your Information: The cut-flower industry

Many cut flowers that are sold for holidays come from great distances. For example, in England, one-fourth of the flowers sold on Valentine's Day are grown in Kenya, and many of the others come from Tanzania, Ethiopia, or Uganda. In North America, a large percentage of cut flowers are grown in Colombia. Many people are concerned about the growth of this industry, because workers are exposed to large quantities of toxic chemicals every day. They also object to growing luxury flowers on farmland that could grow food for hungry people.

A 🔊 **4** Listen to the stress in each sentence. Then listen again and repeat.

1. She wants to go to a private college.
2. We have to pay the electric bill.
3. The bill can be paid online.
4. My family needs the money I make.
5. I'm saving money for a new computer.
6. He wants a Lexus, but he should buy a Toyota.

B 🔄 Underline the content words. Then practice saying the sentences with a partner.

1. Flowers are an important part of life.
2. Delicious grapes can be grown in California.
3. I like diamonds and rubies, but they're very expensive.
4. My future could be very bright.
5. Celia wants to buy a new car.
6. Do you think she should get a small car?

Communication

A Write each item in the appropriate column. Use your own opinion.

> a computer   a car   furniture   shoes   clean water   fresh fruit
> books   flowers   money   a telephone   public parks   the Internet

Luxuries	Necessities

Word Focus

Necessities are things we need, such as food and shelter.

Luxuries are things we don't really need, but they can be nice to have.

B 🔄 Compare your chart from exercise **A** with a partner's chart. Talk about why you think people need (or don't need) the items.

C 🔄 **GOAL CHECK** ✔ **Talk about needs and wants**

What is something you absolutely need? What luxury item do you want very much? Discuss these questions with a partner.

Luxuries   **87**

Discuss What Makes People's Lives Better

Language Expansion

- Have students look at the picture and describe what they see. Ask, *What are these rugs made of? Where are they made?* Write answers on the board to remind students of the passive voice.

- Remind students that irregular verbs don't follow a pattern—they must be memorized one by one. Point out that irregular verbs have irregular past participles (used in forming the passive voice).

- Present the past participles in the box.

A
- Tell students to complete the sentences with past participles. If necessary, explain that *seafood* refers to animals from the ocean that we eat.

- Have students compare answers with a partner.

- Check answers.

Grammar

- Go over the information in the chart about the use of the passive with *by*. Explain that we put the *by* phrase in the sentence only if the information is important.

A
- Tell students to read the sentences and cross out the *by* phrases that aren't needed.

- Have students compare answers with a partner.

- Check answers.

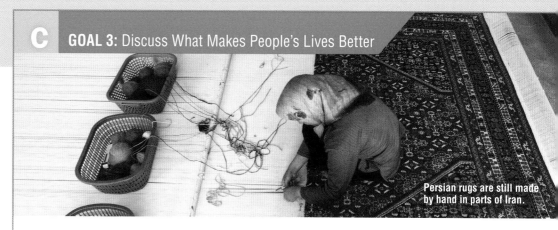

C GOAL 3: Discuss What Makes People's Lives Better

Persian rugs are still made by hand in parts of Iran.

lose – lost   find – found
send – sent   give – given
put – put   freeze – frozen
build – built
know – known

Language Expansion

A Fill in the blanks with the words in the box. Use your dictionary to help you.

1. Many kinds of precious stones can be ___found___ in Brazil.
2. Fresh seafood can be ___flown___ by plane to anywhere in the world.
3. The seafood is ___frozen___ so that it stays cold until it arrives.
4. Iran is ___known___ for its beautiful handmade rugs.
5. Smartphones are ___lost___ every day when they fall out of a pocket or purse.
6. Gifts are often ___given___ to people on their birthday.
7. Ferrari cars are ___built___ by hand, so it takes longer to make them.
8. The watches are ___put___ into special boxes to protect them.

Grammar: Passive voice with *by*

The passive voice is usually used without a *by* phrase.	Cut flowers **are sold** early in the morning. Most of these cut flowers **are imported**.
A *by* phrase is used when we want to say who or what does something (*the agent*).	These blouses **are made** by well-paid workers. Each rug **is made** by a different artist, so no two rugs are alike.

A Read the sentences and cross out the unimportant *by* phrases.

1. The Mercedes-Benz is made in Germany ~~by people~~.
2. This necklace was given to me by my grandmother.
3. King Tut's tomb was discovered by Howard Carter.
4. My car was stolen on April 19 ~~by someone~~.
5. The company was founded by the owner's grandfather.
6. Even during the winter, daisies can be grown in greenhouses ~~by workers~~.

88   Unit 7

Word Bank:
Irregular past participles

begin/begun	make/made
bring/brought	pay/paid
catch/caught	see/seen
do/done	send/sent
drive/driven	sing/sung
grow/grown	take/taken

Grammar: Passive voice with *by*

The *by* phrase (agent) is included in a passive sentence when the agent is important or surprising information.

Hamlet was written by William Shakespeare.

That painting was made by a monkey.

The *by* phrase is omitted where it is not important or when the speaker is trying to avoid naming the person.

Cars are made in Japan ~~by workers~~.

B Re-write each sentence as a question in the passive voice.

1. Children need to be taught good manners.

Why _do children need to be taught good manners?_

2. Money should be kept in a bank.

Why _should money be kept in a bank_ ?

3. Good jobs are often given to people with a good education.

Why _are good jobs often given to people with a good education_ ?

4. Hard work is valued as much as education by some employers.

Why _is hard work valued as much as education by some employers_?

C 🔄 Ask a partner the questions from exercise **B**. Give your own opinions.

Conversation

A 🔊 5 Close your book and listen to the conversation. According to Gary, why is education valuable?
Your life can be improved by education.

Lance: Gary, do you think people's lives are improved by money?

Gary: It depends. Some people don't have enough money to buy necessities. Their lives are definitely improved by having more money.

Lance: What about other people?

Gary: Well, when you have enough money for the basics, I think your life can be improved by education.

Lance: Interesting! Is your education improving your life?

Gary: Sure. I enjoy learning about new things, and I hope to get a good job someday because of my education.

Lance: I see what you mean. For me, though, my life would be improved by having a nice car.

Gary: OK, but nice cars cost money. Maybe you should think about getting a job first.

▲ College campus in the spring

B 🔄 Practice the conversation with a partner. Switch roles and practice it again.

C 🔄 **GOAL CHECK** ✔ **Discuss what makes people's lives better**

Do these things improve people's lives? Have a new conversation about each one and add your own idea.

a big house   fame   nice clothes
electronics   good health _____

Real Language

We use _It depends_ to say that something is not always true. Then we often explain our reasons.

Luxuries **89**

B • Have students change the sentences to questions using the passive voice.
• Check answers.

C • Have students ask a partner the questions.
• Compare opinions with the class.

Conversation

A • Have students close their books. Write the question on the board: _According to Gary, why is education valuable?_
• Play the recording.
• Check answers.
• Go over the information in the Real Language box.

B • Play or read the conversation again for the class to repeat.
• Practice the conversation with the class in chorus.
• Have students practice the conversation with a partner, then switch roles and practice it again.

C 🔄 **GOAL CHECK** ✔

• Divide the class into pairs. Have students talk about other things that make life better, giving their reasons. Have them add another item to the box.
• Compare ideas with the class. Ask, _Does a big house improve people's lives? How does it improve people's lives?_

Grammar Practice: Passive voice quiz

Have students work with a partner. Tell them to think about different occupations and how people do the jobs. Then have them form questions and answers about them using this model:

Who makes bread? (Bread is made by a baker.)

They should write eight questions and answers, asking you for help as needed. When students are finished, combine them to form groups of four. Have the pairs take turns quizzing each other, giving one point for each correct answer. Call on pairs to ask the class their most difficult or interesting questions. Then find out which pair answered the most questions correctly.

Evaluate the Effect of Advertising

- Have students look at the pictures and describe what they see. Introduce the topic of the reading. Ask, *What is perfume made from?*

Reading

A
- Have students answer the questions with a partner. If your students are young, ask if they have ever bought perfume as a gift for someone.
- Compare answers with the class.

B
- Have students read the questions. Remind them to underline key words (the content words) that help them understand the question, so they know what to focus on when they read.
- Point out the definitions in the footnotes.
- Have students read the article. Remind them to use the context and pictures to help them with any new words.
- Have students answer the questions and then compare answers with a partner.
- Check answers.
- Go over the article and answer any vocabulary questions.

C
- Have students work in pairs to list other products people buy to "feel better." If necessary, give examples: makeup, designer jeans, and so on.
- With the class, discuss which (if any) of these products actually do make people feel better about themselves.

D | **GOAL 4:** Evaluate the Effect of Advertising

Reading

A 🔁 Discuss these questions with a partner.

1. Have you ever bought perfume? What brand did you buy?
2. Why do people wear perfume?
3. What do ads for perfume usually show?

B Write answers to the questions.

1. What are the two main ingredients in perfume? <u>aromatic oils and alcohol</u>
2. Why do perfume makers use fixatives? <u>to make a fragrance last a long time</u>
3. Which French city is famous for its flower farms? <u>Grasse</u>
4. What are the four advantages of synthetics? <u>costs less than natural ingredients; for scents that cannot be obtained naturally; for flowers that are too rare to be picked; saves wild animals from being used for their musk</u>
5. What percentage of new perfumes succeed? <u>10 percent</u>

C ⚙ Make a list of other products designed to make people feel better about themselves. Share your list with the class and talk about whether the products really do what they're supposed to do.

▲ "For me, perfume is an indulgence," says Angie Battaglia, an Austin, Texas, businesswoman who owns 30 scents.

90   Unit 7

Grasse, France

PERFUME: THE ESSENCE OF ILLUSION

"Perfume," says Sophia Grojsman of International Flavors & Fragrances, "is a promise in a bottle." We want to believe. We want to be prettier, richer, and happier than we are. Consider the names of the **fragrances** we buy: Joy, Dolce Vita, Pleasures, White Diamonds, Beautiful. "We sell hope," said Charles Revson, founder of the Revlon cosmetics company.

In terms of chemistry, fragrances are a mixture of **aromatic oils** and alcohol. The "fixatives," or oils, that make a fragrance last a long time, traditionally came from animals. Those have mostly been replaced by **synthetic** chemicals. The other ingredients come from plants, especially flowers.

For Your Information: Perfume

The word *perfume* comes from the Latin "per fumum" meaning *through smoke*. The first perfumes were made in ancient Mesopotamia (Iraq) and Egypt. Knowledge of how to make perfume was brought to Europe by the Muslims, and the first European perfume was made in Hungary. In Europe, the original purpose of perfume was to cover the odors of unwashed bodies. By the 18th century, Grasse and Paris had become the world centers for perfume. Today, the job of inventing new perfumes is done by a person called a *nez*—the French word for "nose."

The area around Grasse, France, is famous for growing flowers. Farmers like Joseph Mul have been producing flowers—including roses, jasmine, and lavender—for centuries. Mul's "rose absolute," the fragrant **liquid** he gets from his roses, sells for $3,650 a pound. "Picking roses will never be done by machine," explains Mul. The roses are carefully collected by hand during the early morning. By ten o' clock, the heat of the sun begins to affect the flowers, and the workers are done for the day. "Labor is 60 percent of the cost," says Mul.

The high cost of natural ingredients is just one of the reasons that perfumers today also use artificial ingredients in their fragrances. In addition, synthetics allow perfumers to use scents that cannot be gotten naturally; for example, the scent from the lilac flower. They allow the use of scents from **rare** or endangered flowers, and they save wild animals from being used for their musk—a kind of fixative. According to perfumer Harry Fremont, "Good fragrance is a balance between naturals and synthetics."

Once perfumers have created a lovely fragrance, it's time for the marketing department to work its magic. The industry spends hundreds of millions of dollars each year to convince people to buy something they don't really need. The success rate for new perfumes is low—only about one in ten is successful, so spending money on advertising is a big risk. It's also the only way to let the world know about a fragrance so enchanting that it can make us believe our dreams will come true.

fragrance *perfume* **aromatic oils** *pleasant smelling oil*
synthetic *artificial, man-made* **liquid** *a fluid* **rare** *unusual, unique*

**Flower plantation
in Grasse, France**

Luxuries **91**

After Reading

Web search: Have students do an online search with the term *history of perfume* and find three facts about perfume to report to the class.

Project: Have students bring in a product ad in their native language for a luxury item and work with a partner to translate it into English, using a dictionary as needed. Ask them to write a paragraph in English about the ad: Who is it for? How does it try to convince people? Is it a successful ad?

Evaluate the Effect of Advertising

Writing

A
- Have students read the text and identify the parts of a print ad.
- Check answers.
- Ask, *Why are print ads still important? What are their advantages? Who should print ads appeal to?*

B
- Divide the class into pairs and tell them they are going to market a new perfume. Go over the directions and the questions.
- Have students discuss the questions and then create their ads on a piece of paper.

C
- Have pairs design and write the print ad for the new perfume. Provide paper, pens, etc., as possible.
- Have students display their ads around the classroom. Have a gallery walk: one of the students from each pair stays by the ad and explains the reasons behind the design of their ad while the other walks around to find out about the other ads. Then they switch roles. Encourage students to ask questions about each ad to the student who is presenting it.
- As a class, discuss which ad they think would be most effective and why.

D | **GOAL CHECK** ✔

- Divide the class into pairs and have them discuss the questions.
- Call on student pairs to present to the class their findings on the luxury item they chose.

D | **GOAL 4:** Evaluate the Effect of Advertising

Writing

A Read the information. What are the basic parts of a print advertisement?
a photograph or image, a message, and a design

Even in the digital age, many newspapers and magazine are printed on paper. That means "print ads" are still important to companies with a product to sell. Print ads may be expensive, but they allow companies to choose their audience. In addition, the audience can spend as long as they want looking at the ad.

Print ads normally have three things in common: a photograph or other image, a message, and a design—including colors and fonts. A successful print ad does not need to appeal to everyone—only to people who might buy the product.

B You are in charge of marketing a new perfume. Discuss the questions.

1. Who is your target audience? (men or women, young or old, etc.)
2. What kind of photograph might appeal to that audience?
3. What is your message? (What do you want the audience to think or do?)
4. What are some key words to include in your message?

C Write a print ad for your perfume.

D | **GOAL CHECK** ✔ Evaluate the effect of advertising

Choose a luxury item and talk with a partner about the way it is marketed. What forms of advertising are used? How do the advertisers "convince people to buy something they don't really need"?

92 Unit 7

Teacher Tip: Checking answers

There are many ways to check students' answers to activities.

1. Teacher reads the answers aloud, students check their work—the fastest way, but with the least student involvement.

2. Teacher calls on students to give their answers—also fast, but may make students feel anxious.

3. Students correct each other's work—gives students more responsibility, but they may not correct all mistakes.

4. Volunteers each write the answer to one question on the board—gives the class an opportunity to work with common errors, but takes up a lot of class time.

VIDEO JOURNAL: *Coober Pedy Opals* **E**

Opals mined in Australia

Southern Australia, Australia

Before You Watch

A Match each word in blue with its definition in the box.

1. The ground under Coober Pedy contains opals. ___c___

2. Digging is one thing you can do in the ground. ___e___

3. The Australian outback is very dry and hot. ___a___

4. Very beautiful opals can be worth a fortune. ___b___

5. Miners hope for a big payoff for their hard work. ___d___

a. area that is far away from cities

b. a large sum of money

c. earth, soil

d. the benefit you get from an action

e. to make a hole by taking away earth

While You Watch

A ▶ Watch the video. Circle each word in the box when you hear it.

digging   fortune

outback   payoff   ground

B ▶ Watch the video again. Circle **T** for *true* or **F** for *false*.

1. About three thousand people live in Coober Pedy. (T) F

2. Over eighty percent of all opals come from Australia. T (F)

3. Ninety-five percent of all opals are colorless. (T) F

4. The hope of a huge payoff motivates people to dig for opals. (T) F

5. Most people in Coober Pedy make a fortune eventually. T (F)

Word Focus

miners = people who dig for stones or other minerals

After You Watch / Communication

A ⚡ Some of the tunnels in Coober Pedy are converted into homes. What might be the advantages and disadvantages of these underground homes? Tell a partner.

B 👥 Create a newspaper or Internet job listing for opal miners. Describe the work and the potential rewards. Try to attract new people to Coober Pedy!

Luxuries   93

Video Journal: *Coober Pedy Opals*

Before You Watch

- Have students look at the picture and describe what they see. Point out the map and elicit what they know about Australia. Introduce the topic of opals. Ask what students know about them. Do they, or anyone they know, have opal jewelry?

A • Have students read the sentences and write the correct word for each definition.

- Check answers.

While You Watch

A • Tell students to watch the video the first time and circle the words in **A** that they hear. Point out the definition in the Word Focus box.

- Play the video.

- Tell students they should have all of the words circled.

B • Tell students to watch the video again and choose *true* or *false*. Then have them read the statements.

- Play the video.

- Check answers.

After You Watch / Communication

A • Divide the class into pairs. Have them talk about the underground homes.

- With the class, compile a list of advantages and disadvantages of the homes.

B • Divide the class into groups of three or four. Have them write a job ad to bring miners to Coober Pedy. Remind them that the ad should describe the good things about the job—not the bad! Provide an example of a job ad as a model for students.

- Have groups exchange ads and compare similarities and differences between the ads.

For Your Information: Opals

Opals are beautiful, precious stones that contain a percentage of water trapped inside them. Opals can be white, gray, red, orange, yellow, green, blue, magenta, rose, pink, slate, olive, brown, or black. White and green are the most common opals, and the combination of red and black are the rarest and most expensive. About 97 percent of the opals in the world are mined in Australia. In medieval Europe, opals were considered very lucky. People believed they had the magic powers of all other precious stones combined, because they have all of their colors combined. Today, some people consider opals unlucky to wear, unless they are given to you as a gift—or unless you were born in October, for which it is the traditional birthstone.

Nature

About the Photo

Eiko Jones is a photographer who specializes in dramatic underwater photography. In this photograph, taken at the edge of a marsh, a school of tadpoles suddenly came upon the photographer and provided an opportunity for a striking photo. The tadpoles were swimming through the stalks of lilies growing on a fallen tree log, probably searching for food.

Frogs are born as tadpoles, also known as pollywogs. They live underwater while they undergo a metamorphosis for several weeks to become a frog. The tadpoles breathe through gills like a fish and have long, flat tails to help them swim. They swim in groups called "schools" and feed on algae growing on plants and rocks.

- Introduce the theme of the unit. Ask, *Where can I go near here to spend time in nature? What can I see there?*

- Have students look at the picture and say what they know about tadpoles. Write their ideas on the board.

- Have students discuss the questions with a partner.

- Compare answers with the class.

- Go over the Unit Goals with the class.

- For each goal, elicit any words or ideas students already have and write them on the board.

Tadpoles swimming in the lily stalks

94

UNIT 8 GOALS	Grammar	Vocabulary	Listening
• Use conditionals to talk about real situations • Talk about possible future situations • Describe what animals do • Discuss a problem in nature	Real conditionals in the future If I **have** time tomorrow, I'**ll call** you. Quantifiers (review) Raccoons eat **many** different kinds of food.	Nouns and adjectives to describe animals Adverbs of manner	Listening for general understanding and for specific information A radio program: The bluefin tuna

Unit Theme Overview

- In every country of the world, the needs of the human population are affecting the natural world. In developed countries, the growth of suburban areas around prosperous cities, and the roads needed to connect them, are taking away countless hectares/acres of land every year. In poorer countries, the urgent need to produce more food leads people to build farms in areas that were once wilderness.

- The conflict between human needs and wants and the survival of natural systems is in the news every day. Global warming—the result of human activity—is melting the ice in the Arctic and making it impossible for polar bears to hunt and survive. Overfishing is destroying the populations of many marine creatures and threatening the survival of people in poorer countries who depend heavily on fish for protein in their diets. These and other similar stories will likely be familiar to your students.

- In this unit, students will practice talking about the future results of present activities. They will then examine and discuss one particular problem facing us: the impact of increased fishing. They will learn to describe what particular animals do and will practice expressing their opinions about another human/animal conflict. Throughout this unit, they will be reminded again and again that a single action can have many different results in the future.

UNIT 8 GOALS

1. Use conditionals to talk about real situations

2. Talk about possible future situations

3. Describe what animals do

4. Discuss a problem in nature

95

Speaking	Reading	Writing	Video Journal
Role-playing to promote environmental action to make oceans sustainable **Pronunciation:** Phrases in sentences	**TED Talks:** How Poachers Became Caretakers	Writing a paragraph to give an opinion	**National Geographic:** Happy Elephants

Use Conditionals to Talk About Real Situations

Vocabulary

- Ask students if they have ever been to a zoo. What did they see and do there? How often do they read the informational signs: Sometimes? Always? Never?

- Ask students what they know about polar bears. Where do they live? What do they eat? Write their ideas on the board.

A • Have students read the text about polar bears. Answer any questions they have about vocabulary.

B • Ask students to match the words from the text to their definitions.

- Have students compare answers with a partner.

- Check answers.

Grammar

A • Have students read and think about the sentence and answer the questions.

- Check answers.

- Go over the information in the chart.

- Elicit more examples from the class. Ask, *If you have time tomorrow, what will you do?*

- Write some of the students' sentences on the board.

POLAR BEAR (*Ursus maritimus*) The polar bear is one of eight different __5__ species of bears. Its __4__ habitat is the ice and water near the Arctic Circle. These bears are __3__ predators that eat other animals. Their usual __2__ prey is other arctic animals, such as seals. They __1__ hunt for their food during the day. This bear is __8__ wild and is found in the north of Canada. Polar bears are vulnerable, and there are not many of them left. Their habitat is shrinking. If we don't __7__ protect these bears, they will become __6__ extinct.

Vocabulary

A Read the text.

B Match the words in blue to their meanings.

1. to look for animals and kill them
2. an animal that other animals kill to eat
3. animals that kill other animals
4. the place where an animal usually lives
5. a kind of animal or plant
6. doesn't exist any more, all dead
7. to keep safe from danger
8. in nature, not controlled by people

Grammar: Real conditionals in the future

A Study the sentence and answer the questions.

Condition	Result
If we don't protect these bears, they will become extinct.	

1. Is the condition possible or not possible? _____ possible _____
2. Is the result now or in the future? _____ in the future _____

Real conditionals in the future	
We use the real conditional for situations that can happen in the future.	**If you look** out the train window, **you will see** a group of wild deer.
Conditional sentences have two clauses: the condition clause and the result clause.	Condition: *if* + subject + simple present tense verb Result: subject + *will/be going to* + verb
The condition clause can be at the beginning or end of the sentence.	**If you talk** loudly, the birds will fly away. The birds are going to fly away **if you talk** loudly.

96   Unit 8

Word Bank: Wild animals

camel	gorilla	rhinoceros
deer	kangaroo	squirrel
eagle	lion	tiger
elephant	monkey	whale
fox	panda	wolf
giraffe	penguin	zebra

Grammar: Types of conditionals

English has three types of conditional sentences with *if*.

1. Real situations in the present or future (called the *first conditional*): *If I study hard, I will get a good grade.*

2. Unreal situations (called the *second conditional*): *If I studied hard, I would get better grades.* (but I don't study hard)

3. Unreal situations in the past (called the *third conditional*): *If I had studied hard, I would have gotten a better grade.* (but I didn't study)

B Complete the sentence with the correct form of the verb in parentheses.

1. If an elephant ___lives___ (live) in a zoo, it ___will get___ (get) bored.
2. We ___will be___ (be) very happy if our team ___wins___ (win).
3. If I ___see___ (see) a bear in the forest, I ___will yell___ (yell) loudly.
4. I ___will go___ (go) to the concert if I ___have___ (have) enough money for a ticket.
5. If you ___don't sleep___ (sleep, not) enough, you ___will feel___ (feel) tired.

C 🔁 Discuss these situations with a partner. Write sentences to describe them in your notebook. What will happen if . . .

1. polar bears can't find enough food?
2. the polar bear's habitat disappears?
3. people put more polar bears in zoos?
4. people protect polar bears?
5. polar bears become extinct?

▲ An Alaskan brown bear near Nonvianuk Lake, Katmai National Park, Alaska

Conversation

A 🔊 6 Close your book and listen to the conversation. What is Katie afraid of? *bears*

Mike: Let's go camping in the national park.
Katie: I'm not sure that's a good idea. There are black bears in the park.
Mike: That may be, but there aren't very many, and they stay away from people.
Katie: If I see a bear, I'll be really scared. They're so dangerous!
Mike: Bears won't hurt you if you leave them alone.

> **Real Language**
>
> You can say *That may be (true), but . . .* to show that you disagree with the other person's idea.

B 🔁 Practice the conversation with a partner. Switch roles and practice it again.

C 🔁 Make two new conversations. Choose from the topics below.

1. White Beach/sharks
2. North Campground/wolves
3. the nature reserve/snakes
4. your own idea _____

D 🔁 **GOAL CHECK** ✔ **Use conditionals to talk about real situations**

Look at the problems in the box. How will these issues affect nature? Talk about them with a partner.

> climate change
> human population growth
> energy use
> nature shows/other education

Nature **97**

B • Have students work individually to complete the sentences with the correct form of the verbs in parentheses.
• Check answers.
• Have students compare answers with a partner.

C • Have students work with a partner to write a sentence for each situation.
• Compare answers with the class.

Conversation

A • Have students close their books. Write the question on the board: *What is Katie afraid of?*
• Play the recording. 🔊 6
• Check answers.
• Direct students' attention to the Real Language box.

B • Play or read the conversation again for the class to repeat.
• Practice the conversation with the class in chorus.
• Have students practice the conversation with a partner, then switch roles and practice it again.

C • Have students work with the same partner to make new conversations modeled on the one in **A.**
• Call on student pairs to present their conversations to the class.

D 🔁 **GOAL CHECK** ✔

• Write one of the issues on the board and ask, *How will this issue affect nature?* Write students' ideas on the board.
• Have students work with a partner to talk about how the issues will affect nature.

Grammar Practice: Real conditionals in the future

Tell students they are going to make their own sentences about different situations—and then share the sentences with the class. Write on the board: *We'll be very happy if _____.* Give students one minute to think of a sentence. Then go around the class quickly and have each student say his or her sentence. In large classes, have students share their sentences in pairs.

Continue with:

I'll be very surprised if _____.   *We'll learn English faster if _____.*
I'll have a great time if _____.

Talk About Possible Future Situations

Listening

- Ask students what they know about fish and fishing. Ask, *Do people eat a lot of fish in your country? Where is the fish caught?* etc. Write students' ideas on the board. Tell students they are going to listen to a radio program about a type of fish called the bluefin tuna.

A
- Have students label the map with the bodies of water in the box. Go over the answers.

B
- Tell students to listen to the whole program the first time and circle the three places on the map that they hear mentioned.
- Play the audio one or more times. 🔊 7
- Check answers.

C
- Tell students to listen again to the first part of the program to find the missing information and write it in the blanks.
- Play the audio one or more times. 🔊 8
- Have students compare answers with a partner.
- Check answers.

D
- Tell students to listen again to the second part of the program to find the information. Have them read the sentences and complete them while they listen.
- Play the audio one or more times. 🔊 9
- Have students compare answers with a partner.
- Check answers.

E
- Have students answer the questions with a partner.
- Compare answers with the class.

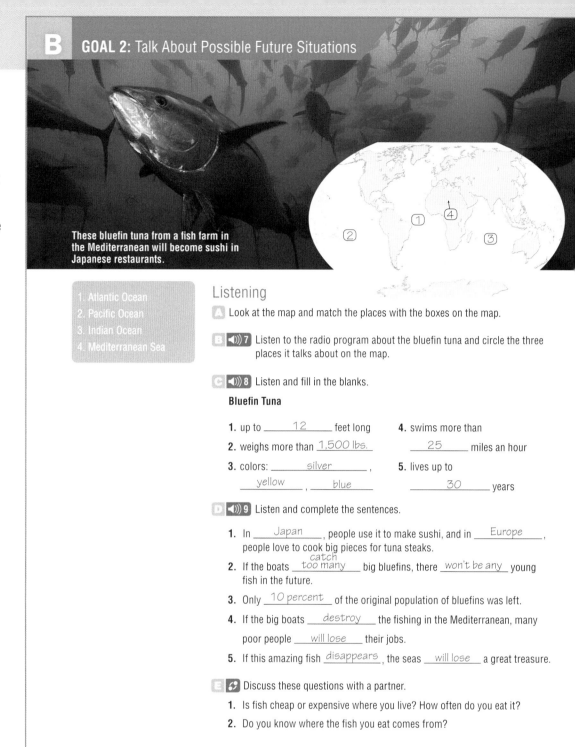

B   GOAL 2: Talk About Possible Future Situations

These bluefin tuna from a fish farm in the Mediterranean will become sushi in Japanese restaurants.

1. Atlantic Ocean
2. Pacific Ocean
3. Indian Ocean
4. Mediterranean Sea

Listening

A Look at the map and match the places with the boxes on the map.

B 🔊 7 Listen to the radio program about the bluefin tuna and circle the three places it talks about on the map.

C 🔊 8 Listen and fill in the blanks.

Bluefin Tuna

1. up to ___12___ feet long
2. weighs more than _1,500 lbs._
3. colors: ___silver___, ___yellow___, ___blue___

4. swims more than ___25___ miles an hour
5. lives up to ___30___ years

D 🔊 9 Listen and complete the sentences.

1. In ___Japan___, people use it to make sushi, and in ___Europe___, people love to cook big pieces for tuna steaks.
2. If the boats ___too many___ ~~catch~~ big bluefins, there ___won't be any___ young fish in the future.
3. Only ___10 percent___ of the original population of bluefins was left.
4. If the big boats ___destroy___ the fishing in the Mediterranean, many poor people ___will lose___ their jobs.
5. If this amazing fish ___disappears___, the seas ___will lose___ a great treasure.

E 🔄 Discuss these questions with a partner.

1. Is fish cheap or expensive where you live? How often do you eat it?
2. Do you know where the fish you eat comes from?

98   Unit 8

For Your Information: Overfishing

Worldwide, the number of fishing boats is estimated to be two to three times larger than the oceans can sustainably support. The main problem is not the number of boats (many of the boats are very small), but the methods used by the largest boats. Trawlers use huge nets that sweep up everything in the ocean—both the species of fish that the fishers want to harvest and a much larger "bycatch" of other types of unwanted fish that are discarded unused. In some places, up to 80 percent of all the fish that are caught are thrown away. Scientists estimate that for large predator fish such as the bluefin tuna, up to 90 percent of the world's stock has already been depleted. When the population of a fish species gets too low, it can no longer reproduce.

Pronunciation: Phrases in sentences

A 🔊 **10** Listen and repeat the sentences. Notice how they're divided into phrases.

1. A bluefin tuna | can swim very fast | and live a long time.
2. My friend's birthday | is June fourteenth.

B Draw lines to divide these sentences into phrases.

1. Jeff and I | saw three big sharks.
2. Cathy isn't here, | but I can take a message.
3. I'll bring my camera | if we go to the zoo.
4. If they catch | all the big fish, | the species won't survive.
5. The family | will have fun | at the national park.

C 🔊 **11** Listen and check your answers. Practice saying the sentences.

Communication

A Read the information. What does *sustainable* mean?

Fish is one of the world's favorite foods. Around the world, the average person eats 36 pounds (16 kg) of fish every year. But many kinds of fish around the world are disappearing because people catch too many of them. Scientists say that 90 percent of the biggest fish are gone now. If we catch too many big fish now, there won't be any baby fish in the future. Our way of fishing now is not **sustainable**—it can't continue for a long time without hurting the environment.

> **Word Focus**
>
> The word **environment** can refer to nature or to everything that's around us.
>
> *Recycling used paper is good for the **environment**.*
>
> *This classroom is a good **environment** for learning.*

B You are members of an environmental group called **Save the Oceans.** You want to take action to solve the fishing problem. Talk about these plans. What will happen if we follow each one?

Plan A: Don't eat fish!	Plan B: Safe fish symbol	Plan C: Strict laws about fishing
Tell people to stop buying and eating fish. Put ads in newspapers and magazines, and make TV commercials to explain why fishing hurts the environment.	Make a special symbol for fish that are caught in a sustainable way. Make commercials to tell people to look for this symbol in supermarkets and restaurants.	Make stronger laws about how many fish people can catch. Send special police in fast boats to all of the fishing areas to make sure that fishing boats follow the laws.

C **GOAL CHECK** ✓ **Talk about possible future situations**

Which is the best plan? Why? Explain your decision to the class.

Pronunciation

A
- Introduce the idea of a phrase— a group of words that have a meaning when used together.
- Have students read the sentences. Then tell them to listen to the pronunciation of the phrases.
- Play the audio. 🔊 **10**

B
- Have students mark the divisions in the sentences.
- Have students compare answers with a partner.

C
- Tell students to listen and check their answers.
- Play the audio one or more times. 🔊 **11**
- Check answers.
- Have students form pairs and take turns saying the sentences. Monitor and help them with the correct pronunciation.

Communication

A
- Have students read the information. Point out the definition in the Word Focus box.
- Ask, *What's the definition of sustainable?* (It can continue for a long time without hurting the environment.)

B
- Divide the class into groups of three or four. Go over the three plans with the class.
- Have students discuss with their groups the different plans and the results of each plan.
- Have students choose the most effective plan. Tell them that they can make changes to a plan if they want to.

C **GOAL CHECK** ✓

- Call on each group to explain their decision and reasons to the class.

Expansion Activity

On the board, write, *People get married at a later age.* Ask the class, *What will happen if people get married at a later age?* Elicit several consequences (for example, *families will have fewer children*) and write them on the board, linking them to the original sentence with an arrow. Then ask about the results of these events, and write the possible consequences, linking them to that event with an arrow. Once students are familiar with the technique, have them break into groups and work on other statements, such as *The earth's climate gets warmer*, or *The population of our city increases to 5 million.* Have someone in each group record the group's ideas to present to the class.

Describe What Animals Do

Language Expansion

A • Have students look at the pictures and say what they know about each animal. Ask, *How does the snail move? Does it move slowly or fast? How does the penguin move?*

• Tell students that adverbs are words that describe (modify) a verb. They give information about how an action is done.

• Have students fill in the correct adverbs.

• Check answers.

• Go over the information in the chart about the formation of adverbs. Elicit more examples from students. Ask, *How do you swim/ drive/speak English?* (*badly/fast/ quickly/happily*, etc.)

B • Have students work together with a partner to write sentences using each adverb in the box.

• Call on student pairs to read a sentence to the class.

Grammar

A • Review the ideas of count nouns (things we count, such as *books, horses, chairs, people*) and non-count nouns (things we don't count, such as *water, rice, air, happiness*).

• Tell students to read about raccoons and their food and identify count and non-count nouns.

• Have students compare answers with a partner.

• List answers on the board.

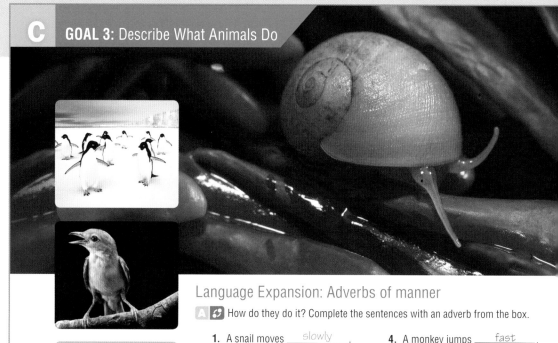

C **GOAL 3:** Describe What Animals Do

Language Expansion: Adverbs of manner

A 🔁 How do they do it? Complete the sentences with an adverb from the box.

beautifully   fast   well
slowly   loudly   badly

1. A snail moves ___slowly___ .
2. A fox hunts ___well___ .
3. A penguin walks ___badly___ .
4. A monkey jumps ___fast___ .
5. A lion roars ___loudly___ .
6. A bird sings ___beautifully___ .

Adverbs of manner	
Adverbs of manner tell us how an action is done. The adverb usually follows the verb.	A snail <u>moves</u> **slowly.** Tigers <u>run</u> **fast.**
Many adverbs of manner are formed from adjectives plus *-ly*.	quick – quickly safe – safely soft – softly careful – carefully
Some adverbs of manner are irregular.	well fast hard
Note: For most adjectives that end in *-y*, change the *-y* to *-i* and add *-ly*.	easy – easily happy – happily angry – angrily

quick   careful
quiet   easy   loud

B 🔁 In your notebook, write sentences using the adverb form of each adjective in the box.

Grammar: Review of quantifiers

A 🔁 Write C for count nouns or NC for non-count nouns.

Raccoons are small (1) ___C___ <u>animals</u> that live in North America, Japan, and a few (2) ___C___ <u>parts</u> of Europe. They are *omnivores*—animals that eat both plants and animals. A raccoon's usual diet is (3) ___C___ <u>nuts</u> and (4) ___NC___ <u>fruit</u>. They also like to eat insects. Sometimes they catch (5) ___NC___ <u>fish</u> or (6) ___C___ <u>frogs</u>.

100   Unit 8

Word Bank:
Animal sounds
In English, animals "say":

cat:	meow
cow:	moooo
dog:	bow-wow
rooster:	cock-a-doodle-doo
sheep:	baaaa

Grammar: Quantifiers

In English, objects are viewed as separate things that we can count (such as *coins*) or as a whole that we can't count (such as *money*). It is how we view the object that determines its countability. Because of this, some nouns can be both count and non-count.

Different sets of quantifiers are used with each class of nouns.

There is too little paper in the copy machine.

There are too few papers for the students in the class.

Quantifiers

Quantifiers					
With count nouns			**With non-count nouns**		
too few a few some	a lot of many too many	eggs	too little a little some	a lot of too much	meat

*Quantifiers tell us *how much* or *how many*.
*Don't use *much* in affirmative sentences: ~~He has much money.~~ He has a lot of money.

B Circle the correct quantifier in each sentence below.

1. Raccoons eat ((many) | a little) different kinds of food.
2. They eat (a little | (a lot of)) nuts.
3. Raccoons will eat ((a few) | a little) insects if they find them.
4. They sometimes eat ((a little) | many) soap.
5. If a raccoon goes in your garbage can, you'll find ((a lot of) | many) garbage all over the place!

Conversation

A 🔊12 Listen to the conversation with your book closed. What does the woman want to see at the zoo? the penguins

Dan: So, which animals do you want to see at the zoo?
Carmen: I love to look at the penguins. I think they're really amazing.
Dan: Why is that?
Carmen: Well, they walk so slowly, but in the water they swim really well. And it's fun to watch them at feeding time.
Dan: Really? What do they eat?
Carmen: They eat a lot of fish and a few shrimp.

B 🔄 Practice the conversation with a partner. Switch roles and practice it again.

C 🔄 Fill in the chart. Add your own ideas. Then make new conversations.

	What they do	What they eat
1. tigers	walk, run	meat
2. elephants	walk, swim, run	leaves, grass, fruit

meat   walk   play
leaves   grass   swim
run   fruit

D ♻ **GOAL CHECK** ✔ **Describe what animals do**

Report to the class. Tell them about your favorite zoo animal. Try to use adverbs and quantifiers.

B • Go over the information in the chart with the class.
- Then tell students to circle the correct word in each sentence.
- Check answers.
- Ask, *Do people ever have this kind of problem with animals in our country? What happens?*

Conversation

A • Have students close their books. Write the question on the board: *What does the woman want to see at the zoo?*
- Play the audio. 🔊12
- Check answers.

B • Play or read the conversation again for the class to repeat.
- Practice the conversation with the class in chorus.
- Have students practice the conversation with a partner, then switch roles and practice it again.

C • Have students work with their partners to fill in the chart with words from the box.
- Check answers.
- Tell students to choose another animal and add a third section to the chart.
- Have students make conversations about the three animals, modeled on **Conversation A.**

D 🔄 **GOAL CHECK** ✔

- Have each student choose a favorite zoo animal and write notes about what it does and what it eats. Remind them to use adverbs and quantifiers.
- Ask students to tell the class about the animal they've chosen. In a class of more than 15 students, you may prefer to divide the class into groups of six and have them tell their group about the animal.

Grammar Practice: Quantifiers

Have students ask and answer questions about their own diets with a partner. Write these items on the board:

meat   fruit   vegetables

eggs   coffee   water

Model the activity. Ask a student, *How much meat do you eat?* Elicit, *a lot/a little, every day/too much*, and so on.

Have students take turns interviewing their partners and answering with the quantifiers they've studied. Then ask the class questions such as *Who has a healthy diet/drinks a lot of coffee?*

Discuss a Problem in Nature

Reading

- Introduce the topic of the reading. Have students look at the photos of John Kasaona and say what they think he does and where he works.

A
- Write on the board: *endangered.* Have students explain what it means and give some examples of animals that are endangered.
- Have students discuss with a partner why some animals are endangered.
- Have several pairs share reasons, and write them on the board.

B
- Have students read the list and check the ways of protecting endangered animals that they think they will read about in the article.
- Have students compare their predictions with a partner.
- Have students read the article quickly to understand the main ideas and check their predictions. Remind them not to worry about new words yet.

C
- Point out the words and their definitions in the footnotes. Then have students read the article again to find the dates.
- Have them compare answers with a partner.
- Check answers.

D
- Have students write down two good things about the community-based conservation program.
- Have them compare answers with a partner.

WANT MORE? Visit **TED.com** for more talks on nature and conservation. We suggest *The Voice of the Natural World* by Bernie Krause.

D **GOAL 4:** Discuss a Problem in Nature

Reading

A ⚡ What are some reasons animals are endangered? Talk about your ideas with a partner.

B ⚡ Look at the list of ways we can protect endangered animals. Check (✓) the ideas you predict you will read about in the article. Compare your answers with a partner.

1. _✓_ stop poaching
2. ____ create advertisements about conservation
3. ____ prevent droughts
4. _✓_ put land under conservation
5. ____ support nature tourism

C Read the article. Write the dates next to the events.

1. __1995__ 20 lions remain in Kunene
2. __1971__ John Kasaona is born
3. __1980s__ drought hits Namibia
4. __1966__ war begins
5. __1990__ war ends

D ⚡ List two good things in your notebook about the community-based conservation program. Compare your answers with a partner.

Many elephants are killed for their tusks.

John Kasaona
Community-Based Conservationist

HOW POACHERS BECAME CARETAKERS

When John Kasaona was a boy growing up in Namibia, his father took him into the **bush** to teach him how to take care of the family's livestock. His father said, "If you see a cheetah eating our goat, walk up to it and smack it on the backside." A cheetah is a very nervous animal. If a person **confronts** it, it will probably run away. John also learned how to deal with a lion by standing very still and making himself look very big. These were useful lessons for a boy who became a wildlife **conservationist.** As Kasaona says, "It is very important if you are in the field to know what to confront and what to run from."

Kasaona was born in 1971. At that time, Namibia had many problems. The country was at war from 1966 to 1990. Because of the fighting, many people had rifles. This caused a secondary problem—**poaching.** For example, poachers killed many black rhinos for their horns, which were very valuable. To make things even worse, around 1980, a terrible drought killed people, livestock, and wildlife. By 1995, there were only 20 lions left in the Kunene region in the northwest of the country, where Kasaona's family lives. Many other **species** were also endangered.

At the same time, positive changes were taking place. A non-governmental organization, the Integrated Rural Development and Nature Conservation (IRDNC), began working in Namibia to protect wildlife. They met with village leaders to ask who would be able to work with them. They needed people who knew the bush well and who understood how wild animals lived. The

---

For Your Information: Namibia and John Kasaona

Namibia is a country on the east coast of southern Africa. It is a very dry country and one of the least populated in the world because of the Namib Desert. Namibia has suffered from war and drought, and due to poaching, many wildlife species have been close to extinction. However, John Kasaona and the Integrated Rural Development and Nature Conservation are working hard to change Namibia's future. The IRDNC has come to the world's attention because of its unique approach to conservation. Kasaona was invited to TED to share Namibia's conservation success story. He firmly believes that conservancy projects must work with the people who use and live on the fragile land. This has meant that those now involved in protecting the land and its wildlife are the former poachers themselves. Conservation is a key issue in all our lives. We need to learn from ideas such as this one and help to protect our planet and its wildlife.

"We knew conservation would fail if it didn't work to improve the lives of the local communities."
— John Kasaona

John Kasaona's idea worth spreading is that there is good news from Africa. Protecting wildlife is a great way to transform communities — and countries. Watch Kasaona's full TED Talk on TED.com.

Reading Tip

Predicting content before reading a text is a helpful reading strategy. It helps students be prepared for the topic they are going to read about by activating any prior knowledge of the topic. Students may understand a text better if they have the opportunity to make predictions before they read. You can use the title of a text, photos or other images, and key words (for example, *endangered*, for this text) as the basis for encouraging students to make predictions before they read.

answer was surprising: work with local poachers. It seemed crazy, but it also made sense. After all, if you spend your time hunting for animals, you will know where they live and how they behave. So IRDNC hired a group of poachers, including Kasaona's own father, to help protect wildlife in Namibia.

Since then, the situation has changed dramatically. The Kunene region now has more than 130 lions. The black rhino, almost extinct in 1982, has come back, and there are now many free-roaming black rhinos in Kunene. Most importantly, more land than ever is under conservation. That protected land generates money from tourism for Namibia to use in education, health care, and other important programs for its people.

John Kasaona explains, "We were successful in Namibia because we dreamed of a future that was much more than just a healthy wildlife." Kasaona created a model for other nations to follow by starting the largest community-led conservation program in the world.

bush *land far from towns and cities*
confront *to challenge (someone) in a forceful way*
conservationist *someone who works to protect animals, plants, and natural resources*
poaching *killing an animal illegally*
species *a group of animals or plants that are similar*

103

After Reading

Web search: Have students research an endangered species online. Ask them to present what they learned to the class or a small group.

Project: Have students work in small groups to research and prepare a brochure about a nature area in their country. They should include information about the land, the wildlife, any environmental problems there, and what visitors can see and do. Display the brochures in the classroom for students to read and enjoy.

Expansion

After reading the article, have students find out more about this conservationist and his work by:

1. watching John Kasaona's TED Talk at TED.com

2. finding out about the documentary *Milking the Rhino* which features Kasaona's work.

Communication

A • Ask, *What problems in nature are there in your country?* Write one idea on the board. Ask, *Why is this happening?* Write one or two ideas on the board.

• Have students think of two or three other problems and discuss with a partner what is happening and what is causing each problem.

• Have pairs share with the class one problem they discussed.

Writing

A • Have students complete the sentences.

• Have them discuss their answers with a partner.

B • Direct students' attention to the Writing Strategy box and the connectors *but/so/even though.*

• Have students complete the paragraph.

• Check answers.

C • Remind students of the problems they identified and discussed in **Communication A.**

• Have students write a paragraph about one of the problems using *but/so/even though.* Remind them to use the paragraph in **B** as a model.

• Have students exchange paragraphs with a partner and check the connectors.

D | 🔁 | GOAL CHECK ✔

• Divide the class into small groups. Have students discuss the problems they identified in **Communication A** with their group. Remind students to say which problem they think is the most important and ways it can be solved.

• Have each group report briefly on the problems they discussed and which one they decided was the most important to solve.

D | **GOAL 4:** Discuss a Problem in Nature

Poaching endangers species in their natural habitats.

Communication

A 🔁 Think about two or three problems in nature in your country. What is happening? What are the causes? Share your ideas with a partner.

Writing

A Complete the sentences about a problem in nature in your country.

Answers will vary.

1. If we believe in conservation, we will _____.

2. If _____, many animals will be saved.

3. If people want to make positive changes, they will _____.

B Write *but, so,* and *even though* in the correct places in the paragraph.

By the 1990s, many species of animals were endangered in Namibia. The situation was serious, (1)____*so*____ conservationists needed to find a way to protect the animals. They found one, (2)____*but*____ it wasn't what you would expect: they asked poachers for help. (3)*Even though* this seemed crazy, I think it was a great idea. If we want to protect endangered species, we need to consider every solution.

Writing Strategy

Conjunctions

Conjunctions are used to connect ideas within sentences.

C Write a paragraph in your notebook giving your opinion about a problem in nature in your country. Be sure to use the connectors in Exercise **B.**

D | ♻ | GOAL CHECK ✔ Discuss a problem in nature

Work with a group. Share your ideas from Exercise **A** about problems in nature. In your opinion, what is the most important problem to solve? What are two or three ways to help?

104   Unit 8

Teacher Tip: Giving students more responsibility

Giving students responsibility for everyday classroom tasks can not only lighten the teacher's workload, but gives students a greater feeling of involvement. Here are some tasks that your students may be able to perform:

• handing back homework

• calling the class to order at the beginning

• checking attendance (with your supervision)

• distributing papers

• setting up audio equipment

• erasing/washing the board at the end of class

VIDEO JOURNAL: *Happy Elephants* **E**

Elephants crossing Luangwa River, Loxodonta africana, Zambia

Before You Watch

A ⟳ Read about the video and check the meanings of the words in **bold** with a partner.

> Elephants are amazing animals. They can use their **trunks** to pick up heavy things. **In the wild**, they live in **herds** in the forest. Today, many elephants live in zoos. Their **trainers** take care of them. But can elephants be happy **in captivity**?

While You Watch

A ▶ Watch the video *Happy Elephants*. Choose the main idea.

1. Elephants are happier in the wild.
2. People and elephants have been together for a long time.
3. Elephant trainers find ways to make elephants happier.

B ▶ Watch the video again. Fill in the information.

1. Elephants and people have worked together for over ___2,000___ years.
2. There is one question that people have been asking: How is it possible to keep elephants happy ___in captivity___ ?
3. Many people who work closely with animals say that they do have ___feelings___ and can experience happiness.
4. That means that they live in families and herds and they ___need___ other elephants.
5. For elephants, communication and social relationships are really ___important___.

After You Watch

A ⟳ Discuss these questions with your partner. Have you visited a zoo or seen a video of a zoo? Do you think the animals like living there? Why or why not?

Nature **105**

Video Journal:
Happy Elephants

- Ask the students what they know about elephants—their food/habitat/behavior. Ask, *Have you ever seen an elephant? Where? What was it doing?* Point out the title of the video: *Happy Elephants.* Ask, *What makes an elephant happy?*

Before You Watch

A • Go over the video summary in the box and explain the vocabulary in bold, if necessary.

While You Watch

A • Tell students to watch the video the first time and find the main idea.
  - Play the video.
  - Check answers.

B • Tell students to watch the video again and find the information to complete the sentences. The answer to Item 5 must be inferred by what the students have learned from the video.
  - Play the video.
  - Have students compare answers with a partner.
  - Check answers.

After You Watch

A • Have students discuss the questions with a partner.
  - Have several pairs share their answers.

For Your Information: Elephants

Elephants are the largest land animals. There are two elephant species now living in Africa and one species in Asia. At birth, a baby elephant can weigh 120 kilograms (260 pounds). An elephant can live as long as 70 years. The largest elephant recorded was killed in Angola (Africa) and weighed more than 12,000 kilograms (26,000 pounds). In many cultures, elephants are a symbol of wisdom, and they are known for their good memories and high intelligence. Female elephants in the wild live in large "families" made up of mothers, daughters, sisters, and aunts. When one group gets too large, a part of it will leave to form a separate group. Male elephants live alone.

Life in the Past

About the Photo

This photo shows visitors at the *Al-khazneh* (or Treasury) in the ancient city of Petra, Jordan. In 1985, Petra was designated a UNESCO World Heritage Site due to its outstanding beauty and cultural value. The city was carved into the rock face more than 2,000 years ago by the Nabataeans, Arabian nomads who settled in the area. Today, Petra is Jordan's most important tourist attraction. The beauty of this city in the rocks is enhanced by the candlelit night in this image taken by Colby Brown. Brown specializes in landscape, travel and humanitarian fine art photography, but is also a photo educator and an author.

- Direct students' attention to the picture. Have them describe what they see.

- Have students work with a partner to discuss the questions.

- Compare answers with the class, compiling lists of the different kinds of changes on the board.

- Ask these questions orally or by writing them on the board for students to answer in pairs: *What things have made our lives better? What things have made our lives worse?*

- Go over the Unit Goals with the class.

- For each goal, elicit any words students already know and write them on the board; for example, how to talk about actions in the past, the names of historical wonders, vocabulary to discuss aspects of life that have changed, etc.

Life in the Past

The ancient city of Petra, Jordan at night

106

UNIT 9 GOALS	Grammar	Vocabulary	Listening
• Discuss life in the past • Contrast different ways of life • Compare today with the past • Talk about a historical wonder	*Used to/Would* Native Americans **used to** make their shoes out of deerskin. Past passive voice Igloos **were built** with blocks of ice.	Activities and artifacts Indian innovations Separable phrasal verbs	Focused and general listening An interview: An archaeologist's excavation

Unit Theme Overview

- In many ways, the past is not what we think it was. For example, people in the 21st century often assume that our ancestors' lives were nothing but endless hard work with almost no time for leisure. In fact, according to some sociologists and historians, our ancestors might have felt sorry for us with our long working hours. Research has found that peasant farmers in medieval Europe, although their work day stretched for 16 hours in summer, took long breaks for breakfast, lunch, dinner, and an afternoon nap—and in fact worked fewer than eight hours a day in the busiest part of summer. In Africa, the Kung people, who still live today by hunting and gathering wild food, work only two to four hours a day.

- Modern inventions and technology may not have made life simpler, but they have certainly changed it. In this unit, students will look at changes within their own country and culture, as well as learn about the past in other countries. They will begin by talking about activities in the past and then contrast different ways of life. They will compare today with the past. Finally, they will talk about historical wonders and share their ideas.

UNIT 9 GOALS

1. Discuss life in the past

2. Contrast different ways of life

3. Compare today with the past

4. Talk about a historical wonder

107

Speaking	Reading	Writing	Video Journal
Discussing daily life in the past based on archaeological discoveries **Pronunciation:** Reduction of *used to*	**National Geographic:** Lord of the Mongols	Writing about one of the New 7 Wonders	**National Geographic:** Searching for Genghis Khan

Discuss Life in the Past

Vocabulary

A • Have students look at the pictures and read the information about each person. Point out the information in the Word Focus box.

• Ask comprehension questions (orally or write them for students to answer), for example, *Where was Marco Polo from? What was Battuta's goal?* etc. Alternatively, in pairs, have students write questions, and then have pairs exchange questions.

B • Have students read the definitions and synonyms, and then have them write the correct word from **A** for each one.

• Have students compare answers with a partner.

• Check answers.

Grammar

• Go over the information in the chart. Elicit more examples from students. Ask, *When you were little, what did you use to do for fun? When you were a child, what did you use to do to celebrate (holidays)?*

▲ Marco Polo

▲ Ibn Battuta

▲ Zheng He

Word Focus

Use **even though** before a clause with a subject and verb.

Use **despite** before a noun or noun phrase.

*They traveled **even though** it was difficult.*

*They traveled **despite** the difficulty.*

Vocabulary

A Read the information about three early travelers.

Long-distance travel can be difficult for anyone, but it used to be even more challenging. Yet despite the difficulty, people have always wanted to see and learn about distant regions. These three brave explorers did exactly that—hundreds of years ago! The result was an exchange of knowledge and culture that changed the world.

Marco Polo (1254–1324) We don't know exactly when and where Marco Polo was born, but he lived in Venice and Genoa, in what is now Italy, and he traveled east—far beyond the borders of Europe into Asia. The stories he published after his travels seem to mix together fact and fiction, but they inspired other European explorers, including Christopher Columbus.

Ibn Battuta (1304–1369) Ibn Battuta was a remarkable traveler. Born in Morocco, he visited most of the Muslim world—North Africa, the Middle East, and East Africa—as well as South Asia, including Sri Lanka and India, and even China. Battuta's goal was to search for knowledge and new experiences, and his stories taught people about other parts of the world at a time when few people traveled.

Zheng He (1371–1433) The explorations of Zheng He took him by sea from China west to the Middle East and Africa. According to stories, Zheng commanded enormous ships more than 400 feet (122 m) long—much, much larger than other ships of the time. The size of the ships was probably helpful for trade, as well as for carrying military people and equipment.

B Write each word in blue next to the correct definition or synonym.

1. _search_ look for
2. _remarkable_ impressive
3. _trade_ buying and selling
4. _beyond_ past a limit
5. _exchange_ giving and taking
6. _ships_ large boats
7. _distant_ far away
8. _published_ printed copies of writing
9. _inspired_ gave enthusiasm or ideas
10. _despite_ even though

Grammar: *Used to*

We use *used to* + base form of a verb to talk about the past.	My father **used to** build ships, but now he is retired from his job.
Used to usually shows a contrast between past and present.	The company **used to** publish travel books. (Now they publish cookbooks.)
In questions and negative statements, use *did/didn't* + *use to*.	**Did** people **use to** see pictures of distant places? They **didn't use to** know much about other places and cultures.

Word Bank: Life in the past

Time expressions: a long time ago, century, decade

Grammar Practice: *Used to*

Have students talk with a partner about these things, using *used to.*

• what they did after school when they were in elementary school

• how they celebrated their birthdays as a child

• what they did during the summer when they were younger

A Complete each sentence with *used to* plus the verb in parentheses and your own ideas. *Answers in second part of sentence may vary.*

1. My grandparents ___used to travel___ (travel) a lot. Now they _(don't travel)_ .
2. Train tickets ___used to be___ (be) cheap. Now they _(are expensive)_ .
3. I ___used to find___ (find) information at the library. Now I _(find it on the Internet)_
4. She ___used to take___ (take) pictures with a camera. Now she _(takes them with her cell phone)_ .
5. People ___used to write___ (write) letters. Now they _(send e-mails/instant messages)_

B Complete the conversations with the words in the box.

Sue: Why did people (1) ___use___ to travel by horse?

Aki: Well, there (2) ___didn't___ use to be other transportation.

Sue: OK, but did everyone use to (3) ___travel___ that way?

Aki: Why do you ask? You didn't use to (4) ___care___ about horses.

Sue: I'm writing about transportation in the past, so I need to include horses.

Aki: You should talk to Mr. Clark. He (5) ___used___ to ride horses when he was younger, and he knows a lot about them.

Conversation

A 🔊 13 Close your book and listen to the conversation. How old are the El Tajín ruins? *over a thousand years old*

Ben: What's up, Patricia?

Patricia: Not much. I'm looking at pictures of the El Tajín ruins in Mexico.

Ben: I've never heard of El Tajín.

Patricia: It's a remarkable archaeological site that's over a thousand years old. It has several buildings, some pyramids, ball courts . . .

Ben: Ball courts? Why are there ball courts?

Patricia: Well, people used to play ball games there. El Tajín was a center of culture and government, and the games were part of the culture.

Ben: Ball games? That's interesting!

Patricia: It is, and there are at least 20 ball courts on the site!

Ben: Are they used for anything today?

Patricia: Actually, people go to El Tajín now for concerts and events.

▲ El Tajín in Veracruz, Mexico

B 🔄 Practice the conversation with a partner. Then describe the historical places in the box or other places you know about. What used to happen at these places? What happens there now?

C 🔄 **GOAL CHECK** ✔ **Discuss life in the past**

How has modern technology changed people's lives? Tell your partner what people used to do in the past, and what they do now. Use the topics in the box and your own ideas.

Life in the Past   **109**

Grammar:
Used to and *would*

Would is also used to talk about things that were true in the past, but are not true now. *Used to* and *would* have the same meaning, but *would* is slightly more formal and is used more often in writing.

A • Have students complete the sentences with *used to* and the verb given, then their own idea.

• Have students compare answers with a partner.

• Check answers.

B • Have students read the conversation and complete it with the words in the box.

• Have students read the conversation with a partner to compare answers.

• Check answers.

Conversation

A • Have students close their books. Write the question on the board: *How old are the El Tajín ruins?*

• Play the recording. 🔊 13

• Check answer.

B • Play or read the conversation again for the class to repeat.

• Practice the conversation with the class in chorus.

• Have students practice the conversation with a partner, then switch roles and practice it again.

• Have students make new conversations about historical places they know about or the ones in the box.

C 🔄 **GOAL CHECK** ✔

• Have students read the directions. Elicit ideas about how technology has changed people's lives, and write some ideas on the board.

• Individually, have students write notes about each topic. Suggest that they draw a two-column chart with the headings *now* and *in the past*. Encourage them to add other topics.

• Assign new pairs and have them discuss how life was different in the past using their notes.

• Compare ideas with the class, and complete a chart on the board.

Contrast Different Ways of Life

Listening

A • Have students look at the picture and describe what they see. Have them look at the map and elicit what they know about that part of the world.

• Have students read the directions and check the things they think people did.

• Have students compare answers with a partner.

• Compare answers as a class.

B • Tell students they are going to listen to a talk about the Sami people. Have them read the options for the main idea. Tell them to listen and choose the best option.

• Play the recording. ◀))) 14

• Have students compare answers with a partner.

• Check answers.

• Direct students' attention to the information in the Word Focus box.

C • Have students read the statements. Tell them to listen again and choose *true* or *false*.

• Play the recording again. ◀))) 14

• Have students correct the false statements. Play the recording again as necessary.

• Have students compare answers with a partner.

• Check answers. Write the corrected statements on the board.

D • Have students discuss the questions with a partner.

• Compare answers with the class.

B GOAL 2: Contrast Different Ways of Life

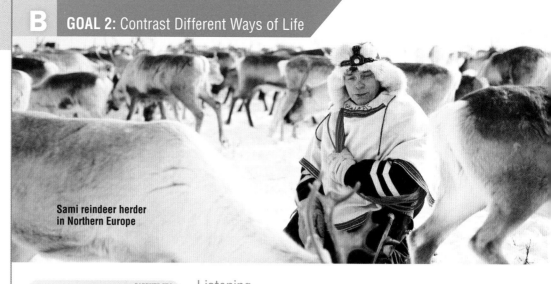

Sami reindeer herder in Northern Europe

Listening

A Look at the map on this page. How do you think people used to live in this part of the world 1,000 years ago? Check (✓) the things you think people did.

1. _____ ate fish from the Arctic Ocean

2. _____ lived on small farms

3. _____ followed groups of animals, such as reindeer

4. _____ lived in houses made of wood

5. _____ had their own language and customs

B ◀))) 14 Listen to a talk about the Sami people and choose the main idea.

a. The Sami people depend on animals, especially reindeer, to make a living.

ⓑ Life is changing for the Sami people, but some of them live in traditional ways.

c. Many young Sami people want to attend a university and choose a career.

C ◀))) 14 Listen again and circle **T** for *true* or **F** for *false*. Correct the false sentences to make them true.

moved from place to

1. Traditionally, the Sami people ~~stayed and lived in one~~ place.   T Ⓕ

2. Reindeer were used by the Sami people for food and clothing.   Ⓣ F

3. Most Sami people still live in the traditional way.   T Ⓕ

Few
4. ~~Some~~ Sami people now raise reindeer on farms.   T Ⓕ

5. New laws affect the way Sami people may use land.   Ⓣ F

D 🔁 Do you think it's important to maintain traditions from the past? Or do you think people should focus on the future? Discuss your ideas with a partner.

Word Focus

Some animal words don't have plural forms:

deer   reindeer   sheep   bison

110   Unit 9

For Your Information: The Sami People

The Sami are the indigenous people who live in the very north of Europe in the Arctic regions of northern Scandinavia and northwest Russia. The area they inhabit is called Sápmi, and it stretches across the northern parts of Norway, Sweden, Finland, and the Kola Peninsula in Russia. The Sami are the only indigenous people of Scandinavia who are recognized and protected under the international conventions of indigenous peoples. There are several Sami languages, but in some areas these languages are threatened and in danger of being lost. The Sami have suffered religious and linguistic discrimination over the years and have had to fight for their land, but their situation is improving; in some areas they now have their own parliaments. In Finland, for example, they have had self-government in cultural and linguistic issues in their homelands since 1996.

Pronunciation: Reduction of *used to*

When we speak quickly, *used to* is sometimes pronounced /yU-st(ə)/.

A 🔊 **15** You will hear each sentence twice. Listen to the full form and the reduced form of *used to*. Listen again and repeat the sentences.

1. People used to make their own clothes.
2. They used to hunt animals and catch fish.
3. Did you use to play baseball?
4. Food used to cost a lot less.
5. My grandfather used to read to me.

B 🔄 Complete the sentences with your own information. Then read the sentences aloud to a partner. Use the reduced form /yU-st(ə)/.

1. When I was younger, I used to _____.
2. As a child, I used to want money for _____.
3. In my country, people used to _____.
4. Before I was born, my grandparents used to _____.
5. As children, my parents used to _____.

Communication

A 🔄 How is life today different than it was 50 years ago? Tell your partner at least four things people used to do and what they do now.

> **People used to make phone calls at home. Now they use cell phones anywhere.**

> **True, and their conversations used to be private. Now everyone can hear them!**

B 🔄 How has your life changed over the years? Tell your partner at least four things you didn't use to know or do.

> **I didn't use to speak English. Now I speak it every day.**

> **I didn't use to get along with my brother. Now we're friends.**

▲ Old Russian telephone in Norway

C 🔄 **GOAL CHECK** ✔ **Contrast different ways of life**

Discuss the differences between the traditional Sami lifestyle and the way most Sami people live today. Consider housing, food, education, language, and transportation.

Life in the Past **111**

Expansion Activity

With the class, make a list of ten things that people use every day (such as cars, telephones, canned food, blue jeans). Then tell students to work with a partner to write sentences about what people used to do before they had these things: *People used to communicate by writing a letter or visiting their friends.* Compare answers with the class.

Lesson B **111**

Compare Today with the Past

Language Expansion

- Review the idea of phrasal verbs: a verb and one or two prepositions that, when used together, have a different meaning than the original verb. Elicit phrasal verbs they already know and some example sentences. Write them on the board.

- Point out the information in the Word Focus box. Compare with the inseparable phrasal verbs they know; for example, *They set out on the trip. Mark grew up in Canada.* Tell students that there are more separable phrasal verbs than inseparable verbs. There is no rule for knowing if a phrasal verb is separable—this information must be memorized.

A • Have students look at the picture and describe what they see.

- Have students complete the sentences with the phrasal verbs, using their dictionaries as needed.

- Have students compare answers with a partner.

- Check answers.

B • Remind students that these phrasal verbs are separable. Model the example with a student.

- Have students ask and answer the questions with a partner.

- Call on pairs to say a question and answer. Then have them say the answer the other way, with the verb and particle together. *(You can bring up children.)*

Grammar

- Review the passive voice—sentences where the focus is on the person or thing that receives the action. Remind students that the passive voice is not a verb tense. It can be used together with different verb tenses to talk about any time.

- Go over the information in the chart.

Word Focus

Separable phrasal verbs can be separated by an object—usually a pronoun.

We **set up** a tent to sleep in.
We **set it up** over there.

> **What can you do with children?**

> **You can bring them up.**

Regular past participles:
invent – invented
pull – pulled
hunt – hunted

Irregular past participles:
eat – eaten
drink – drunk
sell – sold

Language Expansion: Separable phrasal verbs

A Some phrasal verbs are used more frequently than one-word verbs. Complete the paragraph with the phrasal verb closest in meaning to the verb in parentheses.

> bring up   help out   turn on   bring back   put on   figure out

    Hi, my name is Susie, and I live in the Nunavut Territory in Canada. Life in Nunavut hasn't changed as much as it has in other places. It's true—nowadays, we can (1) _turn on_ (start) the furnace when it gets cold instead of building a fire, but we haven't given up our traditional culture. We still (2) _bring up_ (raise) our children in the land our people have lived in for thousands of years. We teach them to (3) _put on_ (don) our traditional clothing to stay warm in the winter. When they're old enough, we teach them to (4) _figure out_ (discover, solve) solutions to everyday problems. We teach them to (5) _bring back_ (return) anything they borrow. And most importantly, we teach them to always (6) _help out_ (aid) their family and their community. Those things will never change.

B Answer the questions. Use pronouns and the separable phrasal verbs.

1. What can you do with children? You can bring them up.
2. What can you do with shoes? You can put them on.
3. How can you assist your friends? You can help them out.
4. How can you understand something? You can figure it out.
5. What can you do with a borrowed book? You can bring it back.
6. What can you do when a computer is turned off? You can turn it on.

Grammar: Passive voice in the past

Passive voice in the past	
Use the active voice in the past to focus on the subject of a sentence.	Parents **raised** their children differently in the past.
Use the passive voice in the past to focus on the object or receiver of a past action.	Children **were raised** differently in the past (by their parents).
Form the past passive with *was* or *were* + the past participle of a verb.	My father **was taught** to always tell the truth.

112   Unit 9

Word Bank: Separable phrasal verbs

hand in	switch on
hand out	take off
look up	throw away
pick up	turn off
put away	wake up
put down	write down

Grammar: Past passive

Because the passive voice is not a tense, it can be used in combination with other tenses to talk about different time periods. The past passive is used for events or processes in a period of time that took place before the present.

A Complete each sentence with the past passive form of the verb in parentheses.

1. Large stones ___were used___ (use) to build the Egyptian pyramids.
2. Igloos ___were built___ (build) from blocks of ice by the Inuit people.
3. Writing ___was invented___ (invent) in Mesopotamia.
4. Wild animals ___were hunted___ (hunt) by Native Americans.
5. Chocolate ___was drunk___ (drink) by the Aztecs.

B 🔄 How did things get done in the past in your country? Complete each sentence with the past passive form of the verb in parentheses and your own ideas.

1. People ___were told___ (tell) about important news by _Answer will vary_
2. Children ___were taught___ (teach) by _Answer will vary_
3. Clothes ___were made___ (make) by _Answer will vary_
4. Important books ___were published___ (publish) by _Answer will vary_
5. People ___were inspired___ (inspire) by _Answer will vary_

▲ An Inuit man builds an igloo.

Conversation

A 🔊 16 Close your books and listen to the conversation. What does Luisa want to find out? _if Carl thinks they need to study history_

Luisa: Hi, Carl. Can I ask you a question?
Carl: Sure. Go ahead.
Luisa: Do you think we really need to study history?
Carl: Of course we do! A lot of important things happened in the past.
Luisa: Like what?
Carl: Well, different systems of government were developed.
Luisa: OK, those are important. What else?
Carl: A lot of remarkable technology was invented—like the telephone.
Luisa: Yes, that's very important!
Carl: And scientific discoveries were made in the past, too.
Luisa: You're right. I do want to know more about the past.
Carl: Good—have fun in your history class!

B 🔄 Practice the conversation with a partner. Switch roles and practice again. Then make new conversations using your own ideas to answer Luisa's questions.

C 🔄 **GOAL CHECK** ✔ Compare today with the past

Talk to a partner. How were things done before the following services were developed, and how are they done now?

public transportation   city water systems   garbage collection service

Life in the Past   **113**

Talk About a Historical Wonder

Reading

A
- Have students look at the pictures and describe what they see. Have them read the title of the article and ask, *Who was the lord of the Mongols?* Elicit *Genghis Khan.*
- Have students read the directions and check the information they think is true.
- Have students compare and discuss their ideas with a partner. Encourage them to say why they think the information is true or not.
- Compare ideas as a class.

B
- Have students read the sentences. Point out the definitions in the footnotes.
- Have students read the article and decide if the sentences are *true* or *false*. Remind them to use the context to help them guess the meaning of new words.
- Have students compare answers with a partner.
- Check answers.
- Go over the article and answer any vocabulary questions.

C
- Have students read the questions and write down their opinions and reasons. Remind them to just write down key words/ideas, not complete sentences.
- Divide the class into pairs and have them discuss their answers to the questions.
- Compare answers and discuss the questions with the class.

D | **GOAL 4:** Talk About a Historical Wonder

Reading

A What do you know about Genghis Khan? Check (✓) the information you think is true. Compare your answers with your partner.

 ✓   He had a difficult childhood.

 ✓   He was a wise leader and a talented general.

_____ He lived in Central Asia in the eighteenth century.

 ✓   He conquered many kingdoms and destroyed their cities.

_____ His empire lasted for hundreds of years.

B Read the sentences and circle **T** for *true* or **F** for *false.*

1. After the Mongol attack, Samarkand was a ruined city.   (T)   F

2. The Mongol Empire covered only a small area.   T   (F)

3. Modern Mongolians think of Genghis Khan as an important leader.   (T)   F

4. Genghis Khan became the leader of his people when he was around 40 years old.   (T)   F

5. People haven't been able to find Genghis Khan's tomb because his soldiers burned it after he was buried.   T   (F)

C Discuss these questions with a partner. How was Central Asia different after the Mongol Empire? In your opinion, were the changes positive or negative? Give reasons for your answer.

For Your Information: Genghis Khan

In the early 13th century, Genghis Khan, the warrior emperor, succeeded in uniting warring tribes in Central Asia and established the Mongol empire, which stretched as far as Europe. Under the rule of Genghis Khan's descendants, this vast empire encompassed lands that are now Russia, China, Iran, and Iraq. Genghis Khan was known for his savagery; his warriors, known as the Golden Horde, were brutal in battle and in their dominance of the people in the lands they invaded. But Genghis Khan is also recognized for his military skills and for being a powerful ruler. For many years in Mongolia, under Communist rule, Genghis Khan and his role in Mongolia's history were ignored; however, in the Mongolia of today, he is considered a hero and a figure of national pride by many.

LORD OF THE
MONGOLS

When the Mongol leader Genghis Khan arrived in 1220, Samarkand was one of Central Asia's greatest cities, with about 200,000 people. Today, there is nothing left of the old city. A visitor can see only grass, ridges, and hills shaped by the wind.

Again and again in the thirteenth century, Mongol armies rode into Central Asia and destroyed its cities, killed its people, and took its treasure. The world has rarely seen so much destruction, but it built one of the world's greatest empires. By 1280, the Mongols controlled territory from the Yellow Sea to the Mediterranean.

The question people usually ask about the Mongols is: Were they only **raiders** and killers? Not in Mongolian eyes. In Mongolia, Genghis is like George Washington; he was the first ruler of united Mongolia. In China, his grandson Kublai is admired for unifying the country. It is also true that the Mongols killed without mercy. They killed opposing armies as well as civilians.

Genghis Khan was born in the 1160s. He was originally named Temujin. When Temujin was born, Mongolia had about thirty **nomadic tribes.** His father was the leader of a small tribe, but he was killed by another tribe when Temujin was only nine. Afterwards, the family struggled to survive.

Despite his difficult beginnings, Temujin grew to be a great **warrior.** He destroyed the enemy tribe that killed his father. In 1206, after many battles, Temujin became Genghis Khan, a name meaning "strong ruler" or "oceanic ruler." In other words, he was ruler of the world. He was about 40 years old.

In August 1227, Genghis died. He was probably 60. Stories say his body was buried in Mongolia, near a mountain called Burkhan Khaldun. Forty beautiful young women and forty horses were buried with him. A thousand horsemen are said to have ridden over the site until it could not be found. It still eludes people who are searching for it.

raider a person who suddenly attacks a place or group   **nomadic** people who move from place to place   **tribe** people with the same language, customs, and beliefs   **warrior** a person who fights and is known for having courage and skill

Many Mongolians are still nomadic and still live in an easily moveable *ger*.

After Reading

Web search: Have students search online using the term *Genghis Khan battles* and report back to the class on one of his famous battles. Tell them to answer the following questions in their report: *When? Where? Against who?*

Project: In small groups, have students research another important historical figure and prepare a poster or information sheet to share with the class.

Talk About a Historical Wonder

Communication

A
- Have students look at the picture and describe what they see. Elicit what they know about the Taj Mahal.
- Have students read the questions and look at the words in the box. Elicit the names of historical wonders in the students' country(ies).
- Divide the class into pairs and have them discuss the questions.
- Have several pairs share their ideas with the class.

Writing

A
- Have students read the information. Ask comprehension questions orally or have students answer them in writing, individually, or in pairs.
- Write the name of one of the New 7 Wonders on the board and have students tell you what they know about it. Write a few ideas on the board. Elicit adjectives to describe personal reactions to the historical site (*amazing, beautiful, impressive*, etc.). Then have students help you begin writing a paragraph about the site on the board. Include a sentence describing your reaction to the site.

B
- Have students research one of the New 7 Wonders and write their own paragraph. Provide vocabulary and help as necessary.

C | 🔄 **GOAL CHECK** ✔

- Divide the class into pairs and have them exchange paragraphs.
- Have students compare the sites they chose and share their reactions to each site.
- Have several students share what they learned from their partner with the class.

D **GOAL 4:** Talk About a Historical Wonder

Taj Mahal in Agra, Uttar Pradesh, India

Bernard Weber wanted to use modern technology to bring the people of the world closer together. He knew that the original Seven Wonders of the Ancient World were chosen by one person, and six of the wonders didn't even exist anymore, so he created a way to let the world determine the New 7 Wonders: an open election using the Internet and text messaging. Anyone could nominate a special site, and anyone could vote.

Millions of votes were cast, and on July 7, 2007, the seven winners were announced in Lisbon, Portugal. They include the Great Wall of China, the Colosseum in Rome, and the Taj Mahal in India. More recently, Weber's Internet-based project has used voting to choose the New 7 Wonders of nature and New 7 Wonders Cities.

Communication

A 🔄 Discuss the questions with a partner.

1. Which words describe your reaction to historical wonders? Explain your choices and add another word of your own.

   amazed   interested   proud   shocked   inspired   _____

2. Tell your partner about some of the historical wonders from your country. What amazing things did people do in the past?

Writing

A Read the information in the box about the New 7 Wonders of the World.

B Use the Internet to research one of the New 7 Wonders historical sites. Write a paragraph with interesting information about the site. Use your own words, including adjectives, to describe your reaction to the site.

C 🔄 **GOAL CHECK** ✔ **Talk about a historical wonder**

Share your paragraph with a partner. Talk about the information that is interesting or surprising to you.

116 Unit 9

Teacher Tip: Sharing students' work

There are a number of ways that students can share their work with their classmates:

- Give oral presentations in front of the class.
- Make large posters to display in front of the class.

- Tape students' papers around the classroom walls and allow time for students to walk around and read their classmates' work.
- Photocopy students' papers into a class magazine/newspaper and make a copy for each student.

Albert Lin in Mongolia

Video Journal: *Searching for Genghis Khan*

Before You Watch

A ⚡ Discuss the questions with a partner. Who is Genghis Khan? Where is he from, and why is he famous? Where do people think Genghis Khan is buried? How is Albert Lin going to find his tomb?

B Fill in the blanks with the correct words from the box.

1. Albert Lin is using the most advanced, or *cutting-edge*, technology to find Genghis Khan's tomb.

2. Genghis Khan was buried in a part of Mongolia that is called the _Forbidden_ Zone, where very few outsiders visit.

3. Because many Mongolians believe Genghis's tomb is ___sacred___, or holy, Lin and his team can't dig there.

4. Instead, they are using ___sensors___, which detect heat, light, sound, and motion.

> cutting-edge
> Forbidden   sacred
> sensors

While You Watch

A Read the sentences and circle **T** for *true* or **F** for *false*.

1. Albert Lin and his team are working only from the United States to find Genghis's tomb. T **(F)**

2. Lin always planned to be an explorer. T **(F)**

3. Lin wants to dig up Genghis's tomb and remove the treasure inside. T **(F)**

4. Many non-scientists are helping with the research by examining satellite images. **(T)** F

After You Watch / Communication

A ⚡ Make predictions with a partner about how new technology can be used in exploration and research. Think about exploration on land, under the sea, and in space.

Life in the Past **117**

Video Journal: *Searching for Genghis Khan*

Before You Watch

A • Have students look at the picture and describe what they see. Ask, *What is he doing?*

• Divide the class into pairs and have them discuss the questions.

• Compare answers with the class.

B • Have students read the sentences and complete them with the words in the box.

• Have students compare answers with a partner.

• Check answers.

While You Watch

A • Have students read the sentences.

• Have students watch the video and choose *true* or *false* for each sentence.

• Play the video.

• Have students compare answers with a partner.

• Check answers. Play the video again as necessary.

After You Watch / Communication

A • Have students read the directions.

• Divide the class into pairs and have them make a list of predictions for each type of exploration.

• Compare predictions as a class, and write lists on the board.

For Your Information: Mongolia

Mongolia is a landlocked country dominated by sparsely populated steppe and semi-desert. It is located in East-Central Asia, with Russia to the north and China to the south, east, and west. Its geography and climate are harsh, and traditionally Mongols led a nomadic or semi-nomadic life herding livestock. Nowadays, however, about a third of the population lives in the capital city, Ulan Bator. The traditional nomadic lifestyle is threatened by climate change and urbanization. Mongolia has been under both Chinese and Soviet rule, but after a democratic revolution in 1990, Mongolia moved to a multi-party system and a free-market economy. Since then, the economy has struggled and the people have suffered from poverty and economic instability. However, due to foreign investment in mineral mining projects, Mongolia is considered to have one of the fastest growing economies in the world.

Life Lessons from Big Cats

Before You Watch

A · Have students look at the picture and discuss the questions with a partner.

· Compare answers with the class and write their ideas on the board.

B · Go over the words in the box. Have students complete the paragraph using the words. Remind them to change the form of the verbs when necessary.

· Have students compare answers with a partner.

· Check answers.

C · Have students read the directions and look at the pictures on page 119. Have them check the information they think they will hear in the TED Talk.

· Have students compare answers with a partner.

· Compare answers with the class. Write their ideas about what they will hear about in the TED Talk on the board.

While You Watch

A · Have students read the three possible main ideas. Tell them to circle the main idea as they watch the talk.

· Play the talk.

· Have students compare their answer with a partner.

· Check answer.

TEDTALKS

Beverly and Dereck Joubert Documentary Filmmakers/ Conservationists, National Geographic Explorers-in-Residence
LIFE LESSONS FROM BIG CATS

Before You Watch

A ↻ Look at the picture and answer the questions with a partner.

> Beverly and Dereck Jouberts' idea worth spreading is that not only do big cats like lions and leopards have big personalities, but getting to know them can help protect Africa. Watch the Jouberts' full TED Talk on TED.com.

1. What kind of animal is in the photo?

2. Where do these animals live?

3. What else do you know about these animals and their habitat?

B Look at the words in the box. Complete the paragraph with the correct word. Not all words will be used.

> **collectively** *adj.* shared or done by a group of people
> **condone** *v.* to allow (something that is considered wrong) to continue
> **crash** *v.* to go down very suddenly and quickly
> **disrupt** *v.* to cause (something) to be unable to continue in the normal way
> **pride** *n.* a group of lions
> **revenue stream** *n.* a flow of money that is made by or paid to a business or an organization

Africa's big cats are endangered, and we are all (1) ___collectively___ responsible. Soon, the (2) ___pride___ of lions may disappear. Because we (3) ___condone___ hunting and other activities that put them at risk, their numbers

have (4) ___crashed___ in the last 50 years. And it's not only the big cats that are in danger—ecotourism brings in a large (5) ___revenue stream___ to Africa. If the cats disappear, so will the money and jobs.

C Beverly and Dereck Joubert are wildlife photographers who publicize the problem of endangered big cats. What do you predict you will hear in their TED Talk? Look at the pictures on the next page. Check (✓) the information you predict you will hear.

✓ **1.** They have spent five years watching a leopard cub grow up.

___ **2.** They are also researching the behavior of giraffes and elephants.

✓ **3.** Their investigations have shown that these lions are essential.

✓ **4.** Lion bones are being sold.

While You Watch

A ▶ Watch the TED Talk. Circle the main idea.

1. It's necessary to study big cats over many years.

2. If the big cats disappear, many other species may disappear.

3. Beverly and Dereck Joubert believe that big cats are beautiful.

Viewing Tip

Remind students that focusing on just the main idea when they first watch the talk will help them. If they try to understand everything, they may feel overwhelmed and frustrated. Tell them that they can focus on understanding specific details when they listen the second time, but it is important to understand the main idea first. Listening for gist (main idea) and listening for specific details are two strategies students should be aware of so that they can decide which strategy is best in a given situation.

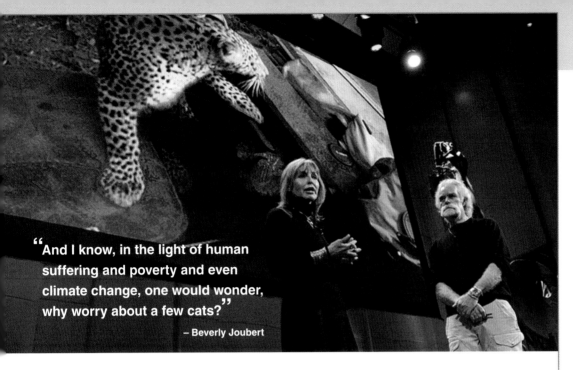

> "And I know, in the light of human suffering and poverty and even climate change, one would wonder, why worry about a few cats?"
>
> – Beverly Joubert

B • Have students read the captions and look at the pictures. Tell them to match the captions to the pictures as they watch the talk again.

• Play the talk again.

• Have students compare answers with a partner.

• Check answers. Play the talk again as necessary.

• Go back to the predictions students made in **Before You Watch C.** Ask, *Were your predictions correct?*

B ▶ Watch the TED Talk again and match the photo that illustrates the TED Talk to the correct caption.

__2__ **a.** If a male lion is killed, the members of his pride may also die.

__3__ **b.** The Jouberts have discovered that some lions hunt in the water.

__4__ **c.** Legadema trusts the Jouberts and lets them come close to her.

__1__ **d.** The Jouberts have studied a young leopard named Legadema since she was a baby.

1.

2.

3.

4.

119

For Your Information: Beverly and Dereck Joubert

Beverly and Dereck Joubert are wildlife photographers and documentary filmmakers who have been studying and documenting wildlife for more than 25 years. They have won five Emmys and many other awards for their films and photography. The Jouberts are National Geographic Explorers in Residence, based in Botswana, and in this role are able to influence public policy and raise awareness about nature, wildlife, and the importance of conservation work. Currently, they are focused on raising awareness about the decline of the big cat population in Africa; they founded the organization Big Cat Initiative to campaign for greater understanding and protection of these amazing animals. If we lose the big cat population, we will lose other species, too, as a result. They urge us to strengthen our connection with nature and not be complacent about the decline of such animals.

After You Watch

A • Have students read the summary and complete it with the words in the box.

• Have them compare answers with a partner.

• Check answers.

B • Have students read the numbers and match them to the phrases according to the information given in the talk.

• Have them compare answers with a partner.

• Check answers.

C • Have students read the statements and circle the ones which express ideas from the talk.

• Have them compare answers with a partner.

• Check answers.

TEDTALKS

Beverly and Dereck Joubert Documentary Filmmakers/
Conservationists, National Geographic Explorers-in-Residence
LIFE LESSONS FROM BIG CATS

After You Watch

A Complete the summary with the words in the box.

> extinction passionate photographing respect survive

Beverly and Dereck Joubert are (1) _passionate_ about protecting the African wilderness. They have spent many years studying and (2) _photographing_ big cats. In the last 50 years, these cats have been pushed to the edge of (3) _extinction_ by hunters. The Jouberts believe that if the big cats are viewed with (4) _respect_, they can survive. And if the big cats (5) _survive_, they can help us maintain our connection to nature and to other human beings.

B Match the phrases to the information from the video.

_c_ **1.** number of lions alive now

_d_ **2.** number of leopards left in the wild

_e_ **3.** years the Jouberts have been filming big cats

_a_ **4.** amount of ecotourism revenue stream

_b_ **5.** number of years the Jouberts followed Legadema

a. $80 billion

b. 5

c. 20,000

d. 50,000

e. 28

C Read the statements below. Circle the ones that paraphrase information in the TED Talk.

(1.) Many kinds of big cats live in the African wilderness.

2. It's important to protect big cats and the humans who live near them.

(3.) There used to be more than 450,000 lions in Africa.

(4.) It is wrong to hunt and kill lions for sport.

(5.) If we aren't connected to nature, we will lose hope.

Project

Beverly and Dereck Joubert want to protect the African wilderness. Use their ideas to write a letter in support of big cat conservation to the editor of a newspaper in your country. Follow these steps.

120

D 🔄 Work with a partner to find facts and opinions from the TED Talk that you can include. Complete the chart below. Choose the ones that support your idea the best.

FACT	OPINION

E 🔄 Write your letter. Use the frame below to organize your ideas. Then show your letter to a different partner. Is your opinion easy to understand? Does he or she have ideas for improvement?

To the Editor:

I am writing to (1) _____. In my opinion, (2) _____. If we don't

(3) _____, we will (4) _____. It is also important to (5) _____. We

will (6) _____ if we (7) _____.

Finally, I think (8) _____. If (9) _____, then (10) _____.

Yours sincerely,

_____

Challenge! 👥 Beverly and Dereck Joubert are working to ensure the long-term survival of big cats. Find out more about the Big Cats Initiative at TED.com and explore ways you can get involved. Share what you learn with the class.

D • Have students read the instructions under the picture. Ask, *What newspaper could you write to?*

• Write on the board:
It is wrong to hunt and kill lions for sport.
The number of lions has dropped from 450,000 to 20,000.
Ask, *Which is a fact and which is an opinion?*

• Divide the class into pairs. Have them complete the chart with facts and opinions from the talk that they can use in their letter to support their ideas.

• Compare answers with the class and complete a chart on the board.

E • Individually, have students write their letter using the outline given. Monitor and provide help as necessary.

• Have students exchange their letter with a partner. Have them give each other feedback on the clarity of their opinion and on how to improve their letter. Encourage them to help each other with spelling and grammar difficulties.

• Have students make improvements to their letter.

Challenge

• Individually or in pairs, have students find out more information about the Jouberts' Big Cat Initiative. (This can be done in or outside of class depending on resources and time.) Have them find out how they can get involved in the project.

• Have each student/pair share what they found out with the class.

Ideas Worth Sharing

• With books closed, have students share what they remember about the Jouberts and their work. Ask, *What is their message? Why do they think understanding big cats is important?* Write their ideas on the board.

• Have students go back to the Ideas Worth Sharing box on page 118. Remind them that they can watch the whole talk at TED.com to help them develop their listening skills.

Travel

About the Photo

This photo shows hikers at the Sossusvlei sand dunes in the Namib-Naukluft National Park in the Namib Desert, Namibia. In the foreground are camel thorn trees and in the background the sand dunes, tinted orange by the early morning sun. The photo was taken by National Geographic photographer Frans Lanting, a wildlife photographer who uses his photography to portray wildlife and our relationship with nature and thus raise awareness of conservation issues. Lanting has received worldwide recognition and many awards for his work as both a photographer and conservationist.

- Introduce the theme of the unit. Ask students, *Where have you traveled? Where would you like to travel in the future?*

- Direct students' attention to the picture. Have students describe what they see.

- Have students work with a partner to answer the questions.

- Compare answers with the class.

- Ask these questions orally or by writing them on the board for students to answer in pairs: *What kind of activities do people do when they go on trips? Have you done any of these things?*

- Go over the Unit Goals with the class. Explain that *pros and cons* means "advantages and disadvantages."

- For each goal, elicit any words students already know and write them on the board; for example, vacation/trip vocabulary from the activities discussed, forms of transportation, etc.

UNIT
10
Travel

Dead camelthorn trees with hikers in Namib-Naukluft National Park, Namibia

122

UNIT 10 GOALS	Grammar	Vocabulary	Listening
• Talk about preparations for a trip • Talk about different kinds of vacations • Use English at the airport • Discuss the pros and cons of tourism	Modals of necessity *I **must** make a reservation.* Modals of prohibition *You **must not** take pictures here.*	Travel preparations Vacations At the airport	Listening for general understanding Conversations: Vacations

Look at the photo, answer the questions:

1 Where do you think these people are? What are they doing?

2 What type of trip would you like to take? Why?

UNIT 10 GOALS

1. Talk about preparations for a trip

2. Talk about different kinds of vacations

3. Use English at the airport

4. Discuss the pros and cons of tourism

123

Unit Theme Overview

- Tourism is believed to be the world's largest industry. If the tourist industry were a country, it would have an "economy" second in size only to the economy of the United States. International travel has increased exponentially in recent decades. The number of international arrivals increased from 25 million in 1972 to 528 million in 1996, according to the World Tourism Organization. In 2012, according to the International Air Transport Association, nearly three billion passengers traveled on flights of its member airlines. More and more people are traveling farther and farther from their homes.

- Travel has many benefits for the people who do it and the workers who serve them. Tourists can enjoy a change of scene and learn about other cultures and environments. And, of course, tourism provides millions of much-needed jobs in developing countries. But there is also a potential negative side to tourism—when it harms the natural environment and causes economic problems. Today, people around the world are calling for the development of new kinds of tourism that will benefit travelers, workers, and the environment.

- In this unit, students look at travel from both a personal perspective—discussing preparations for different kinds of trips and learning language for air travel—and a social perspective—considering the impact of tourism on a place.

Speaking	Reading	Writing	Video Journal
Planning a dream vacation Making your way through the airport **Pronunciation:** Reduction of *have to, has to, got to*	**National Geographic:** Tourists or Trees?	Writing a paragraph about the positive impact of tourism	**National Geographic:** Adventure Capital of the World

Talk About Preparations for a Trip

Vocabulary

- Introduce the topic. Ask, *Are you busy before you go on a trip? What do you do to prepare for a trip?*

- Go over the phrases in the box, explaining the words in bold as necessary.
- Have students write each phrase under the correct picture.
- Check answers.

- Divide the class into pairs, and have them talk about their preparations for a trip. Remind students to tell their partner where they went on their last trip. Point out the Word Focus box: *We make plane, train, and hotel reservations. We buy plane, train, and bus tickets.*
- Have several students tell the class about where their partner went and what he or she did to prepare for the trip.

Grammar

- Go over the information in the chart. Then tell students, *I'm going to (England). Do I need a passport?* Elicit, *You must have a passport.* Continue with a *visa/vaccinations/a lot of money,* and so on.

- Have students read the sentences and circle the correct modal.
- Have students compare answers with a partner.
- Check answers.

Vocabulary

 Label each picture with the correct phrase in the box.

> talk to the **travel agent**
> apply for a **passport**
> apply for a **visa**
> buy a **ticket**
> make a **reservation**
> check the **itinerary**
> get **sightseeing** information
> get a **vaccination**

get a vaccination | get sightseeing information | apply for a visa | talk to the travel agent

buy a ticket | apply for a passport | make a reservation | check the itinerary

 What did you do before your last trip? Use vocabulary from exercise **A.**

Grammar: Expressing necessity

Use *must* + verb in writing or formal speaking to say that something is necessary or is a rule.	Travelers **must apply** for a passport at least six weeks in advance.
Use *have to* or *need to* + verb in informal speaking. Use *have (got) to* + verb for extra emphasis.	We **have to buy** our tickets. I **need to get** a vaccination. Jerry **has got to make** a hotel reservation soon!
Use *don't have to* + verb to say that something is not necessary.	You **don't have to buy** a ticket for a baby. Babies can ride the train for free.
Have to and *need to* can be used with different verb tenses.	We **had to show** them our passports. Someone **will need to** carry Lin's bag.

Circle the correct option for each sentence.

1. Everyone (got to | (needs to)) get a vaccination before the trip.
2. You can't change your reservation online. You ((must) | will must) talk to a travel agent.
3. Last week, we (need to | (had to)) apply for a visa.
4. To get a driver's license, you ((must) | don't have to) pass a driving test.
5. Abdul ((has got to) | have to) apply for a passport now!
6. You (haven't to | (don't have to)) make reservations for the train.

Word Focus

a **plane/train/hotel reservation**
a **plane/train/bus ticket**

Word Bank: More travel vocabulary

alarm clock	map
backpack	money belt
calculator	phrase book
camera	sandals
first aid kit	suitcase
foreign currency	sunscreen
guidebook	swimsuit

Grammar: Expressions of necessity

Must/have to/have got to are all used to say that something is necessary. *Must* is the most formal of the three structures, while *have got to* is mainly used in speaking. To express lack of necessity, *don't/doesn't have to* are used. Students occasionally confuse this structure with *must not,* which expresses prohibition (and will be taught in **Lesson C** of this unit).

Ayers Rock, Australia

You don't have to tell the company where you're going.
You must/have to pay with a credit card.

B 🔄 Look at the car rental rules in the chart. Work with a partner to make sentences using expressions of necessity.

You don't have to make a reservation.
You must/have to be 25 years old.

C 🔄 What are the rules in your English class? Write a list in your notebook. Use expressions of necessity. Compare your list with a partner's list.

1. You *have to* hand in your homework.

Car rental rules	
have a driver's license	☑
make a reservation	☒
tell the company where you're going	☒
be 25 years old	☑
pay with a credit card	☑

You have to have a driver's license.

Real Language

A *hassle* is an informal word for "problem" or "trouble."

Conversation

A 🔊 17 Close your book and listen to the conversation. Where is Peter going on his vacation? *South Africa*

Ed: So, Peter, when are you taking your vacation?
Peter: In September. I'm going to South Africa.
Ed: Wow, South Africa! What a great trip!
Peter: It will be. But first I have to get a new passport, and I have to apply for a visa.
Ed: That sounds like a hassle!
Peter: It's not so bad. I can get the visa from my travel agent. And I don't have to get any vaccinations.

B 🔄 Practice the conversation with a partner. Switch roles and practice again.

C 🔄 Look at the chart. Make new conversations about these countries.

Do travelers need . . .	a passport?	a visa?	vaccinations?
Turkey	Yes	Yes (online)	No
Australia	Yes	Yes (from the embassy)	No
The Philippines	Yes	No	No

D 🔄 **GOAL CHECK** ✅ **Talk about preparations for a trip**

Talk to a partner. Say where you want to go and what you need to do to prepare for the trip.

Grammar Practice: Modals of necessity

Have students work with a partner to write five rules for a sport they both know, using *must/have to/have got to*. If necessary, give examples:

Tennis: *You must hit the ball over the net. You don't have to wear white clothes.*

Call on student pairs to read their rules to the class or have them make posters and display them in the classroom.

B • Point out that many people like to rent a car when they take a trip, but car rental companies have many rules.
• Have students work with a partner to make a sentence about each rule.
• Check answers.

C • Have students work individually to make a list of at least five rules that you have in your English class.
• Assign new pairs and have them compare their lists.
• Call on students to read a rule to the class and write them on the board. Then discuss any surprising ones.

Conversation

A • Have students close their books. Write the question on the board: *Where is Peter going on his vacation?*
• Play the recording. 🔊 17
• Check answers.
• Go over the definition in the Real Language box.

B • Play or read the conversation again for the class to repeat.
• Practice the conversation with the class in chorus.
• Have students practice the conversation with a partner, then switch roles and practice it again.

C • Go over the information in the chart and ask students what they know about these places. Then have students work with a partner to make new conversations modeled on the one in **A**.
• Have pairs present a conversation to the class.

D 🔄 **GOAL CHECK** ✅

• Divide the class into pairs and have them discuss a "dream" trip and how they will prepare for it.

Talk About Different Kinds of Vacations

Listening

- Tell students they are going to hear about three different vacation plans.

A • Have students read the descriptions and tell a partner which kind of vacation they would most enjoy.

- Survey the class to find out which is the most popular kind of vacation.

- Have pairs talk about places for each kind of vacation. Compare answers with the class.

B • Tell students to listen to the interviews and find the names of the countries.

- Play the recording one or more times. 🔊 18

- Have students compare answers with a partner.

- Check answers.

C • Tell students to listen again to find the type of vacation. Review the types of vacations in **A**.

- Play the recording one or more times. 🔊 18

- Check answers.

D • Have students decide which of the three vacations they heard about sound most enjoyable. Have them tell their partner about their choice of vacation and explain why.

- Discuss the most popular vacation and why it was the favorite.

Pronunciation

A • Go over the pronunciation of *have to, has to,* and *got to.* Emphasize that they are always spelled this way—we do NOT write *hafta, hasta,* or *gotta.* Tell students to listen to the pronunciation.

- Play the recording one or more times. 🔊 19

B • Have students take turns reading the sentences with a partner.

B GOAL 2: Talk About Different Kinds of Vacations

Listening

A 🔁 Read the information. Tell your partner which kind of vacation you would enjoy the most. Explain.

1. Adventure vacation	2. Relaxing vacation	3. Learning vacation
Try exciting sports, like mountain climbing, bicycling, and skiing. Have experiences to tell your friends about.	Go to a beautiful place to rest and relax. Sleep late, read, listen to music, and enjoy the scenery.	Learn to do something new, like art or music, or take a class in a subject that interests you.

B 🔊 18 Listen to three people talking about their vacations. Which country are they going to?

Carla: _Italy_

Marcus: _Thailand_

Julie: _New Zealand_

C 🔊 18 Listen again. Which kind of vacation will they take?

Carla: _learning vacation_

Marcus: _relaxing vacation_

Julie: _adventure vacation_

D 🔁 Which of these vacations would you enjoy the most? Explain your reasons to your partner.

Pronunciation: Reduction of *have to, has to, got to*

A 🔊 19 Listen to the pronunciation of *have to, has to,* and *got to.* Notice how they sound like *hafta, hasta,* and *gotta* in fast speech.

I've **got to** finish my homework. (sounds like /ga-ɾə/)
He **has to** clean the house. (sounds like /hæ-stə/)
Do you **have to** work tomorrow? (sounds like /hæ-ftə/)

B 🔁 Practice these sentences with a partner. Pay attention to the pronunciation of *have to, has to,* and *got to.*

1. Sorry, I have to leave now.
2. I've got to apply for a visa.
3. Rosa has to pack her suitcase.
4. They've got to stay after class.
5. He has to be there at six o'clock.
6. Do you have to make a reservation?
7. You've got to answer my questions.
8. Tomorrow, I have to go to the bank.

126 Unit 10

For Your Information: Types of vacations

Adventure vacations are increasingly popular. Activities in this category are trekking (long-distance hiking), whitewater rafting, mountain biking, ice climbing, and scuba diving. Popular destinations include New Zealand, Australia, and the Himalayas.

Relaxing vacations are common. People travel to places such as Hawaii, Southeast Asia, and various Caribbean islands for these vacations.

Learning vacations tend to be more popular with older adults. Examples are cooking schools in Italy or France, and art and photography workshops in the United States and Canada.

Adventure tour in Africa! Travel from Egypt to South Africa in a truck and visit twenty countries. You'll see wildlife and learn about African cultures.

Communication

You and a partner have won a dream vacation in a contest. Read about the three different trips.

Live with a family in London, and take English classes at a language school with students from many countries. Every weekend, you'll take a trip to a famous place.

Stay in a beach house! Swim, relax, or just do nothing. The house has a beautiful garden with a view of the sea, and a chef will cook all of your meals.

A ⟳ Talk with a partner about the three trips and choose which one you will take together.

B ⟳ What do you have to do before this trip? Think of five things.

C ⟳ What will you take along? List fifteen things.

D 👥 GOAL CHECK ✔ **Talk about different kinds of vacations**

Get together with another pair of students. Tell them about your plans. Why did you choose this trip instead of the other two? Explain your reasons.

> If we go to Africa, we'll have to get lots of vaccinations!

> I'll bring a digital camera to take pictures of the animals.

Travel **127**

Communication

- Tell students that in this activity, they are going to choose one of three different vacation trips with a partner. Go over the information about the three trips.

A • Divide the class into pairs. Have them discuss the three trips and then choose the trip they would like to take together.

B • Have students work with the same partners to think about and then list the things they will need to do to prepare for the trip.

C • Tell student pairs to make a list of 15 things they will need for their trip, including any special clothing.

D 👥 GOAL CHECK ✔

- Combine student pairs to form groups of four. Have students talk about where they are going, what they need to do before they go, and what they will take with them. Remind them to explain to each other why they chose that vacation and not one of the others.

- With the class, discuss different groups' decisions. Talk about any unusual items they've decided to take along.

Expansion Activity

As a follow-up to the communication activity, have student pairs imagine their trip and then write a letter or e-mail to their classmates about what they did. Have pairs exchange letters or e-mails. Collect for revision afterwards.

Use English at the Airport

Language Expansion

- Ask students, *Where is the nearest airport? Have you been there? What is it like?*

A
- Go over the vocabulary items with the class.
- Have students number the items in the illustration.
- Check answers.

B
- Have students fill in the blanks with the vocabulary from **A.**
- Have students compare answers with a partner.
- Check answers.

C
- Divide the class into pairs and have them tell each other about an experience at an airport—traveling, meeting someone who is arriving—or a scene from a movie (if students have no personal experience with airports).
- Have several students tell the class about their partner's experience.

Grammar

- Tell students, *You can take most things on an airplane, but you must not take anything dangerous.* For example, you must not take a gun on a plane. And you can't take big animals. Elicit other sentences with *must not/can't* for things that are not allowed on planes.
- Go over the information in the chart.

C **GOAL 3:** Use English at the Airport

Language Expansion: At the airport

A Write the numbers of the words from the box in the correct circles.

1. **departures**	
2. **security check**	
3. **gate**	
4. **terminal**	
5. **boarding pass**	
6. **airline agent**	
7. **baggage claim**	
8. **carry-on bag**	

B Complete the sentences. Use the words from exercise **A.**

1. At the ___security check___, officers look inside your bags.
2. You can take a small ___carry-on bag___ on the plane with you.
3. After your flight, get your bags from the ___baggage claim___.
4. The ___airline agent___ looks at your ticket and gives you a seat.
5. When you are going somewhere, you go to the ___departures___ area.
6. The ___terminal___ is the big building at the airport.
7. The ___gate___ is a door where you get on the airplane.
8. Your ___boarding pass___ is a paper with your seat number.

C Describe an experience at an airport. Use words from exercise **A.**

Grammar: Expressing prohibition

Expressing prohibition		
You	**must not** **can't**	bring a knife on the plane.

Must not and *can't* mean that something is not allowed. There is a law or rule against it.
*This meaning is different from *don't have to.*
You **must not** take pictures here. = pictures are not allowed
You **don't have to** take pictures here. = pictures are OK but not necessary

---

Word Bank: On the plane

aisle	lavatory
beverage cart	overhead bin
captain	passenger
emergency exit	seat
flight attendant	seat belt
in-flight movie	tray table

Grammar: Modals of prohibition

Both *must not* (*mustn't*) and *can't* are used to express the idea that an action is not allowed. *Must not* is stronger and more formal than *can't.*

A Write sentences with *must*, *must not*, and *can't* about the signs on the right.

1. You can't/must not smoke here.
2. You can't/must not bring scissors or a knife here.
3. You must show your passport.
4. You must leave/throw away fruit and plants here.
5. You can't/must not take pictures here.

B Complete the sentences about things to remember when going to the airport. Use your own ideas.

1. You have to _____ .
2. You can't _____ .
3. You must _____ .
4. You don't have to _____ .

Conversation

A 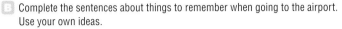 **20** Close your book and listen to the conversation. What time will the traveler get on the plane? 10:15

Check-in agent:	Good afternoon. Where are you flying to today?
Traveler:	To Caracas. Here's my ticket.
Check-in agent:	Thank you. Would you like a window seat or an aisle seat?
Traveler:	A window seat, please.
Check-in agent:	And do you have any bags to check?
Traveler:	Just one. And this is my carry-on bag.
Check-in agent:	OK. Here's your boarding pass. You're in seat 27A. Boarding time is 10:15, but you must be at the gate 15 minutes before that.
Traveler:	I have a question. Is there a restaurant after the security check?
Check-in agent:	Yes, there are two. Thank you, and enjoy your flight!

B Practice the conversation with a partner. Switch roles and practice it again.

C Make new conversations with this information.

1. Seoul | aisle seat | two bags | 15C | 2:30 pm | a place to buy a newspaper
2. London | window seat | two bags | 30E | 4:00 pm | a pharmacy

D **GOAL CHECK** ✔ **Use English at the airport**

Pretend a partner is a foreigner at your local airport. Ask and answer questions about what you have to do to board your plane.

Travel **129**

Margin notes:

A
- Have students write one sentence for each picture.
- Have students compare answers with a partner.
- Check answers.

B
- Have students work individually or in pairs to write sentences.
- Compare answers with the class.

Conversation

A
- Have students close their books. Write the question on the board: *What time will the traveler get on the plane?*
- Play the recording. **◀))** **20**
- Check answers.

B
- Play or read the conversation again for the class to repeat.
- Practice the conversation with the class in chorus.
- Have students practice the conversation with a partner, then switch roles and practice it again.

C
- Have students work with partners to make new conversations modeled on the one in **A**.
- Call on student pairs to present a conversation to the class.

D **GOAL CHECK** ✔
- Divide the class into pairs and assign each student a role: traveler or local person. If some students are not very familiar with the local airport, discuss with the class what people need to do at the airport. Then have pairs role-play the situation and switch roles to practice it again.

Grammar Practice: Modals of prohibition

Have students work with a partner to list three things that travelers *must not* (*mustn't*) and *can't* do in a particular place—in their country or another country. Give them an example, such as *You must not chew gum in Singapore. It's against the law.* Call on students to read a sentence to the class.

Discuss the Pros and Cons of Tourism

Reading

- Introduce the idea of pros and cons—advantages and disadvantages.

A
- Divide the class into pairs and have them discuss the questions.
- Compare answers with the class.
- Tell students they are going to read about a country that has millions of tourists every year. Ask what, if anything, they know about Nepal.
- Point out the vocabulary that is defined in the footnotes.
- Have students read the article. Tell them to circle any words they don't understand. Remind them to try to guess the meaning of new words from the context.
- Go over the article with the class, answering any questions from the students about vocabulary.

B
- Tell students to read the article again and find the information to answer the questions.
- Have students compare answers with a partner.
- Check answers.

C
- Tell students to match the sentence parts to complete the reasons.
- Have students compare answers with a partner.
- Check answers.

Reading

A 🔄 Discuss these questions with a partner.

1. Which places in your country get the most tourists?

2. Do the tourists cause any problems?

B Find the information in the text.

1. What did Khumbu look like 50 years ago?

   a. <u>thick forests</u>
   b. <u>mountains covered with red and</u>
      <u>pink flowers</u>

2. What does much of Khumbu look like today? <u>a desert</u>

3. What problems are caused by tourists in Khumbu?

   a. <u>trails are destroyed</u>

   b. <u>crowded guesthouses</u>
   c. <u>leave water bottles and soda</u>
      <u>cans everywhere</u>

   d. <u>deforestation</u>

4. What actions are people taking in Khumbu?

   a. <u>a program to sell cheap kerosene</u>

   b. <u>planting a million trees</u>

C Match the columns to complete the reasons.

1. Tourists visit Khumbu <u>d</u>	a. because it's too expensive.
2. More tourists go to Khumbu now <u>e</u>	b. because they want hot baths and foreign food.
3. The forests in Khumbu are gone <u>c</u>	c. because the wood was used for tourists.
4. Tourists use a lot of wood <u>b</u>	d. because the mountains are beautiful.
5. People don't burn kerosene <u>a</u>	e. because it's easy to get there.

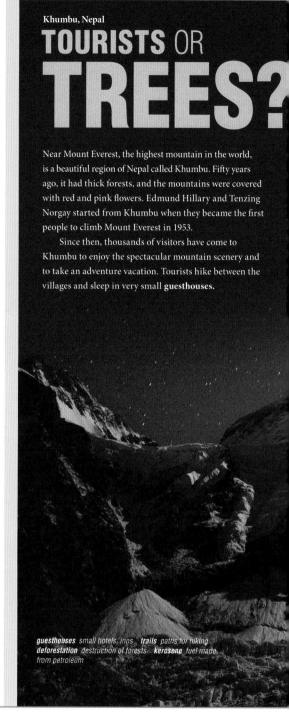

Khumbu, Nepal

TOURISTS OR TREES?

Near Mount Everest, the highest mountain in the world, is a beautiful region of Nepal called Khumbu. Fifty years ago, it had thick forests, and the mountains were covered with red and pink flowers. Edmund Hillary and Tenzing Norgay started from Khumbu when they became the first people to climb Mount Everest in 1953.

Since then, thousands of visitors have come to Khumbu to enjoy the spectacular mountain scenery and to take an adventure vacation. Tourists hike between the villages and sleep in very small **guesthouses.**

guesthouses small hotels, inns trails paths for hiking deforestation destruction of forests kerosene fuel made from petroleum

For Your Information: Nepal

Nepal is a small country in the Himalayas with a population of about 29 million people. The people belong to many different ethnic groups. Nine major languages are spoken there, along with many minor ones. The geography of this small country is very diverse, ranging from hot, humid jungles, to a hilly region, to the Himalaya Mountains. Mount Everest is located on the border with Tibet. Nepal is a poor country with very few natural resources, and tourism plays a very important role in the economy. One study found that 65 percent of the families in the Khumbu region received income from tourism.

Now, however, much of Khumbu has become a desert, partly because over 25,000 tourists pass through every year. Most of them arrive by small plane from Kathmandu, the capital. In the past, the airport there was just a grassy field, but in 2000, a new terminal was built to allow planes and helicopters to bring in more visitors.

"We must reduce the number of tourists," says one local man. "They destroy the **trails** when they all walk in the same place. The guesthouses are crowded. People drop their water bottles and soda cans everywhere."

But the biggest problem of tourism is **deforestation.** Khumbu has lost most of its trees. They were cut down to build tea houses and to use for firewood.

"Tourists don't think about the problems they cause," says one scientist. "Especially about the wood that is used to cook their foreign food and heat water for their baths. One tourist uses as much wood in a day as five local families." Now local people have to walk many miles to find firewood.

One possible solution is to cook and heat water with **kerosene,** but it's too expensive for many local people. "The government has got to distribute kerosene to local people," says the scientist. "It's the only way to save the forest."

People in Nepal are taking action. One group has started a program to sell cheap kerosene. Another group, the Himalayan Trust started by Edmund Hillary, has planted more than a million trees in Khumbu. This will help to save the land and to produce wood products that people can sell. In 30 years, Khumbu may have forests and flowers again.

Climbers ascend through the Khumbu icefall on their way to the summit.

Travel 131

After Reading

Web search: Have students do an online search with the term *ecotourism* and the name of a country to find out about environmentally sound tourism programs in another country. Ask them to present what they learned to a small group or to the whole class.

Project: Have students work in pairs or groups to make a poster with ideas for how foreign visitors can be good tourists in their countries.

Discuss the Pros and Cons of Tourism

Communication

A • Have students look at the picture and describe what they see. Have students look at the pictures of the two people and read their opinions about tourism. Ask, *Which person thinks tourism is good for Venice?*

• Divide the class into pairs and have them take turns explaining one of the opinions. Point out the example in the speech bubble. Have students add more details using their own ideas.

Writing

A • Divide the class into groups of three or four. Have them choose six places that get a lot of tourism, and discuss why they are popular. Tell students to draw a two-column chart. Put the names of the six places in the first column and the reasons why people like to visit them in the second.

• Compare charts with the class.

B • Copy the chart onto the board. Elicit the pros and cons of tourism from the class and complete the chart.

C • Have students write about how to be a good tourist in another country. Remind them to use a clear topic sentence and to explain each idea they mention.

• Have students exchange papers with a partner. Ask them to mark corrections and suggestions for improvements on their partner's paper.

• If desired, have students rewrite their papers, and collect for grading.

D **GOAL CHECK** ✔

• Divide the class into groups of three. Have students read their papers to their group and compare their ideas.

• Compare ideas as a class.

D | **GOAL 4:** Discuss the Pros and Cons of Tourism

Grand Canal at night in Venice, Italy

What does tourism bring to Venice?
• money (shops, hotels, restaurants, etc.)
• energy and activity
• culture from other places

What does tourism bring to Venice?
• crowds, traffic, pollution
• higher prices (food, housing, etc.)
• rude behavior

The older person thinks tourism brings money to Venice. Tourists love to go shopping for souvenirs, and they stay in hotels, and . . .

Communication

A 🔄 Look at each person's picture and opinion. Explain one person's viewpoint to your partner. Add details using your own ideas.

Writing

A ♻ In your notebook, list six places in the world that get a lot of tourism every year. Discuss why people like to visit these places.

B ♻ Brainstorm several positive and negative aspects of tourism to complete the t-chart below.

Tourism PROS (+)	Tourism CONS (−)

C How can tourists help a place they visit and not hurt it? In your notebook, write a paragraph with a topic sentence, three or more good ideas, and details about each idea.

D ♻ **GOAL CHECK** ✔ **Discuss the pros and cons of tourism**

Take turns. Read your paragraph to a small group of students. Discuss each other's opinions.

Teacher Tip: Fillers

Here are some activities to fill in a few extra minutes at the end of a lesson:

• The Blackboard Game (if you have filled the board with vocabulary). Have a volunteer sit with his or her back to the board. Students take turns giving definitions of words on the board. If the volunteer guesses the correct word, erase it. The game ends when all the words are erased.

• Error Quiz. On the board, write ten incorrect sentences from students' work. Have students work to correct the sentences. When the time is up, ask the class for corrections, and rewrite the sentences correctly on the board.

White-water rafting in New Zealand

Before You Watch

A Read about the video and check the meanings of the words in **bold.**

While You Watch

A ▶ Watch the video and circle **T** for *true* or **F** for *false*.

1. Queenstown is a beautiful and quiet place.   T   (F)
2. The jet boat was invented in New Zealand.   (T)   F
3. You can do sixty different activities in Queenstown.   (T)   F
4. Helicopter hikers stay on top of the mountain for a long time.   T   (F)
5. Everyone is happy after they try bungee jumping.   T   (F)

B ▶ Watch the video again. Circle the correct answer.

1. The gap under the jump pod is (300 | (440)) feet.
2. Jet boats were made to travel on (lakes | (rivers)).
3. The mountain hike takes (four | (five)) hours.
4. In helicopter hiking, people walk ((up) | down) the mountain.
5. The world's first bungee-jumping site was a ((bridge) | wire).

After You Watch / Communication

A Which of the activities in the video do you want to try? Why?

B Plan a three-day tour of your country for foreign visitors. What kind of tour will they have? Which places will they visit? What will they do there?

The city of Queenstown in New Zealand is a world center for **adventure** sports. You can ride a fast jet boat through **shallow** water, go bungee jumping off a high **bridge,** or take a helicopter **hike** in the mountains. All of these **pastimes** give travelers a **thrill.** People call Queenstown "the adventure capital of the world."

Travel   **133**

Video Journal:
Adventure Capital of the World

- Tell students they are going to watch a video about New Zealand. Find out what, if anything, they know about the country.

Before You Watch

A • Have students read the video summary. Go over the meanings of the words in bold if necessary.

While You Watch

A • Tell students to watch the video and choose *true* or *false*. Then have them read the statements.
- Play the video.
- Have students compare answers with a partner.
- Check answers.

B • Tell students to watch the video again and circle the correct word.
- Play the video.
- Have students compare answers with a partner.
- Check answers.

After You Watch / Communication

A • Have students tell a partner about which, if any, of the activities they would like to try.
- Survey the class about which activities they would like to try. Ask them to explain their reasons.

B • Divide the class into groups of three or four. Tell them that they are going to plan a tour of their country to sell to foreign visitors.
- Tell them to choose a type of tour and decide on the places and activities for each day. Appoint a secretary in each group.
- Have groups explain their plans to another group.
- Finish with a whole-class discussion of the most interesting/ unusual plans, activities, etc.

For Your Information: Queenstown

Queenstown is located in Otago in the South Island of New Zealand. It is set on a lake surrounded by mountains and has a population of about 10,000 people. It's a center for adventure sports and is famous for skiing, jet boating, bungee jumping, mountain biking, hiking, and fishing. It also has a number of well-regarded restaurants and is in the center of a wine-producing area. It is especially popular with young American and Australian tourists.

Careers

About the Photo

Peter Allinson is a nature photographer, specializing in underwater photography. Photography is a challenging, yet hugely rewarding career. Getting that perfect shot, especially of nature, can take a photographer days of shooting. However, as can be seen from this amazing close up of a whale with the photographer, the challenges are well worth it. Allinson's work has been featured in National Geographic's *Your Shot*.

- Introduce the theme of the unit. Call on students to name as many careers as they can in English. Compile a list on the board.

- Direct students' attention to the picture. Have students describe what they see.

- Have students work with a partner to answer the questions.

- Compare answers with the class.

- Ask these questions orally or by writing them on the board for students to answer in pairs: *Would you enjoy this career? Why or why not? What careers do you think are the most interesting/difficult/exciting/boring? Explain your reasons.*

- Go over the Unit Goals with the class.

- For each goal, elicit any words students already know and write them on the board; for example, vocabulary for professions, education-related vocabulary, tenses to talk about the past and past experiences, etc.

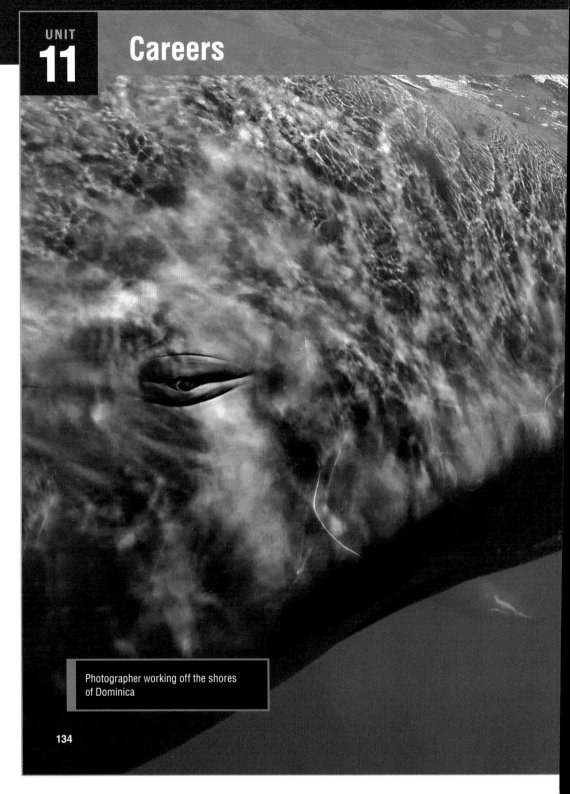

Photographer working off the shores of Dominica

134

UNIT 11 GOALS	Grammar	Vocabulary	Listening
• Discuss career choices • Ask and answer job-related questions • Talk about career planning • Talk about innovative jobs	Modals for giving advice You **should** choose a career that fits your personality. Indefinite pronouns **Everyone** in the audience was laughing.	Career decisions Participial adjectives	Listening for general understanding An interview: A restaurant owner in Thailand

UNIT 11 GOALS

1. Discuss career choices

2. Ask and answer job-related questions

3. Talk about career planning

4. Talk about innovative jobs

135

Unit Theme Overview

• In virtually every country in the world, career patterns are shifting. In countries that once had a system of lifelong employment in the same job, people are now more likely to change employers during their career or even shift to a different field of work entirely. At the same time, in countries where more mobility was customary, people are changing jobs faster than ever. According to experts, the average person in the United States will hold ten different jobs just between the ages of 18 and 38, and every year, about one in three workers changes jobs.

• Whatever the age of your students, it is very likely that they will at some time confront a decision as to a new career or position. In this unit, students will look at the factors involved in choosing a satisfying career and finding a worthwhile job. They will first consider the idea of qualifications for a career and get and give advice about careers that are suitable for a particular person. They will then discuss the attributes of specific jobs and consider the questions asked at a job interview. They will talk about preparation for specific careers and then learn about and discuss the work of two people with unusual careers.

Speaking	Reading	Writing	Video Journal
Role-playing job interviews **Pronunciation:** Intonation in questions	**TED Talks:** Making Filthy Water Drinkable	Writing a letter giving advice	**National Geographic:** Trinidad Bird Man

Discuss Career Choices

Vocabulary

A • Tell students they are going to hear a conversation in a high school. If necessary, explain that in some countries, high school students have part-time jobs after school (such as working for a few hours in a store or fast-food restaurant) and might also do volunteer work (such as reading stories to children in a hospital). Introduce the idea of a *career advisor*—a teacher who helps students choose and prepare for their future careers. Tell students to listen and answer the question.

• Play the recording. 🔊 **21**

• Check the answer.

B • Have students read the notes that the career advisor took during the meeting. Tell students to listen to the conversation again and complete the notes with the words in the box.

• Play the recording. 🔊 **21**

• Have students compare answers with a partner.

• Check answers.

C • Have students discuss the questions with a partner.

• Compare answers with the class.

Grammar

• Continue to talk about Marcy from **Vocabulary.** Ask, *What should she do to start her own business?* Elicit ideas from the class.

• Go over the information in the chart. Then ask students to give more advice for Marcy, using *should/shouldn't/ought to/had better (not).*

A | **GOAL 1:** Discuss Career Choices

Vocabulary

A 🔊 **21** Listen to a conversation between a high school senior and a career advisor. What does Marcy do at the hospital?
She's a family assistant.

B 🔊 **21** Listen again. Then fill in the blanks in Ms. Carter's notes below with the words in the box.

> employee experience owner assistant
> training qualifications volunteer boss

• Marcy has some work ____*experience*____. She went through a ____*training*____ program to become a family ____*assistant*____ at the hospital. It's ____*volunteer*____ work, so Marcy doesn't get paid.

• Marcy would like to be a business ____*owner*____, but she doesn't have the necessary ____*qualifications*____ yet.

• I explained that she could start as an ____*employee*____ at a business. Later, perhaps, she can be the ____*boss*____ when she has her own business.

C 🔄 Talk in pairs. What do you think Marcy should do to prepare for her future? Did the advisor give her good advice?

Grammar: Modals for giving advice

Modals for giving advice	
Use modals of advice to talk about what is or isn't a good idea. Modals are followed by the simple form of a verb.	You **should** <u>choose</u> a career that fits your personality. Miguel **ought to** <u>become</u> an engineer. Linda **shouldn't** <u>take</u> that office job.
Had better is stronger than *should* or *ought to*. It means something bad could happen if the advice isn't followed.	You **had better** <u>talk</u> to the academic advisor before you decide on a major. I'**d better not** <u>miss</u> any more days of work.
Use *maybe*, *perhaps*, or *I think* with modals to make the advice sound gentler and friendlier.	**Maybe** you **should** <u>become</u> a health care worker.

136   Unit 11

Word Bank: Careers

Business: accountant, salesperson

Computers: system analyst, web designer

Education: principal, teacher

Entertainment: actor, musician

Health: dentist, doctor, nurse

Tourism: hotel manager, travel agent

Grammar: Modals for giving advice

English uses a variety of modals for giving advice, and choosing the correct one requires being sensitive to the relationship between the speakers. *Had better* and *had better not* imply a relationship of authority (such as a boss, teacher, or doctor). *Should* and *ought to* are more neutral, but native speakers usually try to soften their advice by adding *I think* or *maybe*, especially when speaking with friends.

A 🔄 Complete the sentences with a partner. Use your own ideas.

> **Career Advice**
>
> - If you want to become a successful businessperson, you should
>   _____ , but you shouldn't _____ .
>
> - If you really like animals, you ought to _____ .
>
> - When you go for a job interview, you had better _____ ,
>   and you had better not _____ . Good luck!

B 🔄 Read one of the problems out loud to a partner. Your partner will give you friendly advice using *maybe, perhaps,* or *I think.*

1. My school is far from my house.
2. I think I may be getting sick.
3. I want to become a doctor.
4. My job doesn't pay very well.
5. My university application was rejected.
6. I never remember my mother's birthday.

> **I don't get along with my co-worker.**

> **Maybe you should avoid him.**

Conversation

A 🔊 22 Close your book and listen to the conversation. Why doesn't Bob like his job? *He does the same thing every day.*

Miranda:	Hi Bob. How's it going?
Bob:	Not so good. I think I need a new job.
Miranda:	You do look stressed out. What is it you do again?
Bob:	I'm an administrative assistant. That's like a secretary, but I have more responsibilities.
Miranda:	Do you have a good boss?
Bob:	Sure. He's the owner of the company, and he's pretty nice, actually.
Miranda:	So what's the problem? Is it the other people you work with?
Bob:	No, my co-workers are fine, but I do the same thing every day.
Miranda:	Maybe you should start looking for a more interesting job.
Bob:	You're right. I can probably find something better.

B 🔄 Practice the conversation with a partner. Then have new conversations about problems that might be nice to have; for example:

I make too much money.   **I have too much vacation time.**

C 🔄 **GOAL CHECK** ✔ **Discuss career choices**

Work in pairs. Choose a career from the box and describe the training, experience, and other qualifications required for that career. Then talk about the advantages and disadvantages of having that career.

> sales representative
> information technology specialist
> lawyer
> health care worker
> computer software engineer

Careers **137**

Grammar Practice: Modals for giving advice

Introduce the idea of an advice column. Ask students if they ever read these columns. Tell them they are going to write a letter to an advice column about a career problem. In pairs, have students write a one-paragraph letter about a work or career problem (real or imaginary). Tell them to include the person's age and a little bit about his or her background. Set a time limit. Then have each pair exchange letters with another pair and write an answer. When students are finished, have them give their letters to the other pair. Call on pairs to read their problems and the advice they received to the class.

A
- Have students work with a partner to complete the sentences with advice.
- Call on students to read a sentence to the class. Comment on appropriate (or inappropriate) use of the different modals—for example, *had better* is quite forceful and indicates that something bad might happen if the advice is not taken.

B
- Assign new pairs and have them take turns telling about a problem and giving advice to solve the problem.
- When all pairs have finished, ask, *Who got some interesting advice? What was it?*

Conversation

A
- Have students close their books. Write the question on the board: *Why doesn't Bob like his job?*
- Play the recording 🔊 22
- Check answers.

B
- Play or read the conversation again for the class to repeat.
- Practice the conversation with the class in chorus.
- Have students practice the conversation with a partner, then make new conversations about the problems.

C 🔄 **GOAL CHECK** ✔
- Divide the class into pairs and have them take turns choosing a career from the box to discuss.
- If necessary, go over the list of careers with the class and describe each one before the students begin the task on their own. (*sales representative:* travels to different places selling a company's products; *information technology specialist:* works with computer systems; *lawyer:* helps people who need legal advice; *health care worker:* takes care of sick people; *computer software engineer:* makes new computer programs).

Ask and Answer Job-Related Questions

Listening

A
- Tell students they are going to hear an interview with a man about his work. Go over the question.
- Play the recording one or more times. 🔊 23
- Check answers.

B
- Tell students to listen again to the interview. Go over the questions.
- Play the recording one or more times. 🔊 23
- Have students compare answers with a partner.
- Check answers.
- With the class, talk about the pros and cons of working in a family business. Ask, *Would you like to have your uncle as your boss? Why or why not?*

C
- Have students work individually to rank the attributes of a good job.
- Have students compare and discuss their answers with a partner.
- With the class, compare answers, and discuss how different people have very different ideas about what makes a "good job."
- Direct students' attention to the Engage! box. With the class, list the advantages and disadvantages of being a business owner versus an employee. Then have students tell their opinions to partners or to a group.

Pronunciation
- Go over the information about the intonation of *yes/no* and *wh-* word questions.

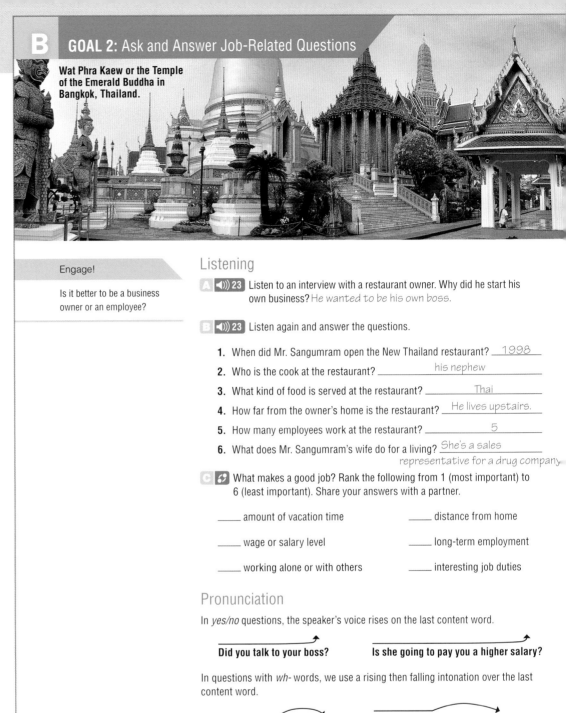

B GOAL 2: Ask and Answer Job-Related Questions

Wat Phra Kaew or the Temple of the Emerald Buddha in Bangkok, Thailand.

Engage!

Is it better to be a business owner or an employee?

Listening

A 🔊 23 Listen to an interview with a restaurant owner. Why did he start his own business? *He wanted to be his own boss.*

B 🔊 23 Listen again and answer the questions.

1. When did Mr. Sangumram open the New Thailand restaurant? ___1998___
2. Who is the cook at the restaurant? ___his nephew___
3. What kind of food is served at the restaurant? ___Thai___
4. How far from the owner's home is the restaurant? ___He lives upstairs.___
5. How many employees work at the restaurant? ___5___
6. What does Mr. Sangumram's wife do for a living? *She's a sales representative for a drug company.*

C ⚡ What makes a good job? Rank the following from 1 (most important) to 6 (least important). Share your answers with a partner.

_____ amount of vacation time   _____ distance from home

_____ wage or salary level   _____ long-term employment

_____ working alone or with others   _____ interesting job duties

Pronunciation

In *yes/no* questions, the speaker's voice rises on the last content word.

Did you talk to your boss?   **Is she going to pay you a higher salary?**

In questions with *wh-* words, we use a rising then falling intonation over the last content word.

When is your job interview?   **What qualifications do you need?**

138   Unit 11

For Your Information: Owning a small business

Many people believe that owning a small business has many advantages, but being a business owner has its negative side as well. A survey found that around the world, small-business owners work an average of 54 hours a week. Globally, 64 percent of small-business owners said that having more control over their work was the main reason for starting their own business, but there were big differences between countries. For example, in Brazil, the most common reason given for starting a business was to contribute to the community, while in China, most business owners said that they wanted to build something that could be passed on to the younger generations in their families.

A 🔊 24 Listen to the following questions. Then listen again and repeat.

Yes/No questions	*Wh-* questions
1. Do you like your co-workers?	6. When is the training?
2. Was your boss in a good mood?	7. How old do you have to be?
3. Is this part of the job?	8. Which company is better?
4. Did you learn any useful skills?	9. What time should I be here?
5. Are you making good progress?	10. How many employees are there?

B 🔄 Imagine you are applying for a job at Mr. Sangumram's restaurant. He needs a waiter, a dishwasher, and an assistant cook. Which job would you apply for? Write questions about the job with a partner.

Yes/No questions	*Wh-* questions
Is the restaurant open late at night?	What are the job duties?
_____	_____
_____	_____
_____	_____

C 👥 Join another pair of students and role-play a job interview. Ask the other pair your questions from exercise **B.** They will answer using their own ideas.

Communication

A Read the career profiles on the right. Choose two careers that might be good for you, but don't tell anyone which jobs you chose.

B 🔄 Ask your partner several questions about the kind of career he or she might want in the future. Then try to guess which two careers your partner chose.

> Do you like to work outdoors?

> How much do you know about medications?

C 👥 **GOAL CHECK** ✓ **Ask and answer job-related questions**

Join another pair of students. Ask each other questions and decide which career is best for each person in the group.

Career Profiles

Commercial Pilot:
Knows about airplane mechanics, weather, radio communication. Works long hours. Often far away from home.

Pharmacist:
Knows about medications. Advises patients about their treatments. Long-term employment. Some vacation time.

Diving Instructor:
Understands and teaches the use of scuba equipment. Works outdoors. Should be a strong swimmer. Salary varies by season.

Retail Sales Clerk:
Manages store merchandise. Assists customers. Should be able to work with others and stand for several hours at a time.

Careers **139**

Expansion Activity

Bring in a page of employment ads from the Internet or from an English-language newspaper and make photocopies for the class. Divide the class into groups of three or four and have them read and discuss the ads. What jobs are available for English speakers? What qualifications are required? Discuss the students' findings with the class. Alternatively, if students have access to the Internet, have them bring in ads for jobs they might be interested in and discuss those.

A
- Tell students to listen to the questions.
- Play the recording. 🔊 24
- Tell students to listen again and repeat the questions.
- Call on students to read a question to the class.

B
- Have students work with a partner to write more questions. Monitor to check questions are correctly formed.

C
- Introduce the topic of job interviews. Ask students if they have ever had one. Discuss the kinds of questions that an employer would ask at a job interview (for example, about education, work experience, qualifications, etc.).
- Join pairs to make groups of four and have them use their questions from **B** to role-play job interviews. Tell students to answer using their own ideas.
- Call on different groups to present one of their interviews to the class.

Communication

A
- Have students read the job profiles. Answer any questions about vocabulary. Tell students to choose two careers that they might want in the future but not tell anyone.

B
- Divide the class into pairs and have them ask each other questions to try and guess which careers they chose. Model the example question and answer with a student, and ask one or two more questions.

C 👥 **GOAL CHECK** ✓

- Have pairs join to make groups of four. Have them ask each other questions and decide which career would be best for each person.
- Have groups report back to the class on the career they decided for each member of the group.

Talk About Career Planning

Language Expansion

🔲 • Write on the board, *firefighter* and *difficult*. Ask, *Which word is an adjective and which one is a noun?*

• Tell students to find and write the nouns that are described by the adjectives in blue.

• Check answers.

🔲 • Write two columns on the board, *someone's feelings* and *something that causes a certain feeling.* Have students tell you in which column to put the first adjective (*bored*) in **A.**

• Have students work with a partner to decide what each adjective does.

• Check answers and complete the chart on the board. Ask, *What do you notice about the adjectives in each column? (-ed vs. -ing ending)*

• Point out the information in the Word Focus box, and have students complete the sentences using the participial adjectives. Have students work in pairs to say the sentences and then explain what might have happened. Model the example in the speech bubbles.

• Have several pairs share their examples with the class.

Grammar

• Write the first two examples from the chart on the board. Underline *she* and *somebody*. Ask, *Which one refers to a specific noun? Which one refers to an unspecified noun?* Show students how *she* refers to the *career advisor*, but *somebody* doesn't refer to a specific person.

• Go over the information in the chart.

Language Expansion: Participial adjectives

🔲 Read the article about A. J. Coston. What nouns do the words in blue describe?
1. A. J. 2. friends 3. helping people 4. the job 5. the moment 6. A. J.

1. A. J.   2. friends

> That was relaxing. Now I feel relaxed.

> I think you went to a park.

Word Focus

Participial Adjectives

That was _____ .
Now I feel _____ .

relaxing/relaxed
embarrassing/embarrassed
tiring/tired
confusing/confused
disappointing/disappointed
exciting/excited
depressing/depressed

A. J. Coston isn't waiting to start his dream job. At age 18, he's a weekend volunteer firefighter in the United States. During the week, he lives at home with his mom, dad, and sister, and does his main job: going to high school. "I always wanted to get into firefighting since I was a little kid watching fire trucks go by," he says. "One day I was bored and on the Internet, and I found out that Loudoun County offered a junior firefighter program."

Some of A. J.'s friends are surprised by his decision to spend weekends at the firehouse, but to A. J., helping people is more satisfying than anything else. The job is never boring, either, since firefighters get called to all sorts of emergencies. One terrifying moment for A. J. was getting an emergency call after four children were struck by lightning. Luckily, all four survived.

A. J. will be off to college next fall, and plans to study what he's most interested in: emergency medical care. "I want to be a flight medic on a helicopter eventually," he says.

🔲 For each participial adjective in blue above, decide whether it describes (1) someone's feelings or (2) something that causes a certain feeling. Then practice the sentences in the Word Focus box with a partner. Guess what might have happened.

Grammar: Indefinite pronouns

Pronouns refer to specified nouns (people, places, or things). Indefinite pronouns refer to unspecified nouns (people, places, or things).	I know the career advisor. **She** lives in my neighborhood. **Somebody** locked the door. *(I don't know who did it.)*
Use *everybody/everyone/everything* to talk about all of a group of nouns.	**Everything** in the book is important. You need to study all of it.
Use *nobody/no one/nothing* to talk about none of a group of nouns.	I want to sell my computer, but **no one** I know wants to buy it.
Use *somebody/someone/something* to talk about an unspecified noun.	You should talk to **someone** at the career counseling center.
Use *anybody/anyone/anything* to emphasize that it's not important to specify a certain person, place, or thing.	You need work experience. **Anything** you do will be helpful. *(It doesn't matter what it is.)*
Use *anybody/anyone/anything* in negative statements and in questions.	I don't know **anybody** at my school. Do you know **anyone** at your school?
Indefinite pronouns always take the singular form of a verb.	**Everyone** has useful skills and knowledge.

Word Bank:
Participial adjectives

amazed/amazing

fascinated/fascinating

frightened/frightening

frustrated/frustrating

motivated/motivating

worried/worrying

Grammar: Indefinite pronouns

Indefinite pronouns are used to refer to an object or person that is unknown to the speaker. *Everything* refers to all members of a group. To refer to one thing or a part of a group, a useful rule is that *something* is used in statements, *anything* in questions, and *nothing* as a negative—although patterns used by native speakers are more complex.

Note that pronouns used with -*body* are more informal than those used with -*one*.

A Complete the sentences with the simple present form of the verb in parentheses.

1. Everybody in my family __enjoys__ (enjoy) eating ice cream.

2. The university is looking for someone who __plans__ (plan) to study nanotechnology.

3. Nothing __is__ (be) more discouraging than doing a job you don't like.

4. Nobody really __knows__ (know) what will happen in the future.

B Take turns reading the situation to a partner. Discuss the choices and circle the correct word.

1. *There are 18 students in the class. One student wants to leave early.*
((Somebody) | Everybody) wants to leave early.

2. *You have never heard of the field of ethnobotany before.*
I don't know ((anything) | something) about ethnobotany.

3. *None of your friends, acquaintances, or family members have a luxury car.*
(Anyone | (No one)) I know has a luxury car.

4. *You want to learn to speak Japanese. You are looking for a tutor.*
I need to find ((somebody) | everybody) who speaks Japanese.

Conversation

A 🔊 25 Listen to the conversation. What is the man planning to do?
 enroll in a training program (to install car stereos)

Parker:	What do you want to do when you finish school?
Kimberly:	I'm not sure, but I want to do something interesting.
Parker:	Of course! Everybody wants that, but you need to start planning.
Kimberly:	OK, what are you planning to do when you finish school?
Parker:	I'm planning to enroll in a training program. They teach you how to install custom car stereos.
Kimberly:	You sound excited about that.
Parker:	I am! You know I've always loved cars, and the program is only four months long, so I can get a job really soon.
Kimberly:	That sounds great! I need to start thinking about my future, too.
Parker:	Mmm hmm. That's what I said before.
Kimberly:	And you're right, as usual.

B 🔄 Practice the conversation with a partner. Switch roles and practice it again. Make a new conversation using your own plans for the future.

C 🔄 **GOAL CHECK** ✓ **Talk about career planning**

Talk to a partner. What kind of career would be interesting and satisfying to you? What are you doing now to prepare for your future career?

Careers **141**

D TEDTALKS

Talk About Innovative Jobs

Reading

A • Write *innovative* on the board and have students explain what it means and give examples.

• Have students discuss the question with a partner. Encourage them to think of other jobs not in the box if they can.

• Compare ideas with the class, and have students explain their reasons.

B • Have students look at the pictures on page 143 and describe what they see. Ask, *What is he doing? What do you think his job is? What are the children doing? Where do you think they are? What do think this man has done that is innovative?*

• Point out the definitions in the Word Bank. Have students read the article and complete the sentences. Tell them to circle any words in the article that they don't understand.

• Have students compare answers with a partner.

• Check answers.

• Go over the article with the class, answering any questions from students about vocabulary.

C • Have students read the directions and list two problems caused by drinking unsafe water.

• Divide the class into pairs. Have them compare their lists and discuss how the water purifying bottle helps prevent these problems.

• Compare ideas with the class.

D GOAL 4: Talk About Innovative Jobs

Reading

A 🔊 What jobs do you think of as especially innovative? Look at the list below or come up with your own ideas. Share them with a partner.

salesclerk	lawyer	inventor
bus driver	designer	researcher
programmer	travel photographer	

B Read the article. Complete the sentences with the correct words in parentheses.

1. Pritchard got his idea for the water purifier when he was __angry__. (happy / angry)

2. Pritchard works __at home__. (at home / in a laboratory)

3. He believes that "old thinking" needs to __change__. (continue / change)

4. Many people have to __boil__ their water before they drink it. (buy / boil)

5. Lifesaver water purifiers are very __efficient__. (efficient / expensive)

C 🔊 List two problems that drinking unsafe water causes. Compare your answers with a partner. How does the water purifying bottle help?

TED Ideas worth spreading

Michael Pritchard Inventor, Problem Solver

MAKING FILTHY WATER DRINKABLE

Like many **innovators,** Michael Pritchard gets good ideas when he sees a problem that needs to be solved. The **inspiration** for his Lifesaver water **purifier** came after the Asian tsunami of 2004 and Hurricane Katrina, which hit New Orleans in 2005. After both disasters, it took days for the people who were affected to get safe drinking water. That was too long, in Pritchard's opinion. It made him very angry.

"Everyone deserves safe drinking water," Pritchard says. Working in his garage and his kitchen, he developed a design for a simple water purifier. It took 18 months and a number of failed prototypes before he successfully created the Lifesaver bottle.

Pritchard believes that "old thinking," the traditional way of responding to disasters by making people travel to get safe drinking water, needs to change. Instead, he "thinks differently," looking for solutions that are simple to use, close to home, and inexpensive to operate.

The water purifying bottle meets all three needs. It can remove **contaminants** from 6,000 liters of dirty water before its filter needs to be replaced. A larger system, in a jerry can, is able to filter 25,000 liters of water. That's enough water for a family of four to drink for three years. It only costs a half a cent a day to operate. Because Lifesaver systems only clean as much water as a person, family, or community needs every day, it is much more efficient than other water purification systems.

Water poverty is the **lack** of a clean, reliable supply of drinking water. An estimated 1.1 billion people are trapped in water poverty. When people have access to clean water, it means that there is less disease.

For Your Information: Michael Pritchard

British engineer Michael Pritchard founded LIFESAVER Systems in 2007 after spending 18 months designing the first Lifesaver bottle. Pritchard believes that everyone deserves safe and easily accessible water. Using nanotechnology, water poverty, which is one of the major problems the world faces, can be solved with low-cost solutions, and that is what LIFESAVER Systems is trying to do. Since the development of the Lifesaver bottle, Pritchard and

LIFESAVER Systems have developed more products that are helping people all around the world produce safe, sterile, drinking water quickly and inexpensively. In addition to being used for humanitarian purposes, their products are also used by the military and for leisure activities, such as camping. As an innovator, Pritchard looks at problems from different angles; he believes that by thinking differently, some of the world's biggest problems could be solved.

> "I'd like to show you that through thinking differently, the problem has been solved."
> – Michael Pritchard

Michael Pritchard's idea worth spreading is that everyone should have access to clean water — and here's a way to give it to them. Watch Pritchard's full TED Talk on TED.com.

They don't have to look for wood or use fossil fuels to boil their water before they drink it. It also means that many girls in developing countries, who are usually responsible for bringing clean water to their homes, can go to school instead. Lives are changed, lives are saved, and community life improves when people have reliable access to clean water.

Innovators like Michael Pritchard who think differently can make a big difference in the world.

innovator a person who creates something new to solve a problem
inspiration something that gives someone an idea about what to do or create
purifier a device used to remove harmful substances
contaminant something that makes a place or a substance unclean
lack the state of not having enough of something

143

After Reading

Web search: Have students go online and search for information on their dream job, using the job title as a search term. Are there any schools, courses, or other programs for people interested in that career?

Project: Have students work with a partner to prepare a poster about a career of interest to your class. The poster should give information about job duties and the qualifications required, and should include pictures of a person doing this work. Hang the posters on the classroom walls.

Writing

A • Have students read the sentences and choose the correct indefinite pronoun.

• Have students compare answers with a partner.

• Check answers.

B • Have students read the directions. Elicit explanations of when we use *should, shouldn't, ought to,* and *had better.*

• Have students complete the advice letter.

• Have students compare answers with a partner.

• Check answers.

Communication

A • Ask, *What other TED speakers have we read about or listened to?* Elicit the different names (have students look through their books if necessary) and write them on the board. For each one, ask, *What's his/ her job? Why is he/she an innovator?* Go over the ideas in the box.

• Assign new pairs and have them discuss what makes each TED speaker an innovator. Remind them to use the words in the box to help them. Provide other vocabulary as necessary.

B 🔗 **GOAL CHECK** ✔

• Combine pairs to make groups of four. Have them compare their ideas from **A.** Have them identify what the innovators have in common.

• Have groups refer to the jobs they identified as being innovative in **Reading A.** Have them discuss whether you can be innovative in every job.

• Compare ideas with the class. Ask, *What do the people we have read about and listened to in TED Talks have in common? What makes them innovators? Are some jobs more innovative than others, or can you be innovative in any job?*

144 UNIT 11: Careers TEDTALKS

D GOAL 4: Talk About Innovative Jobs

▲ An employee shows a powerful new computer that will be able to handle the large amount of calculations needed for nano technology research

Writing

A Circle the correct indefinite pronouns to complete the sentences.

1. An inventor is (nobody | (somebody)) who is interested in problem solving.

2. Pritchard wanted to do ((something) | anything) to solve the problem of unsafe drinking water for millions of people around the world.

3. Pritchard did not work in a high-tech laboratory; he developed his innovation with almost ((nothing) | something).

4. ((Everybody) | Nobody) wants to make the world a better place.

5. I hope to do ((something) | anything) important with my life.

B Complete the letter with *should, shouldn't, had better,* or *ought to.*

I am happy you asked me for advice. If you want to become an innovator, you (1) _should/ought to_ think about a problem you want to solve. Since there are lots of problems in the world, it (2) _shouldn't_ be too hard! Remember, it takes a long time to solve a problem well, so you (3) _had better_ be patient.

community-based conservation

developing world

food systems

undersea exploration

endangered species

non-profit organization

Communication

A 🔗 What other innovators do you know? Look at the other TED readings and TED Talks. What makes them innovators? Use the ideas in the box.

B 🔗 **GOAL CHECK** ✔ Talk about innovative jobs

Share your ideas about innovators. What do they have in common?

144 Unit 11

Expansion Activity

Have students write a letter giving advice to a friend who wants to find an innovative job. Remind students to use the modal verbs for advice. Provide the following outline for them to use:

Dear _____,

I am happy you _____. If you want _____, you _____. I think you _____, too. There are _____ and _____ in the world. Remember, it's _____, so you _____.

Best wishes,

Have students exchange letters with a partner and compare ideas or write replies. Collect letters for grading if desired.

The scarlet ibis is the national bird of Trinidad and Tobago.

Trinidad and Tobago

Before You Watch

A Complete the sentences with a word from the box.

1. A ___hummingbird___ is a very tiny bird.

2. An ___ornithologist___ studies birds.

3. _Paradise_ is a place where everything is beautiful, delightful, and peaceful.

4. Panda bears, honeybees, and dolphins are all examples of ___wildlife___.

5. A ___nest___ is a home that birds build for themselves.

> wildlife   hummingbird
> paradise   nest
> ornithologist

While You Watch

A ▶ Watch the video *Trinidad Bird Man*. Check (✓) Roger Neckles's job qualifications in the box on the right.

After You Watch / Communication

A 🔄 Interview a partner and write down his or her answers in your notebook.

1. What time do you like to get up in the morning?

2. How do you feel about spending a lot of time outdoors?

3. Are you a very patient person? Why or why not?

4. Do you prefer to wear casual clothes or stylish clothes?

5. What do you think is the most interesting kind of wildlife?

B 🧩 Should your partner become a wildlife photographer? Tell the class why or why not.

- ☑ He enjoys being outdoors.
- ☑ He can take photographs.
- ☐ He doesn't mind a low salary.
- ☑ He's very patient.
- ☑ He's enthusiastic about birds.
- ☐ He's an excellent writer.

> **You should become a _____ because . . .**

Careers   **145**

Video Journal:
Trinidad Bird Man

Before You Watch

- Have students look at the picture and describe what they see. Point out the map of Trinidad and Tobago, and tell students they are going to watch a video about a man who works there.

A • Go over the meanings of the words in the box.

- Have students complete the sentences.

- Check answers.

While You Watch

A • Tell students to watch the video the first time and check the man's qualifications.

- Play the video.

- Have students compare answers with a partner.

- Check answers.

After You Watch / Communication

A • Divide the class into pairs and have them take turns asking and answering the questions.

B • Have pairs combine to make groups of four. Have them tell each other whether their partners would be successful and happy as wildlife photographers. Tell them to explain their reasons.

Teacher Tip: Fun with English outside of class

Encourage students to get more practice. Some ideas:

- sing along with English songs on CDs

- read in English on a topic that is well-known in the student's native language (for example, soccer or fashion)

- watch movies with native-language subtitles

For Your Information: Trinidad and Tobago

Trinidad and Tobago is an island nation in the Caribbean, northeast of Venezuela. It consists of two main islands with many smaller islands. Trinidad is much larger than Tobago and has most of the population. The country's economy is based on petroleum, and its culture has spread around the world through the steelpan drum, calypso music, and soca and limbo dancing. The climate is tropical, but there is a wet season and a dry season. Millions of years ago, Trinidad was part of the coast of South America, so it has different plants and animals distinct from other islands in the Caribbean.

Celebrations

About the Photo

This photo shows dancers in costume at the Carnival in Rio de Janeiro, Brazil. Taken by Dutch photographer Robin Utrecht, this photo beautifully reflects the vibrancy and color of the Rio *Carnaval*. Carnival is celebrated in many places in Brazil and throughout the world; however, Rio de Janeiro has become known as the carnival capital of the world. The carnival in Rio lasts for four days and involves processions with floats and dancers. Carnival has its roots in pre-Christian celebrations of spring, the marking of the start of the Christian period of Lent, and, in Brazil, in the music and dance brought to the country by slaves from Africa. The incredible artistic creativity of the Rio carnival make it one of the most interesting cultural events in the world.

- Introduce the theme of the unit. Call on students to name celebrations in their country—both public celebrations, like holidays and festivals, and private celebrations, like birthdays and anniversaries.

- Direct students' attention to the picture. Have students describe what they see.

- Have students discuss the questions with a partner.

- Compare answers with the class, compiling a list on the board.

- Take a class vote for favorite celebration with a show of hands.

- Go over the Unit Goals with the class.

- For each goal, elicit any words students already know and write them on the board; for example, vocabulary for celebrations, adjectives to describe feelings and celebrations, etc.

Carnival is celebrated in towns and villages throughout Brazil. Rio de Janeiro is the Carnival Capital of the World.

146

UNIT 12 GOALS	Grammar	Vocabulary	Listening
• Describe a festival • Compare holidays in different countries • Talk about celebrations • Share opinions about holidays	*As . . . as* *New Year's is **as** exciting **as** National Day.* *Would rather* *I'**d rather** have a big party.*	Festivals and holidays Greetings for celebrations	Listening for general and specific information Discussions: Local celebrations or holidays

Look at the photo, answer the questions:
1 What is your favorite celebration?
2 What do people do there?

UNIT 12 GOALS

1. Describe a festival
2. Compare holidays in different countries
3. Talk about celebrations
4. Share opinions about holidays

147

Unit Theme Overview

- Every culture around the world has special days of celebration. These may be traditional holidays, such as New Year's Day or religious celebrations. Celebrations may include music festivals or craft fairs. Or they may be personal celebrations, such as a birthday or wedding anniversary. In this unit, students will learn about and discuss all three kinds of celebrations.

- Every religion has special holidays marked with religious observances, and many of these have also become occasions for celebration with special foods, music, and gift-giving. Countries mark the anniversaries of important days in their history with patriotic holidays. There are also seasonal holidays that began as celebrations of harvest time or the longest day of the year. In many countries, holidays are combined in sequences to give people a longer break from work—for example, Japan's Golden Week, which includes four holidays from April 29 to May 5. There are even unofficial holidays that are not on the calendar but are widely observed and enjoyed, such as April Fools' Day (April 1) in the United States, a day when people play tricks on one another.

- In this unit, students learn vocabulary and grammar to describe and compare different holidays and then talk about how they celebrate important days with their families. They discuss holiday traditions and, finally, talk about cultural celebrations.

Speaking	Reading	Writing	Video Journal
Comparing different international celebrations	**National Geographic:** Starting a New Tradition	Writing a substantiated opinion	**National Geographic:** Young Riders of Mongolia
Pronunciation: Question intonation with lists			

Describe a Festival

Vocabulary

A
• Ask, *What's special about December 31? What do people usually do in the evening?* Have students look at the picture and describe what they see. Elicit anything they know about New Year celebrations in Scotland.

• Have students read the article about New Year's in Edinburgh. Ask comprehension questions, orally, or write them down for students to answer individually or in pairs; for example, *What are the New Year celebrations in Scotland called? How many days does Hogmanay last? When is the parade?* etc.

B
• Have students match the words in blue in **A** to the meanings.

• Have students compare answers with a partner.

• Check answers.

C
• Have students discuss the questions with a partner.

• Compare answers with the class. Write a list of festivals on the board and discuss what students know about them.

• Direct students' attention to the Engage! box. Have students discuss the question in pairs or small groups.

• Compare responses with the class.

Grammar

• Go over the information in the chart. Choose two celebrations that the class is familiar with and elicit more sentences with *big/old/interesting,* and so forth.

A GOAL 1: Describe a Festival

▲ Hogmany celebration in Scotland

Engage!

How do you celebrate New Year's Day?

Vocabulary

A Read about a special New Year's celebration.

New Year's Day is a holiday around the world, but people in Edinburgh, Scotland, celebrate it in an exciting way. They have a festival called Hogmanay. Hogmanay takes place all around the city, from December 29 to January 1. It starts with a parade on the night of December 29. On December 30, there are concerts and dancing. Finally, on New Year's Eve, there is a street party with fireworks, and people wear very colorful costumes. There is always a big crowd even though it's very cold. One year, more than 100,000 people participated. The celebration in Edinburgh is very well-known, but the annual Hogmanay festivals in other cities in Scotland are popular, too.

B Write the words in blue next to the correct meaning.

1. ____exciting____ delightful, thrilling
2. ____takes place____ happens
3. ____well-known____ famous
4. ____holiday____ a day when people don't work
5. ____crowd____ large group of people
6. ____annual____ happening once each year
7. ____costume____ special clothes for a performance
8. ____festival____ an event with performances of music, etc.
9. ____celebrate____ do something enjoyable for a special day
10. ____participated____ took part in

C Discuss these questions with a partner. What festivals have you participated in? What festivals do you know about? Would you like to participate in Hogmanay in Edinburgh? Why or why not?

Grammar: Comparisons with *as . . . as*

Subject + *be* +	*(not) as* + adjective + *as* +	complement
New Year's Day is	**as** exciting **as**	National Day. (The two holidays are equally exciting.)
Hogmanay is	**not as** popular **as**	Carnival. (Hogmanay is less popular than Carnival; Carnival is more popular than Hogmanay.)

*Use *as . . . as* to say that two things are equal. Use *not as . . . as* to say that two things are not equal.

Word Bank: Holidays

Religious holidays:

Buddhist: Vesak (Buddha's birthday)

Christian: Christmas, Easter

Hindu: Diwali, Holi

Jewish: Chanukah, Passover

Muslim: Eid ul-Adha, Ramadan

Secular holidays:

Valentine's Day, Labor Day

Grammar: Equatives

The construction *as . . . as* can be used with all parts of speech. It can be used with adjectives, adverbs, nouns, or verbs. The form *as . . . as* is normally used with the "stronger" of a pair of adjectives. It is more usual to say *Ed is as old as Joe,* than *Ed is as young as Joe.* If we say *Ed is as young as Joe,* we are emphasizing that both are unusually young. One common use of the construction is to soften a negative statement. Rather than saying *Ed is more intelligent than Joe,* a person would say *Joe is not as intelligent as Ed.*

A Look at the information about the two festivals. Write sentences with *(not) as . . . as.*

	The Spring Festival	**The Harvest Fair**
1. (old)	started in 1970	started in 1970
2. (long)	2 days	4 days
3. (popular)	5,000 people	5,000 people
4. (expensive)	tickets were $5	tickets were $20
5. (big)	10 concerts	23 concerts
6. (well-known)	on a few TV shows	on many TV shows

1. The Spring Festival *is as old as the Harvest Fair* .
2. The Spring Festival *is not as long as the Harvest Fair* .
3. *The Spring Festival is as popular as the Harvest Fair* .
4. *The Spring Festival is not as expensive as the Harvest Fair* .
5. *The Spring Festival is not as big as the Harvest Fair* .
6. *The Spring Festival is not as well-known as the Harvest Fair* .

B  Choose two festivals or holidays. Make sentences with *as . . . as* comparing the celebrations.

Conversation

A 🔊 26 Close your book and listen to the conversation. When is the festival they talk about? *in February*

Dave: Yuki, are there any special festivals in your city?
Yuki: Oh, we have lots of festivals in Tokyo! My favorite is called *Setsubun*.
Dave: Really? What's that?
Yuki: Well, it takes place in February. We celebrate the last day of winter.
Dave: What do you do then?
Yuki: People throw special beans for good luck, and they say "Out with bad luck, in with good luck!" Then you eat one bean for each year of your age. And there are lots of parties.
Dave: That sounds like fun.
Yuki: It is!

B 🔄 Practice the conversation with a partner. Then have new conversations about your favorite holidays and celebrations.

C 🔄 **GOAL CHECK** ✓ **Describe a festival**

Talk to a partner about a special festival in your city. Tell your partner when, why, and how you celebrate this festival.

Celebrations **149**

> Thanksgiving is as enjoyable as Christmas.

> Thanksgiving isn't as expensive as Christmas!

▲ Setsubun procession in Tokyo

A
- Go over the information in the chart. Tell students to write sentences comparing the two festivals.
- Have students compare answers with a partner.
- Check answers.

B
- Divide the class into pairs and have each pair choose two holidays or festivals to compare.
- Call on pairs to present a sentence to the class.

Conversation

A
- Have students close their books. Write the question on the board: *When is the festival they talk about?*
- Play the recording. 🔊 26
- Check answers.

B
- Play or read the conversation again for the class to repeat.
- Practice the conversation with the class in chorus.
- Have students practice the conversation with a partner, then have them make new conversations about their favorite holidays and celebrations.
- Call on several pairs to present one of their new conversations to the class.

C 🔄 **GOAL CHECK** ✓

- Assign new partners and have them take turns discussing a special celebration in their cities. If necessary, suggest that they might want to use the conversation above as a guide for the information they are going to give their partner.

Grammar Practice: Equatives

Divide the class into pairs and have each pair choose two things to compare: two cities, two TV programs, or two sports. Then have them write as many sentences as they can in five minutes, comparing the two things with *as . . . as.* Call on pairs to read their list of sentences to the class. Who has the most correct sentences?

Compare Holidays in Different Countries

Listening

A
- Have students look at the pictures and describe what they see.
- Tell students they are going to hear three people talking about holidays that they celebrate. They should listen for the names of the countries and number them.
- Play the recording one or more times. 🔊 27
- Check answers.

B
- Tell students to listen again to the three speakers and find the missing information to fill in the charts.
- Play the recording one or more times. 🔊 27
- Have students compare answers with a partner.
- Check answers.

Day of the Dead

Country:
_____ Mexico _____

When is it?
_____ November 1 and 2 _____

How do people celebrate it?

a. go to the cemetery with
_____ favorite food and drinks _____

b. bring
_____ orange and yellow flowers _____

What is the special food?

a. sweet
_____ bread _____

b. shaped like skulls
_____ candy _____

Listening

A 🔊 27 Listen to three people talk about a holiday in their country. Number the countries in the order that you hear about them.

a. Japan ___3___   **b.** Mexico ___1___   **c.** United States ___2___

B 🔊 27 Listen again and fill in the charts.

Halloween

Country: _____ United States _____

When is it? _____ October 31 _____

How do people celebrate it?

a. put on _____ costumes _____

b. ask for _____ candy _____

c. watch _____ scary movies _____

What is the special food?

a. _____ chocolate _____

b. _____ apples _____

O-Bon

Country: _____ Japan _____

When is it? _____ August 13 _____

How do people celebrate it?

a. go back to _____ their hometowns _____

b. participate in a special _____ dance _____

c. make big _____ fires _____

150   Unit 12

For Your Information: Halloween

Halloween is a very popular holiday in the United States. Originally celebrated only by children, now it is enjoyed by many adults as well. It comes at the time of a traditional fall harvest celebration, and it incorporates parts of many old celebrations. People decorate their houses with pumpkins that are hollowed out and carved into faces, with a candle inside to light them. Children dress as ghosts, witches, cartoon characters, monsters, and so on. They go to their neighbors' houses, ring the doorbell, and say "trick-or-treat." The neighbors will give the children a treat of candy.

C 🔄 Discuss these questions with a partner.

1. Do you know about any other holidays like this?

2. Why do you think different countries have similar holidays?

Pronunciation: Question intonation with lists

A ◀))️ 28 Listen to the questions. Notice how the intonation rises and falls in questions with a list of choices.

1. Would you like cake, ice cream, or fruit?

2. Is O-Bon in July or August?

B ◀))️ 29 Read the questions and mark the intonation with arrows. Then listen and check your answers.

1. Do you have special food at breakfast, lunch, or dinner?

2. Have you celebrated New Year's in France, Australia, or both?

3. Is your costume red or pink?

4. Is O-Bon in August or September?

5. Do you celebrate with dancing, singing, or gift-giving?

C 🔄 Say each question from exercise **B** to your partner. Give each other feedback on your pronunciation.

Communication

A 👥 Imagine that your group can take a trip to participate in one of the holidays in exercise **A** on page 150. Discuss these questions. Then explain your group's final decision to the class.

1. How are these holidays similar? Think of as many answers as you can.

2. How are they different?

3. What could visitors do at each holiday?

4. Which holiday would you like to participate in? Why?

B 🔄 **GOAL CHECK** ✅ **Compare holidays in different countries**

Take turns. Tell a partner how the different groups' trips will be similar and how they will be different.

C • Divide the class into pairs and have them discuss the questions.

• Compare answers with the class. Point out that many cultures have a special holiday for remembering people who have died.

Pronunciation

A • Have students read the sentences, noticing the lists of items.

• Play the recording. ◀))️ 28

• Point out the pattern: The intonation rises for each item in the list and then falls in the last item.

B • Have students work individually to mark the intonation in the lists in the sentences.

• Play the recording for students to check their answers. ◀))️ 29

• Go over the answers with the class.

C • Divide the class into pairs and have them take turns saying the sentences and questions to each other. Walk around checking for appropriate intonation.

Communication

A • Divide the class into groups of three or four. Have them discuss the questions and then decide which of the three holidays they would most like to participate in.

• Call on each group to explain their decision and reasons. Which holiday was the most popular with the students?

B 🔄 **GOAL CHECK** ✅

• Assign new pairs and have them discuss what the different groups will see and experience on their trips.

Expansion Activity

Have students research and write a paragraph about a holiday from another country. If desired, share the holidays listed in the Word Bank in **Lesson A,** and have students choose one to research.

Talk About Celebrations

Language Expansion

🅐 • Have students look at the picture and describe what they see. Ask, *What would you say to the team after they won the game?* Elicit *well-done/congratulations*, if possible. Elicit any other expressions they know. Ask, *What do you say when someone is starting a new job? Has had a baby?* etc.

• Have students read the expressions and when to use them in the chart.

🅑 • Have students choose the appropriate expression for each situation.

• Have students compare answers with a partner.

• Check answers.

Grammar

• Go over the information in the chart. Ask several students questions, for example, *Would you rather watch a movie at home or go the movie theater? Would you rather do your homework now or later?* etc.

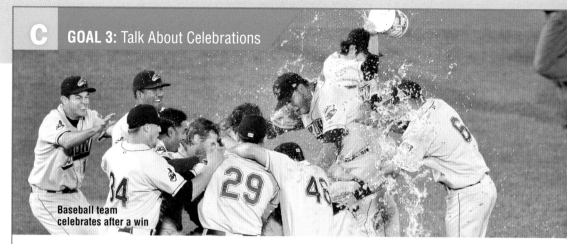

C GOAL 3: Talk About Celebrations

Baseball team celebrates after a win

Language Expansion: Expressions for celebrations

🅐 Read the expressions and their functions.

Expressions and functions
• Congratulations! *(When someone is getting married, having a baby, getting a promotion, winning a game, etc.)*
• Well-done! *(When someone has accomplished something difficult.)*
• Thanks for having/inviting us! *(To thank someone after a party.)*
• Good luck! *(To wish someone a good result or a good future.)*
• Happy Birthday/Anniversary/New Year! etc. *(To greet someone on a holiday or special occasion.)*

🅑 Write the correct expression for each situation.

1. You're leaving someone's house after a dinner party. *Thanks for having us! / Thanks for inviting us!*

2. Your friend has to take a difficult exam tomorrow. *Good luck!*

3. Your neighbor tells you he plans to get married soon. *Congratulations!*

4. Today is your friend's birthday. You see your friend. *Happy Birthday!*

5. Your friend got an excellent grade on an exam. *Well done!*

Grammar: *Would rather*

Use *would rather* + base form of the verb to talk about actions we prefer or like more than other actions.	**I would rather go** to a big wedding than go to a small wedding.
We often use a contraction of *would*.	**They'd rather meet** us at the library.
Use *would rather not* + base form of the verb to talk about things we don't want to do.	**She'd rather not go** to the meeting It's going to be long and boring.
Use *would rather* + base form of the verb in *yes/no* questions to ask people about their preferences.	**Would you rather have** the dinner party at our house or at a restaurant?

152 Unit 12

Word Bank:
Celebration activities

dance	make a toast
give gifts	send a card
go out for dinner	take pictures
have a party	

Grammar: *Would rather* + infinitive

Would rather + infinitive is used to express a preference among alternatives. The second item may be omitted if it is understood from context:

Would you like to have pizza tonight?

No, I'd rather have steak (than pizza).

A Write sentences about things you like to do on your birthday with *I'd rather*.

1. have (a big party/a small party) *I'd rather have a big party.*
2. eat (at home/in a restaurant) _____
3. invite (lots of people/a few close friends) _____
4. get (flowers/presents) _____
5. wear (nice clothes/jeans and a T-shirt) _____
6. (your own idea/your own idea) _____

B 🔄 Ask your partner about his or her preferences. Use the choices in exercise **A** and *Would you rather . . . ?*

> **Would you rather have a big party or a small party?**

> **I'd rather have a big party!**

Conversation

A 🔊 30 Close your book and listen to the conversation. Which celebration is coming soon? *New Year's Eve*

Mike:	New Year's Eve is next week. What would you like to do?
Katie:	Let's go to a party!
Mike:	I'd rather just stay home and go to bed early.
Katie:	That's boring! We could go out for dinner. Or would you rather go to a movie?
Mike:	I'd rather not go out. It's always so noisy and crowded.
Katie:	I have an idea. Let's cook a nice dinner at home and invite a few friends.
Mike:	That sounds like a better plan.

B 🔄 Practice the conversation with a partner. Switch roles and practice it again.

C Make notes. What do you usually do to celebrate these days?

Your birthday	Your favorite holiday: _____

D 🔄 Work with a partner. Make plans to celebrate one of these days together.

E 👥 **GOAL CHECK** ✔ **Talk about celebrations**

Join another pair of students and share your plans.

Celebrations **153**

A • Have students work individually to write sentences about their preferences with *I'd rather*.
• Check answers.

B • Model the example conversation with a student.
• Divide the class into pairs and have them find out about each other's preferences, using the prompts in **A**.
• Have several students share something about their partner's preferences.

Conversation

A • Have students close their books. Write the question on the board: *Which celebration is coming soon?*
• Play the recording. 🔊 30
• Check answer.

B • Play or read the conversation again for the class to repeat.
• Practice the conversation with the class in chorus.
• Have students practice the conversation with a partner, then switch roles and practice it again.

C • Have students work individually to write notes about how they usually celebrate the two days.

D • Assign new pairs and have them make new conversations, modeled on the conversation in **A**.

E 👥 **GOAL CHECK** ✔

• Combine pairs into groups of four and have them talk about the plans they've made.
• Ask the class about any interesting or unusual plans they heard.

Grammar Practice: *Would rather*

Have students carry out an opinion survey about holiday preferences. Divide the class into groups. Have each group plan two questions about preferences for celebrating an event with *would rather*. Allow time for each student to collect answers from three people in class or outside of the school. Then have each group put together the answers they received and give a short oral report for the class.

Lesson C **153**

Share Opinions About Holidays

Reading

A
- Have students look at the picture and describe what they see. Have them read the title and elicit ideas about what they will read about in the article.
- Divide the class into pairs and have them discuss the questions.
- Compare answers with the class. If any of the holidays are new, ask, *Are there any differences between new holidays and old ones? Are new holidays as good as old ones?*

B
- Have students read the information and underline the key words that will help them find the details in the article; for example, *number of people, dates,* etc.
- Have students read the article. Tell them to circle any words they don't understand. Point out the vocabulary that is defined in the footnotes.
- Have students fill in the information.
- Have students compare answers with a partner.
- Go over the article with the class, answering any questions from the students about vocabulary.
- Check answers.

C
- Have students go through the article again to answer *true, false,* or *no information* for each statement. Remind them that for some statements, the answer is not in the reading—they should circle **NI** for those.
- Have students compare answers with a partner.
- Check answers.

Reading

A Discuss these questions with a partner.

1. What are the most important holidays in your country?
2. Are they new or old? How did they start?

B Find this information in the reading.

1. the number of people who celebrate Kwanzaa now __(more than) 5 million__
2. the dates of Kwanzaa __Dec. 26-Jan. 1__
3. the year when Kwanzaa started __1966__
4. the person who started Kwanzaa _____ __Maulana Karenga__
5. three countries where people celebrate Kwanzaa __the United States, Canada, and Jamaica__
6. the most important symbol of Kwanzaa _____ __a candleholder__
7. the colors of Kwanzaa __red, black, and green__

C Circle **T** for *true*, **F** for *false*, or **NI** for *no information* (if the answer is not in the reading).

1. Kwanzaa is celebrated at the end of the year. **(T)** F NI
2. Kwanzaa is a holiday for African Americans. **(T)** F NI
3. Kwanzaa is a very old holiday. T **(F)** NI
4. People in Africa celebrate Kwanzaa. T F **(NI)**
5. People spend a lot of time with their families during Kwanzaa. **(T)** F NI
6. Children receive presents at the end of Kwanzaa. **(T)** F NI
7. Everyone thinks Kwanzaa is an important holiday. T F **(NI)**

STARTING A NEW TRADITION

Shantelle Davis is a nine-year-old girl in New York. On a cold night in December, her family is standing around the kitchen table while she lights a **candle**. The table is decorated with baskets of fruit and vegetables and **ears of corn** for Shantelle and her two brothers.

"This candle represents *umoja*, an African word that means being together," Shantelle says. "That's the most important thing for a family."

More than 5 million African Americans celebrate Kwanzaa every year from December 26 until January 1. It's a time when they get together with their families to think about their history and their ancestors in Africa.

Kwanzaa is very unusual because it was started by one man. In 1966, an American named Maulana Karenga wanted a holiday for African Americans to **honor** their culture and traditions. So he used words and customs from Africa to create a new celebration. He took the name Kwanzaa from the words for "first fruits" in Swahili, an African language. At first, only a few families had celebrations. Now, there are Kwanzaa events in schools and public places, and Kwanzaa has even spread to other countries, like Canada and Jamaica.

The main symbol of Kwanzaa is a **candleholder** with seven candles, one for each of the principles of Kwanzaa. Each night, a family member lights one of the candles and talks about the idea it represents: being together, being yourself, helping each other, sharing, having a goal, creating, and believing. The candles are red, black, and green, the colors of Kwanzaa. The parents also **pour** drinks to honor family members who have died. On the last night of Kwanzaa, there is a big dinner with African food, and children receive small presents.

For Your Information: Kwanzaa and winter holidays

In the Northern Hemisphere, there are many holidays at the beginning of winter, which has become known as the "holiday season." The period begins with Thanksgiving at the end of November; continues through Christmas, Chanukah, and Kwanzaa in December; and ends in January with New Year's Day and the Feast of the Three Kings (January 6). Nowadays, it is quite common to send greeting cards that simply say "Happy Holidays" or "Season's Greetings" to include people of any (or no) religious beliefs.

Today, people can buy Kwanzaa greeting cards and special Kwanzaa clothes. Stores sell Kwanzaa candles and candleholders. Some people don't believe that Kwanzaa is as important as other holidays because it's so new. But other people say that Kwanzaa shows what is important in people's lives.

candle *stick of hard wax burned to provide light*
ear of corn *part of the corn plant* **honor** *show great respect for someone* **candleholder** *device to hold a candle*
pour *make a liquid flow into a container*

Celebrations **155**

After Reading

Web search: Have students search online for information about one of these holidays in English-speaking countries: Thanksgiving, Guy Fawkes Day, Boxing Day, Groundhog Day.

Project: To celebrate the end of the course, have students organize a party for the last day of class. Divide the class into four groups and give them responsibility for food, drinks, decorations, and music/entertainment. Enjoy your time together and congratulate each other for your successes and achievements!

Share Opinions About Holidays

Communication

A • Have students look at the picture and describe what they see. Ask, *Do you think Chuseok is a new holiday or a traditional holiday? What do you think about new holidays? Is it good to start new traditions?*

• Have students read the sentences and write their opinion about each one.

B • Divide the class into groups of three or four. Have them discuss their answers and give reasons for their opinions. Remind them to discuss how their families celebrate holidays.

Writing

A • Have students read the Writing Strategy. If possible, write a paragraph yourself using one of the statements in **A.** Show it to students and have them identify the three sections presented in the Writing Strategy. Alternatively, cut the paragraph up into three and have students work with a partner to put it in order.

B • Ask students to choose one of the sentences from **Communication A** and write their own opinion paragraph. Remind them to include the three elements in the Writing Strategy.

C **GOAL CHECK** ✔

• Divide the class into pairs and have then read each other's paragraphs and answer the questions.

• Have students give their partner feedback on their paragraph by explaining their answers.

• Have students re-work their paragraph to improve it based on their partner's feedback.

• If desired, collect the paragraphs for grading.

D | **GOAL 4:** Share Opinions About Holidays

Chuseok celebration in Korea

Communication

I agree.
I'm not sure.
I disagree.

A Write your opinion about these sentences in your notebook. Use the expressions in the box.

1. A new holiday isn't a real holiday.

2. Some old holidays are not very important now.

3. Our country should start a new holiday.

4. People spend too much money for holidays.

5. It's very important to keep all of the old holiday customs.

B Compare your opinions with the opinions of other students. Talk about things your family does to celebrate holidays.

**Writing strategy:
An effective opinion paragraph**

1. Begin with a strong topic sentence which clearly states your point of view.

2. Support your opinion by giving good, logical reasons for it.

3. End with a brief conclusion related to the opinion and reasons you gave.

Writing

A Read the information about writing an opinion paragraph.

B Choose one of the statements from exercise **A** and write a paragraph about your opinion. Be sure the paragraph contains all three elements from the writing strategy.

C **GOAL CHECK** ✔ **Share opinions about holidays**

Read your partner's paragraph and write answers to the questions. Then explain your answers to your partner.

1. Does the paragraph have a strong, clear topic sentence? Explain.

2. Is your partner's opinion supported with good reasons? Explain.

3. Is there a conclusion that ends the paragraph well? Explain.

Teacher Tip: Self-evaluation

Providing models of texts for students to read and work with prior to writing their own text, as suggested in **Writing A** teacher notes, is very useful for students and will help them produce more appropriate texts. Seeing an example helps them understand better what is expected and what the final product should look like. Furthermore, carrying out activities where they have to put the model text in order or identify the parts of the text are especially helpful for visual and kinesthetic students. It also helps students to understand the organization and structure of a text in English, which may differ from how a text would be organized in their own language.

Young Mongolian riders going to the Naadam Festival.

Mongolia

Before You Watch

A ⚡ Discuss these questions with a partner. What do you know about Mongolia? Have you ever seen a horse race? Describe what you saw.

While You Watch

A ▶ Watch the video *Young Riders of Mongolia*. Write two unusual things about the Naadam horse race.

1. _____ 2. _____

The riders are children, not adults.

They do many things for good luck before the race.

The horses walk a long way before they start running.

People can't see the whole race.

They try to get close to the horses.

There is a prize for the slowest horse.

B ▶ Watch the video again. Circle **T** for *true* or **F** for *false*.

1. In Mongolia today, people ride horses only for special celebrations.   T   **F**
2. The Naadam Festival celebrates traditional sports.   **T**   F
3. The Naadam horse race is very short.   T   **F**
4. People want to get close to the horses for good luck.   **T**   F
5. The winning horses get a lot of money.   T   **F**

After You Watch / Communication

A 👥 Discuss these questions in a small group. What are some traditional sports in your country? Are they still popular?

B 👥 Create a festival to introduce foreigners to the culture of your country. Present your festival to the class.

- Give the festival a name.
- Think of three sports, foods, and shows that will be in the festival.
- Make a poster to advertise your festival.

Celebrations   157

Video Journal:
Young Riders of Mongolia

Before You Watch

A • Have students look at the picture and describe what they see.
- Divide the class into pairs and have them discuss the questions.
- Compare answers with the class. If necessary, describe a horse race.

While You Watch

A • Tell students to watch the video the first time and find two unusual things about the race.
- Play the video.
- Check answers.

B • Tell students to watch the video again and answer *true* or *false*. Then have them read the statements.
- Play the video.
- Have students compare answers with a partner. Check answers.

After You Watch / Communication

A • In groups of three or four, have them discuss the questions.
- Compare answers with the class. Discuss the various traditional sports.

B • Have students continue to work in the same groups.
- Go over the instructions with the class. Emphasize that this festival is for foreigners, so they should choose the most interesting and important sports, foods, and shows.
- Have groups present their festivals, showing their posters. As they listen to their classmates, have students complete a chart with the sports, food, and shows each group includes in their festival, or write a question to ask the presenting group, etc.

For Your Information: Mongolia

The Naadam festival has taken place for centuries and is devoted to the three main Mongolian sports: archery, wrestling, and horse racing. Traditionally, these were known as the "three manly sports." Today, both men and women take part in archery and horse racing, but only men wrestle. The Naadam festival takes place all over Mongolia for two days during the midsummer holidays (mid-July). The festival has its roots in the nomad wedding parties and extravagant hunting expeditions of the Mongol army. Before the sporting events begin, there is a parade with soldiers, monks, musicians, dancers, and the athletes. Naadam has been recognized by UNESCO and in 2010 was added to UNESCO's Intangible Cultural Heritage List.

My Wish–Protect Our Oceans

Before You Watch

A • Have students look at the picture and answer the questions with a partner.

• Compare answers with the class.

B • Go over the words in the box. Have students complete the paragraph using the words. Remind them to change the form of the verbs when necessary.

• Have students compare answers with a partner.

• Check answers.

C • Have students read the directions and look at the pictures on page 159. Have them check the information they think they will hear in the TED Talk.

• Have students compare answers with a partner.

• Compare answers with the class. Write their ideas about what they will hear in the TED Talk on the board.

While You Watch

A • Have students read the three possible main ideas. Tell them to circle the main idea as they watch the talk.

• Play the talk.

• Have students compare their answer with a partner.

• Check answer.

TEDTALKS

Sylvia Earle Oceanographer, National Geographic Explorer-in-Residence
MY WISH—PROTECT OUR OCEANS

Before You Watch

A ⚡ Look at the picture and answer the questions with a partner.

1. Where are these people?

2. Why are they there?

3. What do you think they're doing?

B Sylvia Earle is one of the explorers in the picture. Here are some words you will hear in her TED Talk. Complete the paragraph with the correct word. Not all words will be used.

> **assets** *n.* valuable people or things
> **cope** *v.* to deal with problems and difficult situations and try to come up with solutions
> **depletion** *n.* reduction, shortage
> **drawn down** *v.* reduced
> **enduring** *adj.* continuing to exist in the same state or condition
> **impact** *n.* a powerful or major influence or effect
> **resilient** *adj.* able to become strong, healthy, or successful again after something bad happens

Dr. Sylvia Earle has been exploring Earth's oceans for more than 50 years. She knows how important it is to protect the (1) _____*assets*_____ that are found in the sea. She is worried about

---

> Sylvia Earle's idea worth spreading is that we need to do a better job of looking after our oceans, the world's "life support system." Watch Earle's full **TED**Talk on TED.com.

the (2) _____*depletion*_____ of sea life she has seen—90% of the world's big fish are gone, (3) _____*drawn down*_____ by a growing population, pollution, and wasteful fishing practices. Dr. Earle believes that we must all work together to (4) _____*cope*_____ with this problem by reducing our (5) _____*impact*_____ on the ocean before it is too late.

C Look at the pictures on the next page. Check (✓) the information that you predict you will hear in the TED Talk.

____ **1.** The deep ocean is a dangerous place for humans.

✓ **2.** When we know more about creatures that live in the sea, we can protect them better.

✓ **3.** Human activity has changed the ocean in many negative ways.

While You Watch

A ▶ Watch the TED Talk. Circle the main idea.

①. If we don't protect the ocean, humans will be in danger, too.

2. There are many kinds of fish in the ocean that we don't know about.

3. It is important to develop new ways to catch fish.

Viewing Tip

Encourage students to take notes as they watch the TED Talks. Note taking is a useful study skill for students, as it helps them to focus on key words and ideas and also to remember details for later discussion and analysis. Reading their notes after listening can help them understand ideas that they didn't understand when they heard the talk. The notes can help students make educated guesses about the meaning of new words and the ideas that were expressed.

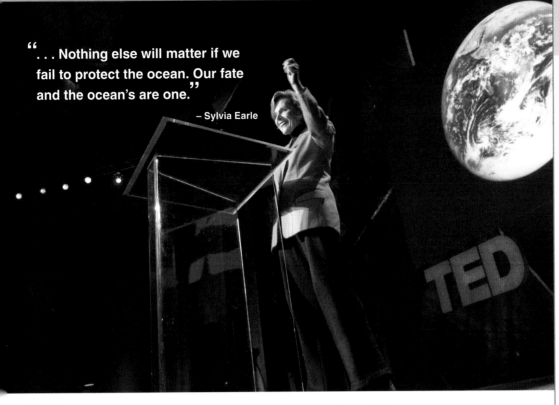

" . . . Nothing else will matter if we fail to protect the ocean. Our fate and the ocean's are one."

– Sylvia Earle

B • Have students read the captions and look at the pictures. Tell them to match the captions to the pictures as they watch the talk again.

• Play the talk again.

• Have students compare answers with a partner.

• Check answers. Play the talk again as necessary.

• Go back to the predictions students made in **Before You Watch C.** Ask, *Were your predictions correct?*

Challenge

• Have students read the directions. Elicit words to describe Earle's work and write them on the board.

• Have students discuss the questions with a partner.

• Compare ideas with the class.

B ▶ Look at the photos. Watch the TED Talk again and write the letter of the caption under the correct photo.

a. Sylvia Earle has developed many devices for underwater exploration.

b. There are many amazing creatures in the ocean.

c. Polar ice is shrinking, and life for polar bears is getting harder.

d. Sylvia Earle loves the ocean and all the creatures that live in it.

1. _d_   **2.** _c_   **3.** _a_   **4.** _b_

Challenge! ↻ How would you describe Dr. Sylvia Earle's work as an ocean explorer? Is her work difficult or easy? Why does she do it? Talk to a partner about Sylvia Earle's career.

159

For Your Information: Sylvia Earle

Dr. Sylvia Earle is an American oceanographer, explorer, author, and lecturer. She is an explorer-in-residence at the National Geographic Society and works relentlessly to raise awareness about the damage that is being done to the world's oceans. She stresses the importance of understanding the oceans and the life within them and how our life depends on the oceans being healthy. Earle has led more than 50 underwater expeditions involving more than 6,000 hours underwater. Her achievements as an ocean scientist have been and continue to be of great significance; she has walked untethered on the sea floor at a depth that no other woman has reached, and started two companies which design undersea vehicles that enable scientists to reach previously inaccessible depths. After winning the TED prize in 2009, she established Mission Blue, an organization that supports ocean conservation projects.

After You Watch

A • Have students complete the summary with the words from the box.
• Have students compare answers with a partner.
• Check answers.

B • Have students match the phrases to the information given in the TED Talk.
• Have students compare answers with a partner.
• Check answers.

C • Have students read the statements and circle the ones that express ideas from the TED Talk.
• Have students compare answers with a partner.
• Check answers.

TEDTALKS

Sylvia Earle Oceanographer, National Geographic Explorer-in-Residence
MY WISH—PROTECT OUR OCEANS

After You Watch

A Complete the summary with the words in the box.

Sylvia Earle is worried about the (1) _____ocean_____ . Even more, she is worried about our planet's (2) _____survival_____ . The ocean is our life (3) _____support_____ system, and if we don't protect it, we will be in (4) _____trouble_____ . Dr. Earle wants us to (5) _____understand_____ the ocean and its creatures better, because if we understand the seas better, we will want to (6) _____protect_____ them.

ocean	protect
support	survival
trouble	understand

B Match the phrases to the information from the TED Talk.

_e_ **1.** percent of the world's oceans that is protected   **a.** 50

_a_ **2.** years that Sylvia Earle has been exploring the ocean   **b.** 90

_d_ **3.** percent of life on the planet that lives in the ocean   **c.** 10

_b_ **4.** percent of large fish species that have disappeared   **d.** 97

_c_ **5.** number of years we have to protect the ocean   **e.** .08

C Read the statements below. Circle the ones that paraphrase Sylvia Earle's ideas in the video.

(**1.**) The loss of fish species in the last 50 years is a problem.

2. People should use the ocean's resources any way they want to.

(**3.**) The oceans make it possible for human beings to live on earth.

4. The creatures that live in the deep ocean aren't as important as those on land.

(**5.**) We only have a short time to protect the ocean.

160

One reason for the depletion of ocean resources is wasteful fishing practices.

Project

Sylvia Earle says that if we don't work to protect the oceans right now, we risk all life on the planet. She works with other scientists and explorers to find ways to protect and sustain ocean environments. What can be done to keep the ocean healthy for future generations?

A Look at these ways we can work to protect the ocean. Which ones are the most urgent? Rank them from most urgent (1) to less urgent (6).

_____ recycle plastics so they don't end up in the ocean

_____ change the way fishermen work so that less fish is wasted

_____ keep oil and other toxic chemicals out of the sea

_____ use less energy (gasoline and electricity) to slow global warming

_____ share the message that protecting the ocean is our collective responsibility

_____ establish conservation/protection zones

B Compare your rankings in exercise **A** with a partner. Do you have the same priorities? Think of some other ways to protect the ocean.

C Use Sylvia Earle's ideas to write a paragraph about ways we can help keep the ocean safe for future generations. Then show your paragraph to a different partner. Are your ideas well organized?

> The oceans are in danger, and everyone can help to save them. If we want to _____, we should start with _____. By doing _____, we can. It is also important to change _____. Finally, we need to _____.

Challenge! Dr. Sylvia Earle has a really big idea worth spreading—one that can change the world and save our oceans. Research what your country's experts are doing to protect oceans and other aquatic environments. Share your ideas with the class.

Research Strategy

Using the search function on web pages

If you want to learn more about a topic on a Web site, use the Web site's search function. You can usually find search windows at the top of the page. They are usually located next to a magnifying glass icon. Sometimes search results can be sorted by relevance, date of publication, or type of resource.

161

Project

- Have students read the project information.

A • Go over the list of ways to help the ocean, explaining vocabulary as necessary. Have students rank them from most (1) to least (6) urgent.

B • Divide the class into pairs and have them compare their rankings.

- Have pairs make a list of other ways to help the ocean.

C • Have students read the directions and the outline for the paragraph. Have them identify the topic sentence, supporting ideas, and conclusion.

- Have students write their paragraphs individually. Provide vocabulary as necessary.

- Have students exchange paragraphs with a partner and identify the three parts of an effective paragraph. Have them help each other improve their paragraphs.

Challenge

- Have students read the information.

- In pairs, have students research TED prizes. Tell them to find out what TED prizes are, when they started giving them, examples of people who have won TED prizes, and whether other oceanographers have won a TED prize.

- Have pairs report back to the class.

- Have students read the information in the Research Strategy box.

- Point out that they can use this strategy to find out about TED prizes at the TED Web site, TED.com.

Ideas Worth Sharing

- With books closed, have students share what they remember about Sylvia Earle and her work. Ask, *What does Dr. Earle do? How long has she been doing it? What is her message? Why are the oceans so important? What's her wish?* Write their ideas on the board.

- Have students go back to the Ideas Worth Sharing box on page 158. Remind them that they can watch the whole talk at TED.com to help them develop their listening skills.

Expansion: Comparing opinions

Have students watch ocean explorer Robert Ballard's TED Talk, *The astonishing hidden world of the deep ocean.* Have students work with a partner and complete a similarities and differences chart to compare and contrast Earle's and Ballard's views on ocean exploration and conservation. Have pairs join together to compare their charts.

GLOSSARY

UNIT 1

beans: a legume plant whose seeds sometimes are different colors, such as black or red, and can be cooked and eaten

climate: normal weather patterns

coast: describes an area near the ocean

corn: a grain that is grown on tall green plants and usually has large yellow seeds that are fed to animals or cooked and eaten by people

crop: a kind of plant grown for food

delicious: something that is good-tasting

disgusting: something that causes great dislike

farmer: person who produces food

flat: describes an area without mountains

fragrant: something that has a pleasant or perfumed smell

geography: the study of the surface of the earth

humid: describes air that is moist

land: areas of earth's upper crust composed mainly of soil and sometimes bodies of fresh water, such as rivers or lakes

lentils: a legume plants whose small round seeds can be cooked and eaten

meal: breakfast, lunch, and dinner

mountain: a tall formation of land and rock higher than a hill

oats: a type of grain usually eaten by animals and people

potatoes: a round starchy root vegetable that can be cooked and eaten

rice: a grain used for food that is usually small and white and grows in watery areas

region: a large area

smelly: something that has a strong or unpleasant smell

soybeans: a legume plant native to Asia, used to make foods such as tofu and soy sauce

staple food: very important food

wheat: a grain usually ground into flour and used to make things such as pasta or bread

yams: a plant with an orange root that can be cooked and eaten, sometimes called sweet potato

yucca: a plant, usually grown in warm climates, whose root can be cooked and eaten

UNIT 2

connect: bring together

culture: people with the same language and way of living

custom: an activity that is usual in a country

formal: very serious and important

gesture: a body movement to show something (a feeling, an idea, etc.)

greeting: the first words or actions used upon meeting someone

informal: friendly and relaxed

misunderstanding: a mistaken idea that causes confusion

rule: the correct way to do something

small talk: conversation about things that aren't important

smile: turn one's lips up at the corners, usually to show good feelings

traditional: the same for a long time without changing

UNIT 3

commute: travel to your job

crowded: too full

east: the direction where the sun comes up—usually at the right of a map

highway: a road where cars go fast

key: (on a map) the section of a map that explains the meaning of the symbols

neighborhood: one area in a city

nightlife: things to do in the evening

noisy: too loud

north: the direction that's usually at the top of a map

population: the number of people who live in a place

public transportation: trains, buses, and subways

rural: in the country

scale: (on a map) the section of a map that explains the distances

south: the direction that's usually at the bottom of a map

traffic: cars moving on a street

urban: in the city

west: the direction where the sun goes down—usually at the left of a map

UNIT 4

artery: one of the large blood vessels going from the heart

bone: a hard, white part of the body that makes up its frame (the skeleton)

brain: the organ in the head used for thinking and feeling

fever: higher than normal body temperature

headache: a pain in your head

heart: the organ in the chest that pumps blood through the body

hiccup: a sharp sound you make in your throat

indigestion: pain in the stomach because of something you have eaten

insomnia: not able to sleep

large intestine: the lower part of the tube in the body that carries food away from the stomach

liver: the organ in the body that helps in making sugar for energy and in cleaning the blood

lung: one of two breathing organs in the chest that supply oxygen to the blood

muscle: a part of the body that connects the bones and makes the body move

nausea: a feeling like you are going to vomit

pimple: a small red swelling on the skin

skin: the outer covering of the body

small intestine: the upper part of the tube in the body that carries food away from the stomach

sore throat: a general feeling of pain in the throat

stomach: the internal body part where food goes after being swallowed

vein: any of the tubes that bring blood to the heart and lungs

UNIT 5

achieve: succeed in making something happen

adventure: something unusual and exciting

amazing: very surprising and wonderful

artist: a person who creates art such as a painter or a musician

break down: something that stops working

business person: someone who works in the business world

challenge: something that is new and difficult to do

equipment: things you need for a particular purpose

explorer: a person who explores unfamiliar areas, an adventurer

give up: stop trying

goal: something you hope to be able to do through your efforts over time

grow up: grow from a child to an adult

keep on: continue trying

mental: something that is related to the mind

political figure: someone who works in a political field, such as a governor, mayor, or president

physical: something that is related to the body

progress: an advancement towards a goal

put up with: accept something bad without being upset

run out of: finish the amount of something that you have

scientist: a person who works and conducts research within the field of science

set out: leave on a trip

skill: an activity that needs special knowledge and practice

watch out: be very careful

writer: a person who makes a living by writing

UNIT 6

adolescence: the part of life when you are becoming an adult

adult: a person aged 20 or over

adulthood: the part of life when you are an adult

baby: a person aged 0–1

child: a person aged 2–12

childhood: the part of life when you are a child

childish: describes a person who is older, but acting like a child (bad)

elderly: describes a person who looks and acts old

in his/her twenties: describes a person who is between 20 and 29 (also **in his teens, thirties, forties,** etc.)

infancy: the part of life when you are a baby

mature: describes a person who is old enough to be responsible and make good decisions

middle-aged: describes a person who is not young or old (about 40–60)

old age: the part of life when you are old

retired: describes a person who has stopped working in old age

senior citizen: an old person (polite term)

teenager: a person aged 13–19

youthful: describes a person who is older, but with the energy of a young person (good)

UNIT 7

build: to make something from different parts or materials

diamond: the hardest gemstone, made of colorless carbon and very valuable

electronics: machines that use electricity such as laptops, televisions, or musical equipment

emerald: a precious green gemstone

expensive watch: a highly-priced small clock worn around the wrist

fame: the state of being well-known and talked about

find: to come across or chance upon something

freeze: to preserve food by keeping it very cold

fur coat: a coat made from the hairy skin of an animal

give: to offer something freely, to make a gift

gold: a precious yellow metal used to make jewelry, coins, and other objects

handmade jewelry: decorative items, crafted by artisans, that people wear such as rings, bracelets, and necklaces

know: to posses knowledge or understand something

lose: to become unable to find

luxury: great comfort at great expense

pearl necklace: a string of smooth, round, white objects, formed naturally in oysters, that is worn around the neck

precious metals: extremely valuable, costly metals such as gold

precious stones: extremely valuable, costly stones such as diamonds

put: to place something

send: to cause to go or move

silk shirt: the material made by silkworms sewn into a piece of clothing worn on the upper body, usually with sleeves, a collar, and buttons

silver: a white, shinny, metallic element used for making jewelry, knives, forks, spoons, and other objects

UNIT 8

badly: the adverb form of *bad*

beautifully: the adverb form of *beautiful*

extinct: doesn't exist any more, all dead

fast: the adverb form of *fast*

habitat: the place where an animal usually lives

hunt: to look for animals and kill them

loudly: the adverb form of *loud*

predator: an animal that kills other animals

prey: an animal that other animals kill to eat

protect: to keep safe from danger

slowly: the adverb form of *slow*

species: a kind of animal

well: the adverb form of *good*

wild: in nature, not controlled by people

UNIT 9

bring back: to take something back from where it was taken

bring up: raise someone and care for until fully grown

beyond: on the other side of

despite: even though, in spite of

distant: far away

exchange: a trade, transaction of ideas or objects

figure out: work through a problem to find a solution

give up: stop doing or having something

help out: do something good for someone

inspired: to motivate or stimulate

published: to print and distribute to the public

put on: (clothing) to dress

remarkable: something that is worthy of attention, extraordinary or outstanding

search: the action of looking for something

ships: large boats used to navigate large bodies of water

trade: an exchange of objects or materials for financial gain

turn on: use a switch to turn on an electrical appliance or machine

UNIT 10

airline agent: a person who works for an airline at an airport

baggage claim: the part of an airport where travelers get their bags back

boarding pass: a card that shows your seat number on an airplane

carry-on bag: a small bag that you can take on an airplane with you

departures: the part of an airport where travelers leave

gate: the part of an airport where travelers get on an airplane

itinerary: a plan for where you will go on a trip

passport: an official document that you must show when you enter or leave a country

reservation: a place that is saved for you in a hotel, airplane, train, etc.

security check: the part of an airport where officers look for dangerous things in travelers' bags

sightseeing: the act of visiting special places as a tourist

terminal: a large building at an airport

ticket: a printed piece of paper that says you paid for a place on a train, airplane, etc.

travel agent: a worker who arranges trips for other people

vaccination: an injection that stops you from getting a particular disease

visa: a stamp or paper that allows you to enter a foreign country

UNIT 11

assistant: someone who helps another person do their work; a word used before job titles to indicate slightly lower rank

bored: a feeling of being uninterested in something

boring: uninteresting

boss: the person in charge of others

computer software engineer: someone who designs computer programs

employee: someone who works for a person, business, or government

experience: understanding gained through doing something

health care worker: someone who gives medical care

information technology specialist: an expert in the theory and practice of using computers to store and analyze information

interested: a feeling of curiosity or a desire to know more about a subject

lawyer: a professional who practices law

owner: someone with a business that belongs to him or her

qualification: an ability that makes someone suitable to do something

sales representative: someone who sells goods and services, usually outside of a store

satisfying: something that meets your wants or needs

surprised: a feeling of pleasure or shock over an unexpected event

terrifying: causing a strong fear in someone

training: a process of education, instruction

volunteer: someone who agrees to do something because they want to, not because they have to

UNIT 12

annual: every year

celebrate: do something enjoyable for a special day

Congratulations!: a greeting you use when someone graduates or gets a new job

costume: special clothes that people wear for a performance or for a holiday

crowd: a very large group of people in one place

exciting: makes you feel happy and enthusiastic

festival: a time with many performances of music, dance, etc.

Good luck!: a greeting used to wish someone a good result

Happy anniversary!: a greeting you use when people celebrate being married for a certain number of years (such as 10, 25, or 50)

Happy birthday!: a greeting you use when someone has a birthday

Happy New Year!: a greeting you use on New Year's Day

holiday: a day when people don't work

participate: take part in

take place: happen

Thanks for having/inviting us!: a greeting used to thank someone for inviting you to their home or party

Well-done!: a greeting used to congratulate someone when they accomplish something difficult

well-known: famous

SKILLS INDEX

GRAMMAR

as + adjective + *as*, 148–149
active voice, 84–84
adjectives
    for age, 72
    comparatives, 44–45
    equatives, 44–45, 136–137
    with *how*, 72–73
    participial, 140
    superlatives, 44–45
adverbs
    already/ever/never/yet, 20–21
    enough/not enough/too + adjective, 60–61
    with *how*, 72–73
    of manner, 100
equatives, 44–45, 136–137
how + adjective or adverb, 72–73
indefinite pronouns, 140–141
infinitives of purpose, 49
modals
    for giving advice, 136–137
    of necessity, 124–125
    of prohibition, 128–129
passive voice, 84–85, 88–89
quantifiers, 100–101
real conditionals in future, 96–97
used to, 108–109
verbs
    future with *will*, 28–29
    irregular, 88
    passive voice with *by*, 88–89
    past continuous vs. simple past, 56
    past continuous with the simple past, 57
    past passive voice, 112–113
    phrasal verbs, 60, 112
    present passive voice, 84–85
    present perfect tense, 16–17, 20–21, 68–69
    simple past tense, 8–9
    simple present vs. present continuous tense, 4–5
    will + time clauses, 32–33
would rather, 152–153

LISTENING

conversations, 9, 18, 21, 33, 49, 61, 73, 89, 101, 113, 129, 141, 153
discussions, 46, 86, 126, 150
interviews, 6, 58, 138
radio programs, 30, 70, 98
talk, 110

PRONUNCIATION

content words, 86
-ed endings, 59
emphatic stress, 30
function words, 86
have/has vs. contractions, 18
intonation in questions, 138–139, 151
linking with
    comparatives and superlatives, 47
    final consonant followed by vowel, 7
phrases in sentences, 99
reductions
    got to/have to/has to, 126–127
    used to, 111
schwa (ə), 70
sentence stress, 86–87

READING SKILLS, 10, 22, 34, 50, 62, 74, 90, 102, 114, 130, 142, 154

READINGS

A Slice of History, 10–11
Arctic Dreams and Nightmares, 62–63
How Food Shapes Our Cities, 34–35
How Poachers Became Caretakers, 102–103
Living Beyond Limits, 74–75
Lord of the Mongols, 114–115
Making Filthy Water Drinkable, 142–143
Perfume: the Essence of Illusion, 90–91
Starting a New Tradition, 154–155
Taking Pictures of the World, 22–23
Tiny Invaders, 50–51
Tourists or Trees?, 130–131

SPEAKING

asking and answering questions, 5, 9, 17, 45, 57, 139
comparing, 4–5
conversations, 5, 7, 9, 17, 19, 21, 29, 31, 33, 45, 49, 57, 61, 69, 71, 73, 85, 89, 97, 109, 111, 137, 141, 149, 153
describing, 9,
discussing, 11, 17, 98,
explaining, 31
ice breakers, 20–21
making plans, 33
role playing, 49, 99
small talk, 18–21
suggesting, 49, 91

TEST-TAKING SKILLS

checking off answers, 29, 34, 44, 59, 65, 74, 102, 110, 114, 145
circling answers, 6, 18, 19, 25, 28, 30, 32, 37, 38, 40, 41, 58, 60, 62, 65, 70, 74, 76, 78, 80, 81, 93, 98, 101, 118, 120, 124, 133, 141, 144, 158, 160
completing charts, 6, 31, 41, 71, 81, 84, 87, 101, 121, 132, 153

TOPICS

VIDEO JOURNALS

VOCABULARY

WRITING

ILLUSTRATION:

8: (tl) Kenneth Batelman; **32:** (t) Kenneth Batelman; **44:** (t, c, b) Sharon & Joel Harris/IllustrationOnline.com; **48:** (1,2,3,4,5) Keith Neely/IllustrationOnline.com; **93, 98, 110:** (inset) National Geographic Maps; **124:** (1,2,4,5,6,7,8) Patrick Gnan/IllustrationOnline.com; **124:** (3) Ralph Voltz/IllustrationOnline.com; **128:** (t) Ralph Voltz/IllustrationOnline.com; **129:** (1,2,3,4,5) Nesbitt Graphics, Inc.; **145:** (inset) National Geographic Maps.

PHOTO:

Cover Photo: ©Jörg Dickmann

2–3: (f) Lannen/Kelly Photo/Alamy; **4:** (t) coolbiere photograph/Getty Images; **5:** (r) KRISTA ROSSOW/National Geographic Creative; **6:** (t) FRANS LANTING/National Geographic Creative; **7:** (t) Farrell Grehan/CORBIS; **9:** (b) foodfolio/Alamy; **11:** (t) © Dan DeLong Photography; **11:** (t) Rusty Hill/Photolibrary/Getty Images; **12:** (t) enviromantic/Getty Images; **13:** (t) IRA BLOCK/National Geographic Creative; **13:** (b) isarescheewin/Thinkstock; **14–15:** (f) Monty Rakusen/Cultura/Aurora Photos; **16:** (t) CORY RICHARDS/National Geographic Creative; **17:** (b) Roc Canals Photography/Getty Images; **18:** (t) Purestock/Alamy; **19:** (b) Fuse/Thinkstock; **20:** (t) © iStockphoto.com/gremlin; **21:** (b) MIKE THEISS/National Geographic Creative; **22–23:** (f) Courtesy of Annie Griffiths; **23:** (t) Annie Griffiths/National Geographic Creative; **24:** (t) Annie Griffiths/National Geographic Creative; **25:** (t) Michael Nichols/National Geographic Creative; **25:** (b) FRANS LANTING/National Geographic Creative; **26–27:** (f) watchlooksee.com/Getty Images; **28:** (t) Mike Theiss/National Geographic Creative; **29:** (b) Sean Pavone/Alamy; **30:** (t) Amy Toensing/National Geographic Creative; **31:** (t) © iStockphoto.com/Plougmann; **33:** (b) Kevin Kozicki/Thinkstock; **35:** (c) TED/James Duncan Davidson; **36:** (t) Louis-Laurent Grandadam/The Image Bank/Getty Images; **37:** (t) Juan Carlos Munoz/Age Fotostock; **37:** (b) Hemis/Alamy; **38:** (t) © Kate Vokovich; **39:** (t, bl, bcl, bcr, br) TED; **40, 41:** (t) TED; **42–43:** (f) Cory Richards/National Geographic Creative; **45:** (t) Dirima/

Thinkstock; **46:** (t) Ingram Publishing/Thinkstock; **46:** (t) Purestock/Thinkstock; **46:** (t) Maksim Shmeljov/Thinkstock; **47:** (r) Pilin_Petunyia/Thinkstock; **48:** (t) Marion C. Haßold/Getty Images; **49:** (b) Alex Mares-Manton/Getty Images; **50:** (m) Kim Kwangshin/Science Source; **50–51:** (f) xrender/Thinkstock; **52:** (t) KidStock/Getty Images; **53:** (t) Tara Moore/Getty Images; **53:** (r) © Sebastian Kaulitzki/Shutterstock.com; **54–55:** (f) © Donald Miralle; **56:** (t) GEORGE F. MOBLEY/National Geographic Creative; **57:** (r) Daniel Milchev/Getty Images; **58:** (l) © Nav Dayanand; **58:** (t) FRITZ HOFFMANN/National Geographic Creative; **58:** (r) Suttiporn Suksumek/Thinkstock; **58:** (t) John Cancalosi/Getty Images; **58:** (r) Joel Sartore/National Geographic Creative; **60:** (t) James A. Sugar/National Geographic Creative; **61:** (r) Valeriya Repina/Thinkstock; **62–63:** (f) Sebastian Devenish/DPP/Icon SMI 547/Newscom; **64:** (t) Arkadiusz Stachowski/Thinkstock; **65:** (t) Mike Hill/Getty Images; **66–67:** (f) Valdrin Xhemaj/epa/Corbis; **68:** (t) © Vivid Pixels/Shutterstock.com; **68:** (t) Leslie Banks/Thinkstock; **68:** (t) FRITZ HOFFMANN/National Geographic Creative; **68:** (t) kali9/Thinkstock; **68:** (l) Patrick Wittmannl/Getty Images; **69:** (t) Andrew Zarivny/Thinkstock; **70:** (t) Gianluca Colla/National Geographic Creative; **70:** (l) Gianluca Colla/National Geographic Creative; **72:** (t) Stephen St. John/National Geographic Creative; **72:** (m) Huntstock/Thinkstock, © StockLite/Shutterstock.com, Robert Ellis/Getty Images, Tom Cockrem/Getty Images, Jacob Wackerhausen/Thinkstock, © DNF Style/Shutterstock.com; **73:** (t) moodboard/Thinkstock; **73:** (b) ML Harris/Getty Images; **75:** (tl, tr, c, bl, br) TED; **76:** (t) Doug Pensinger/Getty Images; **77:** (t) Thomas Mukoya/Reuters/Corbis; **78:** (t) © Maxx-Studio/Shutterstock.com; **79:** (t) James Duncan Davidson/TED; **79:** (2,3,4) TED; **81:** (t) Martin Harvey/Getty Images; **82–83:** (f) David Yoder/National Geographic Creative; **84:** (t) Shafiqul Alam/Demotix/Corbis, Stockbyte/Thinkstock, radu_m/Thinkstock, Jeffrey Hamilton/Getty Images; **85:** (b) Amy White & Al Petteway/National Geographic Creative; **86:** (t) PAUL CHESLEY/National Geographic Creative; **86:** (l) James Forte/National Geographic

Creative; **88:** (t) Kazuyoshi Nomachi/Corbis; **89:** (m) © Jorge Salcedo/Shutterstock.com; **90–91:** (f) Matteo Colombo/Getty Images; **91:** (t) Robb Kendrick/National Geographic Creative; **92:** (t) Tony C French/Getty Images; **93:** (t) Ales Kramer/Getty Images; **94–95:** (f) EIKO JONES; **96:** (t) Ralph Lee Hopkins/National Geographic Creative; **97:** (b) George F. Mobley/National Geograhic Creative; **98:** (t) Brian J. Skerry/National Geographic Creative; **100:** (t) Darlyne A. Murawski/National Geographic Creative; **100:** (t) Stefan Lundgren/National Geographic Creative; **100:** (t) Joel Sartore/National Geographic Creative; **101:** (t) © Lars Christensen/Shutterstock.com; **102:** (b) Ivan Lieman/AFP/Getty Images; **103:** (t) James Duncan Davidson/TED; **104:** (t) Frans Lanting/National Geogrphic Creative; **104:** (c) Gilbert M. Grosvenor/National Geographic Creative; **104:** (b) Martin Harvey/Gallo Images/Getty Images; **105:** (t) Frans Lanting/National Geographic Creative; **106–107:** (f) © Colby Brown Photography; **108:** (t) UIG/Getty Images; **108:** (m) JAMES L. STANFIELD/National Geographic Creative; **108:** (b) Chris Hellier/Alamy; **109:** (m) DAVID HISER/National Geographic Creative; **110:** (t) ERIKA LARSEN/REDUX; **111:** (b) Keenpress/National Geographic Creative; **112:** (t) Paul Nicklen/National Geographic Creative; **113:** (t) Norbert Rosing/Getty Images; **114:** (t) JONATHAN IRISH/National Geographic Creative; **115:** (f) Timothy Allen/Getty Images; **116:** (t) KENT KOBERSTEEN/National Geographic Creative; **117:** (t) CENGAGE/National Geographic Creative; **118:** (t) Beverly Joubert/National Geographic Creative; **119:** (t) James Duncan Davidson/TED; **119:** (1) Beverly Joubert/National Geographic Creative; **119:** (2) Beverly Joubert/National Geographic Creative; **119:** (3) Beverly Joubert/National Geographic Creative; **119:** (4) Beverly Joubert/National Geographic Creative; **121:** (t) Beverly Joubert/National Geographic Creative; **122–123:** (f) Frans Lanting/National Geographic Creative; **125:** (m) Adam Gault/Getty Images; **126:** (t) StockShot/Alamy; **127:** (t) andresrimaging/Thinkstock; **127:** (r) © iStockphoto.com/CampPhoto; **127:** (b) Michael Nichols/Getty Images; **130–131:** (f) Alex Treadway/National Geographic Creative; **132:** (t) Sergey Borisov/Thinkstock;

132: (t) deluigiluca/Getty Images; 132: (b) Katie Garrod/Getty Images; 133: (t) David Wall/Alamy; 134–135: (f) © Dr Peter G Allinson/National News/ZUMA; 136: (t) © Andresr/Shutterstock.com; 137: (b) Bill Varie/Getty Images; 138: (t) chain45154/Getty Images; 139: (t) Monika Wisniewska/Thinkstock; 141: (b) Indeed/Getty Images; 143: (t) James Duncan Davidson/TED; 144: (t) Koichi Kamoshida/Getty Images; 145: (t) Tim Laman/National Geographic Creative; 146–147: (f) Robin Utrecht Fotografie/Corbis; 148: (b) nagelestock.com/Alamy; 149: (b) © Gerard Lazaro/Shutterstock.com; 150: (t) Marcie Gonzalez/Getty Images; 150: (m) Blend Images/Alamy; 150: (b) Sam Abell/National Geographic Creative; 152: (t) © Aspen Photo/Shutterstock.com; 153: (b) Gail Shotlander/Getty Images; 154–155: (f) Hill Street Studios/Blend Images/Corbis; 156: (f) epa european pressphoto agency b.v./Alamy; 157: (f) Gordon Wiltsie/National Geographic Creative; 158: (t) Kip Evans/Mission Blue/TED; 159: (t) TED/Asa Mathat; 159: (1,2,3,4) TED; 160: (t)Shaul Schwarz/Edit/Getty Images; 161: (t) Jeff Rotman/The Image Bank/Getty Images.
T-212: Voronina Svetiana/Shutterstock.com; T-213: urbancow/istockphoto; T-214: Sophie James/Shutterstock.com; T-215: Tyler Olson/Shutterstock.com; T-216: (t) Rich Carey/Shutterstock.com, (b) Igor Plotnikov/Shutterstock.com; T-217: (l) mollypix/istockphoto, (lm) michaeljung/Shutterstock.com, (m) stockphoto mania/Shutterstock.com, (rm) HannaMonika/Shutterstock.com, (r) Kinga/Shutterstock.com; T-218: Stuart Jenner/Shutterstock.com; T-220: (tl) rustemgurler/istockphoto, (tlm) imagehub/Shutterstock.com, (trm) Pushish Donhongsa/Shutterstock.com, (tr) Vladyslav Danilin/Shutterstock.com, (bl) razihusin/Shutterstock.com, (blm) Adisa/Shutterstock.com, (brm) jbmake/Shutterstock.com, (br) Jessimine/Shutterstock.com; T-221: Apollofoto/Shutterstock.com; T-223: Monkey Business Images/Shutterstock.com

TEXT CREDITS

10–11 Adapted from "A Slice of History," by Susan E. Goodman: National Geographic Explorer Magazine, May 2005; 22–23 Adapted from "Connect With Anybody, Anywhere," from National Geographic *Live*, Tuesday, December 11, 2007 at 7:30 p.m.; 34–35 Adapted from "How Food Shapes Our Cities," by Carolyn Steel: TED Talk: www.ted.com/talks/carolyn_steel_how_food_shapes_our_cities.html, October 2013; 50–51 Adapted from "Tiny Invaders," by Kirsten Weir: National Geographic Explorer Public Website, November-December 2006; 58 Adapted from "Jenny Daltry, Herpetologist, Emerging Explorer," National Geographic News Public Website; 60 Adapted from "Alone Against the Sea," by Walter Roessing: National Geographic World Magazine, April 1997; 62–63 Adapted from "Arctic Dreams and Nightmares," by Marguerite del Giudice: National Geographic Magazine, January 2007; 70 Listening text Adapted from "Quest for Longevity Okinawa, Japan," National Geographic Interactive Edition, October 31, 2005; 74–51 "Living Beyond Limits," by Amy Purdy: TED Talk: www.ted.com/talks/amy_purdy_living_beyond_limits.html October 2013; 86 Vocabulary and Listening texts adapted from "Flower Trade," by Vivienne Walt: National Geographic Magazine, April 2001; 90–91 Adapted from "Perfume, the Essence of Illusion," by Cathy Newman: National Geographic Magazine, October 1998; 98 Text and Listening adapted from "Still Waters," by Fen Montaigne: National Geographic Magazine, April 2007; 102–103 Adapted from "How Poachers Became Caretakers," by John Kasaona, TED Talk: www.ted.com/talks/john_kasaona_from_poachers_to_caretakers.html October 2013; 110 Listening text adapted from "Sami: The People Who Walk with Reindeer," by Jessica Benko, National Geographic Magazine, November 2011; 114–115 Adapted from "Lord of the Mongols," by Mike Edwards: National Geographic Magazine, December 1996; 140 Adapted from "Making Filthy Water Drinkable," by Michael Pritchard, TED Talk: www.ted.com/talks/michael_pritchard_invents_a_water_filter.html October 2013

UNIT 1

🔊 3 ## LESSON B, LISTENING

Interviewer: Thank you for talking to us today. I know you're very busy.

Farmer: Yes, I am, but I'm happy to answer your questions.

Interviewer: Wonderful. First, what are those people in the rice paddy doing?

Farmer: They're putting the young rice plants in the ground. That's because we don't plant seeds like other farmers.

Interviewer: Really? Why not?

Farmer: It's simple—we get a much larger crop if we start with young plants.

Interviewer: And why is there so much water in the rice paddy?

Farmer: That's part of growing rice. We need a warm climate and a lot of water. We're getting a lot of rain this year, and that's good news for rice farmers.

Interviewer: I see. And what happens next?

Farmer: Well, the rice grows, of course. Then we have to get the water out of the rice paddy. We let the water run out, then the rice dries.

Interviewer: And when the rice is dry, what happens next?

Farmer: Then we cut the rice plants and clean them.

Interviewer: It's a lot of work, isn't it?

Farmer: It is a lot of work, but we grow a lot of rice, and that rice is food for many people.

UNIT 2

🔊 7 ## LESSON B, LISTENING

CONVERSATION 1

Ken: Hi, my name is Ken Tanaka.

Lisa: It's nice to meet you. I'm Lisa Ortiz.

Ken: Nice to meet you too, Lisa. So . . . are you studying English here?

Lisa: No, not this term. I'm taking a computer class.

Ken: Really? Which class?

Lisa: I'm taking the Web Site Design class. The teacher's name is Mr. Carter. I haven't met him yet, though.

Ken: I've heard that he's a great teacher. One of my friends took his class last year.

Lisa: That's good! It's a difficult subject, but it's really interesting. What about you? What are you studying?

Ken: Well, this term I'm taking Advanced English Writing.

Lisa: Wow, that sounds difficult too!

Nancy: Hi. Are you the new neighbor?

Maria: Yes, I am. My name is Maria Andrews. I'm in apartment 7C.

Nancy: Nice to meet you, Maria. I'm Nancy Chun. I live in 7A.

Maria: Nice to meet you too. So, have you lived here long?

Nancy: Oh, about . . . ten years.

Maria: Wow! I guess you really like this part of the city!

Nancy: It's a great place to live. There are lots of stores, and the park is so relaxing.

Maria: Are there any good restaurants near here?

Nancy: Sure! What kind of food do you like?

◀)) 9 LESSON B, PRONUNCIATION

1. I've never gone skiing.

2. He's been to Colombia three times.

3. Linda has taken a scuba diving class.

4. They have already eaten breakfast.

5. We've had three tests this week.

6. Michael has found a new job.

UNIT 3

◀)) 12 LESSON B, LISTENING

Interviewer: Hello, and welcome to "City Scene." Paris has a very unusual park. It's called the Jardin Nomade, and it's in a very busy urban area in the eastern part of the city. Today we're talking to Isabel Dupont, one of the organizers of the park. Isabel, why is the Jardin Nomade unusual?

Isabel: Our park is amazing because it's so *small*. It was just a piece of empty land between two very busy streets. We wanted a park in our neighborhood, because we wanted a place to grow flowers and vegetables. So in 2003, the city government helped us to start the park. Today, there are 54 small gardens in the park. Families grow things like tomatoes, beans, and lettuce in their gardens.

Interviewer: That sounds wonderful! Has the Jardin Nomade changed the neighborhood?

Isabel: Yes, it has. In the gardens, we got to know our neighbors. Now the park is a meeting place for everyone in the neighborhood. And every month, we have dinner in the park one night. We cook a lot of soup together—vegetable soup! All the neighbors bring tables and chairs to the park, and we have a great time. More than a hundred people come to the dinners.

Interviewer: Imagine I go to the Jardin Nomade tomorrow. What will I see?

Isabel: Well, it's February now, so you won't see any flowers or vegetables. But you'll see kids playing and neighbors talking together. People use the park all year. And in spring, people will start working in their gardens. The city needs more parks like this. Now, there are 40 of these urban gardens in Paris. Next year, we'll help more people start them in their neighborhoods.

UNIT 4

🔊 15   LESSON A, VOCABULARY

Patient: Thanks for seeing me today Dr. Gupta. I really don't feel well.

Doctor: I'm glad you came in, then. Let's listen to your lungs first. Take a deep breath. And now breathe out. Your lungs sound fine. Now I'll listen to your heart. Your heart sounds good, too.

Patient: It might be something I ate. My stomach hurts a little.

Doctor: Hmmm. Does it hurt when I press here?

Patient: No, that doesn't hurt.

Doctor: How about when I press here?

Patient: Ow! Yeah, that does hurt.

Doctor: That's your small intestine. You might have an intestinal virus. Let's take your temperature. Your skin does feel warm.

🔊 17   LESSON B, LISTENING

Speaker A: I guess I'm pretty healthy. I almost never get sick, and I have a lot of energy to do things I enjoy. I don't really do anything special for my health. I eat a good diet, but sometimes I get fast food when I don't have time to cook. I don't work out at a gym, but I walk and I like to spend time outdoors. My mother and my grandmothers were healthy people, too. Maybe I get my good health from them.

Speaker B: I go to the gym three or four times a week. It keeps me in shape, and it gets me away from work. Yeah, my job is pretty stressful. There's a lot of pressure on me, and it seems to take all my energy just to get up in the morning and go to work. I do get sick every couple of months or so—usually just colds or a headache and sore throat. I got the flu last year and had to miss four days of work. My boss was *not* happy.

Speaker C: For me, the key is a vegetarian diet. When I was younger, I ate everything and I felt fine, but then I got older, and I didn't have any energy at all. I read some books about vegetarianism, I started growing my own tomatoes and other veggies, and I started feeling a lot better. Some people think you can't get all the nutrients you need from plant foods, but you can. You just need a little information and a lot of good recipes.

UNIT 5

🔊 20   LESSON A, VOCABULARY

The word **"challenge"** might make you think of **physical** activities like playing sports. But **mental** activities such as learning a new language or a new **skill** can also be a challenge. For me, learning to play a musical instrument is a challenge, but also an **adventure.** You might feel afraid to try it, but it's as exciting as traveling to a new place, and the only **equipment** you need is a violin, a guitar, or in my case—a *koto*.

When I started my *koto* lessons, my **goal** was to learn to play this **amazing** instrument well enough to play for my family. Now, I'm making good **progress** with the help of my music teacher. She thinks I'm getting better every week! I can probably **achieve** my goal soon, and then I'll play the *koto* at my father's birthday party.

🔊 22 LESSON B, LISTENING

Interviewer: Today I'm talking to scientist Jenny Daltry. While Daltry was working in the forests of Cambodia, she discovered some of the last Siamese crocodiles in the world. Ms. Daltry, where did you find these crocodiles?

Jenny Daltry: I found the largest group, about 150 crocodiles, in a remote part of Cambodia. Before I found them, scientists thought this kind of crocodile was extinct. My discovery showed that there are still Siamese crocodiles living in the wild. It also helped people realize that the area is important to wildlife. Over 3 million acres of Cambodian forest are now protected by the government.

Interviewer: That's amazing! And what was your biggest challenge after you discovered the crocodiles?

Jenny Daltry: Well, most people are afraid of crocodiles. They don't think they're as lovable as panda bears or other endangered animals. My biggest challenge was to educate people about the crocodiles. I explained that crocodiles keep the marshes healthy, and the marshes are home to many kinds of birds and animals. Protecting the crocodiles means protecting the environment.

Interviewer: So your discovery is helping to save more than just crocodiles.

Jenny Daltry: That's right, and my next challenge is to help another unpopular animal—the Antiguan racer snake. I was traveling in the Caribbean when I found out about this endangered animal. The Antiguan racer only lives on two small islands in the Caribbean. In fact, it's the world's rarest snake!

UNIT 6

🔊 27 LESSON B, LISTENING

Radio Host: Ushi Okushima is a typical woman from rural Japan. She lives in Okinawa, on an island in the south of Japan, in a traditional house. When we visited her five years ago, she was working on her small farm and growing food for herself and her family. Since then, she has stopped farming. Now she has a job at the market, putting oranges in bags. What's unusual about Ushi? She's 103 years old!

There are many other amazing people like Ushi in Okinawa. More than 700 people there have celebrated their 100th birthday. Ninety percent of these people are women. Now scientists are studying them to try to understand their secrets for a long life. They think it's because of three things: the healthy food in Okinawa, the clean environment, and close relationships with friends and family members.

Ushi's life is a good example of all of these things. She wakes up at six o'clock in the morning. Then she makes a breakfast of vegetables and soup and goes out for a walk. On some days, she goes to her job at the market. Every afternoon she eats lunch with her daughter, and her grandchildren and friends come over to visit. In the evenings, she eats a dinner of mostly vegetables, drinks a cup of rice wine, and goes to bed. When we asked her how to live to be 100, Ushi said, "Work hard, drink rice wine before bed, and get a good night's sleep."

UNIT 7

◀)) 3 LESSON B, LISTENING

Shinobu: Hi, I'm Shinobu. Here in Japan, flowers are a very important part of life. We celebrate the seasons with different kinds of flowers in our houses, and special occasions always call for flowers—weddings, funerals, graduation ceremonies. . . . We do grow some flowers right here in Japan, but we also import many kinds of flowers such as carnations, roses, and orchids. The flowers come from all over the world—from as far away as Kenya and Colombia. Those countries export flowers, and there's always someone here who wants to buy flowers, so everyone is happy.

Rafael: My name is Rafael and I live in Ecuador. Growing flowers in greenhouses is a fairly new business in Ecuador. The greenhouses produce big, beautiful flowers because we get a lot of sunshine all year—not just in the summer months. But to tell you the truth, I don't like working in the greenhouses. I get headaches almost every day from the chemicals we spray on the flowers. Still, my family needs the money I make, and my job pays better than a lot of other jobs.

Peter: Hello, I'm Peter from the Netherlands. You could say we're the world's flower experts. That's because the Netherlands has a long history of developing new kinds of flowers—new colors, new shapes, new sizes. And if you develop the next big hit—the new flower that everybody wants—farmers will pay a lot of money to grow your plant. Today, I'm at the flower auction where buyers choose flowers to export all over the world. I'm watching closely because my rose—well, a rose that I developed—is for sale at the auction today. If people like it, my future could be very bright.

UNIT 8

◀)) 7 LESSON B, LISTENING

Narrator: The bluefin tuna is one of the most amazing fish in the world. It's a different species from the tuna that you buy at the store in cans. A bluefin tuna can grow to be 12 feet long, and it can weigh more than 1,500 pounds. It's a beautiful fish, too, silver-colored with marks of yellow and blue. With its strong body, it can swim more that 25 miles an hour, and it can live for up to 30 years.

Unfortunately, the bluefin tuna is also delicious, because it has a lot of fat in its body. In Japan, people use it to make sushi, and in Europe, people love to cook big pieces for tuna steaks. Every year, fishing boats catch more and more of these fish, and now they are in danger of disappearing. If the boats catch too many big bluefins, there won't be any young fish in the future.

In the past, bluefin tuna also lived in the Pacific Ocean and Indian Ocean. But in the 1990s, almost all of these fish were caught. Only 10 percent of the original population of bluefins was left. So the biggest fishing boats moved to the Mediterranean Sea, and now they catch up to 60,000 tons of bluefin tuna there every year.

There are international rules for fishing, but these boats don't follow the rules. They catch too many fish, and they harm the environment. If the big boats destroy the fishing in the Mediterranean, many poor people will lose their work. Some scientists say that we should stop catching bluefin tuna for several years, so that the population of tuna can grow again. If this amazing fish disappears, the seas will lose a great treasure.

UNIT 9

🔊 13 ## LESSON A, VOCABULARY

Narrator: In today's specialized world we usually buy the things we need—food, clothes, furniture, and houses. Less than 500 years ago many people used simple tools and weapons to do their own farming, hunting, and building. The preparation of daily meals was not easy. Women had to cook the vegetables they farmed and the meat hunted by the men. Many of the everyday things we take for granted today were luxuries for people in the 15th century. Women would use simple hairbrushes and combs made from wood or bone to keep their hair neat. Glass beads were worn as jewelry. Men used to smoke tobacco in pipes for relaxation. And in a world of little entertainment, gambling was popular. Men would play cards and roll dice in games of chance.

🔊 14 ## LESSON B, LISTENING

Narrator (female voice): Imagine living in the northern part of northern Europe—in the cold, snowy land that extends from Norway across parts of Sweden, Finland, and Russia. It's the land of the Sami people, and it stretches to the north far beyond the Arctic Circle.

Traditionally, the Sami people depended on reindeer for much of their food, clothing, and protection from the cold. Instead of living in one place, the Sami people used to follow large groups, or herds, of reindeer as they searched for food. When the reindeer stopped, the Sami people put up tents to sleep in—tents made from reindeer skins.

These days, only a few Sami people herd reindeer in this way, and only a few still speak the Sami language. Some Sami people still raise reindeer, but now they feed the animals on farms with fences so the reindeer can't escape. And like people everywhere, many Sami people don't want to live in traditional ways. They want to explore the world, attend a university, and choose a career for themselves.

For families that maintain a traditional lifestyle, however, life without reindeer is difficult to imagine. They've had to adapt to new technology and new laws for land use, driving long distances in off-road vehicles to make and repair hundreds of miles of fences. Despite these changes, though, the work they do, the food they eat, and the customs they maintain are nearly the same as they have been for thousands of years for the Sami people.

UNIT 10

🔊 18 ## LESSON B, LISTENING

Interviewer: Today's topic is vacations, and we're asking people about their plans for their next vacation trip. May I have your name?

Carla: Carla.

Interviewer: And where are you going for your next vacation, Carla?

Carla: Well, my vacation isn't until September, but I'm really excited already. I'm going to Italy! I've wanted to go there for the longest time!

Interviewer: So, are you planning to go sightseeing there?

Carla: Not really. I'm going to a cooking school there for two weeks. I just love Italian food, and I've always wanted to learn how to make it—not just the easy things like spaghetti. We'll have cooking lessons every day and cook all of our meals. I really like to learn something new on vacation. I get bored if I just sit around.

Interviewer: Sounds like a great trip! Now let's ask this gentleman—excuse me, what's your name?

Marcus: My name's Marcus.

Interviewer: Tell us, Marcus, what are your plans for your next vacation?

Marcus: I just talked to a travel agent and made my reservations yesterday. I'm going to spend a week in Thailand.

Interviewer: Thailand! Sounds great! And what are you going to do there?

Marcus: Nothing! I'm going to do absolutely nothing! I'm going to get up late, and lie on the beach, and look at the ocean, and drink cold drinks, and just relax. My job is really stressful, and I don't want to run around during my vacation. One of my friends went to Thailand last year, and he said it was really peaceful, and that sounds perfect for me.

Interviewer: Well, we hope you have a great time. We have time for one more person—hi! Could you tell us your name?

Julie: I'm Julie.

Interviewer: Hi, Julie. Tell us a little about your plans for your next vacation.

Julie: Well, I've been saving my money for my dream vacation, and this is the year! I'm going to New Zealand for three weeks.

Interviewer: That does sound like a dream vacation! Have you decided on your itinerary?

Julie: I'm going to go hiking for a week in a national park and I want to climb two of the most famous mountains in New Zealand. And I also want to try jetboating. You go down a river in a very fast boat. I'm also going to spend a few days scuba diving. I picked New Zealand because it's a great place for adventure sports, and that's what I love to do.

Interviewer: Sounds exciting. Well, thanks, everyone! And have a great vacation!

UNIT 11

🔊 21 **LESSON A, VOCABULARY**

Marcy: Thanks for seeing me today, Ms. Carter.

Ms. Carter: No problem at all, Marcy. Have a seat.

Marcy: Thanks. I wanted to talk to you about my future. I'm graduating soon, and I still don't know what I want to do with my life.

Ms. Carter: That's what I'm here for. Do you have any work experience now?

Marcy: Not really, but I do have some volunteer experience. I went through a training program at the hospital to become a family assistant at the hospital. I give people information when they come in, and I walk with them to different parts of the hospital. It's a big place!

Ms. Carter: That's great! Maybe you should become a health care worker—a nurse or a doctor, perhaps.

Marcy: Actually, I don't think I want to work in a hospital after I graduate. I think I'd like to be a business owner.

Ms. Carter: Sure—many people have their own business. But most of them start as employees. They work for a boss, and later they open their own business.

Marcy: That makes sense. I could get a job, work for awhile, and build up my qualifications, and then—who knows?

Ms. Carter: That's the idea. Just make sure your job is going somewhere. It should be related to the kind of business you want to get into.

Marcy: You're right. Thanks for the advice, Ms. Carter!

Ms. Carter: Anytime.

🔊 23 ## LESSON B, LISTENING

Interviewer: I'm here in Bangkok talking to the owner of New Thailand, one of the best little restaurants I've found here. Mr. Sangumram, when did you open this wonderful restaurant?

Mr. Sangumram: I opened in 1998, after my children had started their own careers. I was ready to try something new, and I wanted to be my own boss. Besides, my nephew is a fantastic cook!

Interviewer: I agree! This is the best Thai food I've had in Bangkok.

Mr. Sangumram: You know, a lot of restaurants here serve Chinese food or Japanese food, but I wanted to serve our native Thai dishes. And I wanted to work close to home. My wife and I live upstairs!

Interviewer: That's certainly convenient. Does your wife work with you in the restaurant?

Mr. Sangumram: No, she had enough of cooking and serving food when our kids were growing up. I have four employees besides my nephew—two waiters, a dishwasher, and an assistant cook. My wife works as a sales representative for a large drug company.

Interviewer: That's great! Now, I have to ask you one more question if that's alright.

Mr. Sangumram: That's fine. Ask away.

Interviewer: Can I get the recipes for some of the delicious things you cook here?

Mr. Sangumram: Oh, sorry! The recipes are top secret.

Interviewer: I understand. So it sounds like you really enjoy your work.

Mr. Sangumram: Absolutely! This is the best job I've ever had—and I'm the best boss I've ever had!

UNIT 12

LESSON B, LISTENING

Speaker 1: Mexico City is my hometown. There's a special holiday in Mexico called the Day of the Dead, and I enjoy it a lot. It's really two days, on November 1 and November 2. On those days we remember people in our families who have died. We go to the cemetery with their favorite food and drinks. We also bring yellow and orange flowers, so it's very colorful. And we eat sweet bread, and special candy. It's shaped like skulls!

Speaker 2: I'm from Chicago, in the United States. My favorite holiday is Halloween. It takes place on October 31. My friends and I put on strange costumes and go to all the houses in our neighborhood asking for candy. I always get lots of chocolate and apples. We also like to watch scary movies about ghosts and dead people. It's mostly a holiday for children, but some adults like it too. They sometimes have parties on Halloween.

Speaker 3: I come from Osaka, in Japan. We have an annual holiday in summer when we think about people in our families who died before us. It's called O-Bon, and it's on August 13. It's a time for families to be together. Everyone goes back to their hometown, so all of the trains and buses are really crowded and it's hard to travel. People participate in a special dance. And we make really big fires outside. It's beautiful to see!

UNIT 1

VIDEO JOURNAL *FORBIDDEN FRUIT*

NARRATOR: Here in Malaysian Borneo, a seasonal invasion is underway. Staff at hotels watch nervously for a food that is . . . smelly . . . awful . . . and loved by millions. Meet the durian fruit. Its smell is hard to describe.

SOUNDBITE: It smells like a rotten fish and custard.

SOUNDBITE: A rubbish dump.

SOUNDBITE: Bleu cheese.

SOUNDBITE: Perhaps a dead dog.

SOUNDBITE: Like private parts.

NARRATOR: Other cultures love foods that smell strongly. Cheese, a favorite in the West, is actually rotted milk . . . a smell people in Asia find disgusting. Like cheese in France, durian is precious in Southeast Asia. Some believe it's worth killing for. Durian trees don't bear fruit until they're fifteen years old. A single durian can cost as much as fifty dollars American. Here in Kuching, the capital of Malaysian Borneo, hotels are on the front lines of the durian war. When the fruit is in season, hotel managers maintain a constant vigil to keep it out. For them, the problem is really about money. One smelly durian fruit can scare off a hotel full of customers.

EDWARD: So it goes into the curtains. It sticks into the carpet. It sticks into the bedspreads.

NARRATOR: That doesn't stop people from trying to smuggle it in.

AUDREY: We can immediately smell it, and they always deny it, but we know that they've got them.

NARRATOR: Every hotel has its own method of dealing with a durian alert.

EDWARD: There are only two methods of getting rid of the smell we found. One is charcoal. Charcoal absorbs the smell. And the other . . . that takes quite a long time. And the other one . . . we've got an ionizer that . . . it's an industrialized one, and within three hours we can pull the smell out of the room.

AUDREY: Please no durians here, not in the hotel. Outside . . . in the fresh air you can do it. But definitely not in here.

NARRATOR: In Borneo, visitors can decide for themselves if the durian is delicious, or just plain disgusting . . . as long as they do their taste testing outdoors.

UNIT 2

VIDEO JOURNAL *ORANGUTAN LANGUAGE*

NARRATOR: Orangutans. These highly developed primates come from Indonesia and Malaysia. They are so much like humans that their name actually means 'person of the forest' in Malay. They can even communicate through language. And at the National Zoo in Washington, D.C., two orangutans named Inda and Azie are showing the world just how well they can do it. Rob Shumaker is the coordinator of the Orangutan Language Project.

ROB SHUMAKER, ORANGUTAN LANGUAGE PROJECT: We are really adding to what we understand about orangutan mental ability. I also think that we're doing something very, very good for these individual orangutans."

NARRATOR: Shumaker believes that orangutans and other apes in captivity need a stimulating physical and mental environment. The zoo allows its orangutans to move around freely and gives them choices on where to go. Even Shumaker's language program is voluntary for them.

SHUMAKER: It gives the orangutans some choice and some agency about what they do day to day. And I think that's incredibly important for a species that has this much going on mentally. She's just naming the object.

NARRATOR: Shumaker works daily with the orangutans in the program to develop their language skills. Today he's working with Inda, a 20-year-old female orangutan. Inda is learning a vocabulary of symbols that she connects with objects, such as bananas, apples, and cups. Every day, visitors watch as Shumaker and Inda perform certain exercises on the computer to test what language she knows. But even apes have to wait for slow computers!

SHUMAKER: Oh, hold on. The computer's not responding quickly enough, but she's doing it correctly. Try again.

NARRATOR: Inda can identify food and objects using symbols, as well as put symbols together to form simple sentences with a verb and an object. Basically, she can use the symbols to get her point across, which is the essential purpose of language.

SHUMAKER: Each one learns their own way. Each one has their own types of questions that they are better or worse at. And the big emphasis is they are individuals, and their progress is not the same as the other orangutans just because it's orangutan.

NARRATOR: For example, Inda's brother Azie is not as social as his sister. At first, Shumaker thought that Azie was not as intelligent, but that's not true at all. In fact, Azie is very intelligent; he just isn't always as interested in communicating as his sister is.

The Orangutan Language Project is part of an exhibit at the National Zoo called 'Think Tank'. The exhibit explores the process of thinking, and actually involves visitors to the zoo in the program.

LISA STEVENS, THINK TANK CURATOR: What's really nice about Think Tank is that it brings a lot of the behind the scenes activities and research that involve animals right up front where it should be, where people are going to see it.

NARRATOR: Zoo officials hope that exhibits like Think Tank will educate the public and increase conservation efforts. Orangutans could become extinct in the wild in the next 10 to 12 years.

SHUMAKER: Give people a chance to know more about what's going on mentally for orangutans. I know that that increases their regard for them.

NARRATOR: Shumaker personally developed the symbols for the orangutans' vocabulary, but he says that the project has really been successful because of Inda and Azie.

SHUMAKER: I think of this language project as really a team effort between me, and Inda, and Azie. And we all work together on this. This is not my project; it's our project. And I want them to voluntarily participate. When they do that, I know that they're doing it because they enjoy it, and they like it, and they want to be involved with it. And that's important.

NARRATOR: It's easy to see that Shumaker has been successful. The orangutan language team of Inda, Azie, and Shumaker certainly enjoy their work!

UNIT 3
VIDEO JOURNAL *FES*

NARRATOR: This monument to Islamic heritage is getting a new lease on life. The Bouananiya Medersa or Koranic school, was once an architectural jewel of the medieval city of Fes. But centuries of neglect have taken a toll. Restorers are cleaning layers of whitewash off of intricate plaster carvings. It's slow work. But when it's done, they hope the Medersa will shine again, as a masterpiece, and a testament to the grand artistic legacy of their city. Muslim refugees from Spain and Tunisia founded Fes in the 9th century. By the 1300s, it was one of the cultural capitals of the Islamic world, a center for art and learning. Today, its medina, or historic city center, is a living museum of Morocco's Islamic heritage.

DAVID AMSTER, HISTORIC PRESERVATIONIST: Probably the best-preserved Islamic medina in the world right now. There are thousands of traditional houses that are, some of them going back 700 years.

NARRATOR: The medina is culturally rich—but its people are poor. Historic preservation often takes second place to more basic concerns. The people who live in them, usually five or six families renting a room or two each, can't afford to make repairs. Historic homes that aren't falling down are also in danger, of a different kind. This 18th century palace is being sold off, piece by piece, to antiquities dealers. A fountain was the first to go. In theory, the government should protect Fes's historic buildings. But in practice, it's too big a job. And so private citizens have stepped in. They're saving Fes's medina, house by house.

MEHDI EL ABBADI, HISTORIC PRESERVATIONSIT: It's the thing we need to protect. And it's a part of our memory, it's a part of our history, and it's a part of our daily life.

NARRATOR: Private foundations are paying to restore monuments like the Medersa, which will eventually become a museum of Islamic architecture. Fes has realized that its architectural history is too valuable to lose. There's still a lot of work to be done, and not only on restoration. Renovating palaces and historic monuments won't cure poverty, and poverty is the ultimate source of Fes's woes. But preserving the city's architectural heritage ensures that at least these riches will endure.

TODD: I started Improv Everywhere about 10 years ago when I moved to New York City with an interest in acting and comedy. Because I was new to the city, I didn't have access to a stage, so I decided to create my own in public places.

Really one of the points of Improv Everywhere is to cause a scene in a public place that is a positive experience for other people. It's a prank, but it's a prank that gives somebody a great story to tell.

As I started taking improv class at the Upright Citizens Brigade Theater and meeting other creative people and other performers and comedians, I started amassing a mailing list of people who wanted to do these types of projects. So I could do more large-scale projects. Well one day I was walking through Union Square, and I saw this building, which had just been built in 2005. And there was a girl in one of the windows and she was dancing. And it was very peculiar, because it was dark out, but she was back-lit with florescent lighting, and she was very much onstage, and I couldn't figure out why she was doing it. After about 15 seconds, her friend appeared—she had been hiding behind a display— and they laughed and hugged each other and ran away. So it seemed like maybe she had been dared to do this. So I got inspired by that. Looking at the entire facade—there were 70 total windows—and I knew what I had to do.

So this project is called Look Up More. We had 70 actors dress in black. This was completely unauthorized. We didn't let the stores know we were coming. And I stood in the park giving signals. The first signal was for everybody to hold up these four-foot tall letters that spelled out "Look Up More," the name of the project. The second signal was for everybody to do Jumping jacks together. You'll see that start right here. (Laughter) And then we had dancing. We had everyone dance. And then we had dance solos where only one person would dance and everybody would point to them. (Laughter) So then I gave a new hand signal, which signaled the next soloist down below in Forever 21, and he danced. There were several other activities. We had people jumping up and down, people dropping to the ground. And I was standing just anonymously in a sweatshirt, putting my hand on and off of a trashcan to signal the advancement. And because it was in Union Square Park, right by a subway station, there were hundreds of people by the end who stopped and looked up and watched what we were doing. There's a better photo of it.

So that particular event was inspired by a moment that I happened to stumble upon. The next project I want to show was given to me in an email from a stranger. A high school kid in Texas wrote me in 2006 and said, "You should get as many people as possible to put on blue polo shirts and khaki pants and go into a Best Buy and stand around." So I wrote this high school kid back immediately, and I said, "Yes, you are correct. I think I'll try to do that this weekend. Thank you." So here's the video.

So again, this is 2005. This is the Best Buy in New York City. We had about 80 people show up to participate, entering one-by-one. There was an eight year-old girl, a 10 year-old girl. There was also a 65 year-old man who participated. So a very diverse group of people. And I told people, "Don't work. Don't actually do work. But also, don't shop. Just stand around and don't face products." Now you can see the regular employees by the ones that have the yellow tags on their shirt. Everybody else is one of our actors. (Laughter) The lower level employees thought it was very funny. And in fact, several of them went to go get their camera from the break room and took photos with us. A lot of them made jokes about trying to get us to go to the back to get heavy television sets for customers. The managers and the security guards, on the other hand, did not find it particularly funny. You can see them in this footage. They're wearing either a yellow shirt or a black shirt. And we were there probably 10 minutes before the managers decided to dial 911.

So they started running around telling everybody the cops were coming, watch out, the cops were coming. And you can see the cops in this footage right here. That's a cop wearing black right there, being filmed with a hidden camera. Ultimately, the police had to inform Best Buy management that it was not, in fact, illegal to wear a blue polo shirt and khaki pants.

Thank you. So we had been there for 20 minutes; we were happy to exit the store. One thing the managers were trying to do was to track down our cameras. And they caught a couple of my guys who had hidden cameras in duffel bags. But the one camera guy they never caught was the guy that went in just with a blank tape and went over to the Best Buy camera department and just put his tape in one of their cameras and pretended to shop. So I like that concept of using their own technology against them.

I think our best projects are ones that are site specific and happen at a particular place for a reason. And one morning, I was riding the subway. I had to make a transfer at the 53rd St. stop where there are these two giant escalators. And it's a very depressing place to be in the morning, it's very crowded. So I decided to try and stage something that could make it as happy as possible for one morning. So this was in the winter of 2009—8:30 in the morning. It's morning rush hour. It's very cold outside. People are coming in from Queens, transferring from the E train to the 6 train. And they're going up these giant escalators on their way to their jobs.

Thank you. So there's a photograph that illustrates it a little bit better. He gave 2,000 high fives that day, and he washed his hands before and afterward and did not get sick. And that was done also without permission, although no one seemed to care.

So I'd say over the years, one of the most common criticisms I see of Improv Everywhere left anonymously on YouTube comments is: "These people have too much time on their hands." And you know, not everybody's going to like everything you do, and I've certainly developed a thick skin thanks to Internet comments, but that one's always bothered me, because we don't have too much time on our hands. The participants at Improv Everywhere events have just as much leisure time as any other New Yorkers, they just occasionally choose to spend it in an unusual way.

You know, as kids, we're taught to play. And we're never given a reason why we should play. It's just acceptable that play is a good thing. And I think that's sort of the point of Improv Everywhere. It's that there is no point and that there doesn't have to be a point. We don't need a reason. As long as it's fun and it seems like it's going to be a funny idea and it seems like the people who witness it will also have a fun time, then that's enough for us. And I think, as adults, we need to learn that there's no right or wrong way to play. Thank you very much.

UNIT 4
VIDEO JOURNAL *THE HUMAN BODY*

NARRATOR: The human body. No machine can match the feats it performs every day. Our lungs suck in 70 quarts of air each minute when we exercise . . . Our hearts pump two thousand gallons of blood each day . . . And more than 600 muscles keep us moving, in every direction.

Like all living things, human beings are made up of cells—100 trillion of them. Individual cells are organized into tissues . . . like this heart muscle tissue. Different kinds of tissue form an organ, such as the heart. And several organs working together create an organ system. Each of the 10 major organ systems in the human machine performs a special job.

The circulatory and respiratory systems supply energy 24 hours a day. The heart works automatically, and incredibly hard. No other muscle in the body is as strong. It beats 100,000 times a day . . . 36 million times a year, sending blood on a complete trip around the body in less than a minute. The lungs pull in oxygen from the air, delivering breath through 15 hundred miles of airways.

All this work is fueled by food . . . And turning pizza into useable molecules is the job of the digestive system. Swallowing sends food down the esophagus into the stomach. Like a blender, the stomach contracts to break it down, helped out by acid and enzymes. This liquefied food travels into the small intestine, which can be over 20 feet long, where most nutrients enter the bloodstream.

And the brains of this whole operation—is the human brain. A wrinkled blob about the size of a grapefruit, it's the most complex object on earth. The brain contains up to 100 billion neurons, or nerve cells. Neurons send signals rocketing through the brain at over 200 miles an hour. The brain, spinal cord, and nerves make up the nervous system—and all work together to control the body's activities.

The reproductive system creates new life. Each human begins as two single cells—an egg cell from the mother, and a sperm cell from the father. When these two cells meet, they begin to divide . . . And over 9 months, a whole new person is formed. Strands of DNA carried in the original two cells act like a set of blueprints—telling the cells to build a person with blue eyes, curly hair, or a wide smile.

The end result of this genetic scrambling . . . Bodies that take us on a miraculous journey every day. They allow us to push the frontiers . . . Meet awesome challenges . . . And expand the boundaries of human achievement.

UNIT 5
VIDEO JOURNAL *SEARCHING FOR THE SNOW LEOPARD*

NARRATOR: The snow leopards' home is high in the mountains of Central Asia. The snow leopard is an endangered animal, and it's strikingly beautiful. But because of its remote habitat, it is seldom seen by human beings.

NARRATOR: Over the course of 10 months, photographer Steve Winter shot more than 30,000 frames in pursuit of the elusive snow leopard. This is what happened . . .

STEVE WINTER: It was the hardest story I'd ever done physically because of the altitude and steepness of the mountains. Visually, it looks like you're on the moon. The cat's very shy and elusive. They can see for very long distances. We were constantly scanning with binoculars to try to see them and I would be of the opinion that they were looking to see us.

NARRATOR: As few as 3.500 snow leopards may exist in the wild. They've been spotted as high as 18,000 feet and they're notoriously camera shy.

STEVE WINTER: This is where we're going to start our snow leopard expedition. We'll be here a few days to acclimate to the altitudes at 12,000 feet.

And then [we] got the bags in to where the road ends by truck and jeep. And then we had to load everything on horseback and walk in. We took in fourteen remote cameras and a whole camp. Tents, sleeping bags, cots, pads. We brought food from the U.S. and then we bought some in India. At night it was thirty below zero and I've spent my whole career working in jungles. So this was a real switch for me. We looked for locations with the help of the local people that worked with the snow leopard NGO's. They had already ID'd locations where the cat comes to mark.

With this knowledge we were able to find locations to set up cameras where we knew cats would come and visit. Once we knew we were having success in a specific trail then I "mined" that trail with cameras.

It's very interesting for people to realize that no matter where you're working with animals, if there's a trail in the jungle, that's where the cats would walk. They may not hunt on that trail because they're going to hunt wherever they need to go where the scent is for the prey, but they will walk on these trails and you will see areas that they'll mark.

NARRATOR: Snow leopards can leap seven times their own body length. Some have been known to travel 25 miles in a single night and large eyes allow them to hunt in near total darkness.

STEVE WINTER: The first image is a curious cat. Behind him is the trail. He's looking up to see what the flash is and it's just flashing him in the face. It flashed twice, he turned around and he walked away. The next image is on a high ridge. This is a cat at a marking spot where they spray to really give their scent to that location. They mark to tell other snow leopards, "This is my area, not yours." The next image is very important to me and it took five and a half months to get one picture, but I love this image with mountains in the background and the closeness of the animal. It's very intimate to me; I feel like I can just reach out and stroke his fur. Though he'd bite me I'm sure.

This is where the snow leopard lives. He does not roam open areas except for following prey. He will sit in the rocks so he's camouflaged. And one of the reasons the snow leopard has such a long tail, which is the longest tail of any cat in the world, is that when he's on those rocky areas and the blue sheep come in to feed on the small plants that are on the rocks, he will chase them on almost vertical rock faces. And he uses the tail for balance.

NARRATOR: Efforts to save the snow leopard are now taking place in several countries. The key to those efforts is finding ways for humans—especially people who herd animals in the mountains—to live with the snow leopard. If these efforts are successful, the future of snow leopards in the wild will—someday—be more secure.

UNIT 6
VIDEO JOURNAL *NUBIAN WEDDING*

NARRATOR: It is modern—yet connected with the past . . . The Nubian wedding ritual, shared by the entire village . . . For 7 days and nights. The air is perfumed by incense and filled with the sound of beating drums, and joyful Nubian songs. Two years ago Sheriff's family told him it was time to get married. He visited every home in the village . . . looking for the right girl. Then, with one look at Abeer, he ran home to tell his mother he had found his bride. They didn't meet again until just before their Muslim wedding. After the bride and groom sign special legal papers, 7 days of celebration begin. Each day, early in the morning the party moves out into the village streets. The bride is painted from head to toe with henna. One day before the ceremony, the groom's bed is taken outside to be bathed in sandalwood incense. Sheriff is also perfumed . . . the scents, will last for weeks.

The Nubians traditionally lived along the banks of the Nile River in what is now southern Egypt and the Sudan. But in the 1960's that changed. The government of Egypt built the Aswan Dam and the water covered the ancient lands of the Nubian people. This man had to move here at the age of 12. His family left their mud-brick home for one of cement built by the government.

On the final night of the wedding—the village eats a feast of meat and rice in front of the groom's house. Then the groom leaves his parents' home and leads his neighbors through the streets chanting Islamic songs. Well after midnight, the groom at last picks up the bride and they arrive at the party. They spend all night dancing and singing from sunset to noon.

The word "Nubia" comes from an ancient term for "gold"—and refers to the gold mines for which the area was once famous.

That gold still shines today . . . as the bride is draped with jewelry . . . just like a queen.

It's now past 3 in the morning . . . but by Nubian standards the party has just begun.

After the exchange of rings, mother kisses her son and his new bride as they begin their life together . . . carrying on their ancient customs . . . and celebrating a transition in their lives.

TED TALK: HANS ROSLING—THE MAGIC WASHING MACHINE

ROSLING: I was only four years old when I saw my mother load a washing machine for the very first time in her life. That was a great day for my mother. My mother and father had been saving money for years to be able to buy that machine, and the first day it was going to be used, even Grandma was invited to see the machine. And Grandma was even more excited. Throughout her life she had been heating water with firewood, and she had hand washed laundry for seven children. And now she was going to watch electricity do that work.

My mother carefully opened the door, and she loaded the laundry into the machine, like this. And then, when she closed the door, Grandma said, "No, no, no, no. Let me, let me push the button." And Grandma pushed the button, and she said, "Oh, fantastic! I want to see this! Give me a chair! Give me a chair! I want to see it," and she sat down in front of the machine, and she watched the entire washing program. She was mesmerized. To my grandmother, the washing machine was a miracle.

Today, in Sweden and other rich countries, people are using so many different machines. Look, the homes are full of machines. I can't even name them all. And they also, when they want to travel, they use flying machines that can take them to remote destinations. And yet, in the world, there are so many people who still heat the water on fire, and they cook their food on fire. Sometimes they don't even have enough food, and they live below the poverty line. There are two billion fellow human beings who live on less than two dollars a day. And the richest people over there—there's one billion people—and they live above what I call the "air line," because they spend more than $80 a day on their consumption.

But this is just one, two, three billion people, and obviously there are seven billion people in the world, so there must be one, two, three, four billion people more who live in between the poverty line and the 'air line'. They have electricity, but the question is, how many have washing machines? I've done the scrutiny of market data, and I've found that, indeed, the washing machine has penetrated below the air line, and today there's an additional one billion people out there who live above the "wash line." And they consume more than $40 per day. So two billion have access to washing machines.

And the remaining five billion, how do they wash? Or, to be more precise, how do most of the women in the world wash? Because it remains hard work for women to wash. They wash like this: by hand. It's a hard, time-consuming labor, which they have to do for hours every week. And sometimes they also have to bring water from far away to do the laundry at home, or they have to bring the laundry away to a stream far off. And they want the washing machine. They don't want to spend such a large part of their life doing this hard work with so relatively low productivity. And there's nothing different in their wish than it was for my grandma. Look here, two generations ago in Sweden— picking water from the stream, heating with firewood and washing like that. They want the washing machine in exactly the same way.

But when I lecture to environmentally-concerned students, they tell me, "No, everybody in the world cannot have cars and washing machines." How can we tell this woman that she ain't going to have a washing machine? And then I ask my students, I've asked them—over the last two years I've asked, "How many of you don't use a car?" And some of them proudly raise their hand and say, "I don't use a car." And then I put the really tough question: "How many of you hand-wash your jeans and your bed sheets?" And no one raised their hand. Even the hardcore in the green movement use washing machines.

So how come [this is] something that everyone uses and they think others will not stop it? What is special with this? I had to do an analysis about the energy used in the world. Here we are. Look here, you see the seven billion people up there: the air people, the wash people, the bulb people and the fire people. One unit like this is an energy unit of fossil fuel—oil, coal or gas. That's what most of electricity and the energy in the world is. And it's 12 units used in the entire world, and the richest one billion, they use six of them. Half of the energy is used by one seventh of the world's population. And these ones who have washing machines, but not a house full of other machines, they use two. This group uses three, one each. And they also have electricity. And over there they don't even use one each. That makes 12 of them.

But the main concern for the environmentally-interested students—and they are right—is about the future.

What will happen is economic growth. The best of here in the emerging economies—I call them the New East— they will jump the air line. "Wopp!" they will say. And they will start to use as much as the Old West are doing already. And these people, they want the washing machine. I told you. They'll go there. And they will double their energy use. And we hope that the poor people will get into the electric light. And they'll get a two-child family without a stop in population growth. But the total energy consumption will increase to 22 units. And these 22 units—still the richest people use most of it. So what is needed to be done? Because the risk, . . . the high probability of climate change is real. It's real. Of course they must be more energy-efficient. They must change behavior in some way. They must also start to produce green energy, much more green energy. But until they have the same energy consumption per person, they shouldn't give advice to others—what to do and what not to do. (Applause) Here we can get more green energy all over.

This is what we hope may happen. It's a real challenge in the future. But I can assure you that this woman in the favela in Rio, she wants a washing machine. She's very happy about her minister of energy that provided electricity to everyone—so happy that she even voted for her. And she became Dilma Rousseff, the president-elect of one of the biggest democracies in the world—moving from minister of energy to president. If you have democracy, people will vote for washing machines. They love them.

And what's the magic with them? My mother explained the magic with this machine the very, very first day. She said, "Now Hans, we have loaded the laundry. The machine will make the work. And now we can go to the library." Because this is the magic: you load the laundry, and what do you get out of the machine? You get books out of the machines, children's books. And mother got time to read for me. She loved this. I got the "ABC's"—this is where I started my career as a professor, when my mother had time to read for me. And she also got books for herself. She managed to study English and learn that as a foreign language. And she read so many novels, so many different novels here. And we really, we really loved this machine.

And what we said, my mother and me, "Thank you industrialization. Thank you steel mill. Thank you power station. And thank you chemical processing industry that gave us time to read books."

UNIT 7
VIDEO JOURNAL *COOBER PEDY OPALS*

NARRATOR: Beneath the hot skillet surface of the outback, where the baked soil crumbles like ashes, there are treasures to be found.

In endless warrens of burrowing and hope, every hour of every day you can find people digging. And virtually all of these individuals, are like Peter Rowe.

PETER ROWE, OPAL MINER: And I came here to make a million dollars, I heard you could make a million dollars in Coober Pedy, and I come to get my share of it.

NARRATOR: That could only be one thing.

ROWE: To find opal. That's what they came for . . . to find that elusive, beautiful gem that just sort of bounces out and says 'Hey, look at me.'

NARRATOR: The town of Coober Pedy is home to about three thousand people.

It was built on opals. Over ninety percent of the world's opals come from Australia, and the first ones on this continent were discovered right here in 1911.

Finding opal has been turned into as much of a science as the rock will allow. This team has been digging for a year and a half since their last significant payoff. They believe they are only a few feet away from a major find. The problem is, in this town, almost everyone, almost every day believes he is on the verge of finding a fortune.

Something like this: these opals were all cut out of the same fist-sized piece of rock and will sell for at least three hundred thousand dollars, maybe a lot more. But here's the thing, ninety-five percent of all opal is colorless—worthless.

This maze of tunnels did not produce even a dollar's worth of opal. One of the odd benefits of digging so many holes in search of opals, is that some of them can be converted into homes. But it is the motherload payoff that is on everybody's mind.

ROWE: Within a mile of where we're sitting now, there could be millions of dollars. There is millions of dollars. And there's stones that would knock your eye out. Gems that would be just astronomical. And most of them never get seen; never see the light of day.

NARRATOR: Out here, where holes in the ground pass for buildings, most people do not find their fortunes. At the end of this day that started with so much hope, these miners came up empty again. The odds are, as long as they keep questing for opals, this will be the course of their lives for all the hopes, dreams, and hard work—scratching a living out of the ground.

UNIT 8
VIDEO JOURNAL *HAPPY ELEPHANTS*

NARRATOR: Elephants are very large, but they are gentle and intelligent animals. They are important to humans too. Elephants and people have worked together for over 2,000 years. But when they work with people, the elephants are not in the wild. They are usually in captivity and in zoos or circuses.

Over time, people have learned a lot about the way elephants act. However, there is one question that people are still asking: How can people keep elephants happy in captivity?

MIKE HACKENBERGER, ANIMAL TRAINER: OK, everyone, trunk foot salute. Angus. Trunk foot salute.

NARRATOR: Mike Hackenberger is an animal trainer at the Baltimore Zoo. His elephants are very healthy and seem to be happy.

HACKENBERGER: We make sure teeth are where they're supposed to be, don't have ingrown feet . . . this is all that good husbandry stuff.

NARRATOR: He even talks to his elephants.

HACKENBERGER: Oh you're happy . . . hear that? That's a happy sound. That's a good sound.

NARRATOR: But can elephants be happy? Do animals have feelings? If so, are their feelings the same people's feelings? There's a big discussion about this subject.

SPEAKER: Everything's going to be all right.

NARRATOR: Many people who work closely with animals say that they do have feelings and can experience happiness. Other people are not certain. There's one thing that everyone agrees on—elephants seem happier—and safer—if their home in the zoo or circus is very similar to life in the wild. Hackenberger's talk with the elephants may even help comfort them.

HACKENBERGER: Head over, let's go kids. Let's go, Fatman . . . move up . . . here to me . . . watch yourself . . . here to me! We're walking, guys. Come on, Funnyface! Good boy!

NARRATOR: According to Hackenberger elephant training has improved in recent years

HACKENBERGER: I'll tell you that . . . um . . . ten, fifteen, twenty years ago, some of the techniques were a bit barbaric. We've walked away from that, but society's walked away from it.

NARRATOR: Elephants are social animals. That means that they live in families and herds and they need other elephants. If they are alone for a long time, elephants can start to act in an unusual way.
   Hackenberger talks about one elephant, called Limba; Limba was alone for 30 years in a zoo in northern Quebec. She didn't do well by herself.
   Hackenberger then tells how two other elephants came to live with Limba when they were only two days old. Limba 'fell in love' with the two young elephants, he explains, and that's why she became a happier, and more normal elephant.
   When he's training elephants, Hackenberger lets them do the things they do in the wild. And there's one thing elephants love . . .

HACKENBERGER: Do you want to go swimming? Do you? Do you? Do you want to go swimming? I think that's a yes! Absolutely! Let's get in the water.

NARRATOR: So what is the answer to the question: How can people keep elephants happy in captivity? Hackenberger believes that elephants need to learn how to be elephants, just as they are in the wild.

HACKENBERGER: It doesn't get any better . . . no it doesn't. Are they trained? I think so. They're trained to be elephants! Just be an elephant!

NARRATOR: It certainly seems these animals are some very happy elephants!

UNIT 9
VIDEO JOURNAL *SEARCHING FOR GENGHIS KHAN*

NARRATOR: Genghis Khan, leader of the Mongols in the 13th century, rode far across Central Asia with his troops. They conquered city after city, leaving behind death and destruction. But Genghis was more than just a fierce warrior. He unified Mongolia and built an empire that stretched across a continent.
   Dr. Albert Yu-Min Lin is a researcher and engineer at the University of California at San Diego. He is also a National Geographic Emerging Explorer who travels to Mongolia to search for Genghis Khan's lost tomb. It's an exciting career, but it almost didn't happen. Lin was studying materials science and engineering when he realized that

he wanted to do more with his knowledge. He wanted to explore. He also had a personal connection to Mongolia. Lin, whose family is from China, grew up hearing that his family was "from the North." In other words, they were from Mongolia.

Lin's research is focused on looking for ways to use cutting-edge technology such as satellite imagery, ground-penetrating radar, and remote sensors to collect and synthesize data in a way that allows him to conserve archaeological sites, rather than destroying them. Because Genghis Khan's tomb is considered a sacred place, it would be disrespectful to disturb it. The area where it is believed to be located is called "The Forbidden Zone."

Using crowd sourcing, a way to let people from around the world participate in his research, Lin's team is examining satellite images that show where Genghis's tomb might be located. Hundreds of people that Lin calls "citizen scientists" spent months looking at 85,000 images, tagging roads, rivers, and ancient structures that might show where the tomb is located. Now Lin's team is visiting the most promising sites on the ground in Mongolia. How long will it take them to find Genghis's tomb? Only time will tell . . .

TED TALK: BEVERLY AND DERECK JOUBERT—LIFE LESSONS FROM BIG CATS

BEVERLY JOUBERT: We are truly passionate about the African wilderness and protecting the African wilderness, and so what we've done is we've focused on iconic cats. And I know, in the light of human suffering and poverty and even climate change, one would wonder, why worry about a few cats? Well today we're here to share with you a message that we have learned from a very important and special character—this leopard.

DERECK JOUBERT: We found this leopard in a 2,000-year-old baobab tree in Africa, the same tree that we found her mother in and her grandmother. And she took us on a journey and revealed something very special to us—her own daughter, eight days old. And the minute we found this leopard, we realized that we needed to move in, and so we basically stayed with this leopard for the next four-and-a-half years—following her every day, getting to know her, that individual personality of hers, and really coming to know her.

BEVERLY JOUBERT: Well we certainly did spend a lot of time with her—in fact, more time than even her mother did. When her mother would go off hunting, we would stay and film. And early on, a lightning bolt hit a tree 20 paces away from us. It was frightening, and it showered us with leaves and a pungent smell. And of course, we were stunned for a while, but when we managed to get our wits about us, we looked at each other and said, "My gosh, what's going to happen with that little cub? She's probably going to forever associate that deafening crash with us." Well, we needn't have worried. She came charging out of the thicket straight towards us, sat next to us, shivering, with her back towards Dereck, and looking out. And actually from that day on, she's been comfortable with us. So we felt that that day was the day that she really earned her name. We called her Legadema, which means, "light from the sky."

DERECK JOUBERT: We were spending so much time with this leopard and getting to understand her individualism, her personal character, that maybe we were taking it a little bit far. We were perhaps taking her for granted, and maybe she didn't like that that much.

BEVERLY JOUBERT: But when this little cub saw that I had vacated my seat and climbed to the back to get some camera gear, she came in like a curious cat to come and investigate. It was phenomenal, and we felt grateful that she trusted us to that extent. But at the same time, we were concerned that if she created this as a habit and jumped into somebody else's car, it might not turn out the same way—she might get shot for that. So we knew we had to react quickly. And the only way we thought we could without scaring her is to try and simulate a growl like her mother would make—a hiss and a sound. So Dereck turned on the heater fan in the car—very innovative.

DERECK JOUBERT: But really and truly, this was how this little leopard was displaying her individual personality. But nothing prepared us for what happened next in our relationship with her, when she started hunting.

BEVERLY JOUBERT: And on this first hunt, we truly were excited. It was like watching a graduation ceremony. We felt like we were surrogate parents. And of course, we knew now that she was going to survive. But only when we saw the tiny baby baboon clinging to the mother's fur did we realize that something very unique was taking place here with Legadema. And of course, the baby baboon was so innocent, it didn't turn and run. So what we watched over the next couple of hours was very unique. It was absolutely amazing when she picked it up to safety, protecting it from the hyena. And over the next five hours, she took care of it. We realized that we actually don't know everything, and that nature is so unpredictable, we have to be open at all times.

DERECK JOUBERT: Okay, so she was a little bit rough. (Laughter) But in fact, what we were seeing here was interesting. Because she is a cub wanting to play, but she was also a predator needing to kill, and yet conflicted in some way, because she was also an emerging mother. She had this maternal instinct, and so this really took us to this new level of understanding that personality.

BEVERLY JOUBERT: And of course, through the night, they lay together. They ended up sleeping for hours. But I have to tell you—everybody always asks, "What happened to the baby baboon?" It did die, and we suspect it was from the freezing winter nights.

DERECK JOUBERT: So at this stage, I guess, we had very, very firm ideas on what conservation meant. We had to deal with these individual personalities. We had to deal with them with respect and celebrate them. And so we, with the National Geographic, formed the Big Cats Initiative to march forward into conservation, taking care of the big cats that we loved—and then had an opportunity to look back over the last 50 years to see how well we had all collectively been doing. So when Beverly and I were born, there were 450,000 lions, and today there are 20,000. Tigers haven't fared any better—45,000 down to maybe 3,000.

BEVERLY JOUBERT: And then cheetahs have crashed all the way down to 12,000. Leopards have plummeted from 700,000 down to a mere 50,000. Now in the extraordinary time that we have worked with Legadema—which is really over a five-year period—10,000 leopards were legally shot by safari hunters. And that's not the only leopards that were being killed through that period. There's an immense amount of poaching as well, and so possibly the same amount. It's simply not sustainable.

DERECK JOUBERT: There's a burgeoning bone trade. South Africa just released some lion bones onto the market. Lion bones and tiger bones look exactly the same, and so in a stroke, the lion bone industry is going to wipe out all the tigers. So we have a real problem here, no more so than the lions do, the male lions. So the 20,000 lion figure that you just saw is actually a red herring, because there may be 3,000 or 4,000 male lions, and they all are actually infected with the same disease. I call it complacency—our complacency. Because there's a sport, there's an activity going on that we're all aware of, that we condone. And that's probably because we haven't seen it like we are today.

BEVERLY JOUBERT: And you have to know that, when a male lion is killed, it completely disrupts the whole pride. A new male comes into the area and takes over the pride, and, of course, first of all kills all the cubs and possibly some of the females that are defending their cubs. So we've estimated that between 20 to 30 lions are killed when one lion is hanging on a wall somewhere in a far-off place.

DERECK JOUBERT: So what our investigations have shown is that these lions are essential. They're essential to the habitat. If they disappear, whole ecosystems in Africa disappear. There's an 80-billion-dollar-a-year ecotourism revenue stream into Africa. So this is not just a concern about lions; it's a concern about communities in Africa as well. If they disappear, all of that goes away. But what I'm more concerned about in many ways is that, as we de-link ourselves from nature, as we de-link ourselves spiritually from these animals, we lose hope, we lose that spiritual connection, our dignity, that thing within us that keeps us connected to the planet.

DERECK JOUBERT: And Legadema? Well we can report, in fact, that we're grandparents.

UNIT 10
VIDEO JOURNAL *ADVENTURE CAPITAL OF THE WORLD*

NARRATOR: New Zealand is a land of many beautiful and quiet natural places. Queenstown isn't one of them.

BUNGEE INSTRUCTOR: Diving out that way, here we go: five, four, three, two, one, push it out!

NARRATOR: People come from around the world to do adventure sports in Queenstown—especially bungee jumping.

HENRY VAN ASCH, BUNGEE JUMP WORKER: The gap from the underside of that little silver jump pod out there is 134 meters, which is about 440 feet.

NARRATOR: That's a long way down! But the sport must be fun. There are many people waiting for a chance to do it. What do they feel like before a jump?

BUNGEE JUMPER 1: I'm so ready! Bring it on!

BUNGEE JUMPER 2: I'm getting excited actually, yeah.

BUNGEE INSTRUCTOR: Five, four, three, two, one . . .

NARRATOR: If you like exciting adventure sports, New Zealand is the place to do them.

VAN ASCH: New Zealand people have a very immediate lifestyle a lot of the time, and that's what people can experience when they come here.

BRENDAN QUILL, JETBOAT DRIVER: Ha! Nothing like it!

NARRATOR: Riding in a jetboat is a special experience. It's yet another New Zealand adventure invention. There's no propeller, so the boats can work in shallow water.

QUILL: These machines . . . you can spin 'em on a dime!

NARRATOR: Jetboats were especially designed to get around New Zealand's shallow rivers, but they're also really good at giving customers a thrill.

QUILL: Ha ha ha! Yee hee hee! This is one of the number-one pastimes of people coming to New Zealand . . . more importantly probably Queenstown.

NARRATOR: In New Zealand, it seems that nearly every day someone creates another adventure sport.

DAVID KENNEDY, DESTINATION QUEENSTOWN: You know we quite proudly call ourselves 'The Adventure Capital of the World.' There are so many adventure activities to do here. In fact, we worked it out that if you did one of every type of activity you'd be here for 60 days!

GRAHAM BUXTOM, TOUR GUIDE: Okay, we're off.

NARRATOR: One of the newest adventures involves a five-hour hike up a mountain. The best part is, at the end of the hike, the hikers don't have to walk all the way down again.

BUXTOM: We'll stay here for ten minutes or so . . . fifteen minutes. Then we'll jump in the helicopter and fly back to Queenstown.

NARRATOR: The helicopter turns the five-hour hike into a five-minute flight back to the city! These different adventure sports really help the tourism industry in New Zealand. They're also part of an adventurous culture that goes back to the birthplace of adventure tourism in New Zealand—the Kawarau Bridge. The bridge was the world's first commercial bungee-jumping site.

BUNGEE WATCHER: I think it's great—if somebody else is doing it!

NARRATOR: High wire bungee and bridge bungee are both thrilling and slightly frightening sports.

BUNGEE INSTRUCTOR: Here we go Marlene, lean forward: five, four, three, two, one!

VAN ASCH: The people who have to really try hard to jump are the ones that get the most out of it.

NARRATOR: At least that's what some people think.

BUNGEE INSTRUCTOR: How was that?

MARLENE: I'm never bungee jumping again!

NARRATOR: Maybe for some people, jumping once is enough.

BUNGEE JUMPER 1: Cheers!

BUNGEE JUMPER 2: Ah, we deserve that.

BUNGEE JUMPER 3: That was a good one!

NARRATOR: Most jumpers are happy that they did it. Here in the land of adventure, the only question may be: what will they think of doing next? Whatever it is, someone here in The Adventure Capital of the World will be ready to give it a try!

NARRATOR: It's very early morning on the tropical island of Trinidad. Colorful birds are moving around; calling and showing their beautiful colors among the different greens of the trees.

Ornithologist and photographer Roger Neckles is up and moving too. For the past ten years, Neckles has been taking photographs of the island's birds.

ROGER NECKLES: We just got buzzed by a hummingbird. Did you hear that?

NARRATOR: It's clear that he really loves the place. He describes it as being like heaven. He talks about how incredibly beautiful Trinidad is with its many colorful flowers and birds flying everywhere. Neckles feels it's just like paradise . . .

NECKLES: This is the best time of the day for me, getting up at five o'clock in the morning . . . heading off into the sticks up in the mountains. The atmosphere . . .the temperature up here . . . it's just fantastic! You breathe pure oxygen! This is the typical day in the 'office' for me.

NARRATOR: It seems Neckles really has found his own paradise. Neckles works at the Asa Wright Nature Center, which attracts ornithologists and bird lovers from all over the world. Most people go there especially to view some of the world's most attractive and special birds. However, the birds move very quickly. Roger explains he has to be very fast, too or he'll miss his opportunity to photograph them.

NECKLES: Ahh . . .look at that Purple Honey Creeper! Whoa! The color is so unique, a fantastic shade of purple.

NARRATOR: There are about 460 different types of birds on the island and Neckles is trying to photograph them all. But this takes time. He has to wait for just the right moment.

ROGER NECKLES: If you are not prepared to wait for the shot, you won't get it.

NARRATOR: Neckles has studied hummingbird behavior and bird calls for a long time. He knows most things about their way of life, including where they live. Hummingbirds live in very unusual nests that they build themselves.

ROGER NECKLES: And they're really strong, they build them on the edges . . . the very edges of branches, and winds come, hurricanes will come, and gale force winds, and they won't blow down.

NARRATOR: Why has Neckles chosen to study birds in Trinidad and Tobago?

NECKLES: I came here in 1978, and I was so enchanted with the topography of the land here in Trinidad and Tobago that I thought, 'Oh yes! I could do this.'

NARRATOR: Through his research, Neckles has developed a deeper understanding of all the wildlife of the island—even ones that aren't so pretty.

NECKLES: Whoa, you don't want to get your fingers in there!

NARRATOR: However, it's not just any wildlife that brings Neckles into the woods again and again. It's the birds. This morning he hopes to get a photograph of a very small—and very rare—bird.

NECKLES: Look at this! This is the most festive hummingbird in Trinidad and Tobago! The smallest hummingbird in Trinidad and Tobago—the Tufted Coquette. Look at him just sitting there!

NARRATOR: He's been trying to photograph this hummingbird for six weeks. It's been a very long wait, and now it comes down to one chance . . . and he gets it! Neckles has finally gotten the shot that he has been seeking for six weeks!

NECKLES: Yes! I got it! I've got goose bumps all up my arms. This is fantastic!

NARRATOR: Neckles doesn't mind waiting for the perfect moment to take a photograph. Like the birds he follows, he enjoys the day and the beauty around him.

NECKLES: I have no plans to give this up at all because I figure I could do this for the rest of my life. Every time I go out I see something new.

NARRATOR: Apparently, the birds of Trinidad aren't the only ones who have found paradise.

UNIT 12

VIDEO JOURNAL *YOUNG RIDERS OF MONGOLIA*

NARRATOR: Mongolians are very good at horseback riding. They learn to ride when they are very young, and people all over the world think that they're great horsemen. Almost a thousand years ago, Mongolia became a very large and important country, because it had a strong army that rode horses.

Since that time, life in Mongolia has changed a lot. However, horses are still very important to the people here. Mongolians often move from place to place. Because there are few roads and cars there, people still need horses every day for their way of life.

Each year in July, there is a festival called Naadam that celebrates horseback riding and other traditional Mongolian sports. Thousands of people come from all over Mongolia to a place just outside the capital city, Ulan Bator. This festival has important national events in traditional Mongolian sports—especially horse racing. However, the Naadam race is a little unusual. All of the riders in the race are younger than 12 years old!

People start preparing for the race early in the morning. Each horse's tail is covered in leather. Then, the people offer horse's milk to the spirits of nature. Then there are ceremonies protect the riders and their horses from accidents, and to give them good luck. Before the race, the parents join the young riders to walk around a special area.

It's a big race—about 500 riders will participate in it. However, before the race starts, the riders must walk the horses over 15 miles to the starting point. The race begins. Thousands of people wait at the finish line, but they can't see anything. The race is actually happening miles away.

The people who are watching want to get near the winning horses. An old story says that the dust when the horses run is lucky. People believe that it brings happiness and success to anybody it touches. Finally, the first horses and riders appear. These first riders have already been running for nearly 30 minutes!

The first five horses that finish the race get a blue sash for winning. After the winners have arrived, the other horses and riders keep coming in for another hour. Finally, the Naadam race ends in the National Stadium, the country's main sports ground. A famous singer sings about the winning horses and how good they are. The five winners walk around the sports ground. They receive prizes and drink horse's milk. And the slowest horse gets a prize too, so that he will try harder next time.

The Naadam Festival is a happy time. The young riders have shown their skills in one of Mongolia's most important traditions. They are the next great horsemen of their country.

TED TALK: SYLVIA EARLE—MY WISH—PROTECT OUR OCEANS

EARLE: Fifty years ago, when I began exploring the ocean, no one imagined that we could do anything to harm the ocean by what we put into it or by what we took out of it. It seemed, at that time, to be a sea of Eden, but now we know, and now we are facing paradise lost.

I want to share with you my personal view of changes in the sea that affect all of us, and to consider why it matters that in 50 years, we've lost—actually, we've taken, we've eaten—more than 90 percent of the big fish in the sea; why you should care that nearly half of the coral reefs have disappeared; why a mysterious depletion of oxygen in large areas of the Pacific should concern not only the creatures that are dying, but it really should concern you. It does concern you, as well.

I'm haunted by the thought of what Ray Anderson calls "tomorrow's child," asking why we didn't do something on our watch to save sharks and bluefin tuna and squids and coral reefs and the living ocean while there still was time. Well, now is that time. I hope for your help to explore and protect the wild ocean in ways that will restore the health and, in so doing, secure hope for humankind. Health to the ocean means health for us.

I heard astronaut Joe Allen explain how he had to learn everything he could about his life support system and then do everything he could to take care of his life support system; and then he pointed to this and he said, "Life support system." We need to learn everything we can about it and do everything we can to take care of it.

Tim Worth says the economy is a wholly-owned subsidiary of the environment. With every drop of water you drink, every breath you take, you're connected to the sea. No matter where on Earth you live. Most of the oxygen in the atmosphere is generated by the sea. Over time, most of the planet's organic carbon has been absorbed and stored there, mostly by microbes. The ocean drives climate and weather, stabilizes temperature, shapes Earth's chemistry. Water from the sea forms clouds that return to the land and the seas as rain, sleet and snow, and provides a home for about 97 percent of life in the world, maybe in the universe. No water, no life; no blue, no green.

Yet we have this idea, we humans, that the Earth—all of it: the oceans, the skies—are so vast and so resilient it doesn't matter what we do to it. That may have been true 10,000 years ago, and maybe even 1,000 years ago but in the last 100, especially in the last 50, we've drawn down the assets, the air, the water, the wildlife that make our lives possible. New technologies are helping us to understand the nature of nature; the nature of what's happening, showing us our impact on the Earth. I mean, first you have to know that you've got a problem. And fortunately, in our time, we've learned more about the problems than in all preceding history. And with knowing comes caring. And with caring, there's hope that we can find an enduring place for ourselves within the natural systems that support us. But first we have to know.

We can now go to the Arctic. Just ten years ago I stood on the ice at the North Pole. An ice-free Arctic Ocean may happen in this century. That's bad news for the polar bears. That's bad news for us too. Excess carbon dioxide is not only driving global warming, it's also changing ocean chemistry, making the sea more acidic. That's bad news for coral reefs and oxygen-producing plankton. Also it's bad news for us. We're taking out hundreds of millions of tons of wildlife.

This chart shows the decline in ocean wildlife from 1900 to 2000. The highest concentrations are in red. In my lifetime, imagine, 90 percent of the big fish have been killed. Most of the turtles, sharks, tunas and whales are way down in numbers.

But, there is good news. Ten percent of the big fish still remain. There are still some blue whales. There are still some krill in Antarctica. There are a few oysters in Chesapeake Bay. Half the coral reefs are still in pretty good shape, a jeweled belt around the middle of the planet. There's still time, but not a lot, to turn things around. But business as usual means that in 50 years, there may be no coral reefs—and no commercial fishing, because the fish will simply be gone. Imagine the ocean without fish. Imagine what that means to our life support system. Natural systems on the land are in big trouble too, but the problems are more obvious, and some actions are being taken to protect trees, watersheds and wildlife.

With scientists around the world, I've been looking at the 99 percent of the ocean that is open to fishing—and mining, and drilling, and dumping, and whatever—to search out hope spots, and try to find ways to give them and us a secure future. Such as the Arctic—we have one chance, right now, to get it right. Or the Antarctic, where the continent is protected, but the surrounding ocean is being stripped of its krill, whales and fish.

There are still places in the sea as pristine as I knew as a child. The next 10 years may be the most important, and the next 10,000 years the best chance our species will have to protect what remains of the natural systems that give us life. To cope with climate change, we need new ways to generate power. We need new ways, better ways, to cope with poverty, wars and disease. We need many things to keep and maintain the world as a better place. But, nothing else will matter if we fail to protect the ocean. Our fate and the ocean's are one. We need to do for the ocean what Al Gore did for the skies above.

A global plan of action with a world conservation union, the IUCN, is underway to protect biodiversity, to mitigate and recover from the impacts of climate change, on the high seas and in coastal areas, wherever we can identify critical places. New technologies are needed to map, photograph and explore the 95 percent of the ocean that we have yet to see. The goal is to protect biodiversity, to provide stability and resilience. We need deep-diving subs, new technologies to explore the ocean.

And so, I suppose you want to know what my wish is. I wish you would use all means at your disposal—films, expeditions, the web, new submarines—and campaign to ignite public support for a global network of marine protected areas—hope spots large enough to save and restore the ocean, the blue heart of the planet. How much? Some say 10 percent, some say 30 percent. You decide: how much of your heart do you want to protect? Whatever it is, a fraction of one percent is not enough. My wish is a big wish, but if we can make it happen, it can truly change the world, and help ensure the survival of what actually—as it turns out—is my favorite species; that would be us. For the children of today, for tomorrow's child: as never again, now is the time.

UNIT 1 FOOD FROM THE EARTH

Lesson A

A. 1. farmer 2. meal 3. humid 4. flat 5. grasslands 6. mountains 7. crop 8. climate 9. geography 10. coast

B. 2. a. Usually, Claudia eats fish and rice. b. Tonight she is eating a pizza and salad. 3. a. Usually, Claudia drinks water. b. Tonight she is drinking cola 4. a. Usually, Claudia wears a t-shirt. b. Tonight she is wearing a nice dress. 5. a. Usually, Claudia watches TV. b. Tonight she is talking to her friends.

Lesson B

A. 1. regions 2. climate 3. land 4. mountains 5. staple food

B. Answers will vary.

C. 1. He has a brother in Tokyo. 2. I always eats sushi for lunch. 3. We eat a lot of fish. 4. My English teacher is from Australia. 5. Australia has a hot and sunny climate. 6. Rice is the staple food in Korea. 7. What is the staple food in your country? 8. What crops do farmers usually grow in your region?

Lesson C

A.

1. rice	4. corn	7. lentils	10. yucca
2. oats	5. wheat	8. potatoes	
3. black beans	6. soybeans	9. yams	

B.

1. went	5. flew	9. sent	13. ate
2. said	6. took	10. wrote	14. drank
3. bought	7. saw	11. found	15. fell
4. knew	8. told	12. got	16. gave

C. Answers will vary.

D. Answers will vary.

Lesson D

A. 1. Honduras: 2. Mexico: 3. Spain: 4. England: 5. Switzerland:

B. 1. T 2. F 3. F 4. T 5. F 6. F

C. Answers will vary.

D. Answers will vary.

REVIEW

A. Across 4. wheat 7. climate 10. crop 11. wrote 12. gone 13. region 14. coastal 16. told 17. bought

Down 1. knew 2. got 3. meal 5. staple food 6. rice 7. corn 8. saw 9. found 15. said 16. took

B. 1. crops 2. climate 3. staple food 4. grows 5. eat 6. prepare

UNIT 2 COMMUNICATION

Lesson A

A. 1. the weather 2. good 3. the same 4. old 5. good afternoon 6. usual 9. don't understand 10. body

B. 2. I have taken 3. I have read 4. I have gone 5. I have been 6. I have cooked 7. I have brought 8. I have come 9. I have made 10. I have eaten 11. I have given 12. I have heard

C. 2. Have you ever eaten Japanese food?; Yes, I've eaten sushi. 3. Have you ever gone shopping in a Japanese department store?; Yes, I have gone to Sakura Department Store. 4. Have you ever visited a Japanese temple?; Yes, I have visited Toji Temple.

Lesson B

A. 1, 5, 2, 4, 6, 7, 9, 3, 8, 10

B. Answers will vary.

C. Answers will vary.

Lesson C

A. 1. yet 2. already 3. have 4. have 5. already 6. haven't 7. yet 8. never

B. 1. How do you like this weather? 2. Are you enjoying this class? 3. Did you hear about the accident? 4. How long have you been waiting?

C. Answers will vary.

Lesson D

A. 1, 5, 2, 7, 8, 4, 6, 3

B. 5, 1, 2, 3, 4

C. 1. Mortenson talks about his experiences building schools for poor children in Pakistan and Afghanistan. 2. a small village called Korphe 3. Mortenson

D. Answer will vary.

REVIEW

A. Across 2. gone 3. been 5. yet 9. seen 10. eaten 13. eye contact 14. taken

Down 1. culture 2. given 3. bought 4. done 6. greeting 7. informal 8. connect 9. small talk 11. already 12. written

B. 1. culture 2. have been 3. customs 4. greetings 5. went 6. gestures

UNIT 3 CITIES

Lesson A

A. 1. nightlife 2. commutes. 3. urban 4. noisy 5. freeway 6. population 7. rural 8. crowded 9. traffic 10. public transportation

B. 2. Will most people live in the city or in rural areas? 3. Will cities be quiet or noisy? 4. Where will people go shopping? 5. Will young people live in rural areas?

C. Answers will vary.

Lesson B

A. How do you like living in your neighborhood? Well, it has great nightlife, but there are some problems. Like what? It doesn't have good transportation. That sounds like a pretty big problem. But the city is building a subway station now. We'll have better transportation next year.

B. 1. Green space: picture of park bench under a tree. 2. Heavy traffic: picture of a crowded road. 3. serious crime: picture of someone breaking through a door 4. Beautiful old buildings: picture of old residential street with colonial buildings. 5. A lot of noise: picture of loudspeakers.

C. Answers will vary.

Lesson C

A. 1. legend 2. library 3. city hall 4. scale 5. east 6. recycling center 7. key 8. sports center

B. Answers will vary.

C. 2. after 3. after 4. before 5. before 6. after

Lesson D

A. 1. . . . pollution out of the air. 2. They also stop the noise from heavy traffic . . . 3. They make the weather better . . . 3a. . . . they make the air 3-5 degrees cooler 3b. . . . they stop strong winds. 4. They make the city more beautiful. 5. They give people a place to relax and spend time in nature. 6. In hot countries urban forests are cool places for walking and other healthy exercise.

B. 1. Kasugayama 2. Thames Chase 3. Kasugayama and Thames Chase 4. Thames Chase 5. Kasuagayama 6. Kasuyagama

C. Answers will vary.

REVIEW

A. Across 1. shopping center 8. traffic 9. urban 11. before 12. crowded 14. scale

Down 1. skyscraper 2. population 3. nightlife 4. commute 5. neighborhood 6. rural 7. will 10. after 13. west

B. 2. green spaces 3. heavy traffic 4. public transportation 5. definitely 6. after

UNIT 4 THE BODY

Lesson A

A. 1. brain 2. bone 3. lungs 4. artery 5. vein 6. heart 7. muscle 8. liver 9. stomach 10. large intestine 11. small intestine

B. 1. heart 2. brain 3. lungs

C. Answers will vary.

D. Answers will vary.

Lesson B

A. Answers will vary.

B. Answers will vary.

C. 2. My hardest test was in mathematics. 3. Swimming is more relaxing than running. 4. We need a bigger rug in the living room. 5. He's the newest teacher in our school. 6. We're looking for a better restaurant.

Lesson C

A.

1. insomnia	3. pimple	5. headache	7. fever
2. sore throat	4. nausea	6. hiccups	8. indigestion

B. Answers will vary.

Lesson D

A. 1. F 2. T 3. T 4. F 5. F 6. T 7. F

B. 1. f 2. d 3. e 4. c 5. a 6. b

C. Answers will vary.

D. Answers will vary.

REVIEW

A. Across 2. bones 5. blood 9. more interesting 11. skin 12. better 13. heart 14. stomach 16. lungs

Down 1. insomnia 2. brain 3. low in 4. muscles 5. biggest 6. artery 7. headache 8. lifestyle 10. indigestion 13. high in 15. worst

B. 1. exercise 2. diet 3. stress 4. headaches 5. insomnia 6. lifestyle

UNIT 5 CHALLENGES

Lesson A

A. 1. h 2. a 3. e 4. d 5. i 6. g 7. b 8. j 9. c 10. f

B. 2. While we were playing tennis, it started raining. 3. I saw an accident while I was waiting for the bus. 4. She was walking to school when she met her friend. 5. Our boss was talking on the phone when we went into his office. 6. My brother came home while I was watching a movie.

C. Possible answers: 1. Javier found a $100 bill when he was walking on the beach. 2. Mimi's cell phone rang while she was listening to the concert.

Lesson B

A. Answers will vary.

B. Answers will vary.

C. 1. /d/ 2. /t/ 3. /t/ 4. /t/ 5. /ɪd/ 6. /d/ 7. /ɪd/ 8. /t/

Lesson C

A. 1. run out of 2. grew up 3. watch out 4. keeps on 5. give up 6. put up with 7. set out 8. broke down

B. 2. It's too expensive. 3. It isn't loud enough. 4. The water is warm enough. 5. The recipe is easy enough. 6. This backpack isn't big enough. 7. She's too busy. 8. It's too far from my house.

C. Answers will vary.

Lesson D

A. 1. elementary school, 2. spell, 3. word, 4. spell, 5. sits down, 6. last, 7. cities, 8. Washington, 9. winner, 10. four

B. 1. T 2. F 3. T 4. T 5. T 6. F

C. Answer will vary.

D. Answers will vary.

REVIEW

A. Across 1. grew up 4. watch out 7. enough 9. challenge 13. skill 15. run out of 16. too

Down 2. put up with 3. physical 5. achieve 6. keep on 9. goals 10. amazing 11. equipment 12. give up 14. set out

B. 1. challenge 2. decided 3. mental 4. too 5. was taking 6. met 7. give up

UNIT 6 TRANSITIONS

Lesson A

A. 1. b 2. e 3. a 4. c 5. d

B. 2. adulthood 3. old age 4. childhood 6. adulthood

C. 1. have eaten 2. has known, were 3. have worked 4. had 5. have finished 6. have seen, was

D. Answers will vary.

Lesson B

A. **Beth:** Did you hear the big news? Mark is learning to drive.

Julia: But he's 16! That's too young to drive.

Beth: Oh, I don't know about that. He's very careful. And his father is teaching him.

Julia: That's true, but I think he should wait a few years.

Beth: Well, what do you think is the best age to learn to drive?

Julia: I think people should get their driver's license after they've graduated high school.

B. Answers will vary.

C. Answers will vary.

D.

1. important	3. pizza	5. animal	7. listen
2. travel	4. apartment	6. woman	8. transition

Lesson C

A. 1. retired 2. youthful 3. in her thirties 4. childish 5. mature 6. elderly 7. middle-aged

B. 2. How badly does he sing? 3. How wealthy is he? 4. How well does she cook? 5. How difficult was it?

C. 1. How old is he? 2. How hard does he study? 3. How mature is he? 4. How carefully does he drive? 5. How well does he speak English?

Lesson D

A.

Transition	Schulanfang	Quince Años	Coming-of-Age Day
Country	Germany	Mexico	Japan
Age of people celebrating	6	15	20
When	First day of school	15th birthday	Second Sunday in January
Where	School	Church and a restaurant	City Hall
What do people do?	Kids wear new clothes. Parents give Zuckertuete and take pictures. Children meet their teachers, sing, and play games and go to an after school party with coffee and cake.	Girls wear a beautiful and expensive dress. The family goes to church in the morning and has a huge party in a restaurant with music and dancing later.	20-year-olds listen to speeches and get presents from the city mayor. They wear new clothes and many women wear kimonos. Their families take lots of pictures.

B. Answers will vary.

C. Answers will vary.

REVIEW

A. Across 1. infancy 5. mature 6. have seen 7. graduate 8. retired 10. senior citizen 13. teenager 14. have done 15. elderly 16. youthful

Down 2. adulthood 3. get married 4. in his twenties 5. middle-aged 9. got 11. childish 12. move 14. had

B. 1. teenager 2. mature 3. got 4. has already opened 5. bought 6. carefully

UNIT 7 LUXURIES

Lesson A

A. 1. jewelry 2. import 3. silk 4. fur coat 5. export 6. precious metals 7. precious stones 8. Pearls

B. 2. Beautiful jewelry is made in Mexico. 3. A lot of cars are exported by Japanese companies. 4. The best grapes for champagne are grown by French farmers. 5. Precious stones are mined by people in Africa

C. 2. Coffee is grown in Ethiopia. 3. Diamonds are found in The Congo. 4. Pottery is made in Morocco. 5. Movies are filmed in Nigeria. 6. Cotton is produced in Egypt.

Lesson B

A. Answers will vary.

B. Answers will vary

C. 1. k 2. a 3. j 4. g 5. h 6. f 7. c 8. e 9. b 10. i 11. d

D. 1. On Sundays, I can eat dinner with my family in the afternoon. 2. Those fur coats are expensive, but I don't think they're beautiful. 3. Carrie is going to visit her cousins in Mexico during her vacation. 4. Where did you put those new DVDs about animals? 5. We need bread, milk, and eggs from the store. 6. Andy is sad because he failed his big math test.

Lesson C

A. 2. taken 3. used 4. written 5. asked 6. spun 7. flown 8. cooked 9. stolen 10. grown 11. meant 12. checked 13. spread 14. seen 15. dug 16. fixed

B. 3. *by* phrase required 4. OK 5. *by* phrase required 6. OK 7. either response correct 8. *by* phrase required 9. OK 10. *by* phrase required

C. Answers will vary.

Lesson D

A. Top row: 1, 5, 8, 2 Bottom row: 3, 7, 4, 6

B. Answers will vary.

C. Answers will vary.

REVIEW

A. Across 1. flown 6. jewelry 8. import 10. precious stones 13. silk 14. perfume 15. meant 16. dug 17. pearls

Down 2. luxury 3. champagne 4. necessity 5. precious metals 7. export 9. fur coat 11. stolen 12. spread 13. spun

B. Answers will vary.

UNIT 8 NATURE

Lesson A

A. 1. extinct 2. habitat 3. wildlife 4. predator 5. prey 6. wild 7. hunt 8. tame 9. protect 10. species

B. 1. Don't/lose call 2. won't go/tell 3. will disappear/continues 4. cut/will not have 5. go/will see 6. will become/don't stop

C. Answers will vary.

Lesson B

A. Plan 1. a. If they close the beach, hotels will lose money. b. People will be unhappy. c. Answers will vary. Plan 2. a. People will not read it. b. Everyone will feel afraid. c. Answers will vary. Plan 3. a. It will be dangerous. b. The tourists will go home. c. Answers will vary.

B. Answers will vary.

C. 1. Mark and I / went to a national park / last weekend. 2. Do you eat / a lot of fish? 3. This fish / is caught / in a sustainable way. 4. Il send you / an email / about the safe fish project. 5. The zoo has / three African elephants, / four tigers, / and two kangaroos. 6. Fishing laws / are changing / around the world.

Lesson C

A. 1. badly 2. angrily 3. wonderfully 4. slowly 5. well 6. fast 7. loudly 8. interestingly 9. sadly 10. lazily

B. Answers will vary.

C. 1. too many 2. a lot of 3. many 4. too many 5. some 6. a few 7. a little 8. a lot of

D. Answers will vary.

Lesson D

A. Vertically: 7, 5, 1, 2, 4, 3, 6

B. 1. e 2. c 3. f 4. d 5. b 6. a

C. Answers will vary.

D. Answers will vary.

REVIEW

A. Across 1. sustainable 6. prey 7. predator 9. wildlife 10. many 11. fast 12. habitat 15. protect 16. well

Down 2. species 3. badly 4. extinct 5. easily 8. lot 12. hunt 13. tame 14. will 16. wild

B. 1. protect 2. habitats 3. don't 4. will 5. wildlife 6. environment 7. many

UNIT 9 LIFE IN THE PAST

Lesson A

A. 1. inspired 2. trade 3. exchange 4. ship 5. publish 6. distant, remarkable 7. despite 8. search 9. beyond

B. 1. used to play 2. used to make 3. used to get 4. used to travel 5. used to use 6. used to get

C. 2. Did you use to eat 3. Did you use to wear 4. Did you use to walk 5. Did you use to have 6. Answers will vary.

Lesson B

A. Answers will vary

B. Answers will vary.

Lesson C

A. 2. I put on my new shoes before the party. 3. Jennie brought up her little brother after their parents died. 4. I help my friends out if they don't understand their classes. 5. When I wake up, I turn my computer on. 6. I can't figure out this problem.

B. 2. Macbeth was written by William Shakespeare 3. The Great Pyramid of Giza was built by the Egyptians. 4. The telephone was patented by Alexander Graham Bell. 5. The Mona Lisa was painted by Leonardo Da Vinci

C. Answers will vary.

Lesson D

A. 1. T 2. T 3. F 4. T 5. F 6. T 7. F 8. F

B. People making pots, actors, people cooking, staple foods, clothes that people used to wear, a fort, ships, Native American Boats

C. Answers will vary.

D. Answers will vary.

REVIEW

A. Across 2. use to 3. trade 6. help out 8. remarkable 11. exchange 12. distant 15. inspire 17. used to 18. put on

Down 1. search 4. explorer 5. figure out 7. bring back 9. bring up 10. despite 13. turn on 14. beyond 16. ship

B. Answers will vary.

UNIT 10 TRAVEL

Lesson A

A. 1. d 2. e 3. c 4. h 5. g 6. f 7. b 8. a

B. 1. g 2. b 3. d 4. h 5. e 6. a

C. 2. You don't have to have color photographs. 3. You must have a photocopy of your plane ticket. 4. You have to pay $20 cash. 5. You must go to the Visa office. 6. You have to wait two weeks.

Lesson B

A. 1. walk ten miles 2. campgrounds in nature areas 3. local food in pubs 4. hear lectures from famous professors 5. student apartments 6. college dining halls 7. take a bus tour 8. castles 9. the finest restaurants.

B. Answers will vary.

C. Answers will vary.

Lesson C

A. 1. boarding pass 2. baggage claim 3. carry-on bag 4. departures 5. airline agent 6. security check 7. gate 8. terminal 9. arrivals 10. check-in counter

B. 1. ticket 2. check 3. carry-on bag 4. boarding pass 5. gate 6. security check 7. flight

C. 1. must 2. can't 3. don't have to 4. have to 5. can't 6. must

D. Answers will vary.

Lesson D

A. 3, 2, 1

B. 1. Melissa, Lee 2. Carlo, Lee 3. Melissa, Lee 4. Carlo 5. Lee 6. Carlo 7. Carlo, Melissa 8. Lee

C. Answers will vary.

D. Answers will vary.

REVIEW

A. Across 2. ecotourism 6. gate 8. passport 10. security check 12. carry on 13. visa 14. arrivals 15. terminal 16. itinerary 18. must not

Down 1. sightseeing 3. departures 4. boarding pass 5. vaccination 7. ticket 9. reservation 11. have to 17. agent

B. Answers will vary.

UNIT 11 CAREERS

Lesson A

A. 1. assistant 2. volunteer 3. qualifications 4. experience 5. owner 6. training 7. boss 8. employee

B. 1. should 2. had better not 3. shouldn't 4. ought to 5. should

C. Answers will vary.

Lesson B

A. 1. Do you like to work with other people? 2. Is your salary important to you? 3. Do you want a lot of vacation time? 4. Do you need to work near your home?

B. Answers will vary

C. Answers will vary

D. 1. class 2. interview 3. call 4. ask 5. movie 6. Japanese 7. party 8. car

Lesson C

A. 1. terrified 2. interesting 3. surprised 4. pleasing 5. bored 6. satisfying

B. 1. no one 2. anything 3. someone /somebody 4. everything 5. something 6. everyone 7. nothing

C. Answers will vary.

Lesson D

A. Answers will vary

B. Answers will vary.

C. Answers will vary.

REVIEW

A. Across 2. qualifications 7. owner 8. anything 9. volunteer 10. experience 13. bored 15. no one 16. training

Down 1. homemaker 3. assistant 4. terrified 5. satisfying 6. employee 11. boss 12. nothing 14. everybody

B. Answers will vary.

UNIT 12 CELEBRATIONS

Lesson A

A. 1. participate 2. take place 3. celebrate 4. crowd 5. well-known 6. holiday 7. annual 8. colorful 9. festival

B. 1. Thanksgiving is not as long as Hogmanay. 2. The music festival is as well-known as the movie festival. 3. The carnival dance is not as popular as the carnival parade. 4. The Art Fair is as interesting as the music festival.

C. Answers will vary.

Lesson B

A. Answers will vary.

B. Answers will vary.

C. 1. Should we watch the video ↗tonight or ↘tomorrow? 2. Would you like ↗fish, ↗chicken, or ↘pasta? 3. Do you want to make an appointment for ↗Monday, ↗Tuesday, or ↘Wednesday? 4. Would you rather study in ↗Canada or ↘England? 5. What kind of pizza do you want— ↗vegetable, ↗sausage, ↗ham, or ↘cheese?

Lesson C

A. 1. well done 2. thanks for inviting us 3. Happy New Year 4. Happy Anniversary 5. Congratulations 6. Happy Birthday

B. Answers will vary.

C. Answers will vary.

Lesson D

A. 1. F 2. T 3. T 4. F 5. F 6. T

B. 1. Sweden, Finland, Spain 2. Sweden, Finland, Spain 3. Spain 4. Sweden 5. Spain 6. Sweden, Finland, Spain

C. Answers will vary.

REVIEW

A. Across 1. 7. New Year's Day 8. would rather 10. celebrate 12. take place 13. well known 14. annual

Down 2. colorful 3. congratulations 4. day off 5. crowd 6. participate 9. festival 11. good job

B. Answers will vary.

Reasons for Writing

The Writing Program reinforces and complements the lessons in the Student Book. Writing gives students a chance to reflect on the English they've learned and to develop an indispensable academic skill.

The Writing Syllabus

The Writing Activities help students to develop all the building blocks of good writing: words, logical connectors, sentences, transitions, paragraphs, and short essays. As students progress through the levels of the *World English* series, the Writing Activities progress from the word and sentence level to the paragraph and composition level, allowing students to master the basics before they're asked to do more complex writing tasks.

The Writing Activities help students move from sentences to paragraphs as they show relationships between ideas and add detail and precision to their writing with descriptive adjectives.

Writing from Models vs. Process Writing

When students are provided with writing models—examples of completed writing tasks—they have a clear idea of what is expected from them as well as a model on which to base their own writing. Such models give students confidence and a sense of direction and can be found at all levels of the Writing Worksheets.

On the other hand, writers must also learn the writing process. They must generate ideas, plan their writing, perform the writing task, then polish their writing by revising and editing. The Writing Worksheets support process writing by providing activities to stimulate thinking, useful topics and vocabulary, graphic organizers for planning, and opportunities for students to share and refine their writing.

Ways to Use the Writing Program

In general, the Writing Activities are designed to be used after the class has covered all or most of a unit in the Student Book. The Writing Activities often contain grammar, vocabulary, and ideas from the units, which give students solid linguistic and conceptual ground to stand on.

On the other hand, it's not necessary to complete the Lesson D Writing task in the Student Book before using the Writing Activity for that unit. The worksheets complement the writing lessons in the Student Book, but can be used independently.

- **In-Class Discussion**

  Discussion is an important way to stimulate thinking and to help students generate ideas they can use in their own writing. When an activity contains a preliminary matching or listing activity, for example, ask students to share and explain their answers. Ask specific questions about the writing models in order to check comprehension and to elicit opinions about the topics. And be sure to take advantage of opportunities for students to discuss their writing with you and their classmates.

- **Homework**

  Most of the Writing Activities are appropriate for self-study as long as follow-up discussion and feedback are provided later.

- **Vocabulary Practice**

  Many of the Writing Activities contain target vocabulary from the corresponding unit in the Student Book. Ask students to locate vocabulary from the unit in the writing models, or check comprehension by asking students to explain vocabulary words in the context of the worksheet.

- **Grammar Reinforcement**

  Many of the Writing Activities require the use of grammar points found in the Student Book units, and using the grammar in context supports real language acquisition.

- **Pronunciation Practice**

  Although oral skills are not the focus of the Writing Activities, you can do choral repetition of the word lists in the worksheets or use the writing models to practice pronunciation points from the Student Book. Students can also do read-alouds of their finished writing in pairs or small groups while the teacher monitors their pronunciation.

- **Personalization**

  When students complete unfinished sentences, paragraphs, and essays, or when they do less controlled original writing, they bring their personal thoughts and experiences into the classroom and take ownership of the writing task as well as the language they are learning.

- **Real Communication**

  Since the real-world purpose of writing is to communicate, be sure to respond not only to linguistic and technical aspects of student writing, but also to students' ideas. Make comments and ask questions that show genuine interest, either in class or when you collect and give written feedback on the worksheets.

	Writing Tasks	Language Focus
UNIT 1 Time expressions	• Use a graphic organizer • Associate time expressions with verb tenses • Finish sentences about yourself	*yesterday, sometimes, last month, at the moment, every Saturday, right now, etc.*
UNIT 2 A personal profile	• Analyze the use of the present perfect in a model paragraph • List ideas before writing • Finish a paragraph about yourself	*I've had an interesting life.* *I've learned two languages. I've never traveled to another country.*
UNIT 3 Topic sentences	• Read a model paragraph with a topic sentence and supporting details • Choose the best topic sentence • Write your own topic sentence	*My neighborhood is changing fast.*
UNIT 4 Supporting sentences	• Use a graphic organizer to understand supporting details • Identify irrelevant support • Write supporting sentences to finish a paragraph	*sore throat, cough, sneeze, took my temperature, drank some chamomile tea*
UNIT 5 Narrative writing	• Identify sequence in a story • Use the past tense and descriptive adjectives to write a narrative	*interesting, funny, unusual, surprising, unlucky*
UNIT 6 A questionnaire	• Write answers to questions using the simple past and present perfect • Write a mini-questionnaire	*How many times have you moved?* *When did you complete elementary school?*
UNIT 7 Describing a process	• Identify sequence words in a model paragraph • Write a paragraph to describe the process of making soup	*first, second, later, finally, after, next, then,*
UNIT 8 Cause and effects	• Connect effects to their causes • Write compound sentences	*and, so*
UNIT 9 Then and now	• Contrast the past and the present • Write compound sentences	*but, or*
UNIT 10 Pros and cons	• Identify pros and cons • Use a graphic organizer • Write an original paragraph	*losing your camera, trying new foods*
UNIT 11 A job description	• Identify descriptive adjectives in a job description • Write a paragraph about your dream job	*hard-working, reliable, experienced, energetic, interesting, exciting, challenging, creative*
UNIT 12 Giving reasons	• Identify reasons to celebrate • Write a paragraph about a holiday	*because, since, so, to* + verb

UNIT 1 FOOD FROM THE EARTH

TIME EXPRESSIONS

A Time expressions tell us when something happens.

"Right now," tells us that something is happening now.

"Every day," tells us that something happens daily.

"Last night," tells us that something happened late yesterday.

✓ Which verb tenses do you see in these sentences?

B Time expressions can come at the beginning of a sentence or at the end of a sentence. Some time expressions are adverbs (*usually*, *sometimes*, *always*, *never,* etc.), and come after the verb. Notice the placement of the time expressions in these sentences.

1. *Yesterday*, Robert made his family's favorite rice dish.
2. *Every Saturday*, Sofia cooks breakfast for her parents.
3. Sam and Eddie went to Argentina *last month.*
4. *At the moment*, they're shopping for bread and other staples.
5. Walter is playing basketball *as we speak.*
6. *Sometimes*, my brother eats popcorn for dinner.
7. My family moved to this city *last year.*
8. We *usually* eat lunch in the cafeteria.

✓ Read the sentences again, then write each time expression in the correct column.

Now Time expressions to use with the present continuous tense.	**Always** Time expressions to use with the simple present tense.	**Completed** Time expressions to use with the simple past tense.

C Complete the sentences so they are true for you.

1. Yesterday, _____ .
2. Right now, _____ .
3. I usually _____ .
4. _____ last week.
5. _____ every morning.
6. Sometimes, _____ .
7. _____ at the moment.
8. I never _____ .

✓ Check your sentences. Did you use the correct verb tense with each time expression?

Photocopiable © 2015 National Geographic Learning, Cengage Learning

UNIT 2 EXPRESS YOURSELF

A PERSONAL PROFILE

A Read the following paragraph.

My name is Catherine, and I'm 15 years old. I'm a young person, but I've already had a very interesting life. For example, I've learned two languages. My first language is French, and my second language is English. I've never traveled to another country, but I've been in many different cities in this country. I've read many books, and I've taken ballet classes. I've also learned how to change the battery in a car. I think I've done quite a lot for a 15-year-old!

✓ Read the paragraph again and list the things Catherine has and hasn't done.

Catherine has . . .	Catherine hasn't . . .
1.	1.
2.	
3.	
4.	
5.	

✓ Read the paragraph again and underline the present perfect verbs.

B List some things you have and haven't done in your life.

I have . . .	I haven't . . .
1.	1.
2.	
3.	
4.	
5.	

C Write a paragraph about yourself. Use Catherine's paragraph as a model.

My name is _____, and I'm _____ years old. I'm a young person, but I've already had a very interesting life. For example, _____

_____

_____

I've never _____,

but I've _____

_____

_____

I think I've done quite a lot for a _____-year-old!

UNIT 3 CITIES

TOPIC SENTENCES

A Read the following paragraph.

My neighborhood is changing fast. Last year, people had to walk very far to catch the bus. Now, the bus goes right down the main street. I only have to walk one block to catch it. With the new bus service, my neighborhood looks more attractive to new people. Many people are building new houses here. Next year, this neighborhood will be more crowded.

✓ Read the first sentence again. Often, the first sentence in a paragraph is the topic sentence. It gives the topic, or main idea of the paragraph.

✓ Read the other sentences again. What do they say about the topic of change in the writer's neighborhood?

B Read the following paragraph then choose the best topic sentence.

_____ . Residents of large cities need a place to relax and breathe fresh air. City parks have trees and birds, so residents can rest and connect with the natural world. In addition, city parks are a place for family recreation. Parents and their children can run or do other exercises in a park. They can also participate in organized sports such as soccer in some parks.

1. Parks are good places for city residents to get some exercise.

2. Parks are important places for people who live in cities.

3. Parks are a natural habitat for wild animals.

C Read the following paragraph then write a good topic sentence.

_____ . For example, rural areas are usually quiet, so people who live there can sleep well at night. Rural areas are also clean. They are much less polluted than big cities, so residents are healthy and live a long time. Another advantage of rural life is the opportunity to see plants and animals every day. And in rural areas, people don't have to go to the zoo or a park to see the natural world.

UNIT 4 THE BODY
SUPPORTING SENTENCES

A Read the following paragraph and underline the topic sentence. (Remember, the topic sentence gives the main idea of the paragraph.)

Last week, I caught a very bad cold. At first, I only had a sore throat. Then I started to cough and sneeze a lot. My mom took my temperature, and it was warmer than normal. I went to bed early, but I wasn't really tired, so I drank some chamomile tea to help me sleep. The next day, I felt a little better. And after four days, the cold was finally gone.

✓ List the details from the paragraph in the correct columns.

the symptoms	the mother's actions	the writer's actions	the length of the illness

✓ A good paragraph contains a topic sentence and details. The sentences with details are called supporting sentences because they support the idea in the topic sentence.

B Read the following paragraph then ~~cross out~~ the sentence that is NOT a good supporting sentence.

I do several things every day to stay healthy. For example, I always get some exercise. On some days I run or play tennis, and on other days I just go for a long walk. Another thing I do to stay healthy is to watch my diet. I avoid sweets, and I eat as many vegetables as possible. My dad is the best cook in the family. Finally, I get enough sleep at night. That way, I feel good in the morning and I have the energy to exercise.

✓ All of the supporting sentences should give details about the topic sentence.

C Write two more supporting sentences for this paragraph.

My brother Paul has an unhealthy lifestyle. He works too hard, and he never takes time to relax.

In addition, _____

_____ . He also _____ .

_____ .

I worry about my brother because of these unhealthy habits.

UNIT 5 CHALLENGES
NARRATIVES

A Number the supporting sentences in the correct sequence.

Topic sentence: I had a frightening experience last Sunday.

Supporting sentences:

_____ After I got on the bus, I heard some strange sounds.

_____ Fortunately, nobody was hurt, but we were all quite scared!

_____ Every time the bus slowed down, there was a loud squealing sound, and then a low "clunk" when the bus stopped.

_____ I wanted to go downtown, so I took the bus.

_____ After a few minutes, the bus driver tried to stop to pick up some passengers, but the bus kept going!

_____ It didn't stop until the driver went into an area with grass and some small trees.

✓ Compare your answers in pairs and read the paragraph aloud to each other.

✓ Which verb tense does the writer use to tell the story?

B Narratives are a type of writing for telling stories. They describe things that happened, often in the past.

✓ Think of something that happened to you. Choose one of these adjectives to use in your topic sentence:

> interesting funny unusual surprising unlucky

C Now write your own narrative.

I had a(n) _____ [adjective] experience _____ [when?].

_____

_____

_____

_____

_____

_____

_____

✓ When you're finished, check the verbs in your paragraph. Did you use the simple past tense to describe things that happened?

✓ Read your narrative paragraph aloud to a classmate or the whole class.

UNIT 6 TRANSITIONS

A QUESTIONNAIRE

A Read the following questionnaire. Do you understand all the questions?

Questionnaire

1. What's your name? _____

2. How old are you? _____

3. How long have you lived at your current address?

_____

4. How many times have you moved?

_____

5. When did you complete elementary school?

_____

6. When did you begin to learn English?

_____

7. The last time you traveled, where did you go?

_____

8. How many times have you traveled alone?

_____

9. In your opinion, what's the perfect age to get married?

_____

10. In your opinion, what's the perfect age to get a job?

_____

✔ Fill in the questionnaire using your own information. Write complete sentences.

B Write a short questionnaire with four questions. Use the simple past tense for at least one question and the present perfect tense for at least one question.

Mini-Questionnaire

1. _____

2. _____

3. _____

4. _____

UNIT 7 LUXURIES
DESCRIBING A PROCESS

A Writers must sometimes describe a process—how something is done. Sequence words are often used to show the order of the steps in a process.

Sequence Words

| first, second, etc. | later | finally | after | next | then | lastly | later |

B Read the following paragraph and underline the sequence words.

Some of the most expensive clothing in the world is made from cashmere, a very soft, warm fabric. But how is this luxury fabric made? It all starts with special goats. First, the long, soft hair is cut from the animals or removed with combs. Next, the hair is washed to remove any dirt or oils. After the hair is clean and dry, it is made into yarn or thread—very long, thin strings of cashmere that can be woven into fabric for coats or knitted into scarves and sweaters. Finally, the finished cashmere product is sold, usually for a very high price.

✓ Notice how the passive voice can be used to describe a process.

C Look at this recipe for cheese and potato soup. Then, write a paragraph describing the process. Remember to start with a topic sentence and use sequence words.

Step 1: Cook onions, carrots, and celery in a pot with a small amount of oil.

Step 2: Stir in four grams of flour.

Step 3: Add one liter of water or chicken stock to the pot.

Step 4: Put one-half kilo of chopped potatoes into the pot and cook for 20 minutes.

Step 5: Add some milk and one-quarter kilo of cheddar cheese to the pot and stir until the soup is smooth and creamy.

_____

_____

_____

_____

_____

_____

_____

_____

_____

_____

UNIT 8 NATURE
CAUSE AND EFFECT

A Match the effects to their causes. Add two more effects and their causes.

Effects
1. water freezes ____
2. gray hair ____
3. a sunburn ____
4. tiredness ____
5. extinction ____
6. _____
7. _____

Causes
a. too much time in the sun
b. getting older
c. loss of habitat
d. temperatures below 0°
e. too little sleep
f. _____
g. _____

B Writers must sometimes explain causes and effects. Read the following sentences.

1. I had a lot of homework last night, so I started studying right after dinner.

2. I had to do some Algebra worksheets, and I had to read a chapter for History.

3. My brother was talking loudly on the phone, so I asked him to be quiet.

4. He got angry at me, and he took the phone into his bedroom.

5. I finished all of the homework, so I feel ready for my classes today.

✔ Underline the words *and* and *so* in the sentences above. What do those words do in the sentences? What kind of punctuation mark comes before those words?

C Compound sentences have two or more separate clauses. Each clause has a subject and a verb, and the clauses are connected with a word such as *and* or *so*.

Clause: The electricity went out.

Clause: We couldn't watch television.

Compound Sentence: The electricity went out, so we couldn't watch television.

✔ Make compound sentences using the clauses below and *and* or *so*.

1. (and) I like to make cookies. I like to eat them.

2. (so) She makes her own clothes. She doesn't spend a lot of money to look good.

_____

3. (so) Kevin has a terrible job. He's looking for a better one.

_____

4. (and) We'll visit my grandmother at her house. We'll celebrate her birthday.

_____

5. (so) Mrs. Carter is an excellent teacher. You'll enjoy her class.

_____

UNIT 9 LIFE IN THE PAST

THEN AND NOW

A Life in the past was often very different from life today. Label the following *past* or *present*. Add one more activity from the past and one from the present.

1. cooking all your food on an outdoor fire _____

2. using horses for farm work _____

3. texting your friends several times a day _____

4. using large machines for farm work _____

5. cooking on an electric stove _____

6. _____

7. _____

B Writers sometimes must write about the past and the present. Read the following sentences.

1. People used to write letters, but now everyone sends e-mail messages.

2. You can send them quickly, but they're not very personal.

3. People used to visit family members on holidays, or they would stay home when they couldn't afford to travel.

4. My family didn't used to be very big, but my cousins have a lot of children now.

5. As a child, I liked to play games with my friends, or sometimes I stayed in the house and read books.

✓ Underline the words *but* and *or* in the sentences above. What do those words do in the sentences? What kind of punctuation mark comes before those words?

C Remember, compound sentences have two or more separate clauses.

Clause: Native Americans smoked tobacco in pipes.

Clause: Modern smokers smoke packaged cigarettes.

Compound Sentence: Native Americans smoked tobacco in pipes, but modern smokers smoke packaged cigarettes.

✓ Make compound sentences using the clauses below and *but* or *or.*

1. (but) I used to play volleyball. Now I prefer baseball.

_____

2. (or) My grandmother walked to work. She took the bus in bad weather.

_____

3. (but) It's very hard work. You'll be happy when you finish it.

_____

4. (or) I've always done my homework on time. I've gotten permission from the teacher to hand it in late. _____

5. (but) She likes to talk on the phone. She doesn't like to pay the phone bill.

_____

UNIT 10 TRAVEL

PROS AND CONS

A There are good things and bad things about traveling. Write each phrase in the appropriate column.

| sleeping late | losing your camera | trying new foods |
| learning something new | getting vaccinated | paying for everything |

Pros	Cons

B Read the following paragraph then circle the (pros) and underline the _cons_.

Traveling lets you experience new places and meet new people, but it can be stressful. It can be expensive, too, but it's good to get away from work and school. My favorite to do when I travel is to try new foods. I really enjoy discovering a delicious dish that I've never eaten before. Of course, sometimes I eat too much when I travel, and I don't feel well. I'll try to remember that the next time I travel!

C Choose a topic you want to write about. List some pros and cons about the topic, then write a new paragraph with a topic sentence and supporting sentences.

My topic:	
Pros	**Cons**

_____

_____

_____

_____

_____

_____

_____

_____

_____

UNIT 11 CAREERS
A JOB DESCRIPTION

A Imagine that your company needs a new employee. Check the qualities the new employee should have. Use your dictionary to look up new vocabulary.

_____ hard-working	_____ reliable
_____ experienced	_____ energetic
_____ lazy	_____ imaginative
_____ friendly	_____ unmotivated

✓ Writers can make their writing more interesting by using descriptive adjectives.

B Read the following job description and underline the descriptive adjectives.

Job Description

Opportunity in a new and exciting furniture company! Work in a clean, well-lit building. We are looking for employees who are energetic and reliable. Hours are early morning to mid-afternoon, so late sleepers shouldn't apply for the job. If you would like to create beautiful hand-made furniture in a friendly workplace, we are looking for you!

✓ Which adjectives did you find? Does the description make you want to apply for the job?

C Write a paragraph about your dream job. Use some of the descriptive adjectives from the box as well as other adjectives.

> interesting   exciting   beautiful   challenging
> enormous   creative   secure   motivating   friendly

When I have my dream job, I will work in _____

_____

_____

_____

_____

_____

_____

_____

_____

_____

UNIT 12 CELEBRATIONS
GIVING REASONS

A Why do people celebrate? Match the celebrations to the reasons.

1. a birthday _____
2. New Year's Day _____
3. an anniversary _____
4. Independence Day _____
5. Mother's Day _____

a. to begin the new year in a good way.
b. to honor the women who raise children
c. to remember a country's independence
d. to recognize the day someone was born
e. to honor a couple's marriage

B Writers often need to give reasons in their writing. Some common ways to do this are using:

- the word *because*
  *I ran to school **because** I got up late.*
- the word *since*
  *I'll call her tomorrow **since** it's her birthday.*
- the connecting word *so*
  *It's a special day, **so** everyone eats cake.*
- the infinitive (*to* + verb)
  *We pour drinks **to honor** family members who have died.*

C Read the following paragraph and underline the ways the writer gives reasons.

Chuseok is a meaningful holiday for me because it's a time for Korean people to honor their families. At Chuseok time, women make rice cakes shaped like the moon since the date of Chuseok depends on the lunar calendar. Some families take food to the cemetery to honor their ancestors. Most importantly, Korean people want to be with their family at Chuseok time, so it's a very popular time to travel.

D Write your own paragraph about a holiday that is important to you.

_____

_____

_____

_____

_____

_____

_____

_____

_____

	Goals	Language Focus
UNIT 1 Food from the Earth	• Identify common and holiday dishes • Prepare a menu • Describe food	local common dishes, staple foods, holiday dishes, *You should try ____ because ____*
UNIT 2 Express Yourself	• Interview a partner • Ask and answer questions about past activities • Re-tell a partner's information	*Have you ever . . . ?* *I've never . . .* *I've ____ once (many times)*
UNIT 3 Cities	• Ranking urban characteristics • Communicating urban preferences • Giving reasons for selections	*I think ____ should be number 1 because ____* *We decided ____ should be third because ____*
UNIT 4 The Body	• Discuss healthy and unhealthy habits and routines • Give personal opinions about health habits • Support personal opinions	*I agree because . . .* *I disagree . . .* *It depends because . . .*
UNIT 5 Challenges	• Talk about challenges • Describe personal capacity to meet or not meet a specific challenge	*enough, not enough, too ____*
UNIT 6 Transitions	• Respond to a lifetime experience survey • Share your personal information with a partner	*The biggest transition in my life was when . . .* *I have never . . . , but have always wanted to . . . .*
UNIT 7 Luxuries	• Work with a group to brainstorm the marketing campaign for a luxury product • Present and promote a new luxury product to the class	*. . . is made from . . .* *. . . is produced by . . .* *. . . will change your life because . . .*
UNIT 8 Nature	• Select a statement that describes a future plan • State positive and negative consequences to the plan • Support the plan	*If . . . , there will be . . .* *If . . . , you will have to . . .* *Yes, but then . . .*
UNIT 9 Life in the Past	• Describe a common place object without "giving it away" • Guess which object a partner is describing	Past passive voice
UNIT 10 Travel	• Plan an adventure vacation trip • Decide on the necessary items to pack and give reasons for choices	*I need ____ because . . .* *It will be good to have ____ for ____*
UNIT 11 Careers	• Select a volunteer job • Tell classmates about a choice and give reasons	*I am perfect for this job because . . .* *This is the best job for me because . . .*
UNIT 12 Celebrations	• Interview classmates about a special holiday • Report the information collected to the class	*What do you celebrate at , , ,* *Where . . .* *Why do you enjoy it?*

UNIT 1 FOOD FROM THE EARTH

You are the owners of a restaurant in your city. You want to bring foreign visitors to your restaurant, so you are planning a special dinner to introduce them to the food of your country. Follow these steps with your group.

A Make a list of the most common dishes and staple foods in your country. _____

_____

B Are there any special holiday dishes that foreigners might like?_____

_____

C Are there any dishes that foreigners sometimes don't like? Do you think they should try these dishes?_____

_____

D Now choose the menu for your dinner. It should include four dishes and one drink. Write a short description for each one.

Dish #1: _____

Description: _____

_____

Dish #2: _____

Description: _____

_____

Dish #3: _____

Description: _____

_____

Dish #4: _____

Description: _____

_____

Drink: _____

Description: _____

_____

E Tell the class about your dinner!

UNIT 2 EXPRESS YOURSELF

A Talk to your classmates and find out who has done these things. Write in the column the name of the person who has done each thing and get more information from them. When you are finished, sit down in your seat.

	Name	Information
live in another city		
win a prize		
eat an unusual food		
meet a famous person		
read a very long book		
get an unusual present		
read an English magazine		
take a difficult test		

B Tell your group what you found out about your classmates!

Communication Activity T-213

UNIT 3 CITIES

A What are the most important things for a good city? Add your own idea. Then write numbers 1–8 to rank the things, from most important (1) to least important (8).

	Rank
a. A clean environment—no air or water pollution	
b. Interesting nightlife and lots of entertainment	
c. Many beautiful buildings in all parts of the city	
d. Good public transportation everywhere in the city	
e. Plenty of parks and green spaces for people to enjoy	
f. Good jobs and a healthy economy	
g. A beautiful setting like the ocean or mountains	
h. Your own idea:	

B Get together with a partner. Talk about your answers and the ideas you added. Then work together to come to an agreement on the ranking. Make notes about your reasons.

	Rank
a. A clean environment—no air or water pollution Reasons:	
b. Interesting nightlife and lots of entertainment Reasons:	
c. Many beautiful buildings in all parts of the city Reasons:	
d. Good public transportation everywhere in the city Reasons:	
e. Plenty of parks and green spaces for people to enjoy Reasons:	
f. Good jobs and a healthy economy Reasons:	
g. A beautiful setting like the ocean or mountains Reasons:	
h. Your own idea: Reasons:	

C Tell another student pair about your top three items and explain your reasons.

UNIT 4 THE BODY

A What's your opinion about these statements? Mark your answers.

	I agree.	It depends.	I disagree.
1. Modern food is healthier than the traditional food in our country.			
2. Most people worry too much about their health.			
3. Getting enough sleep is as important for health as eating good food.			
4. Medicine that you get from a doctor works better than home remedies.			
5. Most people in this country don't get enough exercise.			
6. All children should have physical education classes in school.			
7. People's lifestyles were healthier in the past than they are now.			
8. A little bit of stress isn't bad for your health.			
9. Walking is the best kind of exercise for everyone.			
10. Eating junk food is as bad for your health as smoking.			

B Get together with another group and compare your answers. Give reasons for your opinions.

UNIT 5 CHALLENGES

A 🔁 Read the descriptions of these challenges. Can you do them? Talk to a partner. Use sentences with *enough*, *not enough*, and *too*.

RAISE MONEY TO FEED HUNGRY PEOPLE!

Join the Great Hike Across Australia. Walk for a day, or walk for a month—people will donate money for every mile you walk.

- You must be 18 years old.
- You must be fit and able to walk 20 miles in a day.
- We will provide meals, accommodations, and a walk leader who will help you with any problems. You need to buy your plane ticket to Australia.

VISIT OUR WEB SITE FOR MORE DETAILS!

Would you like to live on a tropical island and help our scientific research?

We need volunteers ages 16 to 40 to count fish and take underwater photographs near an island in Central America. We will teach you to go scuba diving and use an underwater camera. Fee for participating: $2000. For more information, please call . . .

Cross the Atlantic Ocean with us!

We are looking for eight people to sail from Florida to Spain on our boat next year. You don't need experience—we can teach you everything you need to know. We are looking for people who are friendly, relaxed, and calm. You pay only for your food (about $300) and we pay for everything else. Email us at . . .

TEACH ENGLISH TO CHILDREN IN AFRICA

Our program is looking for volunteers to help in kindergartens in several countries in Africa. It's OK if English isn't your first language. We need people who can tell stories, sing, and play games with the children—in English. You must (1) enjoy children, (2) have good health, (3) come for a training program for one week. We will give you a plane ticket to Africa and pay your living expenses. If you are interested, call . . .

B 🔁 With a partner, choose one of the challenges in activity **A** that you would like to do together.

C Explain your decision to the class.

UNIT 6 TRANSITIONS

A Complete the survey with true information about yourself.

Life Experience Survey

1. The biggest transition in my life so far has been when I _____.

That was in _____. (year)

2. I have never _____, but I have always wanted to.

3. The happiest day in my life was when I _____. I was happy because I _____.

4. I have _____ many times. The last time I _____ was _____. (when?)

5. My biggest mistake was the time I _____.

I haven't _____ since then!

6. I have _____ for a long time.

7. I have never tried _____ because _____.

8. I haven't _____ in many years.

B 🤝 Tell your group about your answers, and listen to their experiences. Be sure to ask follow-up questions to get more information.

C 🔁 Work with a partner from a different group. Tell your partner some of the interesting things you learned about your classmates.

Communication Activity T-217

UNIT 7 LUXURIES

⚙ You are the New Products Department of a company called Luxury Exports. Your boss has asked you to choose an ordinary product from your country and plan a way to sell it in other countries as a luxury product. Follow these steps with your group.

A Answer the questions.

1. What is your product? _____

_____

2. Think of a brand name for your product. _____

_____

3. Who will you try to sell your product to? _____

_____

_____

_____

4. Think of ways to describe your luxury product in advertising.
   - It's made from _____
   - It's produced in _____
   - Its special features are _____
   - It's unusual because _____
   - Everyone wants it because _____
   - It will change your life because _____
   - _____
   - _____

B **⚙** Work together to write a paragraph about your product for an ad. Use some of the ideas from activity **A** to convince people in other countries to buy your product.

_____
_____
_____
_____

C **⚙** Present your product to the class.

UNIT 8 NATURE

A 🔁 Work with a partner. Take turns choosing a sentence. When your partner says a sentence, use if to talk about what will happen. Try to continue the conversation. Cross out the sentence after you talk about it.

Example   A: I've decided to get a dog.
              B: If you get a dog, you'll have to walk it every day.
              A: That's true, but it's good exercise. And also . . .

> I heard we're going to have a test on Monday.

> I love animals, so I've decided to stop eating meat.

> I heard the government is going to put more wolves in the forest.

> I'm thinking about studying overseas next year.

> I heard the government is going to ban all hunting.

> I heard our class time is going to change to 6 a.m.

> The weather report says it's going to rain every day this week.

> I've decided to cut my hair really short.

> I saw on TV that the zoo might get two baby elephants.

> I think I'm going to get a cat.

B 🔁 Present one of your conversations to the class.

UNIT 9 LIFE IN THE PAST

You are archaeologists in the year 2300 A.D. You are looking at these artifacts from the past that were found in an archaeological dig. You don't know the names of the things, but you have some ideas about them.

A 🗘 Choose one of these artifacts. Write sentences about it in the past passive tense.

a.   b.   c.   d.

e.   f.   g.   h.

Artifact: _____

1. It was made _____ .

2. It was _____ .

3. _____

4. _____

5. _____

6. _____

B 👥 Work with a partner and get together with two other student pairs. Read your sentences from activity **A** to the group. Can the other students guess which artifact you wrote about?

UNIT 10 TRAVEL

You are going on an adventure vacation! You will spend two weeks together on your own tropical island, with no other people. There is a kitchen with plenty of food and a comfortable place for you to sleep. Because the boat to the island is very small, you can only bring 10 things with you besides your clothes.

A Work together with a partner to choose the items you will take from this list and write down your reasons.

swimsuit	inflatable boat	a volleyball	MP3 player
deck of cards	a DVD player and DVDs	aspirin	your favorite book
book about tropical plants and animals		sunscreen	insect repellant
magazines	tablet	smart phone	radio
sun hat	flashlight	soap and toothpaste	camera
sunglasses	dictionary	notebook	pictures of your family

Your own ideas: _____ _____ _____

	Item	**Reasons**
1.	_____	_____
2.	_____	_____
3.	_____	_____
4.	_____	_____
5.	_____	_____
6.	_____	_____
7.	_____	_____
8.	_____	_____
9.	_____	_____
10.	_____	_____

B Share your list with another student pair. How many items were the same?

UNIT 11 CAREERS

A ⚙ Read these ads and discuss which volunteer position is the best for each person in your group. Talk about qualifications, interests, and experience.

1. Volunteers needed!

Help children in the hospital. Read stories and do simple art projects with them. You must have experience with children under the age of 12 or be interested in health care. Contact . . .

2. Save the Earth! Clean up our river!

River Day is June 1, and we need people to help clean garbage out of the river. You should enjoy working outside and be able to lift heavy things. For information please call . . .

3. Homework Helper

Are you interested in teaching? We are looking for people who can help in our after-school program at Central Elementary School. Help students practice reading and do their homework. Call . . .

4. Park volunteers wanted

Do you enjoy gardening? Or would you like to learn about it? Neighborhood parks need volunteers to plant flowers and take care of the gardens. If you're interested, please call . . .

5. Help elderly people

Every week, we work in groups to paint people's houses and do small home repairs. If you don't have any experience, we can teach you! You must have free time on Saturday afternoons. Visit our Web site . . .

6. Collect money for AIDS research

You can do volunteer work at home! Help people with AIDS by writing letters to your friends and acquaintances and asking them to give money to the AIDS Foundation. We give you all the information. Call . . .

7. Walk to end world hunger!

Join our walk on July 7. We will walk 18 miles (30 kilometers), and for every mile you walk sponsors will give money to buy food for hungry people. You must be fit and over age 18. Please call . . .

B ⚙ Tell the class about the best volunteer job for you and explain your reasons.

UNIT 12 CELEBRATIONS

A ⚙ Choose an important holiday in your country. Each group should choose a different holiday.

Holiday: _____

B ⚙ In the chart, write two survey questions about how people celebrate this holiday.

	Name:	Name:
Question 1: What _____ _____?		
Question 2: What _____ _____?		

C ⚙ Talk to two classmates. Ask your questions and write their answers. Answer the questions they ask you.

D ⚙ Go back to your group and put together the answers from the students.

E ⚙ Tell the class about the information you got about holiday celebrations.

Unit 1: Food from the Earth

Lesson A

A Circle the correct verb form to complete the sentence.

1. My family (eats | is eating) pizza on Friday nights.

2. It's cold. I'm (wear | wearing) a warm coat.

3. The phone (rings | is ringing). Can you answer it?

4. I (have | am having) a lot of homework.

5. We (cook | are cooking) dinner at the moment.

B Complete the sentences with the correct form of the verb in parentheses.

1. Javi _____ (wake up) at 7 o'clock every morning.

2. He _____ (eat) breakfast at 7:30.

3. At 8 o'clock Javi _____ (go) to school.

4. Javi _____ (speak) English with his friends at school.

5. Now he _____ (speak) to his teacher Ms. Powell.

C Fill in the blanks with the correct form of the verb in parentheses.

There (1) _____ _are_ _____ (be) many students in the library now. Fernanda (2) _____ (use) a computer to do research for an assignment. Gabriela (3) _____ (study) for a test. Carlos (4) _____ (read) a book. Roberto and Andres (5) _____ (do) their homework. Daniela (6) _____ (ask) the librarian a question.

D Complete the sentences with the present continuous form of the verb in parentheses.

1. Tomas usually takes the bus to school but today he _____ (drive).

2. Sandra usually goes out with friends but tonight she _____ (stay) home.

3. We usually cook dinner but tonight we _____ (go) out to a restaurant.

4. Susana usually drinks coffee but this morning she _____ (drink) tea.

5. You usually wear blue shirts but today you _____ (wear) a red one!

E Complete each sentence with the correct form of a verb from the box.

> call   eat   relax
> study   send
> watch

1. Mario and his father _____ a soccer game on TV.

2. Brenda _____ lunch in the cafeteria.

3. Samantha _____ a text to a friend.

4. We _____ for a test.

5. You _____ in the garden.

6. Andres _____ his mother every weekend.

Lesson C

A Complete the chart with the simple past tense forms of the verbs.

be		give	
drink		go	
eat		meet	
fall		see	

B Complete each sentence with a simple past tense verb from the chart.

1. Last year Mia _____ to Peru and _____ Machu Picchu.

2. Yesterday Juan's cell phone _____ out of his pocket.

3. Last weekend Tania _____ green tea and she liked it.

4. The day before yesterday _____ my birthday.

5. Karina _____ her best friend three years ago.

6. Last week Jorge _____ flowers to his mother.

C Complete each sentence with the simple past tense form of the verb in parentheses.

1. Last summer Luis _____*grew*_____ (grow) tomatoes in the garden.

2. Yesterday I _____ (help) Karla with her homework.

3. Tony and Isaac _____ (give) a presentation in class. It _____ (be) interesting.

4. My grandmother _____ (learn) how to drive a car when she was 50!

5. We _____ (ask) the teacher for more time to finish the assignment.

6. You _____ (take) the last cold drink!

D Complete the paragraph with the simple past tense form of the verb in parentheses.

Last weekend Rosa (1) _____ (go) to a Japanese restaurant with her friend Yumi. She (2) _____ (try) new foods. She (3) _____ (eat) sushi and shashimi, and she (4) _____ (like) them. Yumi (5) _____ (show) Rosa how to use chopsticks, and Rosa (6) _____ (learn) how to do it. She (7) _____ (enjoy) the experience very much.

E Complete the paragraph with the simple past tense form of the verb in parentheses.

Yesterday I (1) _____ (arrive) to class 10 minutes late. I (2) _____ (be) late because I (3) _____ (help) a friend. She (4) _____ (lose) her phone on the way to class. She (5) _____ (say) the last time she (6) _____ (have) it was on the bus. But then I (7) _____ (call) her and we (8) _____ (hear) a ringing in her backpack. We both (9) _____ (laugh) and then I (10) _____ (run) to class.

Unit 2: Express Yourself

Lesson A

A Unscramble the words and write sentences.

1. lived / in Brazil / has / Martha _____ .

2. before / has / child / not /on / an airplane / been / The _____ .

3. three / has / to / times / Mexico City / been / Ximena _____ .

4. for / not / country / has / teacher / My / been / to / her / a long time _____ .

5. bought / They / train / have / tickets / the _____ .

B Complete the sentences. Use the present perfect form of the verb in parentheses.

1. Ivan _____ (study) English for two years.

2. We _____ (be) friends for a long time.

3. Mr. Ortiz _____ (not go) to California.

4. You _____ (not do) you homework.

5. I _____ (read) the book.

C Rewrite the sentences as negative.

1. Celeste has been to Montreal. _____ .

2. I have played soccer every day this week. _____ .

3. Jane has finished the assignment. _____ .

4. We have met new friends at school. _____ .

5. The students have spoken to the teacher about the homework. _____ .

D Answer the questions. Use the cues.

1. Have you ever eaten Peruvian food? No, _____ .

2. Have you ever tried writing with your left hand? Yes, _____ .

3. Has your family ever gone on vacation? Yes, _____ .

4. Have they ever seen the ocean? No, _____ .

5. Have you ever written an e-mail in English? Yes, _____ .

E Complete the conversations with the present perfect form of the verb in parentheses.

1. **A:** Have you seen this movie?   **B:** No, I _____, but I want to.

2. **A:** Have you memorized the vocabulary?   **B:** Yes, I _____. I'm ready for the test.

3. **A:** Have you called your family this week?   **B:** Yes, I _____.

Lesson C

A Rewrite the subject and verbs using a contraction.

1. We have had a lot of homework this week. _____

2. They have visited Florida three times. _____

3. She has washed and ironed all of the laundry. _____

4. I have studied English for two years. _____

5. You have done well in this class. _____

B Match the questions and answers.

1. Have you bought milk? _____   **a.** No, they haven't eaten yet.

2. Have the kids eaten yet? _____   **b.** No, she hasn't left yet.

3. Have you ever driven a car? _____   **c.** Yes, he's already washed the car.

4. Has Diana left for school yet? _____   **d.** Yes, I've already bought some.

5. Has he washed the car yet? _____   **e.** No, I've never driven a car.

C Complete the sentences with the correct form of the words in parentheses.

1. (learn, already) The students _____ the simple past tense.

2. (not wake up, yet) The baby _____ from her nap _____ .

3. (not say, yet) The teacher _____ we can leave the classroom _____ .

4. (not go, ever) They _____ to Guatemala.

5. (use, never) Mrs. Sanchez _____ the Internet. She's 80 years old.

D Complete the sentences with *already*, *yet*, *ever*, or *never*.

1. The teacher hasn't given the homework assignment _____ .

2. Have you _____ been to an art museum?

3. Luis is afraid to fly. He has _____ been in an airplane.

4. We're late! The concert has _____ started!

5. I haven't _____ been in a helicopter.

E Read the conversations. Fill in the blanks with *already*, *yet*, *ever*, or *never*.

1. **A:** Have you _____ been on TV?

   B: No, I've _____ been on TV.

2. **A:** Has Sarah walked the dog _____ ?

   B: Yes, she has _____ walked the dog.

3. **A:** Has the bus come _____ ?

   B: No, it hasn't come _____ .

Unit 3: Cities

Lesson A

A Rewrite the sentences as future statements. Use *will*.

1. The airport is crowded. _____ .

2. They play soccer in the afternoon. _____ .

3. I am a student. _____ .

4. We work in an office. _____ .

5. You have a lot of homework. _____ .

B Complete the sentences using *will* and the verb in parentheses.

1. The students _____ (take) a test on Friday.

2. I _____ (send) a text to her.

3. You _____ (call) me tonight.

4. My friends and I _____ (go) to the concert together.

5. She _____ (learn) the vocabulary.

C Complete the sentences about the future. Use the future with *will*.

1. In the future people _____ (no use) cash. All payments _____ (be) electronic.

2. There _____ (no be) as much pollution and waste in cities.

3. People _____ (no work) long days.

4. Students _____ (no pay) for school. Education _____ (be) free.

5. The teacher _____ (no write) on the board. She _____ (use) computer in class.

D Complete the questions and answers using *will*.

1. **A:** _____ you go on vacation this summer?   **B:** Yes, (we) _____ .

2. **A:** _____ you call me later?   **B:** Yes, _____

3. **A:** _____ he meet us at the game?   **B:** Yes, _____

E Complete the conversations with the future tense using *will*. Use contractions.

1. **A:** How will people read books in the future?

   B: They _____ on e-readers or computers.

2. **A:** Where will people buy books?

   B: They _____ buy them online

3. **A:** What will people write on?

   B: They _____ tablet computers to write.

Lesson C

A Read the sentence and answer the question.

1. Carlos will wash the dishes before he goes to work.
   What will he do first? **a.** go to work **b.** wash the dishes

2. The teacher will prepare the lesson before he teaches the class.
   What will he do first? **a.** prepare the lesson **b.** teach the class

3. Marie will call her friends after she does her homework.
   What will she do first? **a.** call her friends **b.** do her homework

4. Joao wants to work in New York City after he finishes college.
   What will he do first? **a.** work in NYC **b.** finish college

B Match the sentence starter with the correct time clause.

1. Before I make a hotel reservation, ____d____   **a.** I'll do my homework.

2. I'll have a cup of coffee _____   **b.** I'll give you some advice.

3. After I have a nap, _____   **c.** before I take the test

4. I'll study hard _____   **d.** I need to buy plane tickets.

5. Before you make up your mind, _____   **e.** after I eat lunch.

C Read the sentence and add a comma, if necessary.

1. After I spend a year in Toronto I'll speak better English.

2. I'll visit my family after I take my final exams.

3. Before I choose a college I'll talk with my parents.

4. Before I get a job I'll travel for a few months.

5. I'll go to bed after I finish reading this chapter.

D Use the prompts below to make sentences with time clauses.

1. practice driving / take the driving test

   After _____ .

2. save money / rent an apartment

   Before _____ .

3. get extra help from the teacher / take another test

   I'll _____ .

4. buy a calling card / call a friend overseas

   I'll _____ .

Unit 4: The Body

Lesson A

A Complete the sentences with the comparative form of the adjective in parentheses.

1. Mexico is _____ than Guatemala. (big)

2. My cousin Perla is _____ than me. (younger)

3. The heart is _____ than the brain. (small)

4. Ms. Garcia's class is _____ than Mr. Rivera's class. (difficult)

5. Today the wind feels _____ than yesterday. (cold)

B Unscramble the sentences.

1. is / expensive / than / espresso / more / coffee _____.

2. than / has / espresso / tea / caffeine / less _____.

3. noisier / the / the / library / is / cafeteria / the _____.

4. plays / better / Miguel / soccer / me / than _____.

5. kilometer / mile / longer / a / than / a / is _____.

C Complete the sentences with the superlative form of the adjective in parentheses.

1. Swimming is the (good) _____ exercise.

2. Soccer is the (exciting) _____ sport to play.

3. Where is the (near) _____ hospital?

4. Javier is the (funny) _____ person in our class.

5. Yesterday was the (hot) _____ day of the summer.

D Rewrite the comparative sentences as equative sentences.

1. Tania speaks English better than Monica. _____.

2. My backpack is heavier than yours. _____.

3. Andre's brother is taller than his father. _____.

4. Running is more difficult than cycling. _____.

5. The lake is deeper than the river. _____.

E Circle the correct words to complete the sentences and questions.

1. Who is the (older | oldest) person in your family?

2. Carlos' sisters are (younger | youngest) than him.

3. Who is (older | oldest) your grandmother or grandfather?

4. Marta studies (most | the most) in this class.

5. David is the (smarter | smartest) person in his family.

Lesson C

A Complete the sentences with the infinitive form of a verb from the box.

> earn   improve   learn   listen   make

1. Ferdinanda put on her headphones _____ to music.

2. Erick studies every day _____ his grades in school.

3. Mrs. Sanchez boils water _____ tea.

4. Alma Rosa reads books in English _____ new vocabulary.

5. Julio works at the pizza restaurant _____ money for school.

B Write a sentence using the prompts *in order to*.

1. Rodrigo / read the chapter / prepare for the test _____

2. Magda / took the bus / get to school _____.

3. Mr. Esteves / learned English / work in the US _____.

4. Jaime / got a job / save money _____.

5. They / got up early / be on time _____.

C Match the phrases to form a sentence.

1. To wake up on time, _____   a. she drinks a lot of water.

2. To stay in shape, _____   b. some students walk to school.

3. To avoid headaches, _____   c. Sam uses email.

4. To keep in touch with friends, _____   d. I set my alarm clock.

5. To save money, _____   e. Ana exercises and does yoga.

D Rewrite the sentences. Begin each one with an infinitive of purpose.

1. Lena gets up at 7 o'clock in order to be at school on time.

   _____.

2. She takes a shower and drinks two cups of coffee to wake up.

   _____.

3. Lena walks to school in order to avoid the crowded bus.

   _____.

4. At school goes to the library to borrow a book.

   _____.

5. She talks to her friends to make plans for lunch.

   _____.

Unit 5: Challenges

Lesson A

A Write the correct past continuous form of the verb in parentheses.

1. Last summer Miguel (learn) _____ English in California.

2. The team didn't play soccer yesterday because it (rain) _____ .

3. The wind (blow) _____ very hard yesterday, too.

4. In class today Mr. Torres (talk) _____ about challenges.

5. At 3 o'clock this afternoon Ivan (wait) _____ for the bus.

B Circle the correct verb form to complete the sentence.

1. The presentation you (gave | were giving) in class was very interesting.

2. Everyone listened very carefully when you (spoke | were speaking).

3. What (were you cooking | did you cook) for dinner?

4. At midnight we (slept | were sleeping).

5. Yesterday at this time Luis (took | was taking) a test.

C Write the correct past continuous form of the verb in parentheses.

1. The students (take) _____ a test when the fire alarm went off.

2. Carmen didn't hear the phone ring because she (dry) _____ her hair.

3. Mexico (win) _____ at half-time.

4. Linda's mother (travel) _____ on a business trip last week so she hasn't seen Linda.

5. Diego (sit) _____ with his friends in the park this morning.

D Match the phrases to form a sentence.

1. Their mother came home _____

2. Juan hurt his ankle _____

3. I was reading your e-mail _____

4. It was snowing _____

5. They were driving home _____

a. when I was in Montreal.

b. while they were cleaning the house.

c. when they saw two police cars.

d. when I got your text. What's up?

e. while he was playing baseball.

E Circle *when* or *while* to complete the sentences.

1. Selina was tried not to yawn (when | (while)) her boss was making a presentation.

2. (When | While) Jorge was waiting in the airport, he read a newspaper.

3. My family was living in Monterey (when | while) my youngest brother was born.

4. (When | While) Tracy moved to Mexico, she didn't speak Spanish.

Lesson C

A Read the information in the box. Then answer the questions. Use *enough*, *not enough*, or *too*.

At this age	A person can do this
5	go to kindergarten
14	get a job
16	get a driver's license
18	vote
65	receive a pension

1. Wanda is 15. Is she old enough to get a driver's license? _____ .

2. What is a 20-year-old old enough to do? _____ .

3. Maria is 14. Can she get a job this summer? _____ .

4. Does your four-year-old nephew go to kindergarten? _____ .

5. Tomas is 17. When will he be old enough to vote? _____ .

B Complete the sentences with the the word in parentheses and *enough*, *not enough*, or *too*.

1. **A:** How did you do in the road race?   **B:** Not very well. I was (fast) _____ .

2. **A:** Do you like the soup?   **B:** No, it's (salty) _____ .

3. **A:** Are you (warm) _____ ?   **B:** Yes, I am.

4. **A:** I want to buy this jacket.   **B:** Do you have (money) _____ ?

5. **A:** Do you want to go to the movies?   **B:** I can't. I have _____ much homework.

C Complete the sentences with *enough*, *not enough*, or *too*.

1. This assignment is _____ difficult. I don't understand it.

2. Carla is _____ to drive. Her fifteenth birthday was last month.

3. When Sam has _____ money he's going to buy a new bike.

4. We can't play tennis. It's _____ hot outside today.

5. There is not _____ snow to go skiing.

Unit 6: Transitions

Lesson A

A Complete each sentence with the *present perfect* form the verb in parentheses.

1. This movie is good. I (see) _____ it before.

2. Arturo (go) _____ to Texas twice.

3. Mr. Hernandez (work) _____ at the company for 23 years.

4. Lee (read) _____ all of the books in the library.

5. Denise (learn) _____ all of the vocabulary for the test tomorrow.

B Complete each sentence with the correct form of the verb in parentheses (*past tense* or *present perfect*).

1. I don't like this song. I (hear) _____ it too many times!

2. Sergio and Alexis (go) _____ to the game last night.

3. Mr. Williams (no buy) _____ a new car for a long time.

4. Valeria (no do) _____ her homework again!

5. Charlie (be) _____ seven years old when he moved here.

C Answer the questions.

1. **A:** Has Mrs. Lopez ever lived in the US?

   B: Yes, _____ .

2. **A:** Have you ever tried sushi?

   B: No, _____ .

3. **A:** Has Jennifer called you yet?

   B: No, _____ .

4. **A:** Have they already gone to the beach?

   B: Yes, _____ .

D Answer the questions using the present perfect and *for* or *since*.

1. **A:** How long have you been studying English?

   B: (2 years, for) _____

2. **A:** Have you known Elena for a long time?

   B: (5 years, for) _____

3. **A:** Has this mall been here for a long time?

   B: (2010, since) _____

4. **A:** How long have you been working at the bookstore?

   B: (last year, since) _____

Lesson C

A Read the sentence. Ask a question with *How* to get more information.

1. Eduardo is a fast swimmer. _____

2. The restaurant was very expensive. _____

3. Adriana reads fast. _____

4. Alex plays soccer very well. _____

B Unscramble the questions.

1. Spanish / does / how / speak / well / Jane _____

2. is / how / grandfather / your / old _____

3. the / mature / students / how / are _____

4. this / how / city / safe / is _____

C Match the statements and questions.

1. My mother retired from her job. _____   **a.** How hard it is?

2. Luis plays soccer often. _____   **b.** How old is she?

3. Arabic is a difficult language to learn. _____ **c.** How well did she do?

4. Karen did well on the test. _____   **d.** How young is he?

5. The tennis player is very young. _____   **e.** How often does he play soccer?

D Read the sentence. Ask a question with *How* to get more information.

1. Elizabeth lived in Los Angeles for a long time. _____

2. My parents are very strict. _____

3. My son is very responsible. _____

4. The actor and actress are very rich. _____

5. Oh no, we're late! _____

E Complete the conversations by asking *How* questions.

1. **A:** I finished writing the essay last night.

   B: Really? I haven't finished yet. I write slowly in English.

   A: _____

2. **A:** Don't ride in Ken's car.

   B: Why?

   A: He drives too fast.

   B: _____

Unit 7: Luxuries

Lesson A

A Unscramble the sentences.

1. are / Precious / underground / metals / found _____ .

2. as / given / are / Precious / stones / gifts _____ .

3. with / metals / precious / Jewelry / such / is / gold as / made _____ .

4. celebrities / by / is / clothing / worn / Luxury _____ .

5. safe / in / Valuable / kept / items / are / a _____ .

B Write the correct passive voice form of the verb in parentheses.

1. The pearl necklace (show) _____ in the store window.

2. Expensive watches (make) _____ in Switzerland.

3. India is where many fine silk clothes (sew) _____ .

4. Luxury clothing (design) _____ by famous designers.

5. Emeralds (import) _____ from Colombia.

C Rewrite the active voice sentences as passive voice sentences.

1. The children wear cotton clothes. _____ .

2. Expensive boutiques sell luxury clothes. _____ .

3. Stores make big profits on luxury items. _____ .

4. The washing machine damaged my silk blouse. _____ .

5. Sheena lost a handmade ring. _____ .

D Use the prompts to write sentences in the passive voice.

1. money / give / gift / at weddings _____ .

2. pearls / produce / oysters _____ .

3. oranges / grow / Florida _____ .

4. silver / find / Mexico _____ .

5. diamonds / import / South Africa _____ .

E Circle the correct words to complete the sentences.

1. Machinery (uses | is used) to separate precious stones from rocks.

2. The restaurant (uses | is used) food from local farms.

3. My mother (makes | is made)) the best tortillas.

4. The best tortillas (make | are made) by my mother.

5. The dressmaker (sewed | are sewn) pearls onto the bride's gown.

Lesson C

A Complete each sentence with the passive voice form of a verb from the box.

> made   need   use   visit   watch

1. Every day the website _____ by thousands of people.

2. Millions of online purchases _____ every day.

3. Credit cards _____ in stores, restaurants, and hotels all over the world.

4. The TV show _____ by millions of people every week.

5. Your user name and password _____ every time you log in.

B Match the two phrases to make a sentence.

1. The principal is known _____   a. by the bakery.

2. The food is served _____   b. by the students.

3. Cakes are made _____   c. by the students.

4. The vocabulary is memorized _____   d. by bees.

5. Honey is made _____   e. by the waiter.

C Read the sentences and cross out the unimportant *by* phrases.

1. The field is used by the soccer team.

2. Corn is grown in Mexico by farmers.

3. English is spoken by people all over the world.

4. Rules are sometimes broken by people.

5. The clothes are ironed by my sister.

D Answer the questions in the passive voice in complete sentences.

1. Are many people's lives improved by education?

   Yes, _____ .

2. Is the illness caused by unclean water?

   No, _____ . It is caused by a virus.

3. Are people's lives improved by television?

   No, _____ .

4. Are people's job opportunities improved by education?

   Yes, _____ .

Unit 8: Nature

Lesson A

A Complete the real conditionals with verbs from the box. Put the verb in the correct form.

> continue   ignore   live   melt   understand

1. Polar bears are going to become extinct if people _____ the problem.
2. Their habitat will disappear if the ice _____ .
3. The ice will melt if the ocean temperature _____ to rise.
4. People will try to protect the polar bears if they _____ the problem.
5. It will be terrible if no more polar bears _____ in the wild.
6. Julio works at the pizza restaurant _____ money for school.

B Complete the sentence with the correct verb form to make real conditionals.

1. (not stop / lose) If the ice _____ melting, the polar bears _____ their habitat.
2. (lose / die) If the polar bears _____ their habitat, they _____ .
3. (become/ be) If they _____ extinct, it _____ a terrible tragedy.
4. (is / hunt) If an animal _____ a predator, it _____ for prey.
5. (find / kill) If a predator _____ prey, it _____ the prey.

C Match the condition and the result to form real conditionals.

1. If people don't protect some species, _____   **a.** they will learn to care about the environment.

2. If scientists learn more about climate change, _____   **b.** some resources will be saved.

3. If children watch nature shows, _____   **c.** they will become extinct.

4. If people use energy carefully, _____   **d.** there will not be enough food.

5. If the population continues to grow quickly, _____   **e.** maybe it can be slowed down.

D Complete the sentence with the correct form of the verb in parentheses.

1. We (play) _____ baseball if the rain (stop) _____ .
2. If the team (win) _____ this game, they (play) _____ in the final.
3. If we (be) _____ quiet, we (not scare) _____ the deer.
4. We (go) _____ to the zoo if it (be) _____ open today.
5. I (call) _____ you if I (find) my cell phone!

Lesson C

A Circle the correct quantifier in each sentence below.

1. Martina watches (a lot of | too much) nature programs.

2. Yoko watches (a few | too much) TV.

3. (Too many | A little) species are endangered.

4. Sandra wants (a few | a little) milk in her coffee.

5. They have (too few | some) problems with pronunciation.

B Match the sentences.

1. There was a lot of food at the party. _____
2. There were a few people I knew. _____
3. There are too many cars on the road. _____
4. Angela wears a lot of perfume. _____
5. I bought too many potatoes. _____

a. There is always a lot of traffic.

b. I ate too much!

c. Do you want some?

d. And there were a lot of people I didn't know.

e. Yes, she uses too much.

C Circle the correct quantifier to complete the sentence.

1. The French class was canceled because _____ students signed up for it.

   a. some   b. a few   c. too few

2. An extra English class was added because _____ students want to learn English.

   a. a few   b. a lot of   c. too much

3. Alain is tired today because he slept _____ last night.

   a. a few   b. too little   c. some

4. He slept for only _____ hours.

   a. a few   b. too many   c. too little

5. The students think the teacher gives _____ homework.

   a. too many   b. too little   c. too much

D Cross out the quantifier that does not fit in the sentence.

1. There are (too few | too much | a lot of) tomatoes in my salad.

2. (A lot of | Too many | A few) students want to study in another country.

3. My friend Yolanda tells (a few | a lot of | too much) good stories.

4. The plane tickets cost (many | a lot of | too much) money.

5. Liv has (a little | some | too little) money in her pocket.

Unit 9: Life in the Past

Lesson A

A Complete the sentences with *used to* plus the verb in parentheses.

1. James _____ (drink) a lot of coffee every morning. Now he has only one cup.

2. We _____ (drive) to school, but now we take the bus.

3. Our class is in the evening. But it _____ (be) in the afternoon.

4. The baseball team _____ (win) a lot of games.

5. The baby _____ (wake up) in the middle of the night.

B Match the sentences.

1. Laura used to wake up on time in the morning. _____
2. They used to eat large meals. _____
3. Carl used to watch movies on TV. _____
4. There used to be fewer planes in the sky. _____
5. Cars used to use a lot of gasoline. _____

a. Now they are more fuel efficient.
b. But now they eat less to lose weight.
c. Nowadays I see many planes.
d. Now she needs an alarm clock.
e. He watches movies on his laptop now.

C Answer the questions with a negative response.

1. Did she used to work at the bank? _____ .

2. Did those actors used to be married? _____ .

3. Did your brother used to drive a red car? _____ .

4. Did he used to wear glasses? _____ .

D Read the prompts. Write a question with *used to* and the information in the sentence.

1. he / live / Miami _____

2. Mr. Lin / teach / science _____

3. you / play / tennis _____

4. she / work / at night _____

E Complete the paragraph with *used to* plus the verb in parentheses.

People (1) _____ (take) photos with cameras that used film. Now most people take photos their phones or a digital camera. But not so long ago it (2) _____ (be) necessary to buy film and load it into the camera. Film was expensive, and also had to be developed. This meant people (3) _____ (bring) a used roll of film to store that did developing, and they (4) _____ (wait)—sometimes hours, sometimes days—for their pictures. Photos (5) _____ (not be) instant!

Lesson C

A Read each sentence. Write *AV* if the sentence is *active voice* or *PV* if the sentence is *passive voice*.

1. The award was given to the student (by the principal). _____

2. The test was graded by the teacher. _____

3. The movie was about a family in Buenos Aires. _____

4. The museum was visited by millions of people last year. _____

5. Millions of tourists visited Venice last year. _____

B Complete each sentence with the past passive form of the verb in parentheses.

1. The book (write) _____ by an explorer.

2. It was very popular and (read) _____ by millions of people.

3. The story explains how parts of Antarctica (explore) _____ .

4. The facts (explain) _____ in a way that was easy to understand.

5. Many interesting things (learn) _____ by the readers.

C Rewrite the active voice past tense sentence in the passive voice past tense.

1. Genghis Khan ruled Mongolia.

_____ .

2. Genghis Khan destroyed many cities and kingdoms.

_____ .

3. For example, Khan's army destroyed the city of Samarkand.

_____ .

4. Many people respected Genghis Khan.

_____ .

5. His soldiers burned his tomb.

_____ .

D Complete each sentence with the past passive form of the verb in parentheses.

1. Long trips (take) _____ by explorers 700 years ago!

2. Marco Polo's stories about his travels (publish) _____ as a book.

3. Other people (inspire) _____ by his stories.

4. Countries from Morocca to China (visit) _____ by the traveler Ibn Battuta.

5. The journey from China east to the Middle East and Africa (make) _____ by Zheng He.

Unit 10: Travel

Lesson A

A Read the pool rules and the sentences below. Write *T* for *true* and *F* for *False*.

> **Pool Rules**
> Swimmers must shower before using the pool
> Swimmers must wear bathing caps
> No food or drink allowed in the pool are
> No running in the pool area
> Children under 12 must be accompanied by an adult

1. Swimmers don't have to cover their hair. _____
2. Swimmers can drink water and juice beside the pool. _____
3. Swimmers have to take a shower. _____
4. A teenager can use the pool without an adult _____
5. Children must run and jump into the pool. _____

B Circle the correct option for each sentence.

1. Passengers (must to | must) remove laptops from their carry-on bags.
2. Passengers (have to | don't have) show boarding passes and passports at airport security.
3. You (don't have to | have to) have a window seat if you prefer the aisle.
4. Tickets (must | have) be paid for in advance.
5. Rob (has to | must to) get a new passport.

C Read the direction. Then rewrite it as negative. Use the pronoun *you*.

1. Check in at the gate. _____.
2. Put your suitcase on the scale. _____.
3. Buy tickets in advance. _____.
4. Take off your shoes. _____.
5. Get a vaccination. _____.

D Use the prompts and the information in parentheses to write present tense sentences.

1. you / wait in line at security (formal) _____.
2. he / check his bag (not necessary) _____.
3. I / e-mail the hotel (informal) _____.
4. children under 10 / travel with an adult (formal) _____.
5. she / wait in that line (not necessary) _____.

Lesson C

A Read each sentence. Write *P* for *prohibited* or *A* for *allowed*.

1. You don't have to take off your shoes. _____

2. Passengers must not use electronic devices. _____

3. We can't use our cell phones at school. _____

4. You can't park here. _____

5. They don't have to pay for parking. _____

B Read the statements. Rewrite them using *must not* (formal) or *can't* (informal).

1. No talking during the movie. _____ .

2. Don't eat the ice cream. _____ .

3. Do not restart the computer. _____ .

4. Don't turn on the TV. _____ .

5. No photos. _____ .

C Read each situation. Write a sentence with *must not* or *can't* prohibiting the action.

1. use cell phones in class _____

2. park a car in a crosswalk _____

3. copy another student's work _____

4. make an omelet without eggs _____

5. go to college without finishing high school _____

D Circle the best answer for each sentence.

1. A person (must not | can't) drive a car without a driver's license.

2. A 17-year-old (must not | can't) vote.

3. Personal information (must not | can't) be given to people you do not know.

4. He (must not | can't) listen to the radio because I am reading.

5. This passport is expired. You (must not | can't) use it again.

Unit 11: Careers

Lesson A

A Match the modal with its use. Answers can be used more than once.

1. should _____
2. maybe, perhaps, I think + modal _____
3. had better not _____
4. had better _____
5. shouldn't _____
6. ought to _____

   a. to talk about something that is a good idea

   b. to say that something bad could happen if the advice isn't followed

   c. to make the advice sound gentler and friendlier

B Complete the sentences with *should*, *ought to*, or *had better* in the affirmative or negative.

1. You _____ read the directions before doing the assignment.
2. This is a good book. You _____ read it.
3. There's not hot water. You _____ take a shower.
4. I told her it was a secret. She _____ tell anyone!
5. It might rain today. You _____ take an umbrella.

C Choose the best modal to complete each sentence.

1. That's a good idea. We (should | had better) invite them to the party.
2. He (shouldn't | had better not) forget to charge his phone.
3. It's getting late. I (should | had better) wake the baby up from his nap.
4. If you're free tonight you (should | had better) come to our house for dinner.
5. People (shouldn't | had better not) use the clothes dryer in the summer.

D Match the sentences.

1. You said something that hurt your friend's feelings. _____
2. There are dirty dishes in the sink. _____
3. The roads are icy. _____
4. Your sister sent you a text. _____
5. You have been late for work twice this week. _____

   a. You should reply.

   b. You should wash the dishes.

   c. You had better not be late again.

   d. You ought to apologize.

   e. You had better not drive your car.

E Unscramble the sentences.

1. you / I / that / should / go to / college / think _____ .
2. money / shouldn't / perhaps / spend / we / a lot of _____ .
3. should / you / a part-time job / get / maybe _____ .
4. talk / you / I / teacher / it /ought to / to / your / think / about _____

Lesson C

A Read each sentence. Does the indefinite pronoun refer to a person or a thing? Circle a or b.

1. Nancy didn't understand <u>anything</u> the teacher said.

    a. person   **b.** thing

2. <u>Nobody</u> is going to wear a shirt like that!

    a. person   **b.** thing

3. <u>Everything</u> his family eats is organic.

    a. person   **b.** thing

4. <u>No one</u> laughed at the comedian's jokes.

    a. person   **b.** thing

5. <u>Everyone</u> in the class has an opinion on homework.

    a. person   **b.** thing

B Choose the correct indefinite pronoun to complete the sentence.

1. Lisa loves to bake cakes. She knows (anything | everything) about making them.

2. Ulli tried on some clothes at the store but she didn't buy (anything | everything).

3. Oscar doesn't like to work at night because there is (anybody | nobody) to talk to.

4. (Somebody | anybody) stole Yuan's cell phone!

5. They don't know (something | anything) about computers.

C Complete the sentence with the correct indefinite pronoun.

1. Marsha took _____ out of her suitcase and put it all in the closet.

2. Tran didn't do _____ fun this weekend.

3. _____ answered the phone at home. They must be out.

4. She has to make _____ to eat for lunch.

5. Have you told _____ else about it?

_____ .

D Complete the paragraph with words from the box.

> anyone   anything   everything   somebody   someone

A few years ago Gus didn't know (1) _____ about marine biology. Then (2) _____ brought him to an aquarium. He was fascinated! He thought (3) _____ about sea life was interesting. (4) _____ at his school suggested that he apply for a semester-as-sea program, and he was accepted. At first Gus didn't know (5) _____ on the boat. But soon he got to know (6) _____ and enjoyed (7) _____ about the experience at sea.

Unit 12: Celebrations

Lesson A

A Use the prompts to write affirmative sentences using the comparison *as … as*.

1. Veterans' Day / important / Memorial Day _____.

2. July 4 in the US / exciting / September 18 in Chile _____.

3. summer vacations / popular / winter vacations _____.

4. soccer / challenging / tennis _____.

5. July / hot / August _____.

B Rewrite each comparison as a negative.

1. My backpack is as heavy as your backpack. _____.

2. This assignment is as difficult as the last one. _____

3. Spain is as interesting as Italy. _____

4. Chocolate ice cream is as delicious as vanilla. _____

5. Tea is as strong as coffee. _____

C Answer the questions.

1. Is your mother as old as your father? _____

2. Is Tina's laptop as fast as Ravi's? No, _____.

3. Are your sunglasses as dark as mine? Yes, _____.

4. Is Boston as big as Houston? _____.

5. Are the Olympics as exciting as World Cup? _____.

D Use the prompts to write sentence with *as … as*.

1. my brother / not tall / me _____.

2. my writing / not good / your writing _____.

3. Lucia's pronunciation / clear / my teacher's pronunciation _____.

4. my job / not interesting / your job _____.

5. My uncle's car / expensive / my mother's car _____.

Lesson C

A Complete each sentence with *would rather* + the verb in parentheses.

1. My father _____ (get up) early than sleep late.

2. Some people _____ (drive) long distances than fly.

3. Jenny _____ (live) in a small town than a big city.

4. Roland _____ (see) the action movie than the documentary.

5. Sylvia _____ (go) to the beach than the mountains for a vacation.

B Answer each question with *would rather*. Use a contraction of *would*.

1. **A:** Are we going to your house tonight?

   B: No, Jackie _____ we go to her house.

2. **A:** Can we handwrite our essays?

   B: No, I _____ you use a computer and print them.

3. **A:** May I call you Mrs. Wong?

   B: No, I _____ you call me Sheryl. That's my first name.

4. **A:** Can we go swimming?

   B: No, I _____ you didn't. It's going to rain soon.

5. **A:** Can I email my homework assignment to you?

   B: No, I _____ you give it to me in class.

C Match the sentences.

1. Sonya would rather not go out for dinner. _____   **a.** It's too windy.

2. Luis would rather not study Greek. _____   **b.** It's a beautiful day outside.

3. We'd rather not sit outside. _____   **c.** I'll walk instead.

4. I'd rather not take the subway. _____   **d.** He thinks it is too difficult.

5. They would rather not work today. _____   **e.** It's too expensive.

_____ .

D Complete the questions with *would rather* and the pronoun *you*.

1. _____ take a test on a computer or on paper?

2. _____ read a book or a magazine?

3. On an airplane, _____ watch a movie or read?

4. _____ study in Europe or North America?

5. _____ have a big house or a small house?

UNIT 1 FOOD FROM THE EARTH

Lesson A

A. 1. eats 2. wearing 3. is ringing 4. have 5. are cooking

B. 1. wakes up 2. eats 3. goes 4. speaks 5. is speaking

C. 1. are 2. is using 3. is studying 4. is reading 5. are doing 6. is asking

D. 1. is driving 2. is staying 3. are going 4. is drinking 5. are playing 6. are wearing

E. 1. are watching 2. eats 3. is sending 4. are studying 5. are relaxing 6. calls

Lesson C

A.

be	was/were	give	gave
drink	drank	go	went
eat	ate	meet	met
fall	fell	see	saw

B. 1. went; saw 2. fell 3. drank 4. was 5. met 6. gave

C. 1. grew 2. helped 3. gave, was 4. learned 5. asked 6. took

D. 1. went 2. tried 3. ate 4. liked 5. showed 6. learned 7. enjoyed

E. 1. arrived 2. was 3. helped 4. lost 5. said 6. had 7. called 8. heard 9. laughed 10. ran

UNIT 2 EXPRESS YOURSELF

Lesson A

A. 1. Martha has lived in Brazil. 2. The child has not been on an airplane before. 3. Ximena has been to Mexico City three times. 4. My teacher has not been to her country for a long time. 5. They have bought the train tickets.

B. 1. has studied 2. have been 3. has not gone 4. have not done 5. have read

C. 1. Celeste has not been to Montreal. 2. I have not played soccer every day this week. 3. Jane has not finished the assigment. 4. We have not met new friends at school. 5. The students have not spoken to the teacher about the homework.

D. 1. No, I have never eaten Peruvian food. 2. Yes, I have tried writing with my left hand. 3. Yes, my family has gone on vacation. 4. No, they have never seen the ocean. 5. Yes, I have written an email in English.

E. 1. have not 2. have 3. have

Lesson C

A. 1. We've had 2. They've visited 3. She's washed and ironed 4. I've studied 5. You've done

B. 1. d 2. a 3. e 4. b 5. c

C. 1. have already learned 2. hasn't woken up; yet 3. hasn't said; yet 4. haven't ever gone 5. has never used

D. 1. yet 2. ever 3. never 4. already 5. ever

E. 1. A: ever; B: never 2. A: yet; B: already 3. A: yet; B: yet

UNIT 3 CITIES

Lesson A

A. 1. The airport will be crowded. 2. They will play soccer in the afternoon. 3. I will be a student. 4. We will work in an office. 5. You will have a lot of homework.

B. 1. will take 2. will send 3. will call 4. will go 5. will learn

C. 1. won't use; will be 2. won't be 3. won't work 4. won't pay; will be 5. won't write; will use

D. 1. **A:** Will; **B:** we will 2. **A:** Will; **B:** I will 3. **A:** Will; **B:** he will

E. 1. They'll read 2. They'll buy 3. They'll write

Lesson C

A. 1. b 2. a 3. b 4. b

B. 1. d 2. e 3. a 4. c 5. b

C. 1. After I spend a year in Toronto, I'll speak better English. 2. no comma 3. Before I choose a college, I'll talk with my parents. 4. Before I get a job, I'll travel for a few months. 5. no comma

D. 1. After I practice driving, I'll take the driving test. 2. Before I rent an apartment, I'll save money. 3. I'll get extra help from the teacher before I take another test. 4. I'll call my friend overseas after I buy a calling card. *or* After I buy a calling card I'll call my friend overseas

UNIT 4 THE BODY

Lesson A

A. 1. bigger 2. younger 3. smaller 4. more difficult 5. colder

B. 1. Espresso is more expensive than coffee. 2. Tea has less caffeine than espresso. 3. The cafeteria is noisier than the library. 4. Miguel plays soccer better than me. 5. A mile is longer than a kilometer.

C. 1. best 2. most exciting 3. nearest 4. funniest 5. hottest

D. 1. Tania speaks English as well as Monica. 2. My backpack is as heavy as yours. 3. Andre's brother is as tall as his father. 4. Running is as difficult as cycling. 5. The lake is as deep as the river.

E. 1. oldest 2. youngest 3. older 4. the most 5. smartest

Lesson C

A. 1. to listen 2. to improve 3. to make 4. to learn 5. to earn

B. 1. Rodrigo read the chapter in order to prepare for the test. 2. Magda took the bus in order to get to school. 3. Mr. Esteves learned English in order to work in the US. 4. Jaime got a job in order to save money. 5. They got up early in order to be on time.

C. 1. d 2. e 3. a 4. c 5. b

D. 1. To be at school on time, Lena gets up at 7 o'clock. 2. To wake up, she takes a shower and drinks two cups of coffee. 3. To avoid the crowded bus, Lena walks to school. 4. To borrow a book, she goes to the library at school. 5. To make plans for lunch, she talks to her friends.

UNIT 5 CHALLENGES

Lesson A

A. 1. was learning 2. was raining 3. was blowing 4. was talking 5. was waiting

B. 1. gave 2. were speaking 3. did you cook 4. were sleeping 5. was taking

C. 1. were taking 2. was drying 3. was winning 4. was traveling 5. was sitting

D. 1. b 2. e 3. d 4. a 5. c

E. 1. while 2. While 3. when 4. When

Lesson C

A. 1. No, she is not old enough. 2. A 20-year-old is old enough to get a driver's license and to vote. 3. Yes, she is old enough. 4. No, he is not old enough. 5. He will be old enough next year. *or* He will be old enough when he's eighteen.

B. 1. not fast enough 2. too salty 3. warm enough? 4. enough money 5. too

C. 1. too 2. not old enough *or* too young 3. enough 4. too 5. enough

UNIT 6 TRANSITIONS

Lesson A

A. 1. have seen 2. has been *or* has gone 3. has worked 4. has read 5. has learned

B. 1. have heard 2. went 3. has not bought 4. has not done 5. was

C. 1. she has (lived in the US.) 2. I have never tried sushi. 3. she hasn't (called me yet.) 4. they have (gone to the beach.)

D. 1. I have been studying English for 2 years. 2. I have known Elena for 5 years. 3. It's been here since 2010. 4. I've been working at the bookstore since last year.

Lesson C

A. 1. How fast does he swim? 2. How expensive was the restaurant? 3. How fast does she read? 4. How well does he play soccer?

B. 1. How well does Jane speak Spanish? 2. How old is your grandfather? 3. How mature are the students? 4. How safe is this city?

C. 1. b 2. e 3. a 4. c 5. d

D. 1. How long did she live in Los Angeles? 2. How strict are they? 3. How responsible is he? 4. How rich are they? 5. How late are we?

E. 1. How slowly do you write in English? 2. How fast does he drive?

UNIT 7 LUXURIES

Lesson A

A. 1. Precious metals are found underground. 2. Precious stones are given as gifts. 3. Jewelry is made with precious metals such as gold and silver. 4. Luxury clothing is worn by celebrities. 5. Valuable items are kept in a safe.

B. 1. is shown 2. are made 3. are sewn 4. is designed 5. are imported

C. 1. Cotton clothes are worn by the children. 2. Luxury clothes are sold by expensive boutiques. 3. Big profits are made on luxury items by stores. 4. My silk blouse was damaged by the washing machine. 5. A handmade ring was lost by Sheena.

D. 1. Money is given as a gift at weddings. 2. Pearls are produced by oysters. 3. Oranges are grown in Florida. 4. Silver is found in Mexico. 5. Diamonds are imported from South Africa.

E. 1. is used 2. uses 3. makes 4. are made 5. sewed

Lesson C

A. 1. is visited 2. are made 3. are used 4. is watched 5. are needed

B. 1. c 2. e 3. a 4. b 5. d

C. 2. by farmers 4. by people

D. 1. Yes, many people's lives are improved by education. 2. No, the illness is not caused by unclean water. 3. No, people's lives are not improved by television. 4. Yes, people's job opportunities are improved by education.

UNIT 8 NATURE

Lesson A

A. 1. ignore 2. melts 3. continue 4. understand 5. live

B. 1. doesn't stop; will lose 2. lose; will die 3. extinct; will be 4. is; hunt 5. finds; will kill

C. 1. c 2. e 3. a 4. b 5. d

D. 1. will play; stops 2. wins; they will 3. are; will not scare 4. will go; is 5. will call; find

Lesson C

A. 1. a lot of 2. too much 3. Too many 4. a little 5. There will be snow tonight.

B. 1. b 2. d 3. a 4. e 5. c

C. 1. c 2. b 3. b 4. a 5. c

D. 1. too much 2. Too many 3. too much 4. many 5. too little

UNIT 9 LIFE IN THE PAST

Lesson A

A. 1. used to drink 2. used to drive 3. used to be 4. used to win 5. used to wake up

B. 1. d 2. b 3. e 4. c 5. a

C. 1. No, she didn't use to work at the bank. 2. No, they didn't use to be married. 3. No, my brother didn't use to drive a red car. 4. No, he didn't use to wear glasses. 5. No, they didn't used to live in an apartment

D. 1. Did he use to live in Miami? 2. Did Mr. Lin use to teach science? 3. Did you use to play tennis? 4. Did she use to work at night?

E. 1. used to take 2. used to be 3. used to bring 4. used to wait 5. didn't use to be

Lesson C

A. 1. PV 2. PV 3. AV 4. PV 5. AV

B. 1. was written 2. was read 3. were explored 4. were explained 5. were learned.

C. 1. Mongolia was ruled by Genghkis Khan. 2. Many cities and kingdoms were destroyed by Genghkis Khan. 3. For example, the city of Samarkand was destroyed by Khan's army. 4. Genghkis Khan was respected by many people. 5. His tomb was burned by his soldiers.

D. 1. were taken 2. were published 3. were inspired 4. were visited 5. was made

UNIT 10 TRAVEL

Lesson A

A. 1. F 2. F 3. T 4. T 5. F

B. 1. must/have to 2. have to 3. don't have to 4. must 5. has to

C. 1. You don't have to check in at the gate. 2. You don't have to put your suitcase on the scale. 3. You don't have to buy tickets in advance 4. You don't have to take off your shoes. 5. You don't have to get a vaccination.

D. 1. You must wait in line at security. 2. He doesn't have to check his bag. 3. I need to/ have to email the hotel. 4. Children under 10 must travel with an adult. 5. She doesn't have to wait in that line.

Lesson C

A. 1. A 2. P 3. P 4. P 5. A

B. 1. You must not talk. 2. You can't eat the ice cream. 3. You must not restart the computer. 4. You can't turn on the TV. 5. You must not take photos.

C. 1. You must not use cell phones in class. 2. You must not park a car in a crosswalk. 3. You must not copy another student's work. 4. You can't make an omelet without eggs. 5. You can't go to college without finishing high school.

D. 1. must not 2. can't 3. must not 4. can't 5. must not

UNIT 11 CAREERS

Lesson A

A. 1. a 2. c 3. b 4. b 5. a 6. a

B. 1. had better 2. should *or* ought to 3. shouldn't *or* ought not to 4. had better not 5. had better

C. 1. should 2. had better not 3. had better 4. should 5. shouldn't

D. 1. d 2. b 3. e 4. a 5. c

E. 1. I think that you should go to college. 2. Perhaps we shouldn't spend a lot of money. 3. Maybe you should get a part-time job. 4. I think you ought to talk to your teacher about it.

Lesson C

A. 1. b 2. a 3. b 4. a 5. a

B. 1. everything 2. anything 3. nobody 4. Somebody 5. anything

C. 1. everything 2. anything 3. Nobody 4. something 5. anyone

D. 1. anything 2. somebody/someone 3. everything 4. Somebody/Someone 5. anyone/anybody 6. everyone 7. everything

UNIT 12 CELEBRATIONS

Lesson A

A. 1. Veterans' Day is as important as Memorial Day. 2. July 4 in the US is as exciting as September 18 in Chile. 3. Summer vacations are as popular as winter vacations. 4. Soccer is as challenging as tennis. 5. July is as hot as August.

B. 1. My backpack is not as heavy as your backpack. 2. This assignment is not as difficult as the last one. 3. Spain is not as interesting as Italy. 4. Chocolate ice cream is not as delicious as vanilla. 5. Tea is not as strong as coffee.

C. 1. Yes, my mother is as old as my father. 2. No Tina's laptop not as fast as Ravi's. 3. Yes, my sunglasses as dark as yours 4. No, Boston is not as big as Houston. 5. No, the Olympics are not as exciting as World Cup.

D. 1. My brother is not as tall as me. 2. My writing is not as good as your writing. 3. Lucia's pronunciation is as clear as my teacher's pronunciation. 4. My job is not as interesting as your job 5. My uncle's car is not as expensive as my mother's car.

Lesson C

A. 1. would rather get up 2. would rather drive 3. would rather live 4. would rather see 5. would rather go

B. 1. 'd rather 2. 'd rather 3. 'd rather 4. 'd rather 5. 'd rather

C. 1. e 2. d 3. a 4. c 5. b

D. 1. Would you rather 2. Would you rather 3. would you rather 4. Would you rather 5. Would you rather